South Africa:
Lost
Opportunities

South Africa: Lost Opportunities

Frank J. Parker
Boston College

LexingtonBooks
D.C. Heath and Company
Lexington, Massachusetts
Toronto

Library of Congress Cataloging in Publication Data

Parker, Frank J., 1940–
  South Africa.

  Includes bibliographical references and index.
  1. South Africa—Politics and government—1978- 2. South Africa—
Politics and government—1961-1978. 3. Blacks—South Africa—Politics
and government. 4. South Africa—Race relations. 5. South Africa—
Economic conditions—1961-   . 6. Namibia—Politics and government.
  I. Title.
DT779.952.P37 1983   968.06   78-20633
ISBN 0–669–02750–2

Copyright © 1983 by D.C. Heath and Company

Published simultaneously in Canada

Printed in the United States of America

International Standard Book Number: 0–669–02750–2

Library of Congress Catalog Card Number: 78-20633

To Rhoda, Hessie, Jack and, of course, Mervyn

Contents

Foreword

The formulation of a foreign policy is predicated on an incisive articulation of two discrete elements: the strategic ends of the national interest to be served, and the character of the objects of the policy. For better or for worse, these tasks must remain separate if the resulting foreign policy is to be operationally effective and politically convincing. Too often the strategist-diplomat attempts to combine the two operations into a single exercise, in which the definition of national interest and the constitution of the diplomatic client define each other. The resulting policy is then flawed by the proximity and interrelationship of the end and the object, to the extent that it is rarely operationally effective and almost never politically convincing. Moreover, it is only through the separation of the two exercises that a foreign policy is made resilient enough to sustain the burden of politics; that is, the contradictions, paradoxes, and irrationalities that the dialectics of diplomacy demand.

Clearly, no single foreign-policy problem better represents these contradictions, paradoxes, and irrationalities than that of South Africa. A vestige of another era and long a pariah state in its own continent, South Africa possesses natural and geographical resources that are essential to the defense of the West; and yet it maintains a system of government that is loathsome in terms of the principles of democracy and pluralism that underpin Western notions of legitimacy and sovereignty. It is such a contradiction that a well-crafted foreign policy must seek to accommodate, if not reconcile.

The great value of the present study is that it takes as a given the independence of defining the national interest and describing the diplomatic clients; further, it addresses the more difficult—from a U.S. perspective—of the two exercises: the description of the diplomatic client. To as large an extent, this book demonstrates that the questions surrounding the South African case are, at this time, too complicated to begin defining U.S. interest there without first understanding the nature of the indigenous problem.

What Father Parker has admirably sought to answer instead are the antecedent questions that are revealed only after a careful and copious examination of both the historical tradition of the country and the context of the dilemmas that have evolved over the past five turbulent years of South African politics. In spite of the ideological contentions that set the tone of nearly all debate on the South African question, Father Parker has produced an admirable study that presents the evidence fully and objec-

tively, and allows the reader and policymaker to arrive at independent conclusions on the strategic principles that should constitute a foreign-policy
prescription for the United States.

Beginning with a well-researched analysis of the status and activities of
current political parties in the country, Father Parker sets the tone for the
reader by vividly describing the last five years of South African politics. The
internal political development, he confirms, is not progressing at the break-
neck pace of many of South Africa's neighbors, but is proceeding excruci-
atingly slowly. His thorough description provides a penetrating analysis of
the political dilemma, and this is followed by a rehearsal of the history of
the Namibia dispute, which made South Africa an outlaw in the international community. Returning to the current situation in South Africa,
Father Parker presents perhaps the most contemporary summary of the
status of the South African economy currently in print. He then concludes
with an overview of the U.S. government and corporate relations with the
Pretoria government.

With neither praise nor criticism for the policies of the last two administrations, this book serves the student, scholar, and policymaker as a
research tool on the contemporary history of South African politics. It
represents a noble effort to digest the huge amount of information on the
topic, a point of departure for anyone attempting—in theory or practice—
to define U.S. interests in the region in terms of the contingencies that face
any well-formulated, resilient U.S. foreign policy toward South Africa.

W. Scott Thompson

Preface and Acknowledgments

South Africa is a country of many baffling contrasts. There have been few societies in history in which so much dedicated enthusiasm for the promotion of a cause has been manifested by one section of society while another section complained so persistently to be suffering from a sense of indignity, and pain as a result of policies ostensibly designed for their long-term benefit.
T.R.H. Davenport, *South Africa: A Modern History* (Johannesburg: Macmillan, 1977), p. 277

South Africa: Lost Opportunities subscribes to and continues for five more years the sentiments expressed in the opening quotation from Davenport. Little has changed for the better in the period of time on which this book concentrates. Those possessing an optimistic frame of mind might argue that avoiding all-out racial war in South Africa for five more years is, in itself, a singular achievement. Given the seriousness of the rift between the white and nonwhite and the potential cataclysm lurking, optimism hardly seems in order; neither side could afford five more years of stalemate, but they occurred.

This book examines events in South Africa from 1977 to 1982, and concludes that the situation did not greatly change during this five-year period. Such a state of affairs is highly unsatisfactory, and the world can only hope that in the future those involved will do better.

Acknowledgments

A great many people gave their time and professional expertise in assisting me with the writing of this book. My only fear in compiling a list of those to thank is that I have forgotten someone. The usual disclaimers concerning all errors, omissions and opinions being mine alone, of course, apply.

I received academic guidance from Jay Katzen, without whose help and encouragement this book would never have been completed; and, also, from Kees Schager, Frank Cappiello, Robert Kiley, Jim Burlage, Winslow Martin, Reed Wheedon, Bill Hickey, Eugene Martel, William Henze, Mary Lee Garrison, and Nobel Peace Price winner, Sean MacBride. I wish to thank all of them.

Research and manuscript-preparation assistance of various types were provided by Virginia Burlage, Stacie Beck, Dorian Skeete, Jan Swanbeck, Richard Coughlin, Ellen Schiller, Katherine Kissen, Elaine Bregman, Sandra Tedlock, and my mother, Louise Parker. I am most grateful to all. I also acknowledge with thanks the generous support provided by the Academic Support Fund of the Jesuit Community at Boston College and the cooperation of the Barat Jesuit Community at Boston College.

1

The Continuing State of Political Stagnation

If the Republic of South Africa were a true republic, in the accepted sense of the word, it would be proper to expect that the years between 1977 and 1982 would have been full of movement and excitement. Since South Africa is not a republic, however, it is more understandable that this expected state of flux on a constant basis did not occur. The white minority government in Pretoria kept a close check and heavy hand on all expressions of political dissent. It mattered not if the perpetrator were white or not. As a result, many of the trappings of a police state under siege were present. Close resemblances to a republic fall away in such a time. This chapter examines the limited role of black and white political expression in the Republic of South Africa from the end of 1977 until the beginning of 1983.

Political Activity in the Nonwhite Community

The Appearances of Unity

In 1977 it appeared likely that a unity movement would occur among groups opposed to the South African government. What better motivation could exist than the recent triple cataclysm of political disasters: the Soweto riots, the Steven Biko killing, and the mass arrests of politically involved people on October 19, 1977? Hindsight is often a great teacher. Today, it is clear that the divisions among the groups of opponents were so massive that it was not realistic to assume that unity could have prevailed. At the time, however, it did appear likely that the South African government would be presented with a reasonably unified nonwhite death-struggle opponent.

Intense stirrings in the nonwhite political community began to take place at the start of 1978. The Labor party, the main colored political party in the country, announced that it intended to join forces with the largest black political party, Inkatha. If such a political coupling succeeded, two major results would take place. The South African government would not only face a threat from a broad-based political party of nonwhite opposition but also, for the first time, a black political leader of true nationwide substance would have emerged, who could not be easily detained as a political prisoner. This man is, of course, Chief Gatsha Buthelezi, hereditary prime minister to the Zulu king, head of the Buthelezi tribe and president of Inkatha.

Immediate speculation began that the leading Asian political parties would be brought into the grouping. On paper, such a tripartite alliance appeared formidable. Many of those opposed to the South African government hoped that it would come to fruition. Other more-skeptical observers were less enthusiastic. In their eyes, those involved were hopelessly conservative. These critics believed that events had passed such voices of appeasement, as they viewed them. To these younger people of all nonwhite skin colors, an Inkatha/colored/Asian alliance was a roadblock in the path of the armed confrontation between white and nonwhite in South Africa that they believed must come.[1]

A similar movement toward possible grouping with Inkatha began to take place in the Indian community. Again, those accustomed to wearing rose-colored glasses began to speculate on the possibility of peaceful political negotiation leading to an eventual power sharing within South Africa. If the main political party for the more than 750,000 Indian people within South Africa could be joined with Inkatha and its colored associate parties, then the forces of change stood a chance. While these utopian dreams were being advanced, it seemed appropriate to complete the cycle and recall Chief Buthelezi's stillborn attempts of early 1977 aimed at drawing closer to the white-opposition Progressive Federal party.[2] Early 1978, then, was a time for imbibing heady wines of united political opposition. Since no one doubted that the cause was just, it seemed to those hoping for an alliance that such an event simply must take place. Their hopes were dashed for a variety of reasons, many of which are sketched in the rest of this chapter.

Chief Buthelezi Runs into Trouble

The first clear warning that nonwhite unity would be a difficult task occurred on January 29, 1978, at Jabulani Stadium in Soweto. Chief Buthelezi had received government permission to address the crowd concerning the upcoming election in his native Kwazulu. Observers noted that among the 9,000 who attended, very few were under forty years of age. Such a statistic served warning that Chief Buthelezi might not be able to control the black youth of the country in succeeding years. Many Soweto youth leaders were openly critical of the appearance by Chief Buthelezi. They pointed out that he had not appeared in Soweto until after the leading Soweto blacks in the so-called Committee of Ten had been detained or banned in the political actions taken by the government on October 19, 1977. All along, Chief Buthelezi had been trying to avoid the tag of being the leader only of the 5.5

million Zulu-tribe descendants in the nation and not of all blacks in the nation. The circumstances surrounding the Jabulani Stadium speech indicated that his attempts to become a nationwide black leader—to say nothing of being the premier nationwide nonwhite leader—were not yet successful.[3]

During March 1978, Chief Buthelezi's problems became worse. For the first time, he was directly and openly insulted, and his leadership was challenged. This event took place at a memorial service for Robert Sobukwe, the founder of the Pan Africanist Congress (PAC). Chief Buthelezi was forced to leave the Graaff Reinet service in fear of his life. Without doubt, some of the violence that occurred was spontaneous. It is equally true that other participants were opposed to the presence of the chief whom they viewed as a turncoat and white appeaser. Three black teenagers were wounded by gunshots. Other spectators, including a white photographer, were injured by thrown stones. On regaining the comparative safety of his limousine, Chief Buthelezi said, "This is a disaster. It does not augur well for our liberation."[4]

In retrospect, it probably was unwise for Chief Buthelezi to attend the Sobukwe memorial service. In the wake of the 1960 Sharpeville massacre that had led to sixty-nine deaths, the South African government had kept Sobukwe in jail or under house arrest until he died. Such treatment was in direct contrast to the respectful manner in which the government has dealt with Chief Buthelezi, the head of Inkatha. Given the emotions of the moment, it is not surprising that Chief Buthelezi was driven from the service or even that some people threatened to kill him. Even in the best of times, there is serious fragmentation among black people in the heavily politicized atmosphere of South Africa. What the event did illustrate is that Chief Buthelezi could not assume that being the number-one political-party leader of black South Africa would guarantee that the mass of black people in the country would support him or allow themselves to be led by him.

The next blow to the aspirations of Chief Buthelezi to become the leader of all nonwhite opposition took place during September 1978. Sonny Leon, the leader of the Labor party, resigned his post. In his role as titular leader of the more than 2.5 million colored people in South Africa, he had led his people along a path of dialogue with the government in a manner similar to that advocated by Chief Buthelezi. The cooperation between Inkatha and the Labor party had sprung from this congruence of views. As had happened in the black community, however, the younger people in the colored community were not pleased with a stance that they would see as appeasement. Leon was not able to hold his consensus, and finally, citing ill health, he resigned. The largest loser in the incident may well have been Buthelezi. Late 1978 was the time in which National party unity was shattered by a political payoff scandal in the government. Prime Minister Vorster, who had won a landslide election victory in November 1977, was driven from office, a victim of the Muldergate scandal, a mere ten months later. If the nonwhites had been united at that time, there is no telling what political concessions could have been obtained and what trends could have been set in motion. Unfortunately for them, they were united in disunity alone. A golden opportunity for progress slipped away.

Relations between Botha and the Nonwhite Communities

As Pieter Willem Botha began his service as the tenth prime minister of South Africa since 1910 and as Pieter G. Koornhof assumed the right-hand-man role of minister of plural relations and development, the nonwhite community was forced to reassess their attitudes and opposition strategies. During the first six months of their tenure, enough signs of flexibility could be detected that many nonwhites were hopeful for the first time in recent memory. Especially responsible for this brief era of good feeling was the successful January 1979 meeting between Prime Minister Botha and eight homelands leaders at Capetown and the simultaneous easing of the government position on housing resettlement at Crossroads near Capetown. The group least willing to go along with the new, hopeful attitude was made up of expatriate African National Congress (ANC) leaders carrying on their opposition from outside the borders of South Africa. To this group, cooperation, or even a wait-and-see attitude, smacked of treason. Attention was focused upon Chief Buthelezi as typifying this unacceptable trend. Much behind-the-scenes negotiating and peacemaking was carried out between ANC and Inkatha leaders to keep the split from becoming both public and irreparable. Chief Buthelezi exacerbated the tension by choosing this period to speak out in public on a frequent basis to encourage continued Western investment in South Africa. He viewed Western investment as the best way to break down apartheid, a view not shared by most ANC leaders.

As months passed, the honeymoon began to end. The roots of apartheid were entrenched so firmly in the South African soil that even the perceived reasonableness of Botha-Koornhof policies had little permanent success. By April 1979, the conciliatory-minded secretary general of the South African Council of Churches, a black man named Bishop Desmond Tutu, felt compelled to remark, "There is an outside chance—just an outside chance—that we may be able to turn the trick (and avoid violence) but I say this with a wavering certainty as each day passes."[5]

Fueding in the Black Political Movements

The lack of cohesion in the nonwhite political groupings was emphasized on June 12, 1979, when David M. Sibeko, age forty, was assassinated in Dar Es

Salaam, Tanzania. He had been one of the three men to assume joint control of the PAC presidency when Potlako Leballo had resigned for health reasons the previous month. A longtime exile for political reasons from South Africa, Sibeko had been most influential in publicizing the state of affairs in South Africa among U.S. and U.K. apartheid opponents. His forced elimination from the political scene pointed out once again how fragile was the consensus for cooperation among the various opposition political factions involved in the South African liberation struggle.[6]

In the wake of the Sibeko assassination, a power struggle broke out in the ranks of the (PAC). Eventually, Vusumzi Make rose to the top of this banned organization now headquartered in Dar Es Salaam. He began his presidency tenure by attacking former leader Potlako Leballo. He charged that Leballo had harbored reactionary counterrevolutionary tendencies and had been an ineffectual leader.[7]

Within South Africa, disagreement among the various groupings also continued. As might be expected, given the enormous size of Soweto, much of the disagreement centered in that city. Attempts by the Committee of Ten to keep harmony among the groupings did not always succeed. The external-based ANC remained perpetually jealous and suspicious of all black politicians living within South Africa. The PAC was even more hostile. Within Soweto, youth leaders continued their school boycott. Such an action was fraught with the possibility of outright violence that could dwarf the 1976 riots and, not incidentally, destroy the leadership potential of this broadly based Committee of Ten.

Another element of disunity was caused by the South African-government-recognized local-ruling framework for Soweto. David Thebehali was the elected black chief executive for Soweto. He had been selected in a government-supervised election that had been boycotted widely by the black electorate; only 6 percent of eligible Soweto voters participated.

It had been hoped originally that the municipal-government scheme in Soweto could serve as a buffer between black and white hostility and perhaps eventually lead to the incorporation of Soweto as a true city, legally distinct from Johannesburg. By the time of Thebehali's election in September 1979, it was clear that these hopes would not be realized. Electrification was proceeding slowly, and the much heralded ninety-nine-year lease program was so enmeshed in red tape that by that time only ten families had been accepted. Under such circumstances, it was understandable that many blacks in Soweto and elsewhere looked on David Thebehali and the municipal-government structure in Soweto as nothing more than another divisive element in the equation.[8]

Still another element to be considered was provided by the tendency of many younger blacks to gravitate toward exclusionary, black consciousness groups. The Azanian Peoples Organization (AZAPO) led by Curtis Nkondo quickly was becoming the most prominent of these groups. The avowed purpose of AZAPO in its current incarnation was to prevent the formation of a black middle class that could be manipulated by the white government and used as a force to blunt the thrust toward the coming revolution.[9]

In a situation of political repression such as currently exists in South Africa, or existed in Rhodesia during its Universal Declaration of Independence (UDI) days, dissident political groups come and go with great rapidity. As a result, it is a mistake to place great weight on quick-rising, star newcomers like a Curtis Nkondo, for example. Staying power becomes a virtue, as Robert Mugabe and Joshua Nkomo demonstrated in Rhodesia before it became Zimbabwe. A similar observation can be made concerning Chief Buthelezi and imprisoned leaders such as Nelson Mandela and Walter Sisulu. For a variety of reasons, some of them not always clear to observers, men like these three are able to retain long-term positions of significance where others are not. As the Committee of Ten attempted to establish itself as such a force, it became necessary for it to situate itself properly in relation to these personages of perennial political significance.

At the end of 1979, relations between the Committee of Ten, located principally in Soweto, and Inkatha, located principally in Natal, suffered through a series of tense confrontations. At one point, Dr. Nthato Motlana, the chairman of the Committee of Ten, suggested that Chief Buthelezi was a traitor. Motlana later apologized for the remark, but the head of Inkatha was not in a forgiving mood. Chief Buthelezi came to Soweto on October 21, 1979, and attacked Motlana in a public speech in the harshest terms of opprobrium. He even suggested a possible romantic relationship between Dr. Motlana and Mrs. Winnie Mandela, the wife of longtime imprisoned black leader Nelson Mandela. Buthelezi also claimed to be hearing a telepathic message from Nelson Mandela and Walter Sisulu in prison. According to the chief, both men were urging him to keep to his present course.

Hurried efforts at reestablishing peace were made. A group of Inkatha representatives went to London to meet with Oliver Tambo and other ANC leaders. Within South Africa similar meetings between representatives of the Committee of Ten and Inkatha took place. An uneasy truce, one destined to last into the middle of the following year, occurred. Talk of the Committee of Ten's becoming a national organization began to subside, an event that had to please Chief Buthelezi since he was not keen on sharing the leadership spotlight with more people than necessary.

Free Nelson Mandela

Political stirrings in the South African black community began again to rise during the first part of 1980. Such an event was a natural consequence of the end of white rule of Rhodesia and the ascension to power of a black-ruled Zimbabwe led by Robert Mugabe. Under such circumstances of renewed hope, it is natural that agitation to free Nelson Mandela was heard once again throughout South Africa. Born in 1918, this lawyer and Tembu royalty descendant was found guilty of sabotage in 1964. Since then he had been imprisoned on Robben Island, situated off Capetown. His release would serve as a rallying cry to those looking for a charismatic leader. Observers noted with interest that, at best, the support of Chief Buthelezi for the Free-Nelson-Mandela campaign was restrained.

The leading Black spokesperson in the move to free Mandela was the editor of the *Johannesburg Post*, Percy Qobosa. In a number of speeches and articles, he called for the release of the famous black leader. Qobosa asserted that such a move by the South African government could lead to the start of peace negotiations among all races in South Africa. He warned that the alternative would be a prolonged state of war that would dwarf the Rhodesian civil war and make it appear to be a "tea party" in comparison.[10]

In the United States, the Free-Nelson-Mandela campaign picked up some official support. Senators Paul Tsongas (D.–Mass.) and Mark Hatfield (R.–Ore.) and seventeen members of Congress sent a joint letter in support of Mandela to Donald Sole, the South African ambassador to the United States. The point was made that Mandela "personified the Black man's struggle against apartheid." The senators requested that the South African government release Mandela so the peace process in South Africa could proceed at an increased pace.[11]

The groundswell of support for Nelson Mandela taking place within and without South Africa did little to move Prime Minister Botha. Speaking at the University of Stellenbosch during April 1980, he called Mandela an avid Marxist who supported violence and made it clear that he had no intention of shortening the life prison sentence being served. Many blacks felt that the campaign would have had more chance of being successful if Chief Buthelezi had been more energetic in supporting it. The best that the head of Inkatha could bring himself to say was that "if the people chose Mandela as a leader, I would be prepared to serve him if that were their will."[12]

In June 1980, the ANC broke its truce with Chief Buthelezi. The perceived lack of support for freeing Nelson Mandela, the longtime standard bearer of their party, was too much for them to support. In a statement issued in London, the ANC accused Buthelezi of throwing in his lot with the South African government, failing to support the school boycotts, and not working with vigor to free Mandela. The ANC also felt that his support of foreign investment in South Africa was at odds with recent opposition attempts to disrupt the South African white-controlled economy by means like recent guerrilla raids on government-sponsored coal-to-oil conversion plants.

Chief Buthelezi reacted with well-publicized disbelief to the ANC charges and discounted them because the head of the organization, Oliver Tambo, had not presented them as his own opinion. Since the ANC statement was incontrovertibly official in nature, such distinctions seem to have little validity. The public split had caused a breach in black unity that would be difficult to heal.

In the wake of the weakening of universal support for Buthelezi and the failure to free Mandela, speculation arose that Bishop Desmond Tutu might assume a leading black political role. As an outspoken opponent of apartheid, observers thought that he might have more credibility in the larger black community than Chief Buthelezi, while simultaneously, he might be equally acceptable to the South African government for the role of chief black spokesperson as Chief Buthelezi.

Although the idea of Bishop Tutu as a major political leader had much of surface merit to recommend it since he has consistently preached the need for unity among the various black political groups and since he was an outspoken advocate of support for the colored and black student boycotts, few expect him to become the top black political leader in the country. One reason is that the trend toward violence among youth groups within Soweto and Capetown and guerrilla activities operating from outside South Africa make it hard to maintain close cooperation with a church leader preaching a message of conciliation. The second reason is totally extrinsic but, nonetheless, important. Blacks in South Africa were horrified by the perceived favoritism toward whites and against black liberation groups that Bishop Abel Muzorewa of Zimbabwe displayed during his prime ministership in that emerging country. Unfair generalizations to the effect that Bishop Tutu would act in an equally unsatisfactory manner were made with frequency. The end result was to make it likely that Bishop Tutu would, in the future, be confined largely to a role of moral support to the black liberation movement—not a role of leading policymaker.[13]

Some relief from the continual squabbling among black leaders was provided in mid-1980 when they were able to agree to oppose the Botha government idea of replacing the Senate with a president's council. Since blacks would not be allowed full participation in the scheme, even those blacks who advocated cooperation with the South African government found they could oppose this Botha plan with vigor.

The Buthelezi Plan

In a contemporaneous move that softened opposition to Chief Buthelezi in other black groups, he chose June 1980 to propose and attempt to promote an ambitious scheme for power sharing in Natal. Since citizens of his Kwazulu homeland did not wish to lose their South African citizenship, and since white farmers in the area did not wish threats of violence and worker strikes, it seemed that a multiracial entity encompassing Natal and Kwazulu within a federated South Africa might have some hope of eventual serious consideration. Chief Buthelezi selected a forty-man multiracial commission to study the proposal.[14] Given the tribal homogeneity in Kwazulu on the black side and the industrial and agricultural diversification on the white side in Natal, this region would appear to be the outstanding testing place for ideas of confederation.

Prime Minister Botha rejected the Buthelezi plan out of hand. He moved ahead instead with his idea of a president's council. Since the black population of the country was destined to have an advisory role alone and not a participatory one in the new governing scheme, the message was clear for all to see. The South African government remained determined to deny the black members of the population a meaningful say in the running of their government and, by extension, of their own lives. Chief Buthelezi seemed to sum up the matter as well as anyone. "Who can deny," he said, "that the president's council, which will sit without blacks, brings us closer to violence than to peaceful change?"[15]

By provoking Prime Minister Botha into a public condemnation of the Natal-Kwazulu confederation, Chief Buthelezi regained some stature as an independent black leader not overly committed to agreeing with the government on its terms. Others were not so sure. The public criticism of Buthelezi by the ANC that had begun in June 1980 continued in following months. In response to the original defense by Chief Buthelezi, pointing out that ANC President Oliver Tambo had not joined publicly in the statements made, this omission was soon remedied. Subsequent statements were issued in the name of President Tambo. Most notable in this regard was one that criticized the head of Inkatha for the role he was playing in suppressing the struggles of workers and students against the fascist-racist regime.

Allusions in the statement of condemnation were undoubtedly being made to the refusal of Chief Buthelezi to support the student boycott when it spread to Kwamashu, a black township near Durban that had been gerrymandered into Kwazulu. The ANC statement also seemed to be criticizing the statements of Chief Buthelezi encouraging outside corporate investment and discouraging black worker strikes as being counterproductive and self-defeating.

Chief Buthelezi and his Inkatha cohorts were equally as skillful as ANC members in hurling bombs of provocative rhetoric. Oscar Dhlamo, the minister of education in Kwazulu and the general secretary of Inkatha, clearly was speaking with the approval of his superior when he spoke in Buthelezi's defense. Dhlamo proclaimed himself as being disgusted with those who criticized Chief Buthelezi as a person who fostered the hated concept of Bantu education. He warned that "Inkatha was now ready to shed blood when it comes to dealing with those people who make it their hobby to discredit the stature of Chief Buthelezi as our leader."[16]

Mr. Dhlamo went on to voice a fear that continued tension between ANC supporters and Inkatha supporters eventually could lead to a tribal war between the Xhosa tribe (largely ANC) and the Zulu tribe (largely Inkatha).[17] Such a dire warning brought to the surface a hidden fear of both blacks and whites within South Africa. Blacks feared that such a tribal-based feud would cost many lives and would hinder significantly the drive toward independence. The recently completed war in Rhodesia-Zimbabwe was an all-too-fresh reminder of what could happen among black groups when tribal considerations came to the forefront. White people also could draw a lesson from Zimbabwe, or an even more-pointed example from Zaire during the first half of the 1960s, to know that when the tribal element begins to dominate in a liberation struggle, the chances are high of random violence spilling over and engulfing people of all skin colors in an arbitrary manner.

Mr. Dhlamo also made references to criticisms of Chief Buthelezi made by black consciousness leader Steven Biko in the last days before his death. Biko had objected to Chief Buthelezi continuing in his role as chief administrator in the Kwazulu homeland and had accused him of being a South African government puppet. The chief's position had always been that as long as he did not follow the Transkei, Bophuthatswana, and Venda into supposed independence, he was not cooperating with the South African government in a manner harmful to the eventual liberation of all South Africa from minority rule. Chief Buthelezi and his followers felt the path chosen was the best interim way for them to walk. The road was slow and frustrating and the role Inkatha had to play was often a demeaning one, but it seemed to them a wiser method in which to proceed than the one usually followed by the ANC.

Dhlamo criticized the ANC in scathing terms. In his opinion, the armed struggle had gone nowhere in twenty years. With biting sarcasm, he pointed out that people in the movement have been content with throwing a Molotov cocktail at a post office once a year and using this act as justification for saying the struggle is continuing.[18]

Difficulties Worsen

The last months of 1982 and the first few months of 1983 were not pleasant ones in the nonwhite community. The South African government moved with determination on a number of fronts. The first target was the ANC. In

Maputo, Mozambique, prominent author and ANC supporter Ruth First, was killed by a letter bomb.[19] It was widely assumed that South African security forces had been responsible for the assassination. Within South Africa, a second white woman, Barbara Hogan, was convicted of high treason for being an ANC member.[20] Both the First killing and the Hogan conviction were publicized widely by the South African communications media. The government was serving clear notice that the ANC would be contested on all fronts.

This message was reenforced by the predawn events of December 9, 1982. The South African Defense Forces staged an audacious raid in the suburbs of Maseru, the capital of Lesotho. Best estimates are that thirty to forty people were killed in this attack upon the neighboring, sovereign nation.[21] The target was supposedly ANC activists using Lesotho as a staging point for raids into the territory of South Africa; however, most of the victims turned out to be refugees and Lesotho women and children. The Reagan administration criticized the attack with sharpness.[22] One must wonder if this was not a price the South African government was willing to accept for getting its message across to its opponents.

On the domestic scene, the South African government used the last months of 1982 to force a wedge of unparalleled proportions between blacks, coloreds and Indians. This state of affairs was achieved by the surprising support for the new national constitution that surfaced in the colored and Indian communities. Both of these nonwhite communities were to have their own houses of parliament and representation in the president's council that would be a part of the new constitution due to take effect in 1984.[23] No provision was made for the 25 million blacks of the nation. Understandably, black leaders were furious with the Botha government and also with the Reform party (Indians) and the Labor party (colored), since strong evidence was emerging that the three groups would cooperate in an attempt to make the new constitution work.[24]

Black groups saw this plan as a buyout of the Indian and colored populations by the Botha government. They were certain that these groups would never achieve true parity.[25] By implementing the president's council idea, the Botha government would extinguish any remaining hope that blacks would ever be brought to a state of freedom and equality in their own country. In the short term, Chief Buthelezi lost most from the Indian and colored interest shift.[26] The Natal–Kwazulu confederation idea could not coexist with a president's council that excluded black participation. Those who advocated revolution as the only way to bring human rights to the black population in South Africa would seem to have received added ammunition for their position. The future for racial peace looks most bleak.

Political Activity in the White Community

Vorster in Control

For John Vorster, in many ways, the most satisfactory month of his tenure as prime minister was November 1977. It is unlikely that he ever conceived that he was less than ten months away from dismissal and onrushing ignominy. Why should Vorster have been apprehensive? The white voters of the country had returned his government to power by a landslide margin in the recent election. Vorster had seemed to have ridden out the bad effects, politically speaking, caused by the Soweto riots and the death of Steven Biko. If the first rumblings of a political fallout from the Muldergate scandal were audible, the volume level must have been most muted.

Business as usual clearly was to be the rule of the day in the new Vorster government. Eighteen of the nineteen appointees to the new cabinet were Afrikaners. Only the talented minister of finance, D.P.F. Horwood, was a member of the English-speaking portion of the white electorate. Many observers were less concerned with the number of Afrikaner cabinet members than with the ideological rigidity of those chosen. Given the widespread criticism of the brutality displayed by Minister of Justice Jimmy Kruger during his insensitive handling of the Steven Biko case, the Kruger reappointment was seen as a deliberate slap in the face to the more-liberal elements of the electorate.

The only step taken to address the social problems of the country by the vehicle of cabinet-level appointments occurred in the decision to separate the ministry of Bantu Administration, Development and Education. Black education and training areas henceforth would be handled by a new, cabinet-level ministry to be headed by Willem Cruywagen. For an Afrikaner, he was considered to be on the moderate side. Less appealing to those who followed the subject was the selection of hardliner Andries Treurnicht, known unaffectionately as the ayatollah of the North, as deputy minister. Treurnicht, a then rising star, was a firm supporter of Prime Minister Vorster.

Information Minister Connie Mulder was asked to add the portfolio of minister of black administration to his current assignment. It appeared that he was moving into the position of being the undisputed heir apparent to Prime Minister Vorster when he eventually chose to relinquish power. Few observers thought that such a change would come at any time in the near future.[27]

The Prime Minister Resigns

Ten months later, these predictions of a continued long reign for Prime Minister Vorster came to an unexpected and startling end. Twelve years and one week after Vorster became prime minister, he submitted his resignation. To all outward appearances, the decision to leave office was totally voluntary. Vorster cited rising ill health as the reason. On August 20, 1978, the holder of the largely ceremonial post of president, Nicolaas Diederichs, had died at the age of seventy-four.[28] Few eyes were raised when John Vorster assumed this position. Interest had shifted swiftly to which of the leading candidates would replace the prior prime minister in his all-important position. Most agreed that it would be either Defense Minister Pieter W. Botha or Black Affairs and Information Minister Connie Mulder or, perhaps, Foreign Minister Roelof F. Botha—often called by his nickname, Pik.[29]

As the political campaigning began in earnest, some observers still found the time to step back one step and appraise the twelve-year rule of Prime Minister John Vorster. Results were mixed, at best. It must be admitted that he brought whites in South Africa together in a state of unity rarely experienced in the past. No hope of addressing the question of apartheid and discrimination could be entertained until some sort of unity among the white population had been achieved. Under Vorster, at least, the outline of a single white position, however rigid, could be detected legitimately.

Petty apartheid was reduced during the Vorster years. A start was made toward lessening racial barriers on the playing fields and in hotels and restaurants. Such steps were, of course, monumentally inconsequential when measured against the all-pervasive denial of human rights being practiced in major areas such as housing, education, health, freedom of speech, freedom of association and the like. The only favorable interpretation that could be placed on the reduction of petty apartheid would be that it was the first step in the long process of achieving equality and that any step is better than no step at all. More-favorable appraisals were not possible as long as draconian pieces of legislation such as the Group Areas Act, the Population Registration Act, and the Mixed Marriages Act remained in force.

Until the Muldergate scandal broke, it appeared that Vorster was leaving the leadership of the country in a smooth state even if the economic health of the country could not be termed vigorous. Investor confidence, shaken by the Soweto riots, had not yet been restored. South Africa was economically in recession. Over two million people were unemployed. Disaffection among blacks was dangerously high, and the attempts at agreement between the prime minister and the Indian and colored executive councils had not been successful. The Namibian situation was no closer to settlement than it had been a dozen years before. Soweto had put an end to the highly publicized *ostpolitick* of Vorster that had aimed to bring cooperation between the black nations of Africa and South Africa. Only if a peaceful settlement does occur one day in South Africa among the races is it likely that John Vorster will be judged as having taken the first steps toward racial peace and, as a result, will receive words of praise for his actions as prime minister. In any other eventuality, it is more likely that history will remember him as the man who, during his time as justice minister, had introduced the practices of banning orders and detention without trial and who, during his time as prime minister, had taken few significant steps toward dismantling the apartheid system.[30]

The passing from the political scene of John Vorster was termed by *The Economist* as being the end of "an era of lost opportunities."[31] Reference was made to his magnetic leadership qualities and his ability to inspire trust in the white electorate. *The Economist* felt he could have led the white community toward making power concessions to the other color groups. Instead, he chose to emphasize Afrikaner unity. As a result, *The Economist* ventured the opinion that any succeeding prime minister will have a much harder time in bringing about racial harmony, assuming of course, that he would desire to do so.

Botha becomes Prime Minister

At the end of September the power handover became complete. Pieter Willem Botha, who had been defense minister, became the eighth prime minister of South Africa since 1910 and Mr. Vorster became the fifth president (counting J.F.T. Naude who had served in an acting capacity from May 31, 1967, until April 10, 1968) since the post was established in 1961.[32] Mr. Botha was significantly older than the fifty-three-year-old Connie Mulder or the forty-six-year-old Roelof F. Botha. At sixty-two, and as a long-time National party and government minister, Pieter Botha seemed unlikely to be a beacon of steady change and apartheid dismemberment. During his twelve years as defense minister, he had supervised the war in Namibia and the ill-fated 1975 invasion of Angola.

Connie Mulder was the clear loser in the government shakeup. As the campaigning within the National party for the prime ministership became heated, John Vorster had started to criticize his presumed heir apparent, Mulder, in an open manner. Such criticism sounded the death knell for the political ambitions of the longtime information minister, without doubt, but more centrally, public hints were now present for all to see that the rumors of a scandal concerning the Bureau of Information undoubtedly contained some truth.[33]

In the new South African governmental framework, Pieter G. Koornhof, then fifty-three, replaced Connie Mulder in his function as minister of plural relations and development—commonly known as minister of black affairs. In the Vorster government, Koornhof had served in a less-important position as minister of sports. Under his leadership, the Ministry of Sports had removed a significant number of petty racial barriers preventing competition among the races.[34]

The anticipated liberalization of black regulations under Koornhof had been given its starting impetus by Connie Mulder. As the Muldergate, or Informationgate, scandal began to surface, few observers paid attention to the record compiled by Mulder during his ten months as minister of plural relations and development. His performance had not been bad. Mulder had displayed a receptivity to new ideas from the nonwhite community. Critics, however, were not convinced that he listened when the feedback came from other than polite sources such as community councils or chiefs' assemblies. It was questionable if he would have worked in harmony with the more-militant parts of the black, colored, or Indian communities.

In the wake of the Botha victory, the first signal fractionalization within the National party began to occur. During late November 1978, this discontent crystalized in Transvaal. Andries P. Treurnicht, the notorious hardliner, was elected as National party leader for this political unit that included Johannesburg. He defeated the slightly more-liberal minister of labor, Stephanus P. Botha and, as a result, replaced the now disgraced Connie Mulder as the National party leader in the Transvaal.

The Economist characterized Treurnicht as a man who would oppose whites and nonwhites playing rugby together because such contact might lead the men to become friends. Once this horrid event occurred, miscegenation between female companions of the players of one race and the male players of the other would be the inevitable next step.[35]

John Vorster had employed Treurnicht as a junior minister in his administration. He had been assigned the role of deputy minister for black affairs. Botha also wished to keep Treurnicht away from the seat of power. For the moment, he had been bypassed effectively as Koornhof assumed the direction of black affairs and as another *verligte,* moderate, Punt Janson became the minister of black education.[36] For the moment, Treurnicht and his supporters had been checkmated. They refused to remain quiescent for long.

Pieter Koornhof stepped into the limelight at the start of the Botha administration. First, he became involved personally in the Crossroads housing dispute near Capetown. Most observers were surprised at the relatively moderate tone he set. This impression was strengthened by his facility for issuing statements to the world press that promised a hopeful future.[37] Never, however, did he place these statements in a temporal context.

The Situation Appears to Improve

As late 1978 passed into early 1979, world opinion looked with optimism, perhaps simple-minded optimism some would think, at events taking place in South Africa. Even as normally a level-headed observer as the *Christian*

Science Monitor allowed itself to be carried away on the breezes of optimism. Its reporter was impressed by a meeting that took place between Prime Minister Botha and the eight homeland leaders in Capetown. Botha took this occasion to promise that he would reexamine the 1936 land-distribution act that had awarded 87 percent of the land of the country to the white population. On the whole, the chiefs appeared satisfied with the results of the meeting. Chief Lennox Sebe of the Ciskei homeland stated for publication that he was pleased to meet with Botha, a man who has "a philosophy and not an ideology."[38] Not to be outdone, the South African prime minister replied that his country must be prepared to eliminate "wornout practices and restrictions."[39]

Vorster and Mulder Fall into Disgrace

Although the two events were unrelated, some observers were amused that during the first months of 1979 the political fortunes of former Information Minister Connie Mulder fell at a rate of decline equal to the rate of rise in price that gold simultaneously was experiencing. Mulder could not arrest the onslaught of criticism he received on all sides. Late in January, he resigned from Parliament. In his parting words, he sounded like a thoroughly broken man. He still had not told his side of the Muldergate story, and as a result, he followed the head of the Bureau of State Security, General van den Bergh, into obscurity and disgrace. Both Mulder and van den Bergh had been World War II, pro-Nazi detainees and were loyal to John Vorster to the end. The parallels between their fate and those of many cronies of Richard Nixon were quite striking. It was clear that both Mulder and van den Bergh intended to keep silent as long as possible. This resolve continued even after the National party expelled Mulder from its ranks in April. It must be remembered that in South Africa the National party carried with it heavy overtones of religious and patriotic observance. Expulsion from the ranks of the National party carried with it a degree of social stigma that should not be underestimated.[40]

The parallels with Watergate continued with startling similarity. During May 1979, Mulder began to talk and to implicate Vorster. He told the press that he had lied to the press on the orders of the prime minister when he had testified concerning the scope of secret propaganda projects undertaken and financed, in a clandestine fashion, by the Pretoria government. On June 4, 1979, John Vorster resigned as president of South Africa. This time nothing was said about ill health. Vorster had joined the ranks of disgraced politicians, a familiar category worldwide.[41]

The Erasmus Commission report dealing with the Ministry of Information scandal was the proximate cause of the Vorster presidential resignation. The report accused him of giving false information to the investigating committee. The commission concluded that he knew all there was to know concerning the basic financial arrangements for dispensing Ministry of Information funds in a clandestine fashion. The commission asserted that then Prime Minister Vorster had been consulted about the usage of the secret funds and about the goals of the projects. Passing unfavorable judgments upon the actions of Vorster, the Erasmus Commission concluded that the prime minister had not revealed irregularities that came to his attention and, furthermore, that he had concealed them from the cabinet and had delayed taking purposeful steps to end this wrongful state of affairs. The government support of the newspaper, *The Citizen,* was cited in this regard.[42]

The president of the South African Senate, Marais Viljoen, replaced John Vorster in his largely ceremonial post as president of South Africa. This change was only the start of a more-fundamental shakeup. Prime Minister Botha used the opportunity to replace Jimmy Kruger as minister of justice. This hardliner, who had been so insensitive in his handling of the Steven Biko matter, had become a continuing source of embarrassment to the more-moderate current regime. Now that Viljoen had abandoned his post as president of the Senate to become president of the country, the perfect opportunity to place Jimmy Kruger in an inconsequential position of honor presented itself. The former minister of justice became the new president of the South African Senate.

At the same time, Botha chose to bring the troublesome, supercritical Andries Treurnicht on to his team in a full-fledged manner. This blatant, hardliner segregationist was selected as minister of public works, statistics, and tourism. No longer a junior minister, Treurnicht now would be included in the criticism of the Botha regime that was being indulged in with increasing frequency by the more-reactionary elements in the country.[43]

Botha also took the occasion of the disgrace of the Vorster-Mulder element of the National party to introduce laws restricting coverage of police activities. For a while it appeared that newspapers would be prohibited from writing about corruption within the South African government. At the last moment, the Botha regime decided not to enact the strict press-censorship rules that had been contemplated. The government did, however, enact a new law that provided for five-year jail sentences and fines in excess of $11,000 for editors and journalists who published false reports concerning police activities. The burden of proof that the law had not been violated was placed upon the editor or journalist in question. A similar prohibition concerning the false reporting of news about the South African prisons had been in effect since 1959.[44]

The rout of the Vorster-Mulder branch of the National party continued. On August 1, 1979, Connie Mulder pleaded innocent to formal charges that he had refused to testify fully before a committee of judicial inquiry. If found guilty, he could have been sentenced to a term of up to six months in prison and/or a fine of up to $118.[45] Two months later Mulder was acquitted of the charges, but the damage had been done. Neither he nor Vorster have again played a part of note in South African political life. In this regard, statements of Dr. Eschel Rhoodie, the mastermind of the scheme, did not help matters. While being held in custody in France, awaiting extradition to South Africa for trial in the scandal, Rhoodie inculpated Prime Minister Botha. If Rhoodie can be believed, Botha, while minister of defense, had smuggled large arms caches into Mozambique in an attempt to overthrow the Samora Machel government. Similarly, according to Rhoodie, Botha had paid longtime Rhodesian (Zimbabwean) liberation leader James Chikerema the handsome sum of $475,000 in hopes that he would succeed in the struggle to become the first black ruler of Zimbabwe.[46] Botha reacted with fury to the charges and, as a result, seemed to work harder to purge the effects of the Vorster regime from the day-to-day running of his government. By neutralizing the Treurnicht-led hardliners and by ostracizing the equally rigid supporters of Vorster and Mulder, Prime Minister Botha was able to develop a consensus that could have permitted him to make significant steps toward easing apartheid, if he were so disposed. Unfortunately, his movement toward easing restrictions was modest at best.

Activities of the Progressive Federal Party

In the white community, the only effective opposition to the apartheid-oriented policies of the Botha government was provided by the Progressive Federal party. Some felt that Frederik van Zyl Slabbert, an Afrikaner academic in a country in which 60 percent of the voters in the country are Afrikaners, could become a force for positive change. van Zyl Slabbert was scheduled to replace English-speaking Colin Eglin as the leader of the political party that could claim 17 members in Parliament—a small number in comparison to the 135-member National party. Nonetheless, the liberal Progressive Federal party did provide some hope for the coming of a multiracial future to South Africa. This party had replaced the United party as the official opposition party in Parliament at the 1977 election.[47]

Subsequent proddings from van Zyl Slabbert, now firmly established as leader of the Progressive Federal party, did little to move Botha toward making major changes in the South African apartheid system. As the first year of the Botha reign ended in October 1979, those looking for indications of future, meaningful, change could find a few straws in the wind to enforce their perhaps unrealistic hopes. The Botha government had made moves toward examining the land tenure system and to consider whether to permit blacks to possess ninety-nine-year leaseholds. The government also promised to study the abolishment of the so-called heartbreak laws and to take advice from black and colored groups. Such changes were no doubt better than none at all, but the heart of the apartheid system remained in effect. The Group Areas Act still specified where people could live and work, and the Pass Laws and Homelands concept further restricted the right of the black person to freedom and happiness.[48]

It was all well and good for outsiders to think that the changes in the apartheid system engineered by the Botha government were minor in nature. To many members of the National party, including some of the leaders, the slight slackening in enforcement was the first step in the direction of the total collapse of their governmental system. It is not surprising that Dr. Treurnicht became the spokesperson of the hardliners within the party. He took every occasion possible to demonstrate that his nickname, Doctor No, was well deserved. He and Botha feuded in public on two different occasions. The first occasion was when Treurnicht suggested that the time to forgive Connie Mulder for his transgressions was at hand and that he should be readmitted to the ranks of the National party. The second disagreement concerned the plan of the Botha government to permit interracial rugby matches.[49]

The demonstrable lack of cohesiveness within the ruling chambers of government coincided temporally with the first days of freedom in Zimbabwe. The utter inability of blacks within South Africa to be able to exploit the momentum generated by this event demonstrated conclusively how far away liberation in South Africa actually was, and, as a corollary, how totally in control the white minority remained. Botha warned that separate development was the cornerstone and salvation of South Africa and that anyone disputing this theory had better watch his or her step. Botha made it clear that any disputes with the Treurnicht hardliners notwithstanding, a repeat of the Rhodesia-to-Zimbabwe transition would not be allowed in South Africa.

Because of governmental restrictions on free speech within South Africa, it is hard to measure public opinion. Knowledgeable observers, however, like John F. Burns of *The New York Times* felt that the Treurnicht branch was far stronger in Parliament than among the general electorate.[50] He estimated that Treurnicht sympathizers might hold about 60 of the 134 National party seats in Parliament and a similar percentage of supporters among the rank and file of the National party workers. Treurnicht's otherwise strong position was negated because he enjoyed little support among English-speaking voters. If an early general election were forced, it was predicted that Treurnicht would be defeated overwhelmingly by Botha. Burns and most other observers were certain that the English speakers invariably would decide that Botha was the lesser of two evils.

The President's Council Proposal

On May 8, 1980, the long-awaited Botha government plan to restructure governmental operations was announced. Interior and Justice Minister Alwyn L. Schlebusch had headed a parliamentary group formed two years previously as a reaction to heavy criticisms of the findings of a similar group that Botha had chaired.

Under the Schlebusch plan, the upper house of Parliament, the Senate, would be disbanded. Its place was to be taken by a new organization, the state president's council. It was to be composed of sixty members drawn from the white, colored, and Indian communities. The thought was to select experts and community leaders to serve as a consultative body on matters of national interest, including the Constitution. What about the black population? They were to have their own role and group, but specifics were not yet clear.

The Schlebusch plan was a modification of the earlier Botha plan for parliamentary rule. The earlier attempt at modifying the governing structure had proposed separate groups established by race in the form of an Indian Parliament and a colored Parliament. Some provisions for joint groupings with white ruling factions were contained, but in general, the isolation and second-class status of the Indian and colored populations were underlined—to say nothing of the complete ignoring of the black population. At least the Schlebusch plan brought Indian and colored representatives on to the same plane with white members of this new governing body. If blacks were not included at this level, and they most definitely were not so included, nonetheless a mechanism for dialogue with blacks had been devised.

Granted that the Schlebusch plan was an improvement over the Botha plan, significant difficulties remained. First, the Schlebusch plan specifically rejected movement toward the one-man–one-vote concept. The report observed that any such movement would bring disastrous consequences for all races. Second, the Schlebusch plan spent little time discussing the power of the state president's council. The reason was simple: There would be virtually none. Nonwhite groups were quick to label the proposed changes as mere window dressing. Third, it was not clear what impact the Schlebusch plan would have upon the government-promoted separate-homelands policy. Clearly, some entrenchment appeared to be occurring. So far, it was unclear how much.[51]

The Botha government could not have been pleased by the overwhelmingly unfavorable reaction to the Schlebusch plan that occurred. The main white opposition party, the Progressive Federal party, rejected the plan because blacks were excluded. Indian and colored groups agreed and added that even if included, the advisory nature of the council made it useless, no matter who participated. Both Dr. Motlana and Chief Buthelezi refused to have any part of the plan and warned of total ostracism by their supporters toward any political leader of no matter what color who chose to participate in the state president's council.[52]

In general, worldwide reaction to the Schlebusch plan was unfavorable. *The New York Times* reaction was typical. In an editorial cynically entitled "Reform, South African Style," the failure of Botha to carry out promises made in the first days of his administration were decried. If the status quo was maintained, the newspaper concluded that "no peaceful development seemed conceivable."[53]

Botha Shakes up His Cabinet

The reluctance of Botha to move in the direction of meaningful governmental reform was matched by a tendency on his part to allow the professional military a larger role in directing the government. No doubt, the years of service by the prime minister as military overseer in his role as defense minister had preconditioned him to accept their views. This shifting of emphasis tended to diminish the role played by the upper echelon of National party leaders in decisions of state. No longer were they the insiders. The military, and especially General Magnus Andre de Merindol Malan, seemed to have become the unquestioned power behind the throne. Malan was a compulsive anti-Communist and was believed to be the voice that urged Botha to strong military action in Namibia and the southern part of Angola.[54]

Seeing that his conceptual changes were meeting with widespread opposition, the prime minister moved to an area in which he was more in control of his own fate. He chose to shake up his cabinet. Botha resigned his portfolio as minister of defense, a move that freed him full time for the position of prime minister. It is not surprising that General Malan took over the defense position in this late–August 1980 move. A clear statement was being made for all to see. The professional military would be in charge of the ultimate self-defense of the nation. The previously all-powerful National party was being taught a lesson.

Within the National party, Botha used this late-1980 cabinet shakeup to isolate himself from the Treurnicht-led reactionary wing of the party. Botha removed Treurnicht from his post as minister of public affairs and tourism and assigned him to supervise the civil service as the minister of state administration. This post was new and had not been cabinet rank previously. At first, it seemed a strange appointment. Since the civil service was, in general, as conservative as Treurnicht himself, it appeared that Botha had provided Treurnicht with a tailor-made base of power. On further reflection, this explanation seemed doubtful because a part of Treurnicht's job was to explain the actions of the Botha government to the Afrikaner hardliners in the civil service. Treurnicht might therefore begin to be seen as a turncoat by those who would like to see him act in the most rigid of all possible modes.

In another move motivated by the desire to stop Treurnicht, Dr. Gerrit Viljoen was appointed as minister of education. He had been serving as administrator in Namibia and was a popular politician. Like Treurnicht, he came from the Transvaal Province. It was likely that at some future date he would challenge the more-conservative Treurnicht for the important post as province leader of the National party. Viljoen previously had defeated Treurnicht for the leadership position in the Broederbond.

Botha used the ministerial shakeup to complete still another piece of business. A competent bureaucrat, J. Chris Heunis, was named as minister of internal affairs. In this position Heunis would supervise governmental dealings with the 2.5 million colored and 750,000 Indian inhabitants of South Africa. Heunis, who had been minister of transportation, was considered to be capable of displaying the same sort of reasonableness in this domain that Dr. Pieter Koornhof had shown in dealing with blacks in his role as minister of cooperation and development. Marais Steyn, who had been minister of internal affairs, was transferred to the post of ambassador to Great Britain. Steyn had been criticized roundly for his intransigent handling of the June 1980 colored-students strike. The Indian and colored populations were not enthusiastic and pointed out that for all his sweet-sounding statements, Koornhof had done little of note to assist the black population. They feared Heunis would perform in a similar manner as internal affairs minister.[55]

During September 1981, Prime Minister Botha kept on with his plan to establish a state president's council. Clearly, he saw the council as the principal method to forge a wider consensus within his country and perhaps sometime to lead it toward a true confederation. The chairman of the commission responsible for the plan, Alwyn L. Schlebusch, was appointed as state vice-president and chairman of the state president's council. He had served previously as minister of interior and justice. Under the new constitution he was to retain his cabinet rank. Even though Schlebusch was now sixty-one years old, some felt that he was firmly in line to become the next prime minister if the state president's council idea succeeded. Botha surrounded Schlebusch with three other cabinet-minister appointments to the new grouping. Some colored and Indian leaders did join the ranks, but at least at the start, the true leaders of these communities were conspicuous by their absence.[56]

General Elections Are Called

On January 28, 1981, Prime Minister Botha called for the first general election in the country since his ascendency to power. This full-scale referendum on the Botha years was scheduled to occur on April 29, 1981. The prime minister was expected to press for a vaguely worded mandate from the electorate that would encourage him to keep the ship of state steady on the course charted. In this regard it seemed that recent unwillingness by the South African government to move toward significant accommodations at the Geneva Conference for Namibian independence was designed to keep the main part of the South African electorate on his side. Gradual progress that would keep both the black community and the Afrikaner hardliners unhappy but unwilling to risk a total break seemed to be the Botha plan. The upcoming election would show whether or not the electorate agreed with him that this was the best strategy in the present circumstances.[57]

Only in a nation like South Africa could Prime Minister Botha be perceived as a moderate candidate. True, he was less rigid than Treurnicht, but once this concession had been made, little more could be said. Remarks made by Botha in Parliament shortly before he announced the forthcoming general election demonstrated how hardline he truly was. When asked if the state president's council was a prelude to granting full citizenship to Indian and colored residents, he stated, somewhat enigmatically, "It is dangerous to make full citizens of Coloreds and Asians at the cost of full citizenship for Blacks." When the questioner pressed to inquire if Botha foresaw the day when blacks would receive full citizenship, he responded with the brusque reply "No."[58]

At the April 29, 1981, election, held two years before necessary by constitutional requirements, Prime Minister Botha won a clear victory.[59] Nonetheless, the margin of victory was disappointing from his perspective. The National party received 131 of the 165 seats in Parliament. Less encouraging, it only managed to capture 53 percent of the popular vote as opposed to 68 percent of the total in the 1977 general election held during the prime ministership of John Vorster. Although its members did not succeed in capturing a seat in the Parliament, the white supremacist Herstige National party (the reconstituted National party) made significant gains in attracting electorate support. This National party breakaway group founded in 1969 by Albert Hertzog waged a vituperative campaign that charged Botha with being a traitor who had sold out the white heritage of South Africa. A significant number of voters obviously agreed.

Paradoxically, even though the left-wing (so-called) element in South African politics, the Progressive Federal party, also made significant gains in the April 1981 election, it was less likely that the Botha government would be affected by their gains. The Progressive Federal party did raise its number of seats in Parliament from 17 to 26 and for the first time was successful in defeating a sitting National party member of Parliament. Nonetheless there seemed to be upper limits to the amount of support that could be garnered in South Africa for any political group positioned to the left of the National party. This statement is particularly true when it is remembered that much of the strength of the Progressive Federal party comes from the minority English-speaking part of the white population. Liberal opposition to National party rule in South Africa has a long and relatively respectable history. Without attempting to diminish the importance of this activity, it still must be stated that it is unlikely that in the end any political party dominated by English speakers will play a crucial rule in the eventual outcome of the South African political crisis. For better or worse, it will be the political parties populated by Afrikaners that will settle the white response to black pressures. For this reason, the burgeoning strength of the Herstige National party becomes so significant.[60]

Even though Prime Minister Botha was still undeniably well ensconced in power, he could not deny that the Afrikaner electorate had sent him a clear message by the electoral vote. Reform might be alright in order to avoid a complete race war in South Africa. Nonetheless, there were definite limits to what would be acceptable. When even a hardline National party member like Truernicht had to scramble to defeat an even farther to the right opponent like the Herstige National party candidate opposing him, Jaap Marais, it must be clear to Botha that the sort of accommodations to the black majority being urged upon him by the Progressive Federal party were totally out of the question. Within the spectrum of acceptable Afrikaner political conduct, Botha felt himself being pushed to the left side of the middle; for him, a new and uncomfortable sensation.[61]

At the beginning of August 1981, Prime Minister Botha addressed the newly constituted Parliament at their opening session in Capetown. He took the occasion to proclaim that he was a strong leader and "not a jellyfish."[62] Clearly, he was reacting to the charge that the recent general-election results had indicated the white population doubted his ability to direct the nation in troubled times.[63]

The leaders of the Progressive Federal party mounted a strong rebuttal in their parliamentary remarks. They excoriated Botha for his lack of direction and his refusal to take steps to end apartheid. Botha, for his part, indicated that he would continue to act in the future as he had done in the past. He made it clear that he would rely on the state president's council that he had instituted in February 1981 for ideas on methods to change the constitutional system in South Africa. Such a tactic was looked on by many of his critics as a method to delay action and to avoid responsibility. Given the lack of credibility with which the nonwhite community regarded many of their so-called representatives, it was highly questionable if the president's council could serve as an effective vehicle for change.[64]

The Botha handling of the Namibia controversy serves as an example of the method employed by Botha to procrastinate when he wishes to preserve the status quo. First, the South African military launched a massive attack into Angola at the end of August 1981. Then, with much fanfare, the troops were withdrawn. As worldwide criticism of the activity mounted, Botha announced that he and U.S. Secretary of State Haig had agreed in principle to a withdrawal timetable. When attentions turned elsewhere, South Africa regretfully announced that new difficulties have arisen that again cast peace attempts in Namibia into doubt. Another half-year passed, and little of substance had been accomplished.[65]

Within South Africa, the Botha government, as did the predecessor Vorster government, employs the stall tactic to equal perfection. Commissions to study the burning problems of the nation are announced with enormous publicity. Promises of a new day soon to come are issued from Pretoria with great regularity. Often an interim report is issued and discussed interminably, and then the commission is asked to deliberate some more. A final report one day appears. Further debate occurs, and speedy Parliament action is promised. This announcement usually is the last step. The report dies a swift, honored, but useless death. In actuality, the situation has not changed. Perhaps it can be objected that the Wiehahn Commission report dealing with labor reform and, to a lesser degree, the Viljoen Committee report on black housing have been carried through to the end of the process and some implementation. Even if true, the Riekert Commission report dealing with manpower usage, the De Lange Commission report dealing with education, and probably the Schlebusch Committee report that led to the state president's council terminated far short of their hoped-for goals. The sum total of these projects is that the status quo still reigns supreme.

The Treurnicht Split

Outside observers might feel that Prime Minister Botha was moving toward racial progress in an overly lethargic manner. Such an opinion, however, was not shared by Treurnicht and those of similarly reactionary-conservative views. In their opinion, Botha was abandoning over three decades of tried and proven apartheid policies. A revolt had been rumored for years. During late February 1982, the definitive split began to take place. In an unheard-of show of disunity within the National party, twenty-two of its Parliament members, of which two held cabinet posts, voted against the prime minister on a motion of confidence proposed in a National party parliamentary caucus. Botha was clearly furious and gave the dissenters until the following Wednesday to change their vote. He promised disciplinary action would be taken if they refused to do so. One hundred National party members of Parliament had voted their confidence in the prime minister. Eighteen, including Andries Treurnicht, the man widely considered to be leading the dissidents, abstained. The forthcoming report of the president's council that was rumored to suggest sweeping change of constitutional governing structures so that colored people again would be given some type of parliamentary representation was suspected as the motivating cause for the timing of the rupture.[66]

The split widened. The leadership by Treurnicht of the conservative wing became totally clear. Botha decided to challenge the dissenters head-on. He insisted that Dr. Treurnicht be ousted from his policymaking role as member of the National party executive committee. By a vote of 172 to 36, party leaders complied. As a result, control of the National party apparatus in the Transvaal fell from his hands. A vote of confidence for the right of the prime minister to interpret National party policies in important issues carried by the same wide majority. A few days later, sixteen National party members of Parliament, including two ministers in the cabinet, Treurnicht and Ferdinand Hertzenberg, formally disassociated themselves from the National party and took a symbolic walk across the aisle at the opening of Parliament in Capetown in order to sit with the opposition members. The largest split in the previously monolithic National party rule of South Africa had occurred.[67]

The Treurnicht revolt is, of course, noteworthy. It is possible however, to exaggerate its importance except as a signpost indicating future political turmoil ahead. Prime Minister Botha is still very much in charge and can count on 126 of the 177 votes in Parliament. In many circumstances, he still may be able to count on the Treurnicht-led Afrikaner hardliners. This point was emphasized by Treurnicht when he said, "We are independent Nationalists. We have no intention of being anything but Nationalists.[68]

Treurnicht pledged his basic support to the traditional principles of the National party and intimated the break came because the ruling Botha wing had lost its bearings. Given the circumstances, it was not surprising that former Prime Minister John Vorster rose from political obscurity and disgrace to lend his support to Treurnicht and his hardliners.

The Treurnicht split came on the same day that the liberal Progressive Federal party and reactionary right-wing Herstige National party both scored marked increase in voter support at local elections held throughout the country. In a major surprise, the Progressive Federal party outpolled the National party for council seats in the city of Johannesburg. Granted that the largest city in South Africa is a stronghold of English-speaking liberalism and granted also that the National party was able to retain control of the city council by arranging a coalition with seat winners from minor parties and independent persuasions, the relatively poor showing made by the National party was another strong indication that all was not well within Afrikanerdom.[69]

With the political events of February to March 1982, it is safe to say that political power within white South Africa is fragmented more than it has been at least since 1948. Some liberal Afrikaners are moving toward the Progressive Federal party at the same time that some conservative English speakers are moving toward the National party and that some conservative National party members are joining with the Treurnicht-led faction of Afrikanerdom. In what was a political monolith, the diversity is quite confusing and hard to interpret. Two political analysts, one of whom became assistant secretary of state for Africa, Chester A. Crocker, discussed this phenomenon and the reasons why it occurs in a recent paper.

"Political collapse as the Iranian case demonstrates, is not only found in states that are objectively 'weak'—stated another way, the definition of weakness may vary over time and place. Twenty-five-to-thirty-year-old governments such as that of the National party in South Africa and the Neo-Destourian autocracy of Tunisia or post-Neguib Egypt may also be vulnerable to at least temporary political upheaval, offering openings to external manipulation."[70]

Recent events have confirmed these opinions and could well explain the seeming confusion and lack of purpose that has characterized white politics in the recent past. If the president's council proposal leads to a significant increase in authority for Prime Minister Botha, the negative reaction to this assumption of added power could lead to even more instances of the type of instability discussed by Crocker and his coauthor, Howard Samuels.

The Treurnicht group carried through with its threat to form a new political party. In late 1982, the Conservative party came into existence. It presented itself as an alternative to the philosophies of the National party. In opening remarks, Treurnicht rejected the concept of an open society and pledged total opposition to multiracialism and social or political integration in South Africa. Treurnicht summed up his views with the observation, "There is a difference between love of your neighbor—that is imperative— and national suicide."[71]

South Africans were obliged to wait another two months before receiving the details of the president's council's plan that had been the immediate cause of the Treurnicht split and the founding of the Conservative party. When a draft of the plan was disclosed, it still was unclear how fundamental would be the changes in the South African governing structure if they were adopted. It seemed clear that the Botha government was floating a trial balloon in hopes that the colored and Indian populations could be enticed to join the white side against the blacks.[72]

The results were surprising. The leading Indian and colored political parties fell into line without a whimper.[73] Many younger, people in both groups did not agree with the president's council plan, but they were outvoted by their elders who opted for a small piece of the political pie rather than none at all. Botha must have been delighted that his strategy was working.[74] The blacks were furious, but he had expected this outcome.[75]. The Treurnicht followers were opposed on the right and the van Zyl Slabbert followers were opposed on the left. As a result, Botha had seized the center firmly for himself. He was placing his trust in the mainstream of the National party populace and was banking that they would support his moves to bring slow, gradual change to the racial situation in South Africa.

Given all the black-white animosity and bloodshed that had already occurred in South Africa it seems almost incredible that the government would believe that measures of reform as timid as the president's council plan could bring racial peace to South Africa.

Notes

1. June Goodwin, "South Africa Political Linkup a Threat to White Regime," *Christian Science Monitor,* January 5, 1978.

2. Caryle Murphy, "Challenge to South Africa," *Washington Post,* January 12, 1978.

3. June Goodwin, "Buthelize Makes Leader Bid in South Africa," *Christian Science Monitor,* January 30, 1978.

4. "South African Militants Attack Chief," *Washington Star,* March 12, 1978.

5. Gary Thatcher, "South Africa's Bishop Tutu—Time for a Peaceful Solution Is Short," *Christian Science Monitor,* April 26, 1979.

6. Associated Press, "David M. Sibeko, 40, South African Exile Murdered in Tanzania," *The New York Times,* June 13, 1979.

7. Reuter News Service, "South Africa Black Unit Chooses New Chairman," *The New York Times,* October 11, 1979.

8. Gary Thatcher, "Soweto: The Mayor Who Isn't," *Christian Science Monitor,* September 18, 1979.

9. Gary Thatcher, "Black Political Movement Reappears in RSA," *Christian Science Monitor,* October 24, 1979.

10. Caryle Murphy, "Blacks Push to Free Activist," *Washington Post,* April 14, 1980.

11. "Congressmen Urge Pretoria to Free Black Rights Leader," *Baltimore Sun,* April 25, 1980.

12. Caryle Murphy, "Blacks Push to Free Activist."

13. John F. Burns, "Black Bishop and South Africa Wage War of Nerves," *The New York Times,* May 4, 1980.

14. "South African Zulu Chief Pushing Power Sharing Plan," *Baltimore Sun,* June 8, 1980.

15. Gary Thatcher, "South African Council Bars Blacks; Turns to Other Non-Whites," *Christian Science Monitor,* September 30, 1980.

16. Joseph Lelyveld, "Zulu Leader Faces a Challenge as Voice of South African Blacks," *The New York Times,* November 30, 1980.

17. Ibid.

18. Ibid.

19. Alan Cowell, "New Conflict Feared Along Africa's Last Color Frontier," *The New York Times,* September 5, 1982.

20. Paul Van Slambrouck, "South Africa Warns Whites Not to Join Banned Black Group," *Christian Science Monitor,* September 21, 1982; Paul Van Slambrouck, "Court Conviction Signals South African Clampdown," *Christian Science Monitor,* October 21, 1982.

21. Paul Van Slambrouck, "South Africa Raid on Black Nationalists Winning a Battle but Losing the War?", *Christian Science Monitor,* December 10, 1982.

22. Editorial, "Bully," *Washington Post,* December 11, 1982.

23. "South Africa Bars a Black Role In 3-House Parliamentary System," *The New York Times,* November 10, 1982.

24. William Raspberry, "Out of South Africa's Frying Pan," *Washington Post,* January 10, 1983.

25. Allister Sparks, "Minority Split in South Africa on Charter Decision," *Washington Post,* February 8, 1983.

26. Ibid.

27. "Vorster Cabinet Shift Hints No Change in Policy," *Washington Post,* January 26, 1978.

28. Associated Press, "South Africa's President Dies at 74," *Baltimore Sun,* August 22, 1978.

29. Caryle Murphy, "Ailing Vorster Quits," *Washington Post,* September 22, 1978.

30. Tila Luuk, "Vorster Policies United Whites but Ignored Ghettoes," *Washington Star,* September 24, 1978.

31. "Vorster's Missed Chance," *The Economist,* September 23, 1978.

32. "Botha Succeeds Vorster as South African Premier," *Baltimore Sun,* September 29, 1978.

33. "South African Leader Quits in Funds Scandal," *Baltimore Sun,* November 8, 1978.

34. John F. Burns, "New South African Premier Picks Moderate as Black Affairs Chief," *The New York Times,* November 15, 1978.

35. "South Africa, Right and Left," *The Economist,* November 18, 1978.

36. John F. Burns, "Racial Hardliner at Transvaal Helm," *The New York Times,* November 26, 1978.

37. "Humane Footsteps in South Africa," *Christian Science Monitor,* December 4, 1978.

38. Humphrey Tyler, "Some Good Words for Botha From Blacks," *Christian Science Monitor,* January 24, 1979.

39. Ibid.

40. Humphrey Tyler, "South Africa's Own 'Gate' Scandal Won't Go Away," *Christian Science Monitor,* January 29, 1979.

41. John F. Burns, "Scandal Exposes Rifts in South Africa Leadership," *The New York Times,* April 18, 1979.

42. "Vorster Accused of Role in Scandal, Quits as President," *The New York Times,* June 5, 1979.

43. "South Africa Shuffles Cabinet Posts; Drops Press Curb Proposal," *Washington Post,* June 15, 1979.

44. "Hopes that Flicker and Die," *The Economist,* June 23, 1979.

45. Reuter News Service, "Mulder Pleads Innocent in Funds Scandal Case," *Washington Post,* August 2, 1979.

46. Gary Thatcher, "South Africa Charged with Paying Off Black Rhodesian Leaders," *Christian Science Monitor,* August 9, 1979.

47. Humphrey Tyler, "Party Revolt in South Africa Ousts Leader," *Christian Science Monitor,* August 22, 1979; John F. Burns, "South Africa White Liberals Pin Hopes on New Leaders," *The New York Times,* September 9, 1979.

48. Carey Winfrey, "Premier's New Ideas Surprise South Africa," *The New York Times,* October 28, 1979.

49. Humphrey Tyler, "South Africa's Doctor No May Split Ruling Party," *Christian Science Monitor,* March 11, 1980.

50. John F. Burns, "Botha Fights a Challenge from South African Right," *The New York Times,* April 13, 1980.

51. John F. Burns, "South Africa Giving Blacks a State Role," *The New York Times,* May 9, 1980.

52. Gary Thatcher, "Plan to Change Constitution Disappoints South African Blacks," *Christian Science Monitor,* May 12, 1980.

53. Editorial, "Reform, South African Style," *The New York Times,* May 21, 1980.

54. Caryle Murphy, "South African Military Exerts Greater Influence on Policy," *Washington Post,* May 30, 1980.

55. John F. Burns, "South Africa's Whites Are Debating Plan to Share Power," *The New York Times,* June 15, 1980; "South African Cabinet Shake-up," *Christian Science Monitor,* August 28, 1980; Caryle Murphy, "Botha Shuffles Cabinet," *Washington Post,* August 27, 1980.

56. Humphrey Tyler, "Botha's Dangerous Gamble Risking Right Wing Ire to Promote Council," *Christian Science Monitor,* September 30, 1980.

57. Joseph Lelyveld, "South African Leader Calls Vote; Move against Party Foes Is Seen," *The New York Times,* January 29, 1981.

58. "Botha Rules Out Grant of Equality for Blacks," *Baltimore Sun,* January 27, 1981.

59. Gary Thatcher, "An Afrikaner Who Wants to Be South Africa's Ronald Reagan," *Christian Science Monitor,* February 25, 1981.

60. Joseph Lelyveld, "Major South African Party Suffers Setback Despite Election Victory," *The New York Times,* May 1, 1981.

61. Caryle Murphy, "Wide Discontent with Botha Seen in South African Vote," *Washington Post,* May 1, 1981; Gary Thatcher, "Ruling Party Wins in South Africa but Many Whites Bolt Ranks," *Christian Science Monitor,* May 1, 1981.

62. "South Africa Splits Healthily under Botha," *The Economist,* May 9, 1981.

63. Robert I. Rotberg, "South Africa: A Mandate for Change," *Christian Science Monitor,* May 8, 1981.

64. Marsh Clark, "Botha Dashes Hope that South Africa Nears Racial Reform," *Washington Star,* August 6, 1981.

65. Benjamin Togrund, "South Africa Stalk," *New Republic,* November 18, 1981; J.D.F. Jones, "The Way of the Tortoise," *Financial Times,* November 16, 1981.

66. Allister Sparks, "South Africa's Ruling Party Split by Conservatives' Revolt," *Washington Post,* February 26, 1982.

67. Joseph Lelyveld, "Pretoria Premier Defeats His Rival," *The New York Times,* February 28, 1982.

68. Allister Sparks, "South Africa Ruling Party Splinters over Race Policies," *Washington Post,* March 4, 1982.

69. Ibid.

70. Chester Crocker, and Howard Samuels, *Soviet Activity in Africa* (Washington, D.C.: Center for Strategic and International Studies, Georgetown University, 1979).

71. Joseph Lelyveld, "Afrikaner Founds Right Wing Party," *The New York Times,* March 26, 1982.

72. Antero Pietila, "South African Whites Stunned by Proposals for Colored Reforms," *Baltimore Sun,* May 14, 1982; Joseph Lelyveld, "South Africa Gets Mixed Power Plan," *The New York Times,* May 13, 1982.

73. Paul Van Slambrouck, "Coloreds, Many Whites Rallying Round South African Power Sharing Plan," *Christian Science Monitor,* January 6, 1983.

74. "A Small Step for Mr. Botha," *Financial Times,* January 11, 1983.

75. Gatsha Buthelezi, "An Ally's Act of Betrayal," *Washington Post,* February 3, 1983.

2 Five More Years of Apartheid

An Oppressive Atmosphere

The stagnation that has occurred in the political spectrum, both black and white, has been matched in other areas. During the period under inspection, efforts have been made to improve housing, education, and job availability for the South African nonwhite population. Government-sponsored commissions have been operating in these three fields. Studies have been made, debated, and the findings even occasionally followed. Unfortunately, the sum total of gains has been small and more than neutralized by the unstopping growth of the nonwhite population. The period 1977–1982 stands as proof that apartheid, even a sanitized version, is doomed to failure.

By 1977, the South African government officially had shelved the term *apartheid* and had resorted to euphemisms such as *separate development* and *plural democracies*. Whatever the system of regulations was called, its scale of operation was still massive. The traditional government policy of assigning the black population to nine homelands comprising 13 percent of the national acreage, areas that some day were to become independent, was still in effect.

The Group Areas Act still controlled where people in the country could live. Section 10 of the Bantu (urban areas) Consolidation Act still made it illegal for a black to remain in any urban area like Soweto for more than seventy-two hours unless he has lived there continuously since birth or has worked continuously with one employer for ten or more years. Wives, unmarried daughters, and sons under eighteen were permitted to remain with a legitimate resident unless he lost his job and was endorsed out to a homeland that he well may previously have never seen.[1]

The massive wave of arrests and bannings undertaken by the government on October 19, 1977, at the very start of our study period, served warning that the current regulatory system, under whatever name it was denominated, would not tolerate strong criticism. Thus, those South Africans, white and black, who agitated for better housing, education, and jobs for the nonwhite population undertook such activity at their own risk. In this particular raid, seventy-five blacks were detained. Six blacks were banned, as were two prominent whites: Donald Woods, the editor of the

33

East London Daily Dispatch, and clergyman Beyers Naude. Black newspaper editor Percy Qobosa of *The World,* one of the strongest voices for change in South Africa, also was banned in the October 19, 1977, sweep. Eighteen dissident organizations and one newspaper were closed.

The press within and without South Africa were quick to condemn the governmental actions. In both cases the protests rose beyond the level of mere objection to the confinements that were carried out in such an arbitrary manner. Observers recognized that detentions, bannings, and closings of this nature had a more-profound and widespread purpose—namely, they were intended to insure that the government approach for providing housing, jobs, and education for nonwhites would continue to be carried out at the snail's pace satisfactory to the government. Agitation from outside of governmental circles aimed at applying pressure to speed progress in these domains would not be tolerated.

The *Cape Times* observed that the banning and detention orders were the actions of foolish and frightened men who lacked the courage to face the truth of their own disastrous failure when it is spelled out to them in plain and forceful language. The *Rand Daily Mail* echoed this view when it observed that these bannings and detention orders were the most gravely authoritarian action that the National party government has ever taken.[2] U.S. and U.K. papers developed the same theme.

The pressure placed upon the South African government by the Soweto riots, student strikes, the death of Steven Biko, and the universal criticism caused by their October 19, 1977, banning and detention orders seemed to persuade the Vorster government that the time to ease pressure, at least momentarily, had arrived. On November 3, 1977, the South African government decreed that blacks, upon leaving their tribal homelands, no longer had to carry with them the so-called reference books supplied by the government. Instead, henceforth, they would be able to utilize identification documents issued by their own tribal homeland. For the most part, the change appeared to be cosmetic rather than substantive in nature. What little convenience would be gained by the rural black population would seem to be canceled by the further dependence upon the homeland authorities that the legislation imposed. Since the whole homelands concept is at base root an affront to South African black solidarity and eventual unified independence, it is not surprising that the reaction to the new legislation was unfavorable.[3]

An editorial in the *Baltimore Sun* concluded that the South African reforms, although significant, would not succeed in diminishing protest.[4] The newspaper felt that the apartheid system still practiced the control of human movement in an infamous manner similar to that practiced in the Peoples' Republic of China and in the USSR.

The *Baltimore Sun* went on to say that neither the Transkei nor Kwazulu was affected by the new travel and identification regulations.⁵ The Transkei is considered by South Africa as being a separate country. Kwazulu did not participate because Chief Buthelezi refused to take part in the concept of separate development as defined by the Pretoria government. For people from the Transkei and Kwazulu, the reference-book system or its equivalent was still much in evidence and effect. The only good point to the new regulations seemed to be that families of black breadwinners were given permission to live with their working member in what was technically a white area of the country. Such a gain could be largely illusionary, however, since the government retained the authority to move these people whenever desired.

School Strikes

Even though the Vorster government had taken steps to ease the housing and travel restrictions upon blacks to some extent, the massive problems within the nonwhite educational system continued to fester. The widespread student strike in Soweto pointed out the unfairness inherent in the South African educational system. No matter how much the South African government claimed that separate but equal educational facilities and opportunities were the wave of the future, it was clear to all detached observers that such a policy was doomed to failure. In order for the policy to succeed, infusions of Pretoria government money beyond any amount that could be expected reasonably would have to be spent. Clearly, the white population was not in the mood to make any such expenditures. At the base of the problem was the reality that better education for blacks would lead inevitably to better jobs for blacks and then to demands for better housing, better apportionment of land, and eventually, full participation in the government of the nation. The one-man–one-vote idea would be then only a step away. As a result, the only answer from the point of view of the Pretoria government would appear to necessitate drawing the line on the question of education. Separate but equal, perhaps in theory, but even this much of an extension of equitable treatment to the black population would appear to pose insupportable problems for the white minority in South Africa.

In the middle of 1977, a massive student strike began in Soweto. Forty schools with a total enrollment of 27,000 students were obliged to close. Half of the 700 high school teachers in Soweto handed in their resignations to demonstrate sympathy with the actions of the black students. The motive for the strike was the continuing obligation for blacks to learn Afrikans, the language of the oppressor as they considered it. In the wake of the June 1976 Soweto riots, the government had promised to take steps to rectify abuses in the educational system. The refusal to lift the Afrikans language requirement during the subsequent year was taken as proof by the Soweto students that the government had no intention of keeping its word.

The strike spread through the nonwhite population of the country with great speed. At its height, more than 200,000 students throughout South Africa joined the strike in sympathy with the aims of the Soweto students. The massive walkout drew attention to the inequities in the South African white versus nonwhite educational systems. The disparities were striking. By 1978, fewer than 10,000 blacks in the country's history had earned university degrees. The three black universities operating within South Africa had fewer than 5,000 students and did not possess faculties of engineering, art, music, dentistry, or medicine. Fewer than 400 qualified medical doctors could be found among the black population. Fifteen additional black medical doctors were qualifying each year at the white University of Natal. At the same time, early 1978, approximately 100 black lawyers and 1 black dentist were practicing in South Africa.

In 1976, at the time of the Soweto riots, government per capita expenditure was $763 for each white child and $48 for each black child. During the 1977–1978 school year, $135 million was destined for white education expenditure. This amount was roughly approximate to 7 percent of the amount being spent on South African military defense.[6]

Dropout rates among black children are enormous. Almost 20 percent of black children who entered school in 1972 failed to reach the second grade. Nearly 40 percent of the black students who first enrolled in 1972 had withdrawn before the start of the fourth grade. At the time of the Soweto student strike it was estimated that only 35 percent of these 1972 black beginners would complete primary courses and that two of each one hundred would finish high school.

As depressing as these statistics unquestionably are, it should be recalled that in South Africa more than half of the black population possesses no formal education. Such cultural deprivation at the adult level places their children in a disadvantageous position even if they are able to attend school. Education fees are beyond the capacity of most black parents to pay. Charges in early 1978 were $67 for a primary school student and $97 for a secondary school student.

Shortly after the Soweto riots, the then minister of Bantu education, Michael C. Botha, promised that schooling for blacks in the primary grades would be made free and compulsory as soon as possible, perhaps before 1980. Such a goal seemed beyond the financial commitment that the government was willing to make. Even though the Pretoria government record in providing education for blacks left much to be desired, it should be stated in its behalf that during the first twenty-five years of National party rule (1948–1973), the population percentage of blacks who were between seven and fifteen years of age rose from 40 percent to 75 percent of the total black population in South Africa. The number of black teachers in the system rose from 700 to 2,100 during these twenty-five years. In the five years ending with the 1977 Soweto students' strike, the black education budget outlays had increased by 350 percent.

Even with the enormous number of black children who never attend school excluded, the figures for blacks who do attend are staggering; 4,500,000 children seek instruction. Such numbers lead to marked overcrowding. Often, black teachers are required to teach daily two sessions of fifty or more students apiece. White teachers normally instruct at one session for about twenty students. In 1978, the maximum white teacher's salary was $8,370 a year. His or her black counterpart was restricted to a maximum of $4,485 a year.

Beyond the irrefutable conclusion that the educational opportunities provided for black students are insignificant when compared to those offered to white students is the deeper problem of lack of qualifications among the black teachers. In Soweto, where the situation was reputed to be better than elsewhere in the country, less than 10 percent of the black teachers at the time of the 1977 strike had completed secondary school. These people were sensitive to calls by the Soweto Students Representative Council to make the nation's education system a unified one. They feared that any such amalgamation of white and black teachers under a one-ministry education system might lead to the loss of their positions.[7]

The same sort of built-in excessive funding of the white educational system to the disadvantage of the black educational field has been duplicated in the area of government expenditures for sports. In 1977, 4.4 million whites received $4.9 million, and 18.5 million blacks received $50,000—a 38-to-1 discrepancy in absolute terms.[8]

As 1978 passed by, the student strike in Soweto continued. The government became increasingly displeased and cracked down on black leaders who dared to speak out in public on the subject. During August, Dr. Nthato Motlana, the chief of the Committee of Ten, was banned for one month as he prepared to speak in public on the education system.[9] Banning remained a most effective method of controlling dissent and movements that could spark revolt whether by design or by accident.

Finally, almost two and one-half years after educational dissatisfaction in Soweto provoked the June 1976 uprising, the government revealed draft legislation to improve black education. The first steps were taken toward making primary school mandatory for blacks. A single salary scale for white and black teachers was promised. Health services were to be provided in black schools for the first time. Advisory black teachers councils would be recognized, but any teacher who ran for public office was to be dismissed.

The draft educational legislation clearly has as one of its purposes the neutralizing of the potential of teachers to be opinion leaders capable of fomenting dissent and revolt. Teachers who disobeyed orders, criticized the government in public, or boycotted classes could be fined sums of up to $230 under the proposed legislation. In addition, the intention was to have the capacity to fine a teacher up to $575 or to send the person to prison for up to one year if any education not approved by the government is given to pupils. Such a vaguely worded statute could easily provide the government with the ammunition needed to keep black dissidence under control. Nothing in the bill spoke of closing the vast disparity in the amount of funds spent by the government to support the two different educational systems. Needless to say, blacks were most unhappy with what they perceived as the limited scope of the proposed changes.[10]

First Actions of the Botha Administration

The overwhelming dimensions of the black education problems were at least as depressing as those in the black housing area—but no worse. The government remained unwilling to solve the land-tenure and housing problems for the nonwhite population, both black and colored. Both in specific instances and in overall policy matters, the government of South Africa continued to apply the apartheid system with vigor.

In early January 1978, to give but one example of how the rules for control of movement by nonwhites in white areas is connected to the housing situation in a direct manner, the South African government dismantled the squatter shantytown of Unibell. By this action, 2,000 shacks housing 20,000 blacks were destroyed. Most of the dispossessed were Xhosa tribeswomen and their children. They had moved without permission into white-denominated areas in order to live with their husbands who were employed on farms or in factories outside of their Transkei homeland.[11]

After John Vorster was returned to the position of prime minister by a landslide vote at the November 1977 election, some observers felt that the government would make a true attempt to improve nonwhite housing within South Africa. The Unibell case was one of many indications that such hopes were soon to be dashed.

Connie Mulder took over direct control of Bantu administration in what was to become the last Vorster cabinet. Mulder was sitting on a powder keg, the Muldergate scandal. His time in the new position was so short that it is hard to evaluate accurately his impact. Mulder did preside over a name alteration for his ministry, from Bantu Administration and Development to the Department of Plural Relations and Development. Life might not have improved significantly for black residents, but at least they were no longer forced to deal with the hated word, Bantu, at every turn.

The record compiled by Mulder most definitely was mixed. His first activities in his new post were handled with more strictness than his middle-of-the-road image as justice minister would have suggested. Mulder proposed a Bantu Laws Amendment Bill, known colloquially as the idle Bantu bill. Under its terms, blacks who were resident in a city while being unemployed for more than 122 days in a calendar year would be subject to arrest and detention in a rehabilitation center or prison colony. This piece of legislation was proposed at a time when 12.4 percent of the labor force was unemployed.[12]

The other new law proposed by Mulder was the Bantu Citizenship Bill. It proposed that any citizen of the Transkei or Bophuthatswana homeland would not be entitled automatically to South African citizenship by surrendering homeland citizenship. It was widely believed that taken together, the purpose of the Mulder bills was to start toward the goal of making every South African black a citizen of one or other homeland and not of South Africa itself, even though 60 percent of the blacks in the country did not live in homeland areas.[13]

Even though the long-range plans may have been to isolate the blacks in a more-thorough manner than in the past, no matter how gently this task was to be accomplished, on a day-to-day basis some loosening of strictures could be detected during the Mulder tenure in office. Theater audiences and sports clubs could be integrated. Churches were permitted officially to take black worshipers into white parishes. Black children received permission to attend white private schools. In all these cases the decision whether or not to admit the blacks was left strictly in the hands of the white membership of the organization in question. True progress in these areas seemed unlikely to occur in the near future.

Other changes that took place in 1977 and early 1978 included the continuing rise in the number of black students studying at white universities even though this action had been banned officially since 1959. Urban-dwelling blacks also were informed that they would be given practically full ownership of their houses rather than the limited tenancy they had possessed in the past. Townships were scheduled to be given full municipal status.

Conditions of Black Life

Early in 1978 a survey appeared that stated 17 people lived in the average four-room matchbox in Soweto. Other statistics on the quality of life for blacks were equally depressing. The infant mortality rate for whites in 1974 was 18.4 per 100,000; for colored inhabitants it was 115.5 infant deaths per 100,000. For blacks the numbers were not computed, but enormous. In 1976, the Johannesburg City Health Department had reported that 58 percent of black patients under ten years of age and 80 percent of those under two years of age at city hospitals were suffering from malnutrition. Department of Health statistics released in 1975 reported that 18 white people per 100,000 suffered from tuberculosis, South Africa's leading cause of death, while 285 blacks per 100,000 and 327 per 100,000 colored people were listed as suffering from this disease. It was admitted that the number of cases within the black population was significantly and perhaps even overwhelmingly understated.[14]

During the end of 1977 and at the start of 1978, housing and education deficiencies attracted headlines. The controversies occurring at District 6 near Capetown emphasized the huge dimensions of the housing-development problem. District 6, a traditional, even historic, colored housing area of Capetown was marked for extinction by the government. The land was needed for more white housing. In came the bulldozers, and the long-term residents were offered no choice but to leave and take up residence farther from the center of Capetown. Until new housing was provided, these people were forced to stay in temporary housing. One such area, the Free Ground, was visited by well-known American writer Tom Wicker. He termed conditions at this spot as "disgraceful." His mood was not improved when he discovered no whites had yet moved into the vacated homes in District 6.[15]

Population statistics released during 1978 made it clear that with the ever-increasing number of nonwhite children being born, it was logical to expect that problems would continue within South Africa for decades to come. Government estimates were that the mid-1978 population of 26.2 million people would be superseded in the year 2000 by a national population of 50 million people, assuming birth rates remain constant in the intervening years. Stretching the same birth rates for twenty more years until the year 2020, the total population would be 70 million people. At 2.7 births per 1,000 per year, South Africa's birth rate has been among the highest in the world. The black birth rate is twice that of the white birth rate.

Best estimates are that the black population in South Africa, which totaled 18.6 million in 1978, will rise at current rates to 35 million by the year 2000 and to 55 million by the year 2020. Taken together it is estimated that the colored and Indian populations will rise to 6 million by the year 2000 and to 9 million by the year 2020. The 4.4 million white people residing in South Africa should, at current rates, rise to 7 million by the year 2000.

Migration to the cities is programmed to continue. The current estimates are that the 48 percent of the population now living in urban areas will rise to 80 percent of the population in the year 2000. At current rates, 15 million of these 22 million new urban dwellers will be black.

Mortality in South Africa is significantly below the continent average. Access to better medical assistance is given as the main reason for this population-raising factor. Given the bad conditions under which a large number of the black population in South Africa must subsist, the statement concerning health care must be taken in a relative sense. In 1978, in South Africa, the mortality rate was computed as being 16 deaths per 1,000.

City planners estimate that 500,000 new homes a year will be needed each year for at least the next two decades. The South African government obviously was not listening to the message. In 1978, it was calling for 90,000 new black township homes over the next five-year period. It is estimated that 2.8 million white-collar jobs will be available in 1990, but at that time less than 1 percent of those entering black schools will complete twelve grades. Black unemployment in South Africa has grown from 580,000 people in 1962 to 1 million in 1970 to 2 million in 1978. The number of unemployed blacks was growing in 1978 at the rate of 10,000 new members a month.[16]

Speaking at the South African Institute of International Affairs in Johannesburg during February 1979, George McGovern of South Dakota listed five steps that South Africa must take before it could be accepted by the world community. First, black education must be improved. Second, passbook and influx-control laws must end. Third, the system of detention and banning without just cause must be eliminated. Fourth, the free-enterprise system must be extended in a meaningful manner to the black population. Fifth, all citizens must be able to participate in the political system in the same manner. McGovern warned that if such steps were not taken, the apartheid system would "go out in a sea of blood."[17]

It should be remembered that at the time of the McGovern speech two and one-half years had passed since the Soweto riots. If the sort of massive changes that he prescribed as being necessary were to take place, it would seem that they would have been in process by February 1979. However, no evidence existed of any such movement.

Changing Political Directions

The Wiehahn Commission Report

The first half of 1979 was marked by the long-awaited release of the Wiehahn and Riekert Commission reports. First came Wiehahn at the start of May 1979. The fourteen-man study group had been charged with making suggestions to improve black working conditions. The commission, headed by industrial-relations professor Nicholas Wiehahn, was composed of representatives for management, labor, and blacks.

In theory, upon adopting major recommendations proposed by the Wiehahn Commission, the government agreed to give to black unions the same rights and privileges that it had extended traditionally to white unions. The most important of these rights was the right to strike. Labor Minister Stephanus P. Botha was quick to add that all unions would remain under the guidance of the government, a polite way of saying the government had no intention of allowing black unions to wield their latent political power in a potent manner.

In accepting major recommendations of the Wiehahn Commission report, the government agreed to end its formal policy of extending preferential job opportunities to whites on a widespread basis. To make such a concession meaningful, it would seem that the government would have to link the move to the installation of a strong apprenticeship program to educate black workers. Otherwise, the concession was hollow and white workers, for the most part, would continue to receive job preference because of their higher level of education and training. However, no such black apprenticeship program was announced.

The government also did not find persuasive other Wiehahn Commission suggestions. For example, it would not form a national manpower commission. It also refused to change the name of the ministry from the Department of Labor to the Department of Manpower. In a similar action, the government would not establish a new labor court with power to settle worker-management disputes. The labor minister, Stephanus P. Botha, accurately summarized the state of affairs when he commented, "We are on the move, but major reform of labor laws must come in stages."[18]

Given the all-pervasive white determination to retain its privileged status, swift and vociferous objections to the Wiehahn Commission recommendations were to be expected. The chief secretary of the all-white, 38,000-member Iron, Steel and Allied Industries Union, Wessel Bornman, termed the recommendations as being "a slap in the face to every white worker in the country and the biggest embarrassment to white unions in the history of South Africa."[19]

Impartial observers felt that Bornman was giving the Wiehahn Commission and the South African government credit for reforms that they only partially deserved. Nonresident black workers, a number that exceeded 2 million men, did not qualify for union membership. In addition, the proposed statutes would be permissive rather than mandatory in nature—that is, white unions would not be obliged to accept black members. In like manner, the government was requiring neither that employers pay black workers at rates equal to those paid to white workers nor that a company must integrate its facilities. Labor Minister Stephanus P. Botha summed up the feelings of the government by saying, "The wishes of the employer must be respected."[20]

The Riekert Commission Report

Immediately in the wake of the Wiehahn Commission report, the Botha government saw fit to release the findings and recommendations of the Riekert Commission report. In substance, it suggested that controls be eased on the entry of nonwhite persons into areas of the country marked out for white occupation. The report also suggested that an end be called to governmental limits on the number of visits by nonwhites lacking the proper authorization to places in officially defined urban areas. In the same thinking mold, it was suggested that wives without permits be allowed to reside in these areas with properly documented husbands and that whites should be allowed to register homes in black areas that they purchased for use by their black employees. Economics Minister Chris Heunis was quick to label the suggestions as being, on the whole, acceptable to the government.

Within the most definite limits of the South African situation, this era of good feelings appeared to have few limits. In a separate development, Botha cohort Pieter Koornhof, the replacement for Connie Mulder, attempted to form black advisory committees. Their stated charge was to assist him in his work. Reaction from the black community was most guarded. Fears of more window dressing were expressed. Although the advisory councils did not get off the ground, conceptually speaking, they did serve as forerunner to the State President's Council—a later, major government initiative, one little more successful than the stalking horse, it must be added. The best that can be said concerning the advisory councils is that they indicated the government was willing to take some steps, however small, in the direction of race-relations progress. Blacks took at least slight encouragement in this trend and added to this viewpoint a sense of satisfaction caused by the government's allowing Alexandria to become a 40,000-person black residential area for families. It had been feared that the space would be designated exclusively as being a complex for single workers. Community roots would be impossible to establish in such circumstances.[21]

The honeymoon of good feelings did not last long. By mid-June 1979, the government already had begun to back away from supporting the Wiehahn Commission recommendations. The first step was to state it would permit, not demand, that unions be integrated. It also announced that it would disqualify from membership all black migrants and black commuters—a group comprising 80 percent of the black work force.

Among the English-speaking press in South Africa and abroad the governmental change in direction was criticized. The *Johannesburg Star* termed recent moves as being "a cruel cynical attitude that will make friends of

South Africa weep.''[22] It was pointed out that the government was ignoring the advice that it had sought in the first instance. Such actions were said to dash hopes that had been nurtured recently in the nonwhite population by the Pretoria regime.

At the end of the same month, the Botha government completed the apartheid-loosening rollback by announcing that upon further reflection it had decided to retain criminal penalties to punish blacks found illegally in white areas. The original Riekert Commission intent was to punish the employers and landlords, instead. It had been felt that they had encouraged or even required the blacks, as part of the terms of employment, to remain illegally in the white area. The Botha government simultaneously announced that it also had decided to retain the regulation prohibiting blacks from remaining for more than seventy-two hours in an urban area without a permit.[23]

Actions taken by the South African government at home to keep the apartheid system in operation often were downplayed by high-level cabinet ministers when they went abroad. Pieter Koornhof, for example, sounded as the soul of reasonableness when he spoke at the National Press Club in Washington, D.C. The time of the speech was virtually contemporaneous with the rollback of the concessions proposed by the Wiehahn and Riekert commissions and seemingly approved by Botha, Koornhof, and the National party government.

During his Washington speech, Koornhof advanced the opinion that apartheid was dead. Compulsory separation of the races was at an end, and present South African racial policies were not the alpha and omega of government thinking. He promised that dramatic changes in government policy were coming and that South Africa eventually might become a confederation of states that would involve white South Africa and the various homelands in a federal form of administrative structure.

The conservative right of the National party were appalled at these statements made by Koornhof. In their view, he had gone back on his promise to emasculate the impact of the Wiehahn and Riekert Commissions recommendations. The outcry against the Koornhof statements was so strong that, for the moment at least, the government was driven back into its protective shell.[24]

The Puzzling Moves of Koornhof and Botha

During the middle of 1979, Botha and Koornhof received a buffeting from both sides. The nonwhites and their white liberal supporters felt equally as provoked as did Treurnicht, but of course in the opposite direction. Talking on the subject of the proposed confederation, Dr. Nthato Motlana observed he could not conceive that blacks would "fall for that kind of cheap trick."[25] Motlana also would not support the Koornhof advisory committee because he thought that the life of urban blacks would be improved to some minimal degree at the expense of rural blacks.[26]

The theme of the remarks by Dr. Motlana was seconded by Nobel Prize academic nominee Dr. Es'kia Mphahlele in published remarks. Mphahlele pointed out that homelands leaders like Chief Buthelezi "had their backs against the wall." If they did not keep the leadership in their hands, then less-forceful leaders would replace them. Under such circumstances, the South African government might succeed in denationalizing homelands residents and declaring their territories independent. To counter this governmental action, Dr. Mphahlele requested that black rural and urban leaders adopt a more-cooperative and flexible attitude.[27]

Perhaps Koornhof and Botha received the message. In July 1979, they once again backtracked and began to introduce reforms along the lines of those advocated by the Wiehahn and Riekert Commissions. Were they choosing liberalism over conservatism? It is impossible to say. Their stop-and-start track record was spastic to the extreme. Pragmatism and the urge of the moment seemed to dictate whether or not they would take any particular action. When they alarmed the conservative white population they would move backward, and when the blacks became alarmed they would move forward ever so slightly. Steady progress toward a goal of complete integration appeared beyond hope. Even Koornhof, for all of the overseas pronouncements of prospects for change, always stopped short of full integration promises.

Koornhof in the Spotlight

Writing on August 4, 1979, in *The New York Times,* Koornhof resorted to the words of Abraham Lincoln in justifying South African racial policies, "You cannot help the poor by destroying the rich."[28] Koornhof claimed that privilege should be based on merit, not skin. All well and good, perhaps, if opportunity for education and advancement are equal. In South Africa, however, the white population has no intention of allowing nonwhites access to equal education and advancement. As a result, the discrimination is as pernicious as if based on race alone.

A curious sense of timing appears to be a Koornhof trademark. *The New York Times* statement, filled as it was with equivocations and assurances that the pleasures of the old order would endure, came as Botha and Koornhof finally seemed to be taking concrete steps toward racial equality. This situation of progress was the exact opposite to what had occurred in mid-June. At that time, the government was retrenching and dashing the hopes of those who had supported the Wiehahn and Riekert commissions. Koornhof chose that moment, while in Washington, to contradict his colleagues and to predict the complete end of apartheid. His unambiguous declarations in June were notably lacking the restrictions contained in his August pronouncement on the subject. The sum total of the puzzle would seem to indicate that promises count for less than deeds among the South African high officials.

Despite his words of caution written a month later, Koornhof's actions during July 1979 had been significant. He announced that any black who had been working illegally in a white area for three or more years or for a white employer for one or more years had a three-month grace period to register and become a legitimate resident. It was estimated that 500,000 blacks currently under threat of immediate removal from Johannesburg would benefit by the new ruling. The number so affected throughout the country might reach 2 million black people. In order for whites to feel compelled to make sure their black employees registered, the government raised the fine a white must pay for employing an unregistered black from $118 to $590 per violation. Some critics of the government thought the scheme was devised to iron the rough spots from the apartheid system. They did not see any fundamental change in the new system. Others felt it was a significant step for the better.[29]

The positive steps taken under the direction of Koornhof in the personal-liberty and housing areas were matched in the labor field. On September 25, 1979, a fifty-year governmental policy concerning the right of migrant and commuter blacks to organize was changed. Minister of Labor Fanie Botha announced that migrant and commuter blacks would have the same rights to form and promote labor unions as permanent resident working blacks. Under the new regulations, the only blacks who would be forbidden to organize would be residents of other sovereign nations such as Mozambique, Malawi, Swaziland, Lesotho, or Botswana. The intent was to keep the ready supply of mine labor from the underdeveloped neighboring countries available as a steady source of cheap labor and as a brake upon the demands of better pay that the black-constituted unions were sure to make.

The South African government was quick to point out that the new status for the blacks from the homelands was granted on a conditional basis. The government promised to keep close supervision over the activities of these black labor unions. The unspoken assumption was that the government would be quick to act if it perceived that wage demands or strikes had gotten out of bounds. Given the past history of non-white unions in South Africa, it was understandable that blacks feared the government would have a short fuse. As with the concessions of Koornhof concerning the need for homeland citizens to carry reference books, it was feared that the liberalization of rules for black labor unions was intended to make supervision more efficient rather than looser.

A number of newspapers including the *Washington Post* pointed out that the South African government was still treating the right to organize for blacks as a privilege, not a right.[30] The consensus was that until blacks are allowed into the same union as whites and to compete on equal terms for the same jobs, true equality was far in the future. The road to its achievement seemed long and rocky.

During the first two months of operation, the new black labor-union rules seemed to operate with some success. Five black unions applied to the government for registration. Eight previously all-white or all-colored unions applied to receive permission to enroll black members. About a dozen other all-black unions indicated that they would register with the government if they could retain their unity within an industry and not be obliged to subdivide by job classification within an industry in order to obtain government recognition. Some white companies that had worked hand in glove with the white unions in their plants encouraged these unions to form parallel branches so as to dilute the potential power of all-black unions that might spring up in competition.[31]

Should the march toward true racial equality accelerate, 1979 no doubt will be looked upon as having been a crucial year in this movement. The Wiehahn and Riekert commissions' suggestions and their follow-up by the government will be given prominence as the first indications of wide-scale future changes. More likely, the path will not be smooth, and a number of disturbances, perhaps even total race war, will take place. In such a case, the government activities in 1979 will be looked upon correctly as one more missed opportunity and still another cruel tease that promised the black population freedom the white population had no desire to grant.

In either case, whether 1979 will be judged as the first step toward racial peace or as still another step on the path to race war, 1980 must be judged as more of the same. New initiatives were slight. The so-called trinity of oppression—housing, education, and jobs—staggered along, sentencing the average black to a life of unhappiness and degradation. It is rather remarkable that large portions of the white population seemed satisfied that true progress was occurring and that the situation would resolve itself peacefully and satisfactorily to all concerned. Such deeply felt white optimism strikes most outside observers as being naive in the extreme.

The Situation in 1980

During 1980, three expert U.S. observers traveled independently to South Africa. All were appalled with what they saw. More crucial, they concluded that full-scale war was virtually inevitable. Roger Wilkins, writing in the *Washington Post,* observed "the iron core of apartheid has not been dented, bent or even nicked."[32] Writing in *Foreign Policy,* MIT professor Robert I. Rotberg, an acknowledged African studies expert, observed, "What is considered rapid change by white South Africans is glacial in American terms."[33] Rotberg also pointed out that many of the South African cities currently possessing twice as many black residents as white ones soon will possess four times as many should current population trends continue. Such demographic realities would seem well worth pondering even by the blissfully confident white South African population.

David Halberstan developed the same theme in an *Atlantic Monthly* article. He pointed out that young blacks believe in their ultimate triumph over their white overseers. The present generation is less accepting of their plight than their parents are. Halberstan found them more politicized and less Christian than the previous generation. Resorting more to rhetorical cuteness than closely reasoned argument, Halberstan found young blacks to be "impatient for a better life in this world rather than in the next one."[34] The famed author appeared on firmer analytical grounds when he reminded his readers that a society depending as heavily upon black labor as the South African one does could be asking for trouble since terrorists easily could infiltrate the ranks of true workers in order to preach and incite revolution.

The government was not listening to the message being delivered, and 1980 was another year of tinkering, seemingly bereft of true initiative. The legislation read as if new, striking steps were being taken, but in the execution, delay and obfuscation occurred.

On the black education front, the Soweto student strike continued. The rhetoric level rose as months passed. "We will not return to school until the gun toting soldiers are gone from the classroom." Translated, the statement by the students meant that they wished no more white teachers in the Soweto black schools.[35]

In March 1980, the colored student population called their own strike. Coordination among the two student groups was for the most part loose, but the discontent of one group fanned the flames of discontent for the other. Figures of the number of colored students on strike varied widely. Estimates all the way from 25,000 on one end to 100,000 on the other were advanced by outside observers. The total colored student population in South Africa was approximately 725,000. The strike came as the colored population was dropping in percentage of the total South African population and as Botha was making it clear that their second-rate status would remain. In a 1979 meeting dealing with the abolition of the Colored Persons Representative Council, the prime minister was quoted as saying, "One man, one vote, is out. That is to say never."[36]

The colored student strike called to mind the desperate situation of this

South African racial group. Nearly half of all colored births are illegitimate. They are leading other racial groups in alcoholism and crime commission statistics. Disease and malnutrition are rampant. Social programs are few. An estimated 200,000 of their number live in squatters' shacks. The government is engaged in the forced movement of many to less-desirable living situations. School-dropout rates are enormous. Less than 1 percent of those entering school graduate from high school. The government spends four times as much on colored education per student than upon black education per student, but less than one-third the amount per student is spent upon a colored student as upon a white student.[37]

In its usual meandering fashion, the government did address the school question during November 1980. Education Minister Ferdie Hartzenberg announced a mandatory schooling plan for the 8 million black students starting in 1981. Such a program would be easier to announce than to bring to fruition. By the end of 1980, only half of the school-aged black children were enrolled. The government announced the plan would be enacted in and around Johannesburg, then would spread through the rest of the Transvaal and finally the whole country. Whether or not the speed of implementation for the government plan would match the ever-rising black birth rate was a question for the future to answer.[38]

Housing and Employment Difficulties

The jerking stops and starts that typified the governmental reaction to black education problems during 1980 were matched in the housing and jobs fields. In housing, the first government impetus showed promise. Minister of Cooperation and Development Pieter Koornhof announced during February that, as an experiment, the hated seventy-two-hour law would be waived—that is, blacks without jobs and their dependents would not have to leave within seventy-two hours of entrance to an area in which they did not reside.[39] A similar, slight but significant, step forward was recorded in the employment field during April. For the first time, black building workers were given permission to perform skilled-work tasks in white areas. Even though there was a significant skilled-labor shortage in South Africa, Minister of Manpower Utilization Fanie Botha was criticized widely for lowering standards by taking this action.[40]

In both the housing and employment areas, the day-to-day activities of the South African government proceeded at a slow pace in implementing the directions of the government ministers. No doubt, this slowness reflected the ideological convictions of the civil-service employees. This group was overwhelmingly hardline Afrikaner in composition. Ministers who had to operate under the glare of international publicity and pressure might well have to adopt a liberal front. The well-entrenched civil servants saw no need to adopt a similar posture. As far as they were concerned the status quo would serve very well.

For example, the government commitment to rebuild the disputed Crossroads development seemed to be flagging. The promise to construct 2,575 new houses during the first year of the program had not been kept. The goal was later reduced to 1,662 new houses. What the government had not disclosed when announcing the program was that the rents for these units would be three to four times higher than they had been for the destroyed units. Such a rate scale was beyond the means of most of the former residents.[41]

The government stood by, for the most part, as the expected white backlash against black labor militancy developed. Johannesburg crushed the black municipal workers' strike during August 1980. The leaders of the job action were detained in tin huts and then shipped back to their homelands. The strike collapsed soon afterward. At the Carltonville mine, owned by Gold Fields of South Africa, a strike was broken by means of a work-or-be-dismissed order. The issue had been the death of nineteen workers during a riot at a demonstration called to protest housing conditions near the work site.

In a pay dispute at the Finsch diamond mine owned by DeBeers in the northern part of the cape province, several hundred protestors were dismissed. The strike at the new Sasol construction site ended with mixed results. Most of the black employees accepted the offered pay hike, but seventy strike leaders, dissatisfied with the solution, were shipped back to their homeland against their will.

The overall results of these management-labor disputes would seem to indicate that the spirit of the Wiehahn Commission recommendations was not being observed fully. Neither management nor government seemed inclined to make life acceptable for the newly emboldened black labor unions. Employers made it clear that they intended to deal only with labor unions they considered sympathetic. Perhaps it could be said that the automobile manufacturers were dealing in good faith with their unions. Elsewhere, especially in the case of municipal unions, the record was far worse. Employers were quick to ask the government to detain and expel to the homelands the militant black union leaders who did not know their place. The South African government showed itself appallingly ready to accede to these requests.[42]

During August, 1980, the residency policy of the government came under attack from a surprising source: the South African Appeals Court. The Section 10 Residency Permits authorized by the Bantu (Urban Areas) Act of 1945 were invalidated as being beyond the intent of the act. This was the law that permitted a wife, unmarried daughter, or son under the age of eighteen to remain in an urban area as long as he or she ordinarily resided with a native who had been born there or had been employed continuously in the area for more than fifteen years. The Section 10 permits were handed out to people who the government defined as ordinary residents. Without such a permit, no black was considered an ordinary resident in the terms of the statute. In its decision, the South African Appeals Court found the definition of ordinary resident to be overly broad. Parliament could, and undoubtedly would, pass new legislation in swift order to remedy the deficiency. Nonetheless, the crack in the usually monolithic government approach to racial problems was interesting to observe.

In part, as a response to the appeals-court action but more likely as one in a number of acts to perfect separate development, the government introduced the Black Community Development Act on October 31, 1980. This new piece of legislation replaced thirty-six currently operating racial laws. Minister Koornhof defined the new act as an attempt to place some blacks on a par with white people. Most critics did not agree and viewed the Black Community Development Act as still another attempt by the government to destroy black unity and to co-opt a small group of urban blacks whose new-found relative affluence would separate them from those confined to the homelands.[43]

The main thrust of the new legislation was to permit the descendants of any person legally resident in a particular urban area to remain with the legally resident person for as long as this status is retained. Such black servants and employees who qualify as legal residents also in the future will be able to stay in any other urban area for thirty days in a year as long as the visit is in an attempt to obtain work in that other area.

Dr. Koornhof claimed with certain justification that the new legislation was a marked improvement over the now-antiquated seventy-two-hour pass legislation. Under the new legislation, in the minister's opinion, blacks would be able to move as freely as whites within South Africa.[44]

Although critics of the government agreed that the new legislation was an improvement over its predecessor, they charged that this was a small blessing and the step forward a small one. Whites do not have to submit proof that they have received a new job or found new housing in order to move to a different area. The new legislation will not help the large majority of the nonwhite population whose documents are less than perfect. In fact, it was feared that more blacks will be endorsed out to the homelands under the streamlined, more easily administerable legislation.

The legislation also attempted to give city councils more authority in black urban areas. The main target was, of course, Soweto. In addition, it was promised that the ban concerning blacks being present in white areas between the hours of 10 P.M. and 6 A.M. would be lifted in 1981. The same promise was made concerning the ending of sweeping police power to arrest blacks standing idly in white areas. Such legislation, if enacted, would reduce the enforcement burden currently carried by the police. In 1979, 120,000 pass-law violators had been arrested. The government also speculated that the day would come when the hated reference books for blacks would be replaced by identity cards.[45]

Government Intentions in Question

How serious was the South African Government in its efforts to bring racial equality to the nation? The answer is difficult to formulate. Some of those working toward progress in South Africa believed that true equality and amalgamation of the races must come. Others believed that equality and amalgamation would never be possible but that the separate-but-equal concept was viable and could come about in the foreseeable future. A midway group could be characterized by the following: Equality and amalgamation, perhaps; separate but equal, definitely; but in any case, not yet. No, not yet. In contradistinction to the three trains of thought leading toward progress would be the point of view that all moves toward liberalization are bad. The only steps to be taken are those to improve and facilitate the operation of the current system of apartheid.

The length that South Africa must go to reach meaningful progress was underlined by the governmental reaction to the Buthelezi plan that intended to change Natal Province and the Kwazulu Homeland into a self-ruling regional confederation without apartheid. Professor Jan Lombard of the economics department at the University of Pretoria was the developer of the plan. Durban, Kwazulu, and the white-owned rural land along transport routes would be divided into subsectors, each with its own legislature, executive structure, and prohibition against racial discrimination. A regional Natal-Kwazulu authority would execute directives passed by a legislature elected from the three subsections. If such a plan could succeed in this area of the country, it was proposed to extend it to eight regions encompassing the whole country.

It would seem reasonable to an outside observer to believe that a government interested in finding a solution to the horrid discord within South Africa would take the Buthelezi plan seriously. Granted, the visionary aspects of the plan tended to obscure the many practical difficulties. For example, what would happen when the white citizens of Natal were forced to surrender their privileged status was a matter most open to conjecture. It was understandable that the Pretoria government would feel that such a plan might lead to civil disorder whether inside or outside of the Natal-Kwazulu region. Strict supervision upon its implementation would be understandable. The absolute refusal of the Pretoria government to consider trying it out is another matter entirely. Those who claimed that the white power establishment was not truly interested in a solution to the South African racial problems would seem to have received more ammunition to support their position. At the very least, the observation of Afrikaner historian Dr. Hermann Gilomee, made at the time of the government refusal to consider the Buthelezi plan, seemed accurate: "There is no longer a coherent ideological blueprint effectively guiding or determining South African policy."[46]

The Situation in 1981

The year 1981 brought more of the same. Every so often the government would announce a bold new initiative. Then the government would fall into a pout when outside analysis demonstrated that the new act would provide little of true assistance to the nonwhite population. Then, as if to confirm the opinion of the critics, the government would withdraw the legislation for further study; a weakened piece of legislation was invariably the result that finally followed.

The optional desegregation of restaurants legislation announced by the government during January 1981 is an apt example of a new law that has a less-sweeping effect than was apparent at announcement time. No longer would international-class restaurants, motels, and hotels need to receive Pretoria permission before desegregating. Dr. Motlana replied for the black community that such proposals are "a mere nibbling away at apartheid." He also observed that no one in the National party was prepared to eliminate apartheid and to write race out of the constitution. It would seem that Motlana was correct. Permissive gestures to alleviate surface manifestations of apartheid were of little true usefulness. They did not attack the heart of the discriminatory system: housing, education, and jobs. The changes in the new legislation were so small that as of 1981, no motel, hotel, or restaurant of international class that did not want to serve nonwhites would be forced to do so. For all practical purposes, the white-only concept was definitely still alive and well.[47]

An occasional white voice could be heard to warn that halfway measures would never succeed. One such dissenter was General Hendrik van den Bergh, the former head of the South African Security Police and an Afrikaner traditionalist of impeccable credentials. He accused the current national party government of living in a "fool's paradise."[48] Van den Bergh observed that once blacks were given better housing, education, training, and jobs, they would not be satisfied until they attained full political equality—another description of majority rule.

Similar views were espoused by Dr. Erika Theron, a well-known former sociologist at Stellenbosch University. She had been the head of the first multiracial commission of inquiry into conditions experienced by colored people in South Africa. Dr. Theron also had been a member of the Group Areas Board. For this reason, her opinions were most important. She stated that the Group Areas Act was "cruel and socially destructive," and thought that the act should be scrapped for the sake of peace and social harmony.[49] The Theron statement came as Professor Michael Savage of the University of Capetown announced that his research showed that 12,586,622 people had been arrested or prosecuted during the first thirty-two years of the National party enforcement of the Pass Laws.[50]

As 1981 continued, examination of the situation in the employment, housing, and education fields indicated how massive are the problems that remain. In the mining field, for example, during 1980, less than 1 percent of the 426,320 black men employed were able to be housed with their families. The South African government has set a 3 percent limit on the number of blacks who can live with their families near the mines. Even this low number will be hard to reach because the government makes it difficult to solve the red-tape requirements necessary to obtain the permit. In this regard, it should be noted that the difficulty in living with one's family near the mines came as the percentage of South African and homeland residents rose in a dramatic fashion. In 1973, foreign blacks had accounted for 79 percent of the mining labor force. By 1981, this figure had dropped to 44 percent.[51]

Housing difficulties for blacks in the mine areas are more than equaled by their continuing salary difficulties. In 1980, the average black salary in the mines was $2,546 a year as opposed to $16,630 a year for whites. Apologists point out that according to these figures white miners earn only 6.6 times as much as blacks; substantial decline from the 8 to 1 differential in 1978 and the 21 to 1 differential in 1970. The free housing received by white miners and their families is not included in the wage computation. Because blacks have not been able to obtain the blasting certificates needed to obtain higher-paying jobs in the mines, the hope for a significant further reduction in the black-white pay differential appears beyond fulfillment.[52]

The housing situation in Soweto also was not improving at the pace promised by the government. Despite major efforts to provide the district with electricity, telephone service, better schooling, and more ownership-type rights, the rising population resident in the district has doomed governmental efforts to failure. Nearly half of the estimated 102,000 residences in Soweto were built between 1957 and 1968. It is estimated that less than 5,500 new homes have been built in Soweto since 1970. Estimates of the number of people living in the 102,000 Soweto homes range from 1.1 million to 1.5 million people, or an average of between nine to twelve residents per home. By the most minimal of estimates, Soweto was, in 1981,

32,000 houses short of the number needed to satisfy population needs. Given natural population growth, at least another 115,000 houses will have to be built by the year 2000 to provide for the Soweto population. Any such building level is most unlikely.[53]

Government claims to be truly interested in assisting the housing needs of all the residents were placed further in doubt when the Crossroads situation, a continuing problem to the government, was examined anew. This colored neighborhood near Capetown used to have 40,000 residents. The governmental removal policy had reduced this number to 10,000 residents by the start of 1980 and to 3,000 residents by the start of 1981. No colored residents were left in Crossroads by the start of 1982.[54] The move to make Crossroads a white neighborhood had started in 1967.

The failure to provide for adequate education for nonwhite parts of the population clearly took its toll and slowed the economic expansion of the economy that had lasted through 1980. At that time, only seventeen qualified black communications technicians were in the country. One hundred forty-two Indian and colored people had qualified in this trade. For the two million black students, there are only five technical high schools in South Africa. To give a specific example of the educational weakness for the nonwhite population, Uitenhage, the home of many automobile plants, had only eleven blacks in its high school population by the start of 1981.[55]

At the time of the twentieth anniversary independence celebration during June 1981, Cardinal Owen McCann of Capetown announced that the Catholic Church would not participate in the event. The Botha government, having promoted the event with vigor was furious. McCann justified the boycott by pointing out that the blacks in the country, the people the Catholic Church primarily serves, "are deprived and oppressed and have no meaningful say in the government, nor full citizenship."[56]

In the wake of the celebration for the twentieth anniversary of full independence in South Africa, militant black labor unions began to increase pressure and to suggest that locals in various plants represented by the same union join together to compel the struck employer to grant demands. Multiplant strikes by the same black militant union could inspire cooperative strikes among militant black unions that are completely independent and that represent workers in different industries. Such a close linkage across industry lines is not easy to accomplish. Competition and jealousy exist among the various black unions. Some are more committed to political action and violent overthrow of the white government than others. The white-owned corporations are more accommodating to some black unions than to others. The government is quicker to arrest and ban some black union leaders than others. These factors militate against a smooth amalgamation of black union activity across the board at this time. To illustrate the point, it should be noted that the ANC call for a labor boycott to protest the twentieth anniversary celebration had been greeted with minimal response by black union leaders and black workers.[57]

During August 1981, the government demonstrated that it had not experienced any significant change of heart. Over 2,000 squatters were arrested at the black camp at Nyanga near Capetown and were carried off to prison. The campsite was burned by the police, as was the one at Crossroads. In the labor arena, Minister of Police Louis Le Grange admitted that there had been close supervision and even encouragement to businesses to bust unions. One such event took place in conjunction with strikes called by radical unregistered black canning and food unions in East London.[58] At the start of September 1981, the sudden arrests of 205 black workers who were returning from union picketing at East London to their homes in the Ciskei homeland proved that the idea of black unions was one whose time had not yet come.[59]

The Situation in 1982

The true attitude of the government toward advancement by black labor unions was thrown into doubt once again by the early February 1982 death of Dr. Neil Aggett. This twenty-seven-year-old white doctor was active in black labor movements, and at the time of his death he was serving as Transvaal Province secretary of the Black African Food and Canning Workers Union. Dr. Aggett had been in detention since November 1981 and was found dead in his cell. The government decreed death by hanging and pronounced his demise as suicide. Many government opponents asserted that Dr. Aggett was well balanced and would not, under any conceivable circumstances, kill himself. They charged another Biko-type murder had taken place.

Regardless of the manner in which Dr. Aggett died, it cannot be denied that the government was taking steps to keep black labor unions under control, whether or not they chose to register with the government. During 1981, 306 people active in black labor unions were arrested. Police Minister Louis Le Grange denied that the purpose of the arrests was to restrict the black labor movement in his country. Rather, he stated, "We detain them because they are directly involved in threatening internal security and especially because they are involved in alleged African National Congress activities."[60] Dr. Aggett was reportedly the first white and the forty-sixth person to die in detention since 1963. The symbolic nature of a white man's dying for black rights in South Africa was important and was an act bound to bring pause to even the most black-separatist supporting of radicals.[61] One might hope that apartheid supporters also would be moved by the symbolic nature of Dr. Aggett's case. However, it is questionable that any such reflection took place.

The year 1982 was one in which some progress toward eradicating apartheid was noted. Given the amount that remained, the successes recorded were very modest and infinitely less sweeping than would be needed to prevent additional bloodshed. The slowdown in the economy during 1982 added to the difficulties. Industries had little desire to raise wages in an effort to improve nonwhite living conditions at a time when profits were falling. Every act of social responsibility cost money. Labor unrest, strikes, and firings were the response, especially in the automobile manufacturing and mining industries.[62]

The government became increasingly edgy as black unrest grew. Pretoria also was mindful that the exclusion of blacks from inclusion in the president's council would make them furious. The government began to tighten the regulations. A draft bill was circulated that would have again restricted access for all but authorized blacks to white-zoned urban areas between 10 P.M. and 5 A.M.[63] In a related move, Koornhof stated that allowing spouses to live with the blacks permitted in the urban area was, in his words, "causing problems."[64] The outcry of protest that ensued, impelled the government to back off from the draft bill.[65] The direction in which the Botha government was heading, however, could not have been clearer. As 1983 started, apartheid was alive and well in South Africa.

Notes

1. John Darton, "Apartheid as Real and Painful as Ever," *The New York Times,* October 30, 1977.

2. "Burning in South Africa," *Washington Post,* October 27, 1977; Richard R. Leger, "Defiant Afrikaners: South Africans Say Pressure Stiffens Their Resolves," *Wall Street Journal,* November 14, 1978.

3. "South Africa Alters Black Pass System," *The New York Times,* November 4, 1977.

4. Editorial. "Reforming Apartheid," *Baltimore Sun,* November 4, 1977.

5. Ibid.

6. John F. Burns, "Separate but Equal is Still a Dream in South Africa," *The New York Times,* March 13, 1978.

7. Ibid.

8. John F. Burns, "Compromising on Apartheid," *The New York Times,* March 13, 1978.

9. "South African Barred from Giving Speech," *Christian Science Monitor,* September 8, 1978.

10. John F. Burns, "Blacks Attack South Africa Plan for School Reform," *The New York Times,* November 19, 1978.

11. "South African Blacks Hastily Vacate Shanties," *Baltimore Sun,* January 20, 1978.

12. "Out with the Idle Black," *The Economist,* February 18, 1978.

13. Ibid.

14. Tilu Lukk, "South African Black Deaths Falling into the Pattern of Whites," *Washington Star,* April 21, 1978.

15. Tom Wicker, "Canute in Capetown," *The New York Times,* December 19, 1978.

16. John F. Burns, "Non-white Growth Rate Poses a Challenge to South Africa," *The New York Times,* July 31, 1978; Humphrey Tyler, "The Races in Flux in South Africa." *Christian Science Monitor,* April 10, 1978.

17. George McGovern, "South Africa and the Free World," *Christian Science Monitor,* February 14, 1979.

18. Jack Foisie, "South Africa Accepts Five Black Labor Proposals," *Los Angeles Times,* May 3, 1979.

19. "Labor Reforms," *The Economist,* May 14, 1979.

20. Ibid.

21. Associated Press, "South Africa Commission Proposing Easing Lot of Blacks in Cities," *Washington Star,* May 9, 1979.

22. As quoted in Anthony Lewis, "South Africa Says No," *The New York Times,* June 11, 1979; Gary Thatcher, "South Africa Blacks See Union Reforms Fading," *Christian Science Monitor,* June 13, 1979.

23. John F. Burns, "South Africa Rift on Race Surfaces," *The New York Times,* June 24, 1979.

24. Humphrey Tyler, "South African Faces Row over Racial Liberalization," *Christian Science Monitor,* June 25, 1979.

25. Gary Thatcher, "Apartheid Changing Form but not Effect," *Christian Science Monitor,* July 10, 1979.

26. Caryle Murphy, "South African Leader Caught in Bind over Race Reform Efforts," *Washington Post,* July 16, 1979.

27. Gary Thatcher, "Apartheid Is Not Dead, but in Transition," *Christian Science Monitor,* January 8, 1980.

28. Pieter G. Koornhof, "South Africa's Reforms," *The New York Times,* August 4, 1979.

29. John F. Burns, "Relaxation of Pass System Governing Millions of Blacks Is Creating Measure of Good Will in South Africa," *Washington Post,* September 27, 1979.

30. Editorial. "A Step Forward in South Africa," *Washington Post,* September 27, 1979.

31. "Black Unions Win Some, Lose Some," *The Economist,* November 17, 1979.

32. Roger Wilkins, "South Africa: Changing Words Cannot Prevent Racial Explosion," *Washington Post,* February 17, 1980.

33. Robert I. Rotberg, "How Deep a Change," *Foreign Policy Magazine,* Spring 1980.

34. David Halberstan, "The Fire to Come in South Africa," *Atlantic Monthly,* May 1980.

35. "Soweto Pupils Plan Boycott to Protest White Teachers," *The New York Times,* February 4, 1980.

36. John F. Burns, "South African Colored Seek Fair Share Too," *The New York Times,* May 4, 1980.

37. Ibid.

38. "Schools to Be Compulsory for Blacks in South Africa," *Baltimore Sun,* November 12, 1980.

39. "Two South African Cities to Try Dropping a Black Curfew," *Christian Science Monitor,* February 8, 1980.

40. Associated Press, "South Africa Easing Work Rules for Blacks," *Baltimore Sun,* April 11, 1980.

41. Gary Thatcher, "Nonviolent Protest Earns Reprieve for South African Shantytown," *Christian Science Monitor,* July 2, 1980.

42. "Is South Africa's Strike Busting Doomed by the Boom?" *The Economist,* August 9, 1980.

43. Caryle Murphy, "Apartheid Nursing Tale," *Washington Post,* August 26, 1980.

44. Joseph Lelyveld, "South Africa Plans to Ease Curbs," *The New York Times,* November 1, 1980.

45. Gary Thatcher, "South Africa to Ease Curbs? Blacks Doubt It," *Christian Science Monitor,* November 4, 1980; Caryle Murphy, "South Africa Moves to Control Black Migration to Cities," *Washington Post,* November 3, 1980.

46. Rene de Villiers, "In Place of Apartheid," *Baltimore Sun,* September 11, 1980.

47. "South Africa Plans to Ease Some Racial Curbs," *Baltimore Sun,* January 14, 1981.

48. Gary Thatcher, "South Africa: Can Race War Be Avoided," *Christian Science Monitor,* February 20, 1981.

49. Humphrey Tyler, "Afrikaner Sociologist Calls Apartheid Law a Threat to Safety," *Christian Science Monitor,* April 30, 1981.

50. John Kane Berman, "South Africa Will Not Include Key Town in New Independent Homeland," *Washington Post,* April 18, 1981.

51. "Desolate Black Area Must Give Its Sons to the Mines," *The New York Times,* June 8, 1981.

52. Joseph Lelyveld, "At South Africa Mines, Race Barriers Are

Rigid," *The New York Times,* January 30, 1981.

53. Joseph Lelyveld, "A New Battle of Soweto Flares: Housing vs. Ideology," *The New York Times,* January 30, 1981.

54. Joseph Lelyveld, "Apartheid Is Crumbling on Beaches of South Africa," *The New York Times,* March 12, 1981.

55. "South African Economic Boom Threatened by Worse Ever Shortage of Skilled Labor," *Baltimore Sun,* February 26, 1981.

56. "Police Disperse Demonstrators in South Africa," *Baltimore Sun,* May 29, 1981.

57. "Black Power," *The Economist,* June 6, 1981.

58. Joseph Lelyveld, "South Africa Discloses Bid to Break Black Union," *The New York Times,* August 10, 1981; "South Africa Arrests 2,000 Squatters in Dawn Raid," *The New York Times,* August 20, 1981. See also John Western, *Outcast Capetown* (Minneapolis: University of Minnesota Press, 1981).

59. Caryle Murphy, "Police Arrest 205 Blacks in South African Unions," *Washington Post,* September 9, 1981.

60. Allister Sparks, "Crackdown on South African Unions Seen," *Washington Post,* February 7, 1982; Antero Pietila, "South Africa Shaken by Death of Doctor Activist," *Baltimore Sun,* February 6, 1982.

61. Paul Van Slambrouck, "Why Black Unionists Protest Death of White South African," *Christian Science Monitor,* February 11, 1982.

62. Paul Van Slambrouck, "Firings, Strikes, Gloomy Spring for South African Labor," *Christian Science Monitor,* September 8, 1982.

63. Joseph Lelyveld, "South Africa Threatens New Curbs on Rural Blacks," *The New York Times,* October 8, 1982.

64. Antero Pietila, "South Africa Tightens Curbs on Black City Workers," *Baltimore Sun,* October 17, 1982.

65. Ibid.

3

The Ever-Bubbling
Caldron of Violence

A Continuing Climate of Violence

Sharpeville and Soweto

On March 21, 1960, a crowd of 20,000 blacks gathered in protest against the reference-book system at the police station in Sharpeville, a township near Vereeniging. Members of the crowd threw stones at the police, and it is alleged that three shots were fired by blacks. The police returned the fire with what was later conceded to be an unauthorized volley, and sixty-seven people were killed.

The same evening, blacks staged a similar demonstration at Langa, a township outside Capetown. Bottles were thrown at the police, and again, the police opened fire. This time, three blacks were killed and twenty-nine people were injured. Prime Minister H.F. Verwoerd defended the police action in Parliament by saying that the police had learned its lesson at the Cato Manor massacre. In that incident, on January 24, 1960, five black and four white policemen had been set upon and slaughtered by an angry black mob. The police were searching for illicit liquor in this location near Capetown at the time they were killed. World opinion, however, did not judge Cato Manor to be sufficient justification for the Sharpeville massacre.[1]

On June 16, 1976, a thirteen-year-old school boy, protesting in front of the Orlando West high school in Soweto, was shot in the throat by a police officer. The boy, named Hector Petersen, died. The Soweto riots that claimed 170 black lives in this township and 575 lives, almost all of whom were black, throughout the country had begun. The Soweto riot period was the worst stretch of anti-apartheid violence in the history of South Africa. Once again, world condemnation reached olympian heights.[2]

Sharpeville and Soweto, sixteen years apart, stand as a double warning that full-scale racial violence could erupt at any moment. Without strict police control, it is undeniable that a third major outbreak would have taken place in the past few years. The death of Steven Biko or of Dr. Neil Aggett could have provided the needed spark. So could the student strikes that have multiplied during recent years. Housing disputes like the one at Crossroads or labor strikes like those at the automobile plants could have served the purpose equally as well.

It seems safe to say that an all-out conflict will arise that will dwarf Sharpeville and Soweto; perhaps not, but all the signs are in the opposite direction. If such an outbreak occurs, those who study the situation will be able to point to a continuing level of government repression that indicates matters can only become worse. In chapter 2, the ineffectiveness of governmental efforts to improve the situation for nonwhite housing, employment, and education was outlined. In this chapter the results of these failures are detailed.

A History of Rebellion

Nonwhite dissatisfaction with their housing, education, and situation, all manifesting the underlying denial of human rights, has led to demonstrations, riots, strikes, and occasional political assassinations. The police response to these actions often has been every bit as forceful as the provoking action. Many times the government acted in advance of a nonwhite display of dissatisfaction. Arrests, bannings, illegal resident searches, and press censorship have been used to keep the status quo in effect. This state of affairs, encompassing thrust and counterthrust, is examined in this chapter, as is the homelands situation, perhaps the most potentially violent situation of all.

Riots and rebellions have long stained the history of South Africa. By no means have all been nonwhite against white. Rebellion by whites against whites include the one by Klip River Boers in 1847 (in concert with Zulu Chief Mpande), by Cape Afrikaners during the Boer War, by Afrikaners in World War I, and by white workers on the Rand in 1922. As the racial situation has evolved in South Africa, however, the whites as a privileged minority naturally have drawn together in order to retain their position of status. For present purposes, we are discussing only nonwhite dissent.

As could be expected, nonwhite (mostly, but not exclusively, by blacks) rebellions and riots have sprinkled the pages of South African history from shortly after the appearance of the first permanent white colony at the Cape in 1652 until the present day. The continuity of the struggle between white and nonwhite endures, unabated. Since World War II came to a definitive end in August 1945, rebellions have taken place on the Hurutshe Reserve (1956-1959), in Pondoland (1957-1960), in Sekhukhuneland (1957-1958), to say nothing of the continuing struggle in South-West Africa (Namibia). Riots protesting government actions during these years have occurred in Durban in 1949 when 142 were killed in rioting between blacks and Indians—two equally frustrated groups of oppressed people; in 1951 during the Torch Commando March; at Lady Selborne near Pretoria and at Durban in 1959; at Cato Manor, Sharpeville, and Capetown in 1960; at Paarl in 1962; at Capetown in 1972; and of course, at Soweto and elsewhere in 1976.

The Government Applies Pressure

During 1977–1982, the first confrontational act was committed by the government. On the night of October 19, 1977, as mentioned earlier, seventy-five blacks were detained. Six blacks were banned—in effect, were placed in a state of suspended animation as sanctioned by the Suppression of Communism Act in 1950. None of the six was communists, but all were active in seeking political rights for all people of South Africa, their home country. Two whites, eighteen organizations, and one black newspaper also were banned. Clearly, the government seized the initiative in an attempt to strip the black community of its galvanizing forces. The Soweto riots and the revulsion caused by the Biko death had scared the Pretoria regime. What other creditable explanations could be proposed for such repressive acts taken at a time of high political unrest? A message was being sent to the nonwhite community by means of the October 19, 1977, detentions, bannings, and closings. Under such circumstances, it is not surprising that the nonwhite community was skeptical when the government put forth legislation at the same time to improve housing, education, and employment.[3]

The pressure did not slacken. On November 10, 1977, police arrested 626 blacks in a house-to-house search through the Atteridgeville-Faulsville black township near Pretoria. The six-hour raid was supervised by helicopters that directed the police to spots where they could seize fleeing illegally housed residents. Four hundred ten blacks were arrested for passbook violations. Eight were charged with possession of stolen property. Five were charged with public violence, and 198 children were detained to determine whether they were in need of care. Critics of the government claimed that the raids were in reprisal for the school boycott throughout the country that had touched 300,000 children.[4]

Four days later, on November 14, 1977, riot police clashed with a thousand stone-throwing black demonstrators at Langa township near Capetown. Five people, one a white police officer, were struck by bullets in an exchange of gunfire at the end of the skirmish. In all, eight participants were seriously hurt. A search for illegal residents of the township had provoked the confrontation.[5] Occurrences of this nature seem to be at least a weekly happening in South Africa. Due to restrictions on the press, relatively minor uprisings typically go unreported. In Port Elizabeth, especially, disturbances had been constant occurrences between mid-1976 and mid-1978. Fourteen hundred separate incidents were reported during that period. The whole area of the eastern Cape has been politically active for many years.[6]

In the months that preceded the second anniversary of the Soweto riots of 1976, the government tightened its control. Those in opposition, especially among the black population, were subjected to close supervision and often to arrest, detention, mandatory migration, passport revocation, or banning. Between May 15 and June 15, 1978, more than 4,000 blacks were arrested for pass-law violations—an offense that could carry penalties ranging from a fine of as little as $5.50 to the severe penalty of being endorsed out to rural tribal homeland. In such an extreme case, it was most likely that the entire family would be forced to return to the homeland with the endorsed person.[7]

The increased use of the prison system by the government drew attention to the willingness displayed by the Pretoria regime to lock up those who violated the broadly written criminal laws of the South African Republic. During 1976 alone, 273,395 people, one of each ninety-five residents in the country, were sentenced to prison. More than half of these prisoners were pass-law violators.

The government showed equal quickness in sending to the gallows those convicted of serious crimes under its statutes. Ninety people were executed in 1977. This figure was twenty more than the ten preceding years' average of seventy per year. The 1977 count included sixty-three blacks, twenty-six of mixed race, and one white person. When considered appropriate by the government, wide publicity was given to these executions as a warning to nonwhite potential criminals and political activists that they could anticipate a similar fate if they misbehaved.[8]

Short of executing prisoners, but quite severe in its own right, was the government policy to employ whipping as a criminal punishment. During 1975 and 1976 together, 2,551 people were sentenced to a whipping. Of these people, 84 percent were black. The Soweto and associated riots of 1976 added significantly to the statistics being cited since they alone accounted for 528 whippings, including five lashes administered to an eight-year-old boy for an illegal-gathering attendance offense in the city of Port Elizabeth.

The South African prison population during 1977 averaged 100,000 people a day. Of this figure, an estimated 22,237 people were forced to perform manual labor on rural farms. Often the conditions for work, housing, and food for these forced laborers were poor. Revenues of $10 million a year were earned by the prison system from renting out convict labor. Taken all together, the executions, whippings, and forced labor created a climate in which those who do obtain their freedom after prison service will be, most likely, alienated permanently from the Pretoria regime and quite willing to engage in future political activity as well as, or in preference to, future criminal activity.[9]

Squelching Dissent

In 1978, the South African government concentrated on squelching black group protests. Bannings and conspiracy trials were major elements in this campaign. During June 1978, nineteen leaders of the Roman Catholic Young Christian Workers Union were arrested. Most of these men were black. They had been engaged in educating workers as to their human rights and how to organize their own unions.

During subsequent months, another dozen members of the Roman Catholic Young Christian Workers were also detained. Pressure from the Papal Nuncio and from the local Catholic bishops caused the government to start releasing these social organizers. The president of the group, Pheleo Magane, did, however, spend eighty-five days in prison.[10]

Conspiracy trials are another effective tool of the government. Normally, terrorism, as a violation of the 1962 Sabotage Act and the 1967 Terrorism Act, is the preferred charge. The Bethel terrorism trial was an important one, given wide publicity with government approval and encouragement. Zephania Mothopeng, reputedly one of the leaders of the PAC, was charged with terrorism along with seventeen other defendants. Their offense was that they had conducted PAC meetings over the last fifteen years while the organization was banned. They also were charged with encouraging black youth to leave South Africa in order to obtain military training for the purpose of eventually overthrowing the existing governmental structure. The Bethel terrorism trial followed in the wake of the sentencing of two white academics to prison for twelve and eight years respectively for distributing PAC literature.

Eventually, one of the Bethel defendants was acquitted and the others were found guilty. Zephania Mothopeng was sentenced to a pair of concurrent fifteen-year sentences. The rest received lesser sentences either for establishing PAC front organizations or for recruiting youth to become terrorists.[11]

At Kempton Park, an equally important trial was being conducted during the same time period—the trial of the so-called Soweto Eleven. The defendants were charged with, and eventually convicted of, sedition for their parts in the famous uprising. Observers were surprised that the government had settled for the relatively less-severe charge of sedition. It was the first time since the National party had been in power that the government had foregone the power available to it under the terrorism statutes. Reflecting this break with thirty years of tradition, the court handed out less-strict punishment than would have been expected. Four of the defendants received four-year prison terms, while the rest were credited for time served before verdict, twenty-three months, and were placed on probation. It seemed clear the government was attempting to soften its image in the perception of other nations.[12]

A third important trial during this period concerned Solomon Mahlangu. He had been recruited by the ANC and sent to Mozambique and Angola for guerrilla infiltration training. Two days after returning clandestinely to South Africa through Swaziland, he was arrested by police after a shoot-out in which an accomplice had killed two white policemen. By the common-purpose doctrine, Mahlangu was sentenced to die for the shootings. Voices were raised worldwide in an attempt to save the life of the twenty-two-year-old revolutionary. The World Council of Churches and President Jimmy Carter both interceded on his behalf; to no avail, however. Solomon Mahlangu was executed by hanging at the Pretoria Central Jail on April 6, 1979. In refusing to intercede, Prime Minister Botha stated, "It is not for me to interfere in the process of the law."[13]

The spirit of oppression and tension that so permeated South Africa seemed to breed a climate of violence as a necessary by-product. In such circumstances, there is a thin line between crime and political protest. Americans realize the truth of this statement from events during the Vietnam War days. Housing riots, student strikes, and labor violence walked this line in the South Africa of 1978–1979. Some acts, however, were clearly more political in nature. Attacks on police stations, an increasing activity in South Africa, would fall into this category. On May 3, 1979, in the most serious such incident so far, three black guerrillas, employing AK 47 automatic rifles and a supply of hand grenades, stormed a Soweto police station. One black police officer was killed, and two black police officers and three civilians were injured.[14]

The publicity generated by such acts of open defiance did little to improve the mood of the government. The Soweto police station attack took place only hours before the sentencing of those convicted in the Soweto-Eleven trial at Kempton Park. Since the sentences pronounced were less severe than had been expected, perhaps the attack in this case did not affect the outcome. Nonetheless, the impression that the government was under siege from many quarters was fostered. As a result, the Pretoria regime pushed on with its trials, bannings, and detentions with increased vigor. However, actions like the Soweto police station bombing only encouraged black opportunistic opponents of the Pretoria government to increase their number of acts of public defiance.

The Pitermaritzburg-Twelve trial, and especially the forthcoming execution of James Daniel Mange, became caught up in the escalating forces of protest and counterthrust. Mange was especially defiant in court and frequently interrupted proceedings with slogans and black-power salutes. His attitude provoked the judge to no end and, without question, was involved in the Mange death-sentence pronouncement. The twelve defendants were found guilty of high treason for plotting to overthrow the government by force. Mange's eleven companions received prison sentences ranging from twelve to sixteen years. Only one of the Pietermaritzburg Twelve was convicted of an act of violence. Mange was not this person, but the sentencing judge termed Mange "a thoroughly repulsive and objectionable character in more ways than one" and sentenced him to death.[15]

Violence and Protest Continue

Especially in the Port Elizabeth area, violence and unrest continued at a high level during the rest of 1979. Most of this trouble had labor-union pressure at its base. The move toward a position of authority and power was a slow one for black labor unions. The government was far less willing to accept them in their new role than private industry. As a result, any demonstration of industrial protest was interpreted by a nervous government as an act of criminal, seditious, or terroristic motivation.

Such scenes of continuing unrest were kept from the newspapers by the government as much as possible; thus receiving less attention than they deserved. As a consequence, the spectacular acts of protest and violence committed on a one-time-only basis often received more attention than their long-term worth probably would dictate. The Capetown bank massacre in January 1980 is one example of this tendency. Three black robbers held twenty-five patrons as hostages. They demanded the freedom of Nelson Mandela as part of the negotiating terms. A fierce crossfire took place between the robber-black nationalists and the police. The three perpetrators and two hostage civilians were killed. Within the black community, the robbers were looked upon as revolutionary heroes. More than 20,000 people attended the funeral of one of the three gunmen.[16]

During April 1980, the one-time protest action and the long-term ideological-protest form of action both took place. Rocket-propelled grenades were launched against a Johannesburg police station on the morning of April 4, 1980, but no one was injured. The long-term action was the start of another student strike, this one instituted by colored students at Capetown. Their action was contemporaneous with, but independent from, a government crackdown that saw four prominent black power activists arrested, all with ties to earlier student unrest.[17]

This school boycott gave signs during May 1980 of spreading farther than would have been anticipated. Its participants had grown to a number in excess of 100,000. Indian students, a few white students, and a significant number of black students had joined the boycott. The government was clearly afraid that a united nonwhite front might be in the process of being formed. Botha went to Parliament early in the dispute to say that he would not consider restoring colored voters to the common voter role, a privilege they had lost in 1956. He also warned those who hid behind school children that they could be hurt.[18]

At the end of May, the prime minister rethought his position. Taking as a good omen that some students in Durban had returned to class and that due to fatigue from Soweto and its aftermath, black school-strike support had been less than total, Mr. Botha announced that the grievances of the strikers were in the main justified. He promised to consider the possibility of one unified school system for all children in the country and added he hoped the strike would be postponed in the interim.[19] It is not surprising that given the state of alienation between blacks and whites in South Africa, the call for a truce made to other nonwhite groups caused many blacks to react by joining the strike for the first time.

Trouble at Elsie's River

On May 28, 1980, a series of events that could have started another Soweto began to unfold. Police outside of Capetown at Elsie's River fired into a group of student demonstrators. Two were killed and three wounded in the attack. The two dead boys were estimated to be about fourteen years old. The Elsie's River demonstration had been formed to protest the arrest of sixty-five area students.

Serious unrest continued. In all, 1,200 people were arrested for protesting the strike in various cities and towns throughout the country. At the automobile-manufacturing center of Uitenhage, 275 students were arrested. At the time, they were in the process of marching into the city to protest the earlier detention of four of their classmates. In Johannesburg, a demonstration of church leaders led to the detention of 24 of the 53 participants. Among those arrested were Bishop Desmond Tutu and his wife.

The minister of police, Louis Le Grange, took this highly charged moment to make a peace gesture. He apologized in public for the police killings at Elsie's River. Elsewhere in the world, such a statement would be commonplace under the circumstances, but nonwhite-against-white confrontations in South Africa have little resemblance to what is commonplace elsewhere. In the wake of his announcement, the student committee of eighty-one in Capetown agreed to cancel their strike. They decided nothing would be gained by continuing the strike and that it would be better for them to return to class and wait for the prime minister to deliver on his promises to improve their educational situation.[20]

The Elsie's River powder keg was not yet finished. The respite lasted a mere two weeks. On June 17, serious rioting again broke out. Estimates are that forty-three died and that many more were injured. Most were the victims of police bullets. This time, however, it would be incorrect to blame the student strike for being the direct cause of the trouble. "Skollie elements," the local term for juvenile delinquents, kept stoning the police at every opportunity. Armed retaliation eventually ensued and the battle was on again.

Reverend H.J. Hendrickse, a colored spokesperson and Labor party leader, expressed his frustration in public at the slow pace of change in South Africa. He said that he had warned the Pretoria regime repeatedly of the explosive mood of the nonwhite people in the country but that they had refused to listen. Hendrickse blamed the government for the continuing strife between races and termed its methods as "high handed and arrogant."[21]

The second set of riots at Elsie's River triggered another series of countrywide disturbances. Conflicts with the people were particularly serious at Bloemfontein, where fifteen people died, and at Noordgezich, a colored township near Johannesburg, where twenty people were wounded by police bullets. Committee of Ten leader Dr. Motlana was particularly loud in his condemnation of the government. He was most bitter that the government still tended to blame all agitation on Communist sympathizers. He termed these claims as nonsense.[22]

The potential for outright violence on a massive scale seemed to strengthen when the Sasol conversion plants and an oil refinery came under attack on June 2, 1980. In all, at the two separate locations, eight fuel tanks were destroyed. The externally based ANC claimed credit for the attack. The government doubled security around the plants in the aftermath of the destruction and promised to protect the vital energy interests of the country. Nonetheless, the bombings were one of the most significant cases of economic sabotage in the history of South Africa and could be a preview of coming attractions. It is logical to assume that at some future moment, the external-based guerrillas and dissidents within the country will be able to join together in an effective manner.[23]

The Continuing Disruptions

The list of events that might have caused the fatal spark continues to grow. Fanyana Mazibuko, a black consciousness leader in Soweto, received a three-year banning notice in July 1980.[24] At the end of the same month, two blacks were shot to death by police at a disturbance that took place while a deceased student demonstrator in Grahamstown was being buried.[25] A serious municipal strike in Johannesburg broke out simultaneously with the Grahamstown killings. Heavy-handed police pressure quelled the rioting strikers. A large number of the strike leaders were fired and endorsed out to the homelands.[26]

The heaviest concentration of violence during August 1980 again came from the Capetown area. Three blacks and one white were killed in racially motivated rioting. White motorists were forbidden from driving through nonwhite areas of the region.[27] During September 1980, in the diamond center of Kimberley, sixty-eight black girls and forty-four black boys were arrested after trying to burn the homes of two black policemen.[28]

Reacting to the rising climate of violence, the government closed seventy-seven black schools during September 1980, thereby preventing 55,000 students from attending class. Despite the seriousness of the action, it should be remembered that only 4 percent of the black schools in the country and less than 1 percent of the black students were affected by these closings. Reacting to criticisms of its actions, the government pointed out that it had constructed 156 new nonwhite schools during 1979–1980 and 2,515 new classrooms at presently operating schools. It also started three new teachers colleges and moved toward compulsory schooling for all blacks and equal pay for black and white teachers.[29] Far too little, far too late was the opinion of most critics.

Soweto and Port Elizabeth, perennial locations of trouble, recaptured the headlines as 1980 drew to an end. On October 14, 1980, police were obliged to use tear gas and attack dogs to disperse 3,000 rioters who had gathered to protest the awarding of honorary citizenship in Soweto to Cooperation and Development Minister Pieter Koornhof by the government-selected black mayor of Soweto, David Thebehali. A more-provocative move hardly could be envisioned. In a similar act of violence that took place on Guy Fawkes Day in Port Elizabeth, police killed four blacks and wounded sixteen others. Students of history would find it ironic that a holiday whose purpose was to celebrate the breaking of the 1605 Gunpowder Plot and the preservation of the parliamentary system in the United Kingdom has evolved into a day of protest against white South African domination in South Africa.[30]

At the end of 1980, the government switched tactics and turned its attention to the black journalism scene. Fearing that these newspapers were stirring up added opposition among the nonwhite population, employing a technical registration law, the government suspended the right of the largest black newspaper in the country, the *Post Transvaal,* to print. Two other papers suffered the same fate. Increasing the magnitude of its actions, the government served banning notices on two black newspaper union leaders: Zwelakhe Sisulu, the news editor of the *Sunday Post* and son of ANC-imprisoned activist Walter Sisulu, and Marimuthu Subramoney, a British Broadcasting Company correspondent.[31] Two other black *Post* journalists were banned shortly thereafter. Many politically motivated blacks thought that the white owners of the *Post,* an Argus newspaper, could have been more energetic in protecting the rights and freedom of their black employees.

1980 could be looked upon as the year in which black labor unions began to feel their power. Two hundred seven separate strikes had accounted for 175,000 lost days of work by individual workers. In the previous year, 107 separate black strikes had led to the loss of 67,000 man-days of work. Impressive as these figures might appear, it should be remembered that only 100,000 of the 4 million black workers had been unionized at that point. The important area of black mine workers had hardly been touched.[32]

June 1981 saw more discontent-motivated black dissent. Police in Pietersburg, 190 miles north of Johannesburg, fired on black students who were trying to storm a police station as a protest against independence day celebrations.[33] In Soweto, on June 16, 1981, police dispersed 5,000 demonstrators gathered at Regina Mundi Catholic Church. These blacks were attending a memorial commemoration service on the occasion of the fifth anniversary of the 1976 Soweto riots. Dr. Motlana has used the occasion to call once again for the release of Nelson Mandela from Robben Island. The Soweto leader termed the legendary detainee as "our Jesus Christ on Robben Island."[34] The government, of course, ignored the Free-Nelson-Mandela calls and, perhaps as a response, increased bannings and detentions. It was estimated that in excess of 165 people had been detained under these circumstances since the start of 1981—six months' time.[35] Many of these bannings were aimed at leaders of newly emergent black labor unions, or at black and white student leaders.

Externally launched insurgent attacks against South African energy facilities occurred again during July 1981, a little more than a year after the more-impressive Sasolburg raids. Again, the ANC was blamed. This time, the seven transformers and five generator couplings were damaged seriously at two electrical power stations in the Transvaal. The guerrillas presumably slipped in from Mozambique.[36]

Solutions Remain Distant

The dark side of the black struggle toward independence was underlined during August 1981 when Joseph Gqabi was shot to death outside his Salisbury home by an unknown assassin. The veteran ANC leader was directing the anti–South African government forces living in Zimbabwe. The information minister in the newly free nation blamed "unscrupulous agents of the racist South African regime" for the assassination. Whether he was correct or whether the killing was another example of destructive feuding within the various South African political groups was a question that might never be answered.[37]

On August 19, 1981, housing-related violence broke out again near Capetown. Two thousand men, women, and children were arrested in a dawn police raid on Nyanga township. Illegal squatters, those living without the requisite permission, were the victims of uprooting and forced confinement. The raids came the same day as three ANC members were condemned to death for Sasolburg and Johannesburg police station bombings. Eight hundred squatters in Capetown were arrested a week later.[38]

Little changed as 1982 began. The detention-cell death of Dr. Neil Aggett, although it did provoke marches and condemnation in both the black and white communities, failed to produce the same overwhelming sense of revulsion in the nonwhite community as had the death of Steven Biko. No doubt this reaction is understandable; dedicated as Dr. Aggett was to better treatment for nonwhites, he was white. As a result, he was a rare, almost unique, witness to racial equality and freedom in South Africa. Biko, when he died, was assumed an important symbolic role for a whole people. It is most predictable that the death of a person like Steven Biko would have a greater long-run impact than that of a Dr. Neil Aggett. Only if meaningful reform of the police interrogation system results from the death of Dr. Aggett will it be accurate to say his passing had a widespread impact.

During most of the first half of 1982, the South African electorate and most political observers concerned themselves with the Treurnicht split and the proposals of the president's council, the falling state of the economy, and peace prospects in Namibia. Those who assumed that worries of this nature would cause the government to loosen restrictions on political agitation were proven incorrect when the government filed the Internal Security Bill in Parliament on May 14, 1982. It was hard to detect any slackening in the government's grip in the provisions of the new omnibus act. At best, the legislative regulations enforcing apartheid were streamlined and made easier to follow. It would be hard to justify the opinion that they had been eased significantly. The crisp terms spelling out detention possibilities for agitation against government policy would appear to indicate more clearly the current mood of the Botha government than would the vaguely worded proposal aimed at instituting the president's council.

Well-known liberal Parliament member Helen Suzman denounced the new legislation as being "a totally repulsive measure that perpetuates an undeclared state of emergency in South Africa."[9] The Internal Security Bill repeals twenty-eight earlier pieces of security legislation including the frequently utilized Suppression of Communism Act and the Terrorism Act. Their main provisions, however, were incorporated in the new legislation.

The new security legislation enacted suggestions made by the Rabie Commission, headed by Chief Justice P.J. Rabie. Detention still was permitted virtually on the whim of the government since the enabling legislation was to be as wide as it was under previous legislation. It might even be argued that the scope of offenses enabling detention would be more extensive in the future since the Rabie Commission suggested and the government proposed to the Parliament accompanying legislation to the Internal Security Bill that were entitled the Demonstrations in or near Court Buildings Prohibition Bill Act, the Intimidation Bill Act, and the Protection of Information Bill Act. Taken together, the government was free to detain whomever it wished. New provisions in all four acts, stating that limited governmental review would occur for prolonged detentions and that parole might be given on security-violation convictions, hardly seemed to compensate for the rigidity in most of the other provisions.[40] It was perhaps significant that such a manifestation of current government attitudes came as the government was turning a deaf ear to worldwide pleas for it to spare the lives of three young blacks condemned to death for politically motivated crime—attacking a police station—that had not led to any loss of life.[41]

On June 3, 1982, guerrilla activity against the South African government again commenced after a significant lull. Six explosions seriously damaged the Total Oil Company fuel depot in Paulpietersburg, Natal Province. It was assumed that the attackers were ANC members headquartered in Swaziland.[42] On June 4, 1982, a white man was killed when a bomb exploded in the elevator of a Capetown office building. Ironically, the building housed the president's council, the group that, at least in the eyes of the government, was supposed to start the country on the road to racial power sharing. The bombing came on the day that the government backed down to world pressure and commuted to life imprisonment the sentences of three young black men condemned to death for non-life-taking guerrilla activity.[43]

On June 13, 1982, police seized 250 mourners at a Soweto memorial service to commemorate the recent deaths of three black leaders, one of whom had died in an automobile accident and the other two in a bomb blast of unknown origin in Swaziland. Those held by the police included Dr. Nthato Motlana and Albertina Sisulu, the wife of longtime jailed ANC leader, Albert Sisulu. Three days later at the Soweto memorial services to commemorate the 1976 uprisings, serious rioting broke out that police had to quell with tear gas and warning shots.[44]

At the start of July, concern again grew. At least eight black gold miners were slain, six by police and mine security officers; the others died in an unknown fashion. Projected pay raises were the point at issue.[45] At the time, black miners were averaging salaries of $216 per month, while white miners were averaging $1,080 per month.

Widespread disturbances and a short-lived strike broke out in the wake of the initial rioting. With governmental cooperation, over 1,000 miners were dispatched forcibly to the homelands in an attempt to break up the strike.[46] The death toll rose to ten before the situation quieted. Again, civil rights suffered, and one more potential Sharpeville or Soweto passed the way of Elsie's River—almost, but not quite, the ultimate conflagration spark.[47]

The Homelands

Historical Setting

The housing, education, and employment situation discussed specifically in the last chapter and used as a springboard for an examination of mounting violence within South Africa in this chapter has been considered apart from its impact upon the homelands. Housing, education, employment, and the violence leading from the denial to the nonwhite population of freedom occur also in the homelands. Without doubt, in each case, the evils are worse in these remote areas than they are on the 87 percent of the land that is officially designated for white occupation. In the urban areas around Capetown, Pretoria, Johannesburg, and the like, hard as the life is for the nonwhite population, there is not the cast-adrift feeling, and often the harsh treatment, that occurs in the homelands. In Zimbabwe, the white regime eventually fell because it could not control the rural tribal trust lands population. South Africa is a larger, far more-intricate political puzzle, but the same result could happen here as well. The homelands concept, the hope of the South African government for extracting itself from the grave racial dilemma in which it finds itself, now can be rated as a distinct failure and perhaps even as a ludicrous fiasco. However, the government finds itself so committed to the homelands concept that total abandonment of the idea is unthinkable. In such a situation of chaos and oppression, the move toward all-enveloping violence remains a distinct possibility.

The homelands policy, in its current form, dates back to the term of Dr. H.F. Verwoerd as South African prime minister. In the years after his accession to power on the death in office of Prime Minister Strijdom in 1958, Verwoerd moved toward a form of political independence for the Bantu areas. He also strove to, and succeeded in, making South Africa an independent republic. By setting up independent homelands—strictly under South African government control, of course—a more-defined territorial base was being given to homeland residents by this Bantu Authorities System than was given to the essentially rootless Indian and colored populations, even though they possessed indicia of citizenship that the black population did not.

The Transkei, in 1963, became the first homeland with its own local government. No one could think, however, that Pretoria was in any way surrendering meaningful control by this action. The Transkei homeland constitution was drawn up in Pretoria, the capital of the Republic of South Africa, not in Umtata, the capital of the homeland. Prime Minister Verwoerd was involved actively in the construction of the Transkei homeland constitution. The Transkei was described as being a self-governing territory within the Republic of South Africa. The Transkei Assembly was to be composed of a group of chiefs eligible to sit due to their office and a group of members elected by popular vote. Most of the ministries were to be selected in Umtata. Chief Kaiser Matanzima assumed the premiership in a more-or-less free election.

The trend in forthcoming years was for the Pretoria regime to promote the self-governing territories system, to encourage industrial decentralization, to cut down on the number of blacks legally resident in urban areas, and most comprehensively, by the terms of the Bantu Homelands Citizen-ship Act of 1970, to make every black in South Africa a citizen-member of one of the homelands for domestic purposes. The final step of making all blacks a member of a totally independent homeland for international pur-poses as well was yet to come.

The homeland system based on tribal affiliations spread from its start with the Transkei to a point where ten different homelands at different points of independence, are currently in existence. As late as 1970, the Tran-skei was the only self-governing black territory within South Africa. By mid-1972, seven other black homeland territories also had achieved legisla-tive-assembly status. The homeland territories that joined the Xhosa-speaking Transkei as self-governing homeland territories within South Africa included the Xhosa-speaking Ciskei, the Zulu-speaking Kwazulu, the North Sotho-speaking Lebowa, the Chivenda-speaking Venda, the Tsonga-speaking Gazankulu, the Tswana-speaking Bophuthatswana, and the South Sotho-speaking Qwaqwa. Kangwane and Kwandebele were slower to move toward legislative-assembly status.

In April 1972, Prime Minister Vorster stated to Parliament, "As far as I am concerned, if our Black people become independent, they will become independent in the same way as Lesotho or Ghana or Gabon or any other country in the world."[48] On October 26, 1976, Transkei took the massive step and became independent. Its failure to obtain recognition from the other nations of the world and the similar fate suffered by the other homelands following the Transkei lead is detailed in this chapter since the components of this failure exposed themselves during the period under discussion in this book: late 1977 to the end of 1982.

Bophuthatswana and the Transkei

On December 6, 1977, Chief Lucas Mangope was elected as the first presi-dent of Bophuthatswana and its 2.4 million citizens. Bophuthatswana became the second homeland to become an independent nation. Unfortun-ately, as far as it and South Africa were concerned, no other independent nation in the world extended diplomatic recognition to it. As a result, Bophuthatswana joined the newly independent Transkei in a limbo status of international isolation. Except for South Africa, no one paid any attention to them. As long as this state of affairs continued, the main Pretoria government plan for ending racial strife was doomed to fail.

Whether the homelands should become independent, was a debated question. Many of those resident within the boundaries of the homeland did approve. Their theory was that they possessed nothing, whether indepen-dent or not, so they might as well become independent and further divorce themselves from white control over their day-to-day life. On the other hand, many Tswana tribespeople resident in urban areas of South Africa were opposed violently to full homeland independence because they would lose their South African citizenship by this step. As citizens of a nonrecognized Bophuthatswana, their passports for foreign travel might not be accepted anywhere in the world except in South Africa.[49]

Dr. Nthato Motlana was one of the blacks due to lose his citizenship when Bophuthatswana became independent. He explained to the world press that he had been born just outside Pretoria capital in 1925 and had lived in neighboring Johannesburg since 1933. With scorn in his voice, he said, "I don't even know where this place called Bophuthatswana is."[50]

As Bophuthatswana moved toward independence, its leaders could not have been encouraged by the difficulties experienced by the Transkei since it had declared itself to be an independent nation. During April 1978, the Transkei severed diplomatic contacts with the Republic of South Africa, the only nation that had recognized it originally. Ostensibly, the split came because South Africa assigned the disputed territory called East Griqualand to the white-governed Natal Province of South Africa rather than to the newly independent Republic of the Transkei.

Although the South African refusal to provide farmland that would assist the Transkei was certainly part of the dispute, most observers thought that Chief Kaiser Matanzima took the highly visible step of breaking diplomatic relations with South Africa in order to divert the attention of his Transkei citizens from the severe economic conditions present in the new nation. Chief Matanzima also had been consolidating his hold on power within the Transkei by jailing many of his political opponents. It was said that he was highly frustrated by the lack of outside world political recognition for his republic.

The Transkei possessed an army of 300 men. Threats by Chief Matanzima to make war eventually against the 80,000-strong South African Army caused observers to recall *The Mouse that Roared*. Since South Africa had provided $190 million of the $280 million Transkei budget for 1978, few believed that the Transkei could continue its isolation from South Africa for an extended period of time. Chief Matanzima did continue to threaten and scold the South African government with a ferocity that surprised those who had considered him a mere puppet of the Pretoria regime. "Knowing the strength of the South African government militarily," he said, "the Transkei will bide its time before taking up arms to recover the land that has been cynically raped from it."[51]

The Transkei is composed of three sections that, taken together, are double the size of Israel. It is a land of beautiful mountains, forests, and rivers, leading to a 200-mile-wide coastline on the Indian Ocean. Unfortunately, neither industry nor commercial agriculture has developed. Ninety percent of foodstuffs must be imported from South Africa.

Not all close followers of the South African political situation laughed at the Transkei. Brown University political scientist Newell Stultz, for one, treated it seriously. In an article in *The New York Times* during July 1979, Stultz compared it to "a black-run provincial government in a highly decentralized South African confederal political system."[52] He pointed out that the roots of self-government by blacks for blacks emanating from Umtata were becoming increasingly pronounced as years went on. Stultz thought it was possible that in the future the Transkei might play a marked role in the political future of a South Africa in which it had an undeniable stake.

South Africa and the Transkei renewed political contacts during February 1980. The Pretoria regime promised to consider returning a portion of East Griqualand to the Transkei. One bitter observer in Umtata, Tsepo Letlaka, the minister of finance, suggested that his government should have grabbed a hundred or so white hostages, "called the press, and shot them."[53] He suggested that critics of the South African government would have applauded this move. Instead, when the weak Transkei regime attempted to bargain with the South African government and failed, everyone mocked their ineptitude.

Venda and the Ciskei

On September 13, 1979, Venda, located in the northeast woodland became the third independent homeland in South Africa. At least for the short term, its prospects were dismal. Sixty-seven percent of the job-holding men were obliged to work outside the homeland. Nearly 50 percent of food consumed in Venda must be imported from South Africa. The Republic of South Africa spent $35 million to prepare Venda, a territory situated more than 350 miles from Johannesburg, for independence. It possessed one paved road at the time of independence but no connecting rail links to the outside world.

The local chiefs in Venda, led by Chief Minister Patrick R. Mphephu, are paramount. Mphephu holds power mainly due to the loyalty of the twenty-seven other chiefs and fifteen additional seats he controls in the Venda Parliament. In the 1978 election, the opposition Independence party won thirty-one of the forty-two elected seats. This result was a threat to the paramount chief since despite its name, the Venda Independence party was most lukewarm about total separation from South Africa. In reply, Mphephu locked up eleven of these elected legislators as part of a crackdown on political dissidence that led to the arrest of fifty people overall. The move toward full independence, South African–homeland style, continued without interruption.

Venda is among the smallest of the homelands, and depending on what acreage is ceded to or withheld from other homelands that declare independence in the future, it could be the smallest of all. At the time of independence Venda possessed only one significant industrial plant, a pickle factory. The land does possess farming potential since it is fertile, but so far, much of what is produced has been in the nature of subsistence farming. The potential to extract coke coal also exists. In both cases, a weak infrastructure restricts progress. Domestic industrial development is a necessity. At independence time a maximum of 125,000 jobs could be provided within the territorial confines of Venda. Over 70 percent of all income earned by citizens of Venda came from work in South Africa, not in Venda.[54]

The gloomy picture painted for the third homeland that chose independence, Venda, was replicated in the fourth, the Ciskei. In this case the process was slower and more arduous, but the final result was the same. Leaders in the homeland formed a study commission to suggest methods of heading toward independence. The results of the Ciskei Commission work were most modest. It is not surprising that the majority of residents of this tiny homeland situated south of the Transkei on the shores of the Indian Ocean were discovered to be against full independence from South Africa. As a result, the commission suggested that independence be granted only if the majority of potential Ciskei citizens (resident within and without the Ciskei) voted for independence. The commission advanced other independence conditions. For example, South African citizenship must be retained. A handsome land settlement including much choice white-designated land must be made by South Africa. Ciskei citizens must have continued freedom to work in South Africa on acceptable financial terms. In addition, a multiracial condominium-type land-sharing scheme with the nearby white city of East London was proposed.[55]

The plan proposed by the Ciskei Commission had much to recommend it. Given the state of events in South Africa, however, it is not surprising that the suggestions were ignored by the Pretoria government and that independence moved ahead on terms comparable to those that had been used for the Transkei, Bophuthatswana, and Venda. Bowing to strong pressure from their chiefs and from the South African government, 98.7 percent of Ciskei voters chose independence in the December 1980 election called on this question.[56] The South African government reacted by refusing to allow the neighboring small white city, King William's Town, to become part of the Ciskei.[57]

Writing during May 1981, *Baltimore Sun* columnist Antero Pietila observed that the Ciskei was "a two million acre area of eroded fields and corrugated tin huts."[58] Seven months before full independence was to take place, the Ciskei still had not been given the definitive territorial bounds of its new nation. Less than 600,000 of the 2 million projected citizens of the Ciskei resided within its territory. Forty-seven percent of the land mass was listed as being moderately to seriously eroded. A severe drought had caused widespread starvation. Accurate statistics were lacking, but many children were dying both in the Ciskei and in the neighboring Transkei. The industrial base of the new nation was virtually nonexistent. To emphasize the point, it should be noted that a drive-in movie theater was listed as being the major enterprise of the new capital, Redwoods.[59]

Even as the Ciskei joined the ranks as the fourth independent homeland, it had become clear that Verwoerd's plan was not producing the overall benefits desired by the Pretoria regime. The refusal of Chief Buthelezi to lead Kwazulu toward independence was one factor. The unwillingness of the outside world to accord diplomatic recognition to the new nations was another. A third difficulty concerned the massive financial outlays that Pretoria was obliged to make to keep the new nations afloat. Such stringent monetary subsidies came as the price of gold fell and as the money involved needed to be spent within South Africa proper. Without doubt, the constellation of states around an industrial, white South Africa idea would not work in its entirety. Since 1948, the Pretoria government had moved over 2 million people into the various homelands, resulting in unrelieved suffering. A permanently embittered rural black population will be the long-term legacy. Speaking before the Transvaal Province National Party Congress in September 1980, Prime Minister Botha seemed to admit the failure of the idea. He stated, "We cannot give away the whole of South Africa merely to create economically viable black states."[60]

Homelands Problems Continue

Even if the master plan for the homelands to become independent nations was doomed, the idea of homelands within South Africa continued to be advanced. In 1981, Kwandebele became the latest example of this dubious experiment. This tribe will be given its own homeland in the Transvaal. For the moment it will be a fully dependent homeland. Nine thousand families were moved forcefully to the upper part of Olifant's River to start the new homeland. No industry existed; the only revenue is produced by cattle grazing. At present, housing is available only for new leaders of the government of Kwandebele. The new capital is a shantytown, Siyabuswa, reached by a dirt road eighteen miles from the nearest paved road. Over 300,000 members of this tribe now live on land that was owned by ten white farmers and that housed 32,000 of their people as recently as 1970.[61]

The breakdown of the homelands-to-independent-nations scheme on both theoretical and practical levels led to added unrest in rural areas. The most poverty stricken of homelands residents could sense that little hope existed for a marked short-term improvement in their lives. Even those fortunate enough to possess jobs in the homelands or in neighboring white-controlled areas fell prey to pessimism. Violence in the homelands and in neighboring area factories increased at the end of 1981 and the start of 1982. Repressionary tactics by the South African police and by the equally heavy-handed local constabulary rose to a notable degree. As mentioned in Chapter 2, one such arrest occurred in the Ciskei, where 205 residents who worked in an East London factory were confined during September 1981 in their homeland on returning from a day of picketing at their place of employment in the neighboring white district.[62]

The Transkei, the oldest of the homelands trying to be an independent nation, has been concerned with anti–South African government guerrillas using their land as a base for operations. Since the Transkei came into being through the cooperation and financial support of the South African government, it is not surprising that ANC guerrillas look on the Matanzima brothers who control the Transkei as South African hired hands and as the enemies of liberation groups. It also should be noted that the jailed ANC leader Nelson Mandela is a cousin both of the Matanzima brothers and of their predecessor whom they deposed, Paramount Chief Sabata Dalindyebo. Now living in exile in Lesotho, Chief Dalindyebo had become a supporter of the ANC. Since many within Transkei considered the Matanzima brothers as despotic rulers, it is understandable that the ANC chose this independent homeland as a perfect spot in which to cause trouble. Whether the ANC possessed the capacity to overthrow the Transkei government as was charged by the Matanzima brothers is most questionable. Certainly, the South African government would step in to prevent any such event. In the meantime, the brothers arrested their two top security men, hired a white mercenary to run the army, imposed universal military service for men, and announced their army would be increased from 300 to 10,000 members.[63]

Problems with the Neighbors

The state of unhappiness prevailing in the homelands was matched in the surrounding independent nations of Botswana, Lesotho, and Swaziland. Botswana's mineral resources afforded it some advantage over the other two, but in all three cases poverty is extreme. The unstable political climate throughout southern Africa and the economic advantage to South Africa assured by the conditions of trade in the Southern African Customs Union promise the status quo will continue. In these three countries, political activism by the disaffected youth of the countries is on the rise. This destabilizing factor is compounded by the renewed efforts of externally based black guerrilla forces to use Botswana, Lesotho, and Swaziland as launching pads for strikes against South Africa. The Pretoria regime has warned their neighbors in strong terms against harboring these groups. Especially in

Lesotho, the local government fears that South Africa would assist internal political opposition in bringing down the government of Chief Leabua Jonathan in return for added efforts by the replacement government to keep anti–South African government guerrillas away from their territory.[64]

The homelands issue and the related question of South African relations with an independent Lesotho, Botswana, and Swaziland took a curious and perhaps ominous turn during early 1982. The South African government and the Swaziland government announced that negotiations were taking place with the aim of transferring a substantial amount of land from South African dominion to that of Swaziland.

The area in question included the Swazi ethnic homeland in South Africa, Kangwane, a thirty-five-mile strip adjacent to Swaziland and a part of Kwazulu, the homeland controlled by Chief Buthelezi. The leaders of both homelands were understandably in total opposition. They did not wish to lose land, and their citizens did not want to become citizens of Swaziland. The Botha motivation was clear. By freeing himself of one of the most dependent of the homelands and also of the obligation to support the 750,000 ethnic Swazi residents in South Africa, both in Kangwane and elsewhere, a substantial financial burden would be lifted from the depression-pinched South African economy. Botha also would bind Swaziland closer to South Africa by the action, an event that should allow South Africa to increase the pressure on the eighty-two-year-old Swazi king, Sobhuza, to keep ANC guerrillas from using his kingdom as a main base.[65]

On June 17, 1982, in a major step, the South African government formally notified Kangwane that it would become part of Swaziland. Chief Buthelezi of Kwazulu was informed that his homeland would be deprived of the Ingwavuma district so that Swaziland could obtain a corridor to, and coastland on, the Indian Ocean. By these moves, all 750,000 ethnic Swazi residents anywhere in South Africa, whether in Kangwane or not, automatically would become residents of Swaziland upon the transition date projected for early 1983. The same fate would befall the 135,000 Zulu residents in Ingwavuma. Pieter Koornhof stated that this move "represented the long-cherished ideal of the Swazi people, who have for long been deprived of Swazi citizenship by an accident of history."[66]

Neither Nganani Mazuba, the chief minister of Kangwane, nor Chief Buthelezi, the Zulu leader, would accept Koornhof's reasoning. Mazuba asked a rhetorical question: "It becomes mysterious why, if people are in favor of incorporation, they are not allowed to express their will by means of a referendum."[67] More ominously, Chief Buthelezi warned that actions like this could drive Inkatha together with the ANC since, in this matter at least, they were of one mind.

In the short run it could be seen that South Africa would free itself of an economic burden by cutting loose these Swazi people. Such a move also would bind Swaziland closer to it and by so doing, give the Pretoria regime the right to use Swaziland border territory to set up outposts to deny guerrillas entry onto South African soil proper. From the Swaziland point of view, the incorporation plan would increase its tax base by adding to the rolls those South African Swazi who were gainfully employed. Swaziland would also gain direct access to the Indian Ocean, a step of great potential economic benefit.

On the negative side of the tribal-transfer issue, South Africa was sending a message to all black citizens that they were expendable any time the Pretoria government perceived it in its interest to cut them loose. The homelands-to-independent-nations theory was shown by this action to be flawed seriously, and the South African need to take steps to protect its borders against guerrilla attack was emphasized. For Swaziland, negatives also existed. Almost 900,000 extra mouths must be fed. All are potential participants in future revolutions either in Swaziland or in South Africa, or perhaps in both nations. Swaziland also for the first time will lose its territorial integrity since Kangwane is split in two parts by a stretch of rich farmland, twenty miles wide, that South Africa would retain. Previously, there was no break in the land possessed by Swaziland.

The most serious deficiency in the plan from the Swaziland point of view, however, well could be that the Organization of African Unity would expel this tiny nation, declare it no longer free, and consider it as another of the dependent South African homelands possessing only bogus independence. To run such a risk hardly seems worth the price.[68]

At the end of September 1982, in a surprise move, South Africa's highest appeals court ruled the transfer illegal because the government had failed to consult with the affected tribal leaders.[69] The South African government promised to study the opinion. Given the supreme status of the executive in South Africa, few doubted that the judicial roadblock could be circumvented if the Botha administration truly wished to do so. Whatever was to be decided, it was clear the government had received a massive propaganda setback.

Two months later, the South African government conceded defeat. The Department of Cooperation and Development revoked its act dissolving the Legislative Assembly of Kangwane and agreed to pay all the homeland's legal costs.[70] The South African government would have to look elsewhere in its attempts to stabilize its hold on power and to eliminate continuing problems in the homelands. Both in the cities and in the rural areas, the climate that leads to violence remains very much present.

Notes

1. F.R. Metrowich, *Africa in the Sixties* (Pretoria, South Africa: Africa Institute of South Africa, 1960), pp. 21–23.

2. Peter Hawthorne, "Soweto Memories Nag South Africa," *Washington Star,* June 17, 1981.

3. "South Africa Alters Black Pass System," *The New York Times,* November 4, 1977; Richard R. Leger, "Defiant Afrikaners: South Africans Say Pressure Stiffens Their Resolve," *Wall Street Journal,* November 14, 1977.

4. Associated Press, "626 Blacks Seized in South Africa Raid," *The New York Times,* November 11, 1977.

5. "Riot Hurts 8 Near Capetown, *Baltimore Sun,* November 16, 1977.

6. "Black Unrest Simmers in Port Elizabeth," *Christian Science Monitor,* April 24, 1978.

7. "Over 5,000 Blacks Jailed in South Africa," *Baltimore Sun,* June 21, 1978.

8. "South Africa's Executions Demonstrate Its Justice System's Harshness," *Baltimore Sun,* August 6, 1978.

9. Ibid.

10. "Catholic Group in South Africa Says Police Holds Leaders," *Washington Post,* June 26, 1978; and Caryle Murphy, "Controversial Detentions Go on in South Africa, Despite Ban," *Washington Post,* September 1, 1978.

11. Caryle Murphy, "South Africa Tries 18 for Terrorism," *Washington Post,* July 2, 1978; "17 South Africans in Terrorist Case," *Baltimore Sun,* June 22, 1979.

12. John F. Burns, "South Africa Ends Soweto Riot Trials," *The New York Times,* May 4, 1979.

13. Caryle Murphy, "Black Becomes Hero on Pretoria Death Row," *Washington Post,* February 11, 1979; Gary Thatcher, "South Africa Executes Terrorist," *Christian Science Monitor,* April 9, 1979.

14. Associated Press, "Soweto Searched for Killer of Policeman," *Baltimore Sun,* May 5, 1979.

15. John F. Burns, "Doomed Black Poses South African Issue," *The New York Times,* November 19, 1979.

16. "New Attempt Made to Free Black Leader," *Baltimore Sun,* January 30, 1980; "Several Arrests Reported in Raid at Pretoria Bank," *The New York Times,* February 1, 1980.

17. Gary Thatcher, "South African Guerrilla Raids Keep Pot Boiling," *Christian Science Monitor,* April 8, 1980; Thatcher, "South Africa Cracks Down on Growing School Boycott," *Christian Science Monitor,* April 25, 1980.

18. Gary Thatcher, "Stay away Spreads in South Africa," *Christian Science Monitor,* May 1, 1980; "South Africa Protest Is Forcibly Dispersed." *Baltimore Sun,* April 30, 1980.

19. Robert I. Rotberg, "The End of the Boycott," *Christian Science Monitor,* May 20, 1980.

20. John F. Burns, "South African Police Kills Two Minority Demonstrators," *The New York Times*, May 29, 1980; "South African Students to End Boycott," *Washington Post*, June 6, 1980.

21. "Four Years since Soweto," *Christian Science Monitor*, June 16, 1980; Gary Thatcher, "South African Riots Gain in Political Impact," *Christian Science Monitor*, June 20, 1980; Humphrey Tyler, "South African Riots Reflect Tragic Alienation," *Christian Science Monitor*, June 19, 1980.

22. Gary Thatcher, "South Africa: More Unrest as Peaceful Black Dissent Cut Off," *Christian Science Monitor*, July 17, 1980; "South African Race Riots Reflect Tragic Alienation," *Baltimore Sun*, June 19, 1980.

23. Quentin Peel, "South African Guerrillas Strike at Nation's Oil Lifeline," *Christian Science Monitor*, June 3, 1980.

24. Gary Thatcher, "South Africa Cracks Whip on Black Dissent," *Christian Science Monitor*, July 16, 1980.

25. "Unrest Flares in South Africa," *Washington Post*, July 28, 1980.

26. Joseph Foisie, "3,500 Black Workers Strike in South Africa," *Los Angeles Times*, July 29, 1980.

27. "Riot Police Move in after Deaths at Cape," *Baltimore Sun*, August 14, 1980; United Press International, "Capetown Youth Killed by Police," *Washington Post*, August 15, 1980.

28. "Black Schools Shut in Two South African Districts," *Baltimore Sun*, September 10, 1980.

29. Caryle Murphy, "Black Youths, South Africa, in Test of Wills," *Washington Post*, September 27, 1980.

30. "Police Use Tear Gas, Dogs to Break Up Protests in Soweto," *Washington Post*, October 16, 1980; Gary Thatcher, "South Africa Bomb Blasts Reflect Black Discontent in Soweto," *Christian Science Monitor*, October 16, 1980; "More Political Unrest in South Africa—4 Die," *Washington Post*, November 7, 1980.

31. Humphrey Tyler, "South African Court and Police Crack Down on Black Newspapers," *Christian Science Monitor*, December 30, 1980; Antero Pietila, "South African Press Assails Harsh Ban on Two Blacks," *Baltimore Sun*, December 31, 1980.

32. June Kronholz, "Black Labor Workers in South Africa," *Wall Street Journal*, April 14, 1981; Joseph Lelyveld, "It's One Step Forward and Two Steps Back for South Africa's Black Unions," *The New York Times*, April 12, 1981; Antero Pietila, "South African Unions: An Anti-Apartheid Weapon," *Baltimore Sun*, May 24, 1981.

33. "South African Police Fire on Students Attacking Station," *Washington Post*, June 2, 1981.

34. "Police Break up a Soweto Church Meeting," *The New York Times*, June 17, 1981.

35. Associated Press, "South Africa Imposes New Crackdown on Dis-

sidents," *Washington Star,* July 1, 1981; Antero Pietila, "South Africa Silences Student Leader," *Baltimore Sun,* July 1, 1981.

36. Humphrey Tyler, "South African Saboteurs Go for Strategic Targets," *Christian Science Monitor,* July 23, 1981.

37. Jay Ross, "Black Nationalist from South Africa Slain in Zimbabwe," *Washington Post,* August 2, 1981.

38. "South Africa Arrests 2,000 Squatters in Dawn Raid," *The New York Times,* August 20, 1981; "South Africa Sentences 3 to Death for Treason," *Baltimore Sun,* August 20, 1981.

39. Joseph Lelyveld, "South Africa Recasting Its Security Laws," *The New York Times,* May 15, 1982.

40. Ibid.

41. Caryle Murphy, "Africa Death Sentence Commutations Sought," *Washington Post,* May 21, 1982.

42. "South African Rebels Blast Fuel Site, Tracks," *Baltimore Sun,* June 4, 1982.

43. Joseph Lelyveld, "Bomb Kills One in Capetown in Wake of Sabotage," *The New York Times,* June 5, 1982.

44. Antero Pietila, "South African Police Use Bus on Rock Throwers in Soweto," *Baltimore Sun,* June 17, 1982; "South African Police Seize 250 at Memorial Service in Soweto," *Baltimore Sun,* June 14, 1982.

45. "8 Black Miners Killed in Violence at South African Gold Mines," *Washington Post,* July 4, 1982.

46. Colin McKinnon, "White South African Miners Set Vote on Strike, Blacks Continue Riots," *Washington Post,* July 6, 1982; United Press International, "Black Miners Sent to the Homelands," *The New York Times,* July 8, 1982.

47. Edgar S. Efrat, "Terrorism in South Africa," In *International Terrorism,* Yonah Alexander, ed. (New York: AMS Press, 1976).

48. Department of Foreign Affairs and Information, *South Africa 1980–81: Official Yearbook of the Republic of South Africa* (Johannesburg: Chris van Rensburg Publications, 1981), p. 184.

49. Nicholas Ashford, "Feelings of Hostility Face Leader of Latest Independent Homeland," *London Times,* December 6, 1977.

50. "In Apartheid's Grip: Rigid Rules Govern Movement of Blacks," *Wall Street Journal,* November 6, 1978.

51. John F. Burns, "Transkei Breaks Diplomatic Ties, It's Only One, with South Africa," *The New York Times,* April 11, 1978.

52. Newell M. Stultz, "Why Is Transkei Still Portrayed as a Stooge?" *The New York Times,* July 9, 1979.

53. Caryle Murphy, "Transkei, Apartheid's Product, Struggles to Break Isolation," *Washington Post,* August 1978; "Self-Governing Transkei Restores Tie with Parent Country, South Africa," *Washington Post,* February 8, 1981.

54. Gary Thatcher, "South Africa Launches Independent Black State

of Venda," *Christian Science Monitor,* September 11, 1979; "Venda Marks Freedom of South Africa Homeland," *Baltimore Sun,* September 16, 1979.

55. Robert I. Rotberg, "South Africa's Latest Homeland: A New Approach," *Christian Science Monitor,* February 12, 1980.

56. Charles Alexander with Marsh Clark, "Voting for Puppethood," *Time,* December 29, 1980.

57. John Kane Berman, "South Africa Will Not Include Key Town in New Independent Homeland," *Washington Post,* April 18, 1981.

58. Antero Pietila, "The Homelands: Apartheid's New Face," *Baltimore Sun,* May 18, 1981.

59. Ibid.

60. Gary Thatcher, "South Africa Admits Black Homelands Concept Not Feasible," *Christian Science Monitor,* September 4, 1980.

61. Joseph Lelyveld, "Black Homelands, Poverty on the Veld," *The New York Times,* May 17, 1981.

62. Caryle Murphy, "Police Arrest 205 Blacks in South African Union," *Washington Post,* September 9, 1981.

63. Geoffrey Godsell, "South Africa's Black Nationalists Step up Guerrilla Warfare," *Christian Science Monitor,* September 29, 1981.

64. Antero Pietila, "Transkei Plans to Draft an Army out of Fear of Black Nationalism," *Baltimore Sun,* October 6, 1981.

65. Joseph Lelyveld, "South Africa Would Yield Homeland to Neighbor," *The New York Times,* March 3, 1982.

66. Ibid.

67. Joseph Lelyveld, "South Africa Tells Tribe of Transfer," *The New York Times,* June 18, 1982.

68. Ibid.

69. Jack Foisie, "Court Voids South African Plan to Transfer Zulu Tribal Lands to Swazi, *Los Angeles Times,* October 1, 1982.

70. "South Africa Concedes Defeat in Move to Cede Area to Swaziland," *Washington Post,* November 26, 1982.

4 Namibia

This chapter discusses the importance of Namibia, South Africa's closest neighbor and longtime ward. The type of political settlement that eventually takes hold in Namibia will affect the political future of South Africa in the most profound manner. An efficaciously hostile black government on the border of South Africa could provide assistance to both internal and external opponents to the Pretoria government. A severe blow to the South African economy could be dealt if a determined effort were made to prevent the continuation of existing ownership patterns within Namibia. Finally, the Namibia situation is important as a clue to the determination South Africa would show in holding on to power in its own nation. For this last reason, the usual pattern of emphasizing the last five years of events is not used in this chapter. Instead, as a lesson pointing to South African determination when it believes its vital interests are being threatened, a full exposure of the South African involvement in Namibia is given.

Origins of the Namibian Dispute

Geographical and Early History

Namibia is a huge (318,261 square miles), for the most part unpopulated, region located to the northwest of South Africa along the Atlantic seaboard in the southwest corner of the continent. If the 434-square-mile area of the deep-water port at Walvis Bay on the coast is included, Namibia would be nearly four times the size of the United Kingdom and seven to eight times the size of Liberia. Namibia is roughly the same size as Nigeria, but its population is less than 1.0 percent that of its northern neighbor. Namibia consumes nearly 3 percent of the total land area on the African continent, but its total population is certainly less than 0.2 percent of the continent's population.[1] Namibia is divided into three regions: the Namib, the Central Plateau, and the Kalahari Desert. In recent times the mineral wealth of Namibia has drawn great attention to the area, so its importance to Africa not only is strategic and symbolic but also promises wealth beyond what already has been attained. The stakes in Namibia are high since supplies of diamonds, uranium, cadmium, silver, arsenic, copper, lead and germanium are plentiful.[2]

South-West Africa was first visited by Portuguese navigators such as Diogo Cao (1484), Bartholomew Dias (1486), and Gasper Vegas (1534). They did not stay and Namibia remained untouched by white hands until after the settlement of the Cape of Good Hope in 1652. Eighteen years later, in 1670, the Cape colony dispatched the *Grundel* to explore the southwest coast. Another ship followed in 1677. Because of the inhospitable Namib desert, little exploration was done, and hope for using the land in a profitable manner was not held highly.

During the eighteenth century and start of the nineteenth century, exploration of Namibia continued on a sporadic basis. By the end of that century, British and French ships cruising the South Atlantic often stopped and claimed the land they touched as territory for their respective sovereign.

In the nineteenth century, missionaries moved into the Namibia area to Christianize the few native inhabitants there. The most notable group involved in this activity was the London Mission Society. Not until the second half of the nineteenth century was the northern part of Namibia explored. Soon the United Kingdom, France, and the Cape government became interested in the fishing, fish oil, and guano deposits that were found off the Namibian coastline.

Between 1861 and 1866, the government of the Cape of Good Hope took possession of islands off the Namibian coast, and in 1878, Commander R.C. Dyer claimed the area surrounding Walvis Bay in the name of the queen of England.[3]

Neither the United Kingdom nor the Cape colony became involved in the internal wars raging among the nine distinguishable tribes within Namibia. As a result, it was easy for the Germans to arrive almost unannounced in 1883 and to acquire an area of approximately 215 square miles around Angra Pequena from the local Nama chief. Using this as a foothold, Bismarck, in 1884, notified the Cape government that the area had been placed formally under German protection. This was the beginning of the territory of German South-West Africa. In the ensuing year Germany extended its possessory claims to include the territory that today is in conflict between South Africa and the rest of the world. Final settlement of the territory held as German South-West Africa was reached with Portugal, who claimed Angola in 1886, and with the United Kingdom, who claimed Bechuanaland in 1890. The Walvis Bay area was excluded since it had been incorporated into the Cape colony in 1884.[4]

The German Occupation

Today's world has little to thank the Germans for their occupation, since almost a hundred years after the date of their action a solution for Namibia has not yet been reached and the trouble the dispute has caused still could provoke a continent-, or even a world-wide, war. Even by the harsh standards of colonial activity in the late nineteenth century and early twentieth century, German activity in Namibia was a disgrace of the worst order.[5]

Between 1904 and 1907, a cruel war raged between the German colonial rulers and two rebelling Namibian tribes, the Hereros and the Namas. The resulting slaughter of African natives can be termed as nothing but a holocaust. The war began in January 1904 under the leadership of Samuel Maharero. His forces launched a surprise attack on German farms and outposts. Over one hundred Germans were killed. The grievances involved were the traditional colonial ones of exploitation of the natives, seizure of their land, and carnal abuse of their women.[6]

The Hereros were slaughtered with great savagery. The lucky ones, including Samuel Maharero, escaped the country, most going to Bechuanaland. It is estimated that when an armistice was declared in 1905, only 16,000 Hereros remained of what had been a population of 60,000 to 80,000. The Namas continued the war that they had begun in 1904 until 1907. They lost half their population in the fighting. Prisoner-of-war camps for the African natives were so horrible that more than 40 percent of those interned died.[7]

The German genocide in Namibia during the Herero-Nama Wars of 1904–1907 is a sad introduction to a saga of struggle and bloodshed, continuing until the present day. The order to wipe out as many Hereros as possible was given by General von Trotha:

> I, the great general of the German soldiers send the message to Herero people. Hereros are no longer German subjects. They have murdered and robbed and have cut off the ears and noses and other parts of the body of wounded soldiers and now, out of cowardice, they refuse to fight. The Herero people must depart from the country. If they do not, I shall force them to it with large cannons. Within the German boundaries, every Herero whether found armed or unarmed, with or without cattle, will be shot. I cannot accept any more women and children. I shall drive them back to their people. Otherwise, I shall order shots to be fired at them. These are my words to the Herero people.[8]

The South African Takeover

World War I spelled the sudden end to German occupation of Namibia. On January 14, 1915, South African troops, motivated in part by the discovery of copper and diamond deposits, invaded the German colony. On July 9, 1915, the German colony of South-West Africa surrendered to the invading forces. The germs of the current dispute had been planted. At the end of the war, South-West Africa was only one of numerous territories whose status had to be determined. On a worldwide level, South African leader and Lloyd George war cabinet member General Jan Smuts was a strong advocate of the territorial-mandate system. He did, however, make an exception in his own case and wished, first of all, to prevent South West Africa from returning to British hands and, second, to have the territory annexed to that of his own country. He was unsuccessful in convincing the nations participating in the League of Nations to his way of thinking. Smuts realized that his attempts to have the conquered territories in Namibia placed on a different footing than those in the rest of the world were doomed to failure. With surprising good grace, he mentioned this point in a letter written during the peace conference:

> Yesterday we discussed the dominion claims to the German colony. I hope I made a good case to southwest Africa but I don't know. My argument was principally that it was a desert, a part of the Kalahari, no good to anyone, least of all to so magnificent a body as the League of Nations! It was like the poor sinning girl's plea that her baby was only a little one! Not that I consider our claim to southwest Africa either sinful or wrong.[9]

Wrong or not, Smuts failed and the League of Nations placed Namibia in the same mandatory-territory situation that it did so many other countries. This action occurred on May 7, 1919, when South Africa was designated the mandatory power in Namibia and accepted the responsibility of submitting an annual report to the League of Nations on the territory committed to its charge.

At least from the advantageous position of hindsight, Article 6 of the Mandate contained in Article 22, paragraph 8, of the Covenant of the League of Nations, the mandates system, was unclear and certainly would lead to future difficulties. Its wording is as follows:

> There are territories such as southwest Africa, and certain of the South Pacific Islands, which, owing to the sparseness of their position or their small size, or their remoteness from the centers of civilization or their geographical contiguity to the territories of the Mandatory and other circumstances can be best administered under the laws of the Mandatory as integral portions of its territory subject to the safeguard above mentioned in the interest of the indigenous population.[10]

The specific mandate for Namibia in Article 1 and the first section of Article 2 continued the slightly unclear wording concerning the exact status of the newly mandated territory. Article 1 stated, "The territory over which a mandate is conferred upon his Britanic majesty for and on behalf of the government of the Union of South Africa (hereinafter called the Mandatory) comprises the territories which formerly constituted the German protectorate of southwest Africa." The first section of Article 2 stated, "The Mandatory shall have full power of administration and legislation over the territory, subject to the present mandate as an integral portion of the Union of South Africa and may apply the laws of the Union of South Africa to the territory, subject to such local modifications as circumstances may require."[11]

South Africa as Mandatory Power

From 1920 on, South Africa administered the neighboring territory of Namibia under the authority of the unclear documents cited here. In day-to-day dealings the question of status did not arise. Lawyers did squabble over the wording of the mandate, but leaders of nations restricted themselves to the more-immediate political and economic questions of the day.

As is not surprising, given the parallel history in South Africa, the Pretoria government from the outset preferred the welfare of the white settlers in Namibia over those of the native tribes. Occasional violent incidents occurred, like the Bondelzwart insurrection of 1922, when the Pretoria government at the direction of Jan Smuts bombed rebels in the Bondelzwarts tribe; a second uprising in 1925 by the Rehoboth Basters was treated in a gentler manner, perhaps because of the criticism precipitated by the Bondelzwart incident.[12] Some sentiment could be found in South Africa during the 1930s to annex the Namibian territory, but these attempts were never pursued with great seriousness.

After World War II the question of the status of South-West Africa again came to the forefront. The United Nations (UN) was established, and the League of Nations, in a separate action, sputtered slowly toward its death. The question of mandated territories like Namibia again became of interest as once more the victorious nations of the world drew together to split up territories held by the losers. The UN presumed that mandatory territories from World War I would be placed under their trusteeship system. Since the UN was not the legal successor of the League of Nations, the Republic of South Africa refused to cooperate in this effort. The UN charter became active on October 24, 1945, and in April 1946, the League of Nations dissolved voluntarily.[13]

During 1946, in a most perfunctory manner, the South African government consulted the tribes of Namibia and concluded that they wished to be incorporated into the Republic of South Africa. Challenges to the legitimacy of the questioning procedure were raised immediately and loudly. South Africa proceeded to inform the UN that it wished to incorporate Namibia into its own territory and thereby to end the League of Nations mandate.

By a vote of thirty-seven to nothing on December 14, 1946, the UN General Assembly rejected South Africa's request and recommended that Namibia be placed under the trusteeship of the new international organization.[14] South Africa was as quick to reject this decision as the UN had been to spurn their original request. The conflict deepened significantly in 1948 when the National party was successful in the South African national elections and moved into power. The former Smuts government had made reports to the UN partially as a matter of courtesy and partially, no doubt, to keep an avenue of communications open with the UN, to the Trusteeship Committee of the UN. The National party government of Dr. D.R. Malan informed the UN on July 11, 1949, that no further reports would be coming. As the government communiqué stated, "The Union government can no longer see that any real benefit is to be derived from the submission of special reports on southwest Africa to the United Nations, and have regretfully come to the conclusion that, in the interest of efficient administration, no further reports should be forwarded."[15] Soon thereafter, South Africa enacted legislation to bind Namibia in a close manner without, at the same time, ending the territorial administration that had endured since World War I.[16] As Prime Minister Malan stated:

> [We shall] place southwest Africa in a position where it will be invulnerable against that type of propaganda and incitement. Knit southwest Africa and the Union in such a manner, knit them together constitutionally in such a way that the two areas will be in future inseparably bound together. In order to achieve this, let us make use of the unquestionable right which South Africa possesses, the right which South Africa also possessed when the mandate was still in existence and the principle in regard to the mandate had not yet disappeared, and bring about a position of closer affiliation of the two territories, the Union and southwest Africa even if, at least, for the present, we do not go as far as the ultimate limit of incorporating southwest Africa into the Union. Even if we do not go to that limit of incorporating southwest Africa into our country, we can still knit southwest Africa and the Union so closely together constitutionally that they can never again be separated.[17]

In December 1949, the General Assembly officially regretted the refusal of the South African government to submit reports.[18]

The Legal Phase

The Dispute with the UN

As the 1950s began, the combat between the UN and the Republic of South Africa reached a position of intractability and open conflict. In December

1949, the UN General Assembly decided to ask for an advisory opinion from the International Court of Justice. The vote to do so was forty to seven, with four abstentions.[19] In its opinion handed down during July 1950, the International Court of Justice found unanimously that South-West Africa is a territory under the international mandate assumed by the Union of South Africa on December 17, 1920.[20] From there on, opinions on specific questions were divided and rules hard to articulate. All did agree that the UN trusteeship system could be used to fulfill the mandate responsibility as to Namibia. Nonetheless, the majority felt that South Africa was not obliged, if it did not wish to do so, to place its mandated territory, Namibia, under the control of the recently established UN trusteeship system. The court did continue to feel that South Africa did not have the right of its own to modify the international status of the territory, such as by annexing it to the Republic of South Africa.[21]

Without question, the International Court of Justice found much of value in the position advocated by South Africa. Enough dissent did exist that both sides had ammunition to continue arguing their present positions. As could be expected, the UN stressed that the opinion was advisory, and South Africa stressed that the court's advisory opinions normally were given the weight of law by the nations who had submitted to its jurisdiction. The UN continued to oppose the position of South Africa and adopted a resolution and established an ad hoc committee to attempt to carry out this transfer of supervisory powers.[22]

To the surprise of almost no one, the ad hoc committee on Namibia was unable to work harmoniously with the South African government. The decision to hear from dissident advocates seeking change annoyed the Pretoria government. In 1953, the ad hoc committee was made permanent.[23] This committee received no more cooperation from South Africa than had the ad hoc committee. Because Pretoria refused to submit reports to the committee, it was obliged to make investigations on its own. In 1955, the International Court of Justice was asked again by the UN for an opinion on the amount of supervision proper under the UN charter. South Africa refused to participate in the case or to accept the ruling of the International Court of Justice. South Africa stated that this decision was based on its unhappiness with the 1950 opinion of the International Court of Justice—although everyone else had considered the ruling to be favorable to South Africa. The UN again invoked the advisory but persuasive status of the International Court of Justice during 1965 and requested another hearing on the matter.

Seeing that South Africa would not bend to the rule of the UN on the Namibian question, in 1957 a more-diplomatic approach was taken by the international body housed in New York. A Good Offices Committee was established to try to reach an agreement that would continue to accord to the territory of Namibia an international status, but one more acceptable to most members of the UN. The chairman of the committee was Sir Charles Arden-Clarke.[24] In its final report in 1958, the Good Offices Committee attempted to reach a compromise. It suggested that "the Good Offices Committee is of the opinion that some form of partition under which a part of the territory would be placed under a trustee agreement with the United Nations and the remainder would be annexed to the Union, might provide a basis for an agreement, although it is aware that in lending support to such an idea it may be laying itself open to the charge of having exceeded its term of reference."[25]

Whether the Good Offices Committee was open to this charge or not, the General Assembly swiftly rejected this compromise solution.[26] The subsequent discussion at the UN led to a decision ordering the committee to return to South Africa and again to seek the handover on terms acceptable to the UN. The South African delegate at New York walked out when this proposition carried. The Good Offices Committee failed in further attempts during 1958 and 1959 to bring the two sides closer together.

While the Good Offices Committee was at work, the UN Committee on Namibia continued to study the situation and file reports highly critical of South Africa's administration of the territory. In its 1958 report it stated, "The Committee therefore reaffirms its conclusion that existing conditions in the Territory and the trend of the administration represents a situation not in accord with the Mandates System, the Charter of the United Nations, the Universal Declaration of Human Rights, the advisory opinions of the International Court of Justice and the resolutions of the General Assembly."[27]

Ethiopia and Liberia Bring Suit

As the 1960s began, the confrontations between the UN and South Africa became more acrimonious. Conciliation probably never had a chance of succeeding, given the geographic location of South-West Africa, on the very borders of South Africa, especially the depth of its southern and eastern penetration toward the tip of the continent. In June 1960, at the Second Conference of Independent African States held in Addis Ababa, Ethiopia and Liberia, two of Africa's oldest nations and former members of the League of Nations, announced they would institute legal challenge to South Africa's mandate control of Namibia. The UN General Assembly approved this action on the part of two of its members.[28] South Africa defended itself before the International Court of Justice but raised objections to Ethiopia's and Liberia's standing as plaintiffs. It took until the end of 1962, and then by the closest of votes, eight to seven, for the International Court of Justice to decide it possessed jurisdiction to adjudicate the merits of the dispute.[29]

South Africa, by continuing to participate in the case, did in effect submit to the jurisdiction of the International Court of Justice.

By the time the case reached the evidence-taking portion, it was 1965, five years after Liberia and Ethiopia announced their intention to begin the process. In the interim, five new judges were sitting on the International Court of Justice, and composition of the court was reflecting the number of new nations being recognized and bringing a Third World orientation to the bench. On July 18, 1966, the court handed down its decision that, in effect, was not a decision at all. Instead, it returned to the matter everyone thought it had decided in 1962—whether or not the court had standing to hear the dispute, which is another way of asking whether or not Liberia and Ethiopia were proper plaintiffs in the case. The International Court of Justice, by the president casting a vote because the votes otherwise were equally divided, decided to reject the claims of the Empire of Ethiopia and the Republic of Liberia, finding they did not have the proper standing to bring suit. The seven minority judges filed dissenting opinions. The complete lack of accord among the judges gave scholars and politicians ample grounds on which to continue their arguments concerning South Africa's true position as mandatory for the territory of Namibia.[30].

Most legal commentators were agreed that the 1962 decision and the 1966 decision were decided under two very different concepts of legal rights under international law.[31] The 1962 majority was operating under the scope of sociological jurisprudence. Under this theory, international law is subservient to the will of the international community. In the South-West Africa/Namibia case, this theory meant that the desire of South Africa to continue the mandate was less important than the evolving desire of the world community, speaking through the UN, to end the mandate and to establish an independent nation (after an interim period) in the area under dispute.

In the 1966 decision not to hear the case, the majority operated under a different legal theory of international law: legal positivism. In such a view, the will of the paramount sovereign nation involved was supreme. Such a nation did not have to justify its basic system of government before an international organization or tribunal. All that was necessary was to ascertain whether or not the original mandating act was legal. Since no one questioned that this was the case, then the 1966 majority felt it could not hear the case, no matter how deeply it abhorred apartheid as a system of governance.

The UN Terminates the Mandate

As could be expected, the nations composing the UN were furious at the decision of the International Court of Justice. South Africa was jubilant and gave the impression that the International Court of Justice had found the charges launched by Ethiopia and Liberia to be without merit. In truth, the case was that the charges were never breached because the court did not find the plaintiffs had proper standing to bring the suit. Spurred on by the unpopular decision, the General Assembly moved to revoke South Africa's mandate over Namibia. On October 27, 1966, by a vote of 114 to 2, with 3 abstentions, the mandate was terminated. The two nations voting against termination were South Africa and Portugal. The three abstainers were France, Malawi, and the United Kingdom. The United States voted for the resolution.[32] By this General Assembly action, the move away from legal redress to the Namibia problem toward political redress had started in earnest. Many international lawyers questioned whether or not the UN had the authority to terminate the mandate. Most of their concerns were over-ridden in the cry of outrage at the decision handed down by the International Court of Justice. Since South Africa steadfastly had denied the UN authority over the mandated territory, it rejected with ease the authority of the UN to remove the mandate from South Africa.

Now that, at least in the eyes of the UN, South Africa no longer held a mandate to administer Namibia, bureaucratic steps were taken to transfer control on an international level to the UN, and a fourteen-member ad hoc committee for Namibia was established to recommend practical means by which the disputed territory could be administered. This group decided that the date for independence should be June 1968. Since South Africa had no intention of removing its troops or administrators from Namibia, much of this bureaucratic scheming in New York seemed most futile. On May 19, 1967, the General Assembly adopted, by eighty-five votes to two, with thirty abstentions, a resolution establishing an eleven-member UN Council for Namibia. This council was charged with administering the territory until independence.[33] The Security Council for the first time became involved directly in the Namibia situation. It was provoked not only by the International Court of Justice ruling but also by the crackdown against political dissidents and general tightening of the reins of power exhibited by South Africa in the disputed territory. On March 20, 1969, the Security Council ratified the action that had been taken by the General Assembly in declaring South Africa's mandate in Namibia as ended. The resolution stated that the "continued presence of South Africa in Namibia is illegal and contrary to the principles of the Charter and the previous decision of the United Nations and is detrimental to the interests of the population of the territory and those of the international community. The Security Council also invites all states to exert their influence in order to obtain compliance by the government of South Africa with the provisions of the present resolution."[34] Calls for South Africa to withdraw from Namibia were ignored in Pretoria. From then on, the Security Council and South Africa exchanged statements which neither side gave an inch. The Security Council moved to bring the case once again before the International Court of Justice.

The 1971 Court of Justice had undergone still more changes in its membership. Only two of the 1966 majority remained. The South African government nonetheless participated one more time. A new element was that South Africa suggested a plebiscite be held in Namibia in order to determine whether the local inhabitants wished to be governed by South Africa or the UN.

On June 21, 1971, the International Court of Justice ruled that South Africa's mandate for Namibia had been terminated lawfully.[35] Strong dissent to the eleven-to-four majority opinion was filed by British Sir Gerald Fitzmaurice.[36] As could be expected, the Security Council accepted the opinion and moved to implement it, and South Africa again rejected the opinion.

It was clear that South Africa would not surrender Namibia. The UN would be forced to adopt and coordinate actions to coerce South Africa to hand over the territory to an independent government. More than a dozen years later this surrender of sovereignty has still not occurred.

A Statement of Principle

After 1971, the dispute over Namibia shifted to a political contest, both within the mandated territory and without. During the 1960s, political opposition among blacks within Namibia started to surface. Using tactics identical to those employed in South Africa, the Pretoria government and its extension at Windhoek moved to suppress the expressions of freedom being demonstrated. The most notable action in this regard was the trial of SWAPO and the South-West Africa National Union (SWANU) members in 1967. One of the SWAPO leaders, Herman Toivo ja Toivo, on being convicted and sentenced to twenty years in prison, made an eloquent speech. Large portions of this address are quoted in order to highlight the inequities felt by black people in Namibia. This speech easily could have been made for South Africa. It is included here to remind us that Namibia is more than merely a possession to be fought over by the nations of the world. It is a group of people joined together in a particular territory and being controlled by the minority.

> We find ourselves here in a foreign country, convicted under laws made by people whom we have always considered as foreigners. We find ourselves tried by a judge who is not our countryman and who has not shared our background.

> When this case started, counsel tried to show that this court had no jurisdiction to try us. What they had to say was of a technical and legal nature.

The reasons may mean little to some of us, but it is the deep feeling of all of us that we should not be tried here in Pretoria.

You, my lord, decided that you had the right to try us because your Parliament gave you that right. That ruling has not and could not have changed our feelings. We are Namibians and not South Africans. We do not now, and will not in the future, recognize your right to govern us, to make laws for us in which we have no say, to treat our country as if it were your property and use us as if you were our masters. We have always regarded South Africa as an intruder in our country. This is how we have always felt and this is how we feel now and it is on this basis that we have faced this trial.

I speak of we because I am trying to speak not only for myself, but for others as well and especially of those of my fellow accused who have not had the benefit of any education. I think also that when I say "we," the overwhelming majority of nonwhite people in southwest Africa would like to be included.

We are far away from our homes. Not a single member of our families have come to visit us, never mind be present at our trial. The Pretoria goal, the police headquarters at Compol where we were interrogated and where statements were extracted from us and this court is all we have seen of Pretoria. We have been cut off from our people and the world. We all wondered whether the headmen would have repeated some of their lies if our people had been present in court to hear them.

The South African government has again shown its strength by detaining us for as long as it pleased; keeping some of us in solitary confinement for three hundred to four hundred days, and bringing us to its capital to try us. It has shown its strength by passing an act especially for us and having it made retrospective. It has even chosen an ugly name to call us by—one's own are called patriots, or at least rebels. Your opponents are called terrorists.

A court can only do justice in political cases, if it understands the position of those that it has in front of it. The state has not only wanted to convict us, but also to justify the policy of the South African government. We will not even try to present the other side of the picture, because we know that a court that has not suffered in the same way as we have cannot understand us. This is perhaps why it is said that one should be tried by one's equals. We have felt from the very time of our arrest that we were not being tried by our equals but by our masters. And those who have brought us to trial very often do not even do us the courtesy of calling us by our surnames.

Had we been tried by our equals, it would not have been necessary to have any discussion about our grievances. They would have been known to those set to judge us.

It suits the government of South Africa to say that it is ruling southwest Africa with the consent of its people. This is not true. Our organization, SWAPO, is the largest political organization in southwest Africa. We considered ourselves a political party. We know that whites do not think of blacks as politicians, only as agitators. Many of our people, through no fault of their own, have had no education at all. This does not mean that they do not know what they want. A man does not have to be formally educated to know that he wants to live with his family, where he wants to live and not where an official chooses to tell him where to live: To move about freely and not require a pass, to earn a decent wage, to be free to work for the person of his choice for as long as he wants and finally, to be ruled by the people that he wants to be ruled by, and not those who rule him because they have more guns than he has. Our grievances are called "so-called" grievances. We do not believe that South Africa is in southwest Africa to provide facilities and work for nonwhites. It is there for its own selfish reasons. For the first forty years it did practically nothing to fulfill its "sacred trust." It only concerned itself with the welfare of whites.

Since 1962, because of the pressure from inside from the nonwhites, and especially my organization and because of the limelight placed on our country by the world, South Africa's been trying to do a bit more. It rushed the Bantustan report so that it would at least have something to say at the world's court.

Only one who is not white and has suffered the way we have, can say whether our grievances are real or "so-called." Those of us who have had some education, together with our uneducated brethren, have always struggled to get freedom. The idea of our freedom is not liked by South Africa. It has tried in this court to prove through the mouths of a couple of its paid chiefs and paid official, that SWAPO does not represent the people of southwest Africa. If the government of South Africa was sure that SWAPO did not represent the innermost feelings of the people in southwest Africa, it would not have taken the trouble to make it impossible for SWAPO to advocate its peaceful policy.

South African officials want to believe that SWAPO is an irresponsible organization and that it is an organization that resorts to the level of telling people not to get vaccinated. As much as white South Africans may want to believe this, this is not SWAPO. We sometimes feel that it is what the government would like SWAPO to be. It may be true that some member, or even members of SWAPO somewhere refuse to do this. The reason for such refusal is that some people in our part of the world have lost confidence in the governance of our country, and they are not prepared to accept even the good that they are trying to do.

Your government, my Lord, undertook a very special responsibility when it was awarded the Mandate over us after the first World War. It assumed a sacred trust to guide us towards independence and to prepare us to take our place among the nations of the world. We believe that South Africa has abused that trust because of its belief in racial supremacy (that white people have been chosen by God to rule the world) and apartheid. We believe that for fifty years South Africa has failed to promote the development of our people. Where are our trained men? The wealth of our country has been used to train your people for leadership, and the sacred duty of preparing indigenous people to take their place among the nations of the world has been ignored.

I know of no case in the last twenty years of a parent who did not want his child to go to school, if the facilities were available. But even if, as it was said, a small percentage of parents wanted their children to look after cattle, I am sure that South Africa was strong enough to impose its will on this, as it has done in so many other respects. To us, it has always seemed that our rulers wanted to keep us backward for their benefit.

1963 for us was to be the year of our freedom. From 1960 it looked as if South Africa could not oppose the world forever. The world is important to us. In the same way as all laughed in court when they heard that an old man tried to bring down a helicopter with a bow and arrow, we laughed when South Africa said that it would oppose the world. We knew that the world was divided, but as time went on it at least agreed that South Africa had no right to rule us.

I do not claim that it is easy for men of different races to live at peace with one another. I myself had no experience of this in my youth, and at first it surprised me that men of different races could live together in peace. But now I know it to be true, and to be something for which we must strive. The South African government creates hostility by separating people and emphasizing their differences. We believe that by living together, people will learn to lose their fear of each other. We also believe that this fear, which some of the whites have of Africans, is based on their desire to be superior and privileged and that when whites see themselves as part of southwest Africa, sharing with us all its hopes and troubles, then that fear will disappear. Separation is said to be a natural process, but why then is it imposed by force, and why then is it that whites have the superiority?

Headmen are used to oppress us. This is not the first time that foreigners have tried to rule indirectly—we know that only those who are prepared to do what their masters tell them become headmen. Most of those who had some feeling for their people and who wanted independence have been intimidated into accepting the policy from above. Their guns and sticks are used to make people say they support them.

I have come to know that our people cannot expect progress as a gift from anyone, be it the United Nations or South Africa. Progress is something we shall have to struggle and work for, and I believe that the only way in which we shall be able and fit to secure that progress is to learn from our own experience and mistakes.

Your Lordship emphasized in your judgments, the fact that our arms came from Communist countries, and also that words commonly used by Communists were to be found in our documents. But, my Lord, in the documents produced by the state there is another type of language. It appears even more often than the former. Many documents finish up with an appeal to the Almighty, to guide us in our struggle for freedom. It is the wish of the South African government that we should be discredited in the western world. That is why it calls our struggle a Communist plot. But this will not be believed by the world. The world knows that we are not interested in ideologies. We feel that the world as a whole has a special responsibility towards us. This is because the land of our fathers was handed over to South Africa by a world body. It is a divided world, but it is a matter of hope for us that it at least agrees about one thing—that we are entitled to freedom and justice.

Other mandated territories have received their freedom. The judgment of the world court was a bitter disappointment to us. We felt betrayed and we believe that South Africa would never fulfill its trust. Some felt that we would secure our freedom only by fighting for it. We knew that the power of South Africa is overwhelming. But we also knew that our case is a just one, and our situation intolerable—why should we not also receive our freedom?

We are sure that the world's efforts to help us in our plight will continue, whatever South Africans may call us. We do not expect that independence will end our troubles, but we do believe that our people are entitled, as are all people, to rule themselves. It is not really a question of whether South Africa treats us well or badly but that southwest Africa is our country and we wish to be our own masters.

There are some who will say that they are sympathetic with our aims but that they condemn violence. I would answer that I am not by nature a man of violence and I believe that violence is a sin against God and my fellow men. SWAPO itself was a nonviolent organization, but the South African government is not truly interested in whether opposition is violent or nonviolent. It does not wish to hear any opposition to apartheid. Since 1963 SWAPO meetings have been banned. It is true that it is the tribal authorities who have done so, but they have worked for the South African government which has never lifted a finger in favor of political freedom. We have found ourselves voteless in our own country and deprived of the right to meet and state our own political opinion.

Is it surprising that in such times my countrymen have taken up arms? Violence is truly fearsome, but who would not defend his property and himself against a robber, and we believe that South Africa has robbed us of our country.

I have spent my life working in SWAPO, which is an ordinary political party like any other. Suddenly, we in SWAPO found that a war situation had arisen, and that our colleagues and South Africa were facing each other on the field of battle. Although I had not been responsible for organizing my people militarily and although I believed we were unwise to fight the might of South Africa while we were so weak, I could not refuse to help them when the time came.

My Lord, you found it necessary to brand me a coward. During the second World War when it became evident that both my country and your country were threatened by the dark clouds of Nazism, I risked my life to defend both of them, wearing a uniform with orange bands on it.

But some of your countrymen, when called to battle to defend civilization, resorted to sabotage against their own fatherland. I volunteered to face German bullets and as a guard of military installations both in southwest Africa and the Republic, was prepared to be the victim of their sabotage. Today they are our masters and are considered the heros and I am called the coward.

When I consider my country I am proud that my countrymen have taken up arms for their people and I believe that anyone who calls himself a man would not despise them.

In 1964 the ANC and PAC in South Africa were suppressed. This convinced me that we were too weak to face South Africa's force by waging battle. When some of my country's soldiers came back, I foresaw the trouble there would be for SWAPO, my people and me personally. I tried to do what I could to prevent from going into the bush. In my attempts, I became unpopular with some of my people but this, too, I was prepared to endure. Decisions of this type are not easy to make. My loyalty is to my country. My organization could not work properly—it could not even hold meetings. I had no answer to the question, Where has your nonviolence got us? Whilst the world court judgment was pending, I at least had that to fall back on. When we failed, after years of waiting, I had no answer to give to my people.

Even though I did not agree that people should go into the bush. I could not refuse to help them when I knew that they were hungry. I even passed on the request for dynamite. It was not an easy decision. Another man might have been able to say, "I will have nothing to do with that sort of thing." I was not, and I could not remain a spectator in the struggle of my people for their freedom.

I am a loyal Namibian, and I could not betray my people to their enemies. I admit that I decided to assist those who had taken up arms. I know that the struggle will be long and bitter. I also know that my people will wage that struggle, whatever the cost.

Only when we are granted our independence will the struggle stop. Only when our human dignity is restored to us as equals of the whites will there be peace between us.

We believe that South Africa has a choice—either to live at peace with us or to subdue us by force. If you choose to crush us and impose your will on us, then you do not only betray your trust, but you will live in security for only so long as your power is greater than ours. No South African will live at peace in southwest Africa, for each will know that its security is based on force, and that without force he will face rejection by the people of southwest Africa.

My co-accused and I have suffered. We are not looking forward to our imprisonment. We believe, however, that human suffering has its effect even on those who impose it. We hope that what has happened will persuade the whites of South Africa that we and the world may be right and they may be wrong. Only when white South Africans realize this and act on it, will it be possible for us to stop our struggle for freedom and justice in the land of our birth.[37]

The Political Struggle

Continuing UN Pressure

After the 1971 International Court of Justice decision, peacemaking attempts in Namibia were sporadic and, for the most part, unsuccessful. UN

Secretary General Kurt Waldheim did attempt to keep the doors for discussion open. His representatives met with Namibian political forces of all skin colors and tried to work out an agreement with the South African–supported advisory council for the territory. However, the UN, to whom Waldheim had to report, was unhappy with this group because they felt that it was controlled by South Africa and denied any meaningful say to rebels from SWAPO who had been driven from the country. They were attempting at the time to regroup in neighboring nations.

On December 17, 1974, the Security Council unanimously called on South Africa to observe the International Court of Justice ruling of 1971 and to release all political prisoners and allow exiles to return to the country. A May 30, 1975, deadline was given. Some members of the Security Council had wished the proclamation to include seizure of all Namibian products on the high seas. The United States, France, and the United Kingdom vetoed this militant provision.

During 1976, South Africa continued to consult on independence plans with the advisory council for Namibia and with the political groups in Namibia that Pretoria found acceptable. 1976 was also important because Namibia was used as a staging ground for the unsuccessful South African invasion of Angola. Many observers felt that France and the United States had precipitated this action and indeed, if President Ford had been successful in the 1976 election, that a second South African attack on Angola launched from Namibia would have occurred.[38]

The change of government in Angola—the abandonment by Portugal of its colonial colony—served stark warning to South Africa that a handover of Namibia to forces dedicated to liberating South Africa from white rule would cause untold problems. As a result, Prime Minister Vorster increased his support of the Turnhalle constitutional convention taking place in Windhoek and indicated that he would turn over independence to such a group by December 31, 1978. Such a solution was totally unacceptable to the black nations of Africa or to the SWAPO forces fighting a guerrilla war in exile. This, then, was the general state of affairs as we begin our detailed examination of trends that have occurred in Namibia since the end of 1977.[39]

False Hopes of Peace

By the end of 1977, it was legitimate to possess some hope that a Namibia settlement might occur. During that year, five Western nations—the United Kingdom, the United States, France, Canada, and West Germany—had acted as go-betweens for the Pretoria government, SWAPO, and the black African states in the region. SWAPO did agree to take part in free electtions, thereby dropping its claim that it was the only party who could run a newly independent Namibia. South Africa agreed to release political prisoners and to commit itself to a one-man-one-vote political system, with the UN supervising.

As was demonstrated so many times in the Rhodesian crisis, a beleaguered white prime minister's definition of one-man-one-vote and of free, impartial elections was very different from the definition employed by black groups and their supporters advocating a power turnover. In addition, South Africa's refusal to remove its soldiers from Namibia proved an added stumbling block. South Africa felt that without its military on the premises, Namibian independence elections would not be free, and the other side felt that as long as South Africans were present, the election equally would not be free.[40]

In hopes of avoiding a breakdown that would have led South Africa to seek a totally internal settlement unacceptable to the rest of the world, U.S. Secretary of State Cyrus Vance and the foreign ministers of the United Kingdom, France, Canada, and West Germany agreed to February 11 and 12, 1978, talks on Namibia with representatives from SWAPO and South Africa. It was known the Western proposal would be that South Africa retain fifteen hundred troops in the southern part of Namibia during the transition period and that the UN peacekeeping force number between fifteen hundred and three thousand members, plus civilian UN employees to supervise the election.[41]

The talks did not proceed as hoped. After one of the two days of scheduled consultations, South African Foreign Minister Roelof F. Botha left for home. He termed the situation very serious. Insiders said that at the time when military compromise discussions were going badly, SWAPO leader Sam Nujoma chose this moment to raise the equally peevish question of the disposition of Namibia's main port, Walvis Bay. The South African response was total rejection.[42]

At the end of March 1978, a truly shocking assassination took place. Two men shot to death, from ambush, Chief Clemens Kapuuo, the chief of the Herero tribe and one of the leaders of the Democratic Turnhalle Alliance. It was unclear who killed the longtime Namibian leader. As could be expected, South Africa suggested it was SWAPO members from the rival Ovambo tribe, and SWAPO members suggested it was South Africa. In any event, a voice of moderation was silenced by the killing, and settlement between rival forces became less certain than ever.[43]

On May 10, 1978, South Africa used Namibia as a staging point for its armed invasion of Cassinga, 155 miles north of the Namibian border in Angola. The South African government claimed the town housed a Namibian refugee camp. More than 600 people were killed, and 420 were injured by the South African air and ground attack. The peace negotiations with SWAPO that had been due to resume in New York were broken off as a result.[44]

Further illustrating the complexity of obtaining peace in Namibia was the early June 1978 announcement by Zambia, Angola, and Tanzania that they would not agree to the Pan African security force for Namibia in its existing form. Foreign Minister Siteke Mwale of Zambia stated that it was an idea of Western countries with vested interests in Africa. He insisted the force must be established under the jurisdiction of the Organization of African Unity.[45]

On July 8, 1978, the South African government in Pretoria, speaking through Foreign Minister Roelof F. Botha, said it would not under any circumstances consider changes to the Western plan for black majority rule in Namibia. The Western plan envisaged a one-man-one-vote election among the territory's 850,000 people, of whom 90,000 were white. These people could choose a constituent assembly who would write a constitution that would provide for government elections.[46]

The 1978 Luanda Meeting and Its Aftermath

Shortly thereafter, leaders of the five Western nations contact group held a meeting with the parties involved in Luanda, Angola. The negotiators announced that "the parties agree to proceed to the Security Council as soon as possible."[47] This announcement "is the best thing that has hit Southern Africa in years,"[48] enthused the *Washington Post*. The *Washington Star* was less convinced and drew attention to SWAPO's "own lack of total internal democracy."[49] The *Washington Star* was disturbed by the detention of 1,000 SWAPO dissidents in jails in neighboring countries at the request of the Sam Nujoma faction of SWAPO. Special attention in the editorial was called to the imprisonment without trial in Dodoma, Tanzania, of Andreas Shipanga and eleven other rivals to Nujoma within SWAPO. The *Washington Star* also reminded its readers that many people thought SWAPO had been responsible for the assassination within Namibia of Chief Clemens Kapuuo, a possible moderate rival to Nujoma for the first presidency of a free Namibia. Clearly, the *Washington Star* had mixed emotions about the role being played by U.S. peace negotiators.

In the midst of the celebrating, insufficient attention was paid to the comment of South Africa's chief delegate to the conference that his government would renege on its acceptance of the Western independence plan if the UN Security Council tried to decide the status of Walvis Bay. South Africa refused to allow Namibia to take over this port because its administration of Walvis Bay predated the South West Africa mandate.[50]

On July 27, 1978, the Security Council passed two resolutions concerning the Namibia problem. They first requested the secretary general to appoint a special representative for Namibia in order to insure the early independence of the territory through free elections sponsored and controlled by the UN. The second, more-controversial resolution declared "the territorial integrity and unity of Namibia must be assured through the reintegration of Walvis Bay within its territory."[51] This resolution went on to demand that South Africa not use Walvis Bay in any manner prejudicial to the independence of Namibia or the viability of its economy. South Africa accepted the first Security Council resolution but rejected the second, stating that all aspects of the Walvis Bay question must be subject to further negotiation. Sam Nujoma, for his part, counted that Walvis Bay has been, is, and will be an integral part of Namibia. Some relatively impartial observers were wondering if it was wise for the Western powers to tie themselves so closely to the intractable radical Sam Nujoma. It was pointed out that either Herman Toivo ja Toivo, still in prison, or Andreas Shipanga, who recently had been released from prison in Zambia after feuding with Nujoma, might be a national leader better capable of negotiating a phased withdrawal by South Africa from Namibia.[52]

During August 1978, the UN special representative Martti Ahtisaari and a fifty-member UN transitional assistance group visited Namibia in hopes of preparing for coming elections. After touring the country, Ahtisaari stated, "It will be a long time before we can create the atmosphere that would guarantee a free and fair election in the territory."[53]

In the wake of the UN visit to Namibia, Secretary General Kurt Waldheim requested that 7,500 troops and 1,200 officials be sent there. He estimated that the twelve-month venture that must be approved by the Security Council would cost more than $300 million. The main purpose of the civilians would be to control the more than four hundred polling stations in the 318,000-square-mile territory, and the military forces would be sent to keep order. In a parallel move, the army of the Republic of South Africa attacked Namibian forces stationed in Zambia, killing at least sixteen. The attack was in retaliation for a SWAPO attack in Namibia that previously killed nine South African troops.[54] The climate for negotiation and settlement in Namibia seemed strained at best. One possible hopeful light was added when Andreas Shipanga announced that he would return to Namibia after fifteen years in exile.[55] During mid-September 1978, as John Vorster prepared to step down as South African prime minister, he dashed the world's hopes by rejecting the Namibia peace plan. Instead, he said, South Africa would go its own way in implementing independence in Namibia. Vorster cited implementation problems as the reason for South Africa's withdrawal. Plans for an early election in Namibia were made by the South African government. The first date given was November 19, 1978, and the second date, after a short postponement was announced, was December 3, 1978. In New York the Security Council resumed deliberations in hopes of saving its peace plan in Namibia.[56]

The Negotiators Try Harder

Realizing that a serious point had been reached in negotiations, U.S. Secretary of State Vance, British Foreign Secretary David Owen, West German Foreign Minister Hans Dietrich Genscher, Canadian Secretary of State for External Affairs Donald Jamieson, and French Deputy Foreign Minister Olivier Stirn held mid-October 1978 meetings at Pretoria with the new South African Prime Minister Pieter W. Botha. The hopes were to allow South Africa to back off from its aggressive position of holding elections and instead term the forthcoming vote as a referendum leading to consultation with South Africa on methods of bringing true independence in Namibia.[57]

Shortly after the return of the Western leaders from Pretoria, SWAPO rejected the compromise plan for new talks between the UN and the South African government. As a result of this action, Third World calls at the UN for economic sanctions against South Africa seemed likely. The SWAPO position came shortly after Prime Minister Botha had given in to Western pressure and had downgraded the status of the upcoming election in Namibia from a national election to one of an interim consultative nature.[58]

Despite heavy UN pressure and threats of sanctions, the South African–sponsored elections in Namibia began on schedule on December 4, 1978. Speaking in a conciliatory mood, a U.S. State Department spokesman said the United States obviously was gratified by South Africa's announcement that no power would be handed over to the winners of the current elections in Namibia. SWAPO and many moderate groups of blacks in Namibia shunned the elections. South Africa announced that 81 percent of eligible voters had turned out. The South African-government-favored Turnhalle Democratic Alliance received 82 percent of the vote cast and captured forty-one seats of the fifty available in the territory's Parliament.[59]

In the wake of the avoidance of total breakdown in Namibia negotiations, Assistant Secretary of State for Africa Richard Moose called the Namibia negotiations the most successful U.S. undertaking in Africa this year. Given the troubles the United States was encountering at the time with Rhodesian peace negotiations, Mr. Moose might have been correct. However, many observers feared the path to success in Namibia was by no means assured.[60] During early January 1979, South Africa indicated that it would annul the results of its December 1978 election in Namibia if properly held UN-supervised elections were conducted in the near future. Given this concession on their part, the threat of sanctions against South Africa receded. Although not widely admitted, the United States and the United Kingdom probably were relieved that the sanctions threat was less strong. Both nations served to lose a great deal if trade with South Africa was cut off; especially galling would be that the USSR and other socialist nations would demand a large role in policing mandatory sanctions against South Africa.[61]

Immediately before a March 15, 1978, ceasefire was to take place in Namibia, South Africa refused to participate because it objected to the presence of guerrilla forces within the country. Once again, peace was threatened. SWAPO, to emphasize its position, stepped up its attacks within Namibia and also, on a political level, again demanded immediate access to Walvis Bay. Not to be outdone, South African forces again raided SWAPO camps within the territorial limits of Angola.

South Africa made it clear by early May that it would not go along with the Western nations' peace plan. The March 15 deadline was long past. South Africa indicated that Namibia's constituent assembly that had been elected in December 1978 would be receiving extensive executive authority. The arrest of black dissidents increased, and South African military strength seemed to be growing.[62]

South Africa Continues to Stall

Continuing its attention to the new Namibian territory, South Africa changed the administrator, replacing the relatively moderate administrator Judge Marthinus Steyn with a right-wing hardliner, Professor Gerrit Viljoen, who had been principal of the Rand University in Johannesburg.[63] The Western nations peace group kept trying and now proposed a fifty-kilometer demilitarized zone on either side of the Angolan-Namibian border to be patrolled by UN forces. If successful, this plan would keep SWAPO guerrillas from infiltrating Namibia during the pre-elections ceasefire. Both Andrew Young's successor, UN Ambassador Donald McHenry, and U.K. ambassador to the UN in Geneva, Sir James Murray, actively campaigned in southern Africa for the acceptance of this idea. The originator of the demilitarized plan was President Agostinho Neto of Angola, since deceased.[64] The Namibia crisis dragged on. Western nations proposed a November 12–15, 1979, summit at Geneva to discuss Namibia. The participants would be the five Western nations, SWAPO, the South African government, and the five front line states (Angola, Zambia, Botswana, Tanzania, and Mozambique). The South African government refused to appear unless the Turnhalle Alliance members also were represented. This condition was not accepted. Meanwhile, the sporadic but savage guerrilla fighting in Namibia continued.

As 1979 moved into 1980, the situation in Namibia did not change in any essential manner, although the world around it did. Robert Mugabe had taken over in Zimbabwe, and the long civil war somehow had come to an end. The United States was suffering through a hostage crisis in Iran, and the USSR had seized Afghanistan. In Namibia, talks and intermittent diplomatic moves and killings on both sides continued. The visible achievements were few and the hopes of success were muted.

During the middle of June 1980, South African war planes and ground troups once more attacked Angola. Prime Minister Botha claimed that two hundred SWAPO members were killed. If true, this would have been the largest single engagement in the fourteen-year-long guerrilla war in Namibia. Radio Luanda claimed Angolan antiaircraft artillery shot down three South African Mirage fighter-bombers. Government forces (South African) stayed in Angola in order to seize equipment held by the SWAPO guerrillas. They came back with three hundred tons of weapons including Soviet-built trucks and armored personnel carriers and other weapons and ammunition from the USSR, East Germany, Czechoslovakia, Hungary, Yugoslavia, and China. The weapons listed included shoulder-launch ground-to-air missiles and modern large-caliber recoilless rifles, antiaircraft guns, rocket launchers, World War II–era German rifles, Soviet-made assault rifles, and U.S. M1 rifles of Korean War vintage.[65]

During late July 1980, in another South African raid launched into Angola to find Namibian bases, this time a direct military confrontation took place between Angolan and South African forces. South Africa claimed to have killed twenty-seven in this engagement. On the domestic scene in Namibia, the Turnhalle Alliance established a governing council as South Africa continued to cede more power to this local group of its choosing. The world waited with impatience for South Africa to settle finally the Namibia dispute.[66]

During early September 1980, South Africa once more stalled on the Namibia subject. Foreign Minister Roelof F. Botha told Secretary General Kurt Waldheim that in South Africa's opinon, he and the UN were too prejudiced to administer fairly turnover elections in Namibia. As if to emphasize this point, South Africa announced that in the first eight months of 1980 it had killed 823 members of SWAPO. UN Secretary General Waldheim again proposed talks between South Africa and SWAPO, and again, his mediation attempts for the first face-to-face talks between the two groups failed.

The All-Parties Peace Conference

By late October 1980, Western and large African nation pressure compelled South Africa to agree to an all-sides meeting modeled on the 1979 London Lancaster House Conference that had led to the end of the Rhodesian War and the independence of Zimbabwe. Many were certain that South Africa, who had stalled so effectively since peace negotiations by the Western nations had started in 1976, once again would find ways to block independence. All agreed that one more large push must take place.[67]

Hopes were never higher than at the start of 1981. The UN, on January 7, would chair a meeting at Geneva between all the parties involved in the Namibia dispute. At the complicated negotiations, it was agreed that internal political parties in Namibia—namely, the Turnhalle Alliance directed by Dirk Mudge—would sit at the same table with SWAPO negotiators and that only the top South African administrator in Namibia would also participate. The Republic of South Africa would be accorded the same advisor status as the other front-line nations in the region.The agenda of the conference was left slightly ambiguous to placate South Africa. UN officials did not want the coming constitution to be a subject on the agenda because this would allow further grounds for obfuscation by South African officials. Instead, it was agreed that the peace plan and other practical proposals would be on the agenda.[68]

On the first day of negotiations at Geneva, Secretary General Waldheim called for a firm agreement on a ceasefire date that would clear the way to independence for the territory by the end of 1981.[69] As the talks continued, even the most elementary step of the ceasefire became impossible. On January 13, the conference ended, with the South African delegation declaring the West plan premature. SWAPO, for its part, said the conference had failed because of the "intransigent prevarication" of South Africa.[70]

One more time, hopes had been dashed and peace seemed as far away as ever. In many eyes, it was even more so since the Carter administration that had been pledged to an all-out effort to end the Namibia situation was being replaced by the Reagan administration, whose determination on the subject was yet to be put to the test in a conclusive manner.[71]

In an attempt to recapture some of the momentum toward peace that had been lost by the failure of the Namibia peace negotiations in Geneva, the government in Angola began to make noises suggesting that it might be willing to send the Cubans home if the situation to the south changed to its liking. Lucio Lara, the national secretary of the Movimento de Libertacao de Angola (MPLA), summed up the situation succinctly: "The problem of the Cubans is the problem of South Africa. We do not feel safe."[72]

As could be expected, the nations of the world were furious at South Africa's backing off from peace in Namibia. Most observers felt that if the impartiality of the UN had not been the excuse used, South Africa would have been able to find another. It seemed clear that South Africa was not yet ready to give up Namibia. It wanted to see how strong the Reagan administration would be in applying pressure, and it also needed more time to develop Sasol coal-to-oil-conversion facilities. If South Africa could insure its energy supply, even if sanctions on an international level were effec-

tive, the country would for the foreseeable future be relatively self-sufficient. From Pretoria's point of view, it had little to gain and much to lose by
giving up the battle at this late, but still not last possible, date.

The Crocker Approach

As the Reagan administration came into place and Dr. Chester A. Crocker
took over as assistant secretary of state for Africa, diplomatic moves continued to try to bring peace to Namibia. At the same time, African nations
began agitating loudly for further U.S. action in southern Africa on issues
such as aid, Namibia, and disassociating itself from Savimbi's rebel UNITA
forces in Angola. A March 1981 meeting between UN Ambassador Jeane
Kirkpatrick and a visiting South African general was given wide play and
condemnation in the world press. During April 1981, Assistant Secretary of
State Crocker went to southern Africa to discuss U.S. policy with local
governments and also to bring an altered Namibia proposal in which the
various parties would be asked to work out the laws of the country in
negotiation before an election took place. This procedure had succeeded in
Zimbabwe negotiations. It was hoped that the moderate Turnhalle Alliance
group would be more amenable if the system under which they would be
governed was clear before people chose at the polls between themselves and
SWAPO. The Crocker visit took place as planned in April. This southern
African expert had not yet been confirmed by the U.S. Senate. Senator
Jesse Helms of North Carolina had placed a hold on the Crocker confirma-
tion because he had doubts that the assistant secretary designate accurately
represented the views of the Reagan administration. Without question, this
less than total support from Capitol Hill hurt the first Crocker trip. The
prime minister of South Africa refused to meet with him, and black African
leaders showed skepticism. Nonetheless, both Crocker and the Reagan administration kept at Namibian peace negotiations.

Following his two-week African tour, Dr. Crocker went to London
with the five Western nations to continue working on peace negotiations for
Namibia. From a U.S. point of view, such continued efforts were necessary
since otherwise it was feared that a Third World movement to demand mandatory sanctions against South Africa would take place and that, in order to
assist its own economy, the United States and probably the United Kingdom
would feel constrained to veto such a motion. Heavy criticism of the United
States would be sure to follow. An early May 1981 meeting in Rome among
the Western allies brought about a formal agreement to the new plan based
on the Zimbabwe formula.[73] Nonetheless, the feared call for sanctions
at the Security Council did take place and obliged the United States,
the United Kingdom, and France to cast vetoes. Spain and Ireland joined

Third World nations in voting for an embargo on oil supplies to South Africa. Both the United States and France said in explaining their vetoes that they would remain bound by the arms embargo and claimed that such a new embargo would have seriously hurt the ongoing negotiations in Namibia.[74] Many observers felt that the United States was embarking on a reversal of the Carter policy. Instead of settling Namibia and hoping that the Cubans then would be ushered out of Angola, it now seemed that the United States was at least hinting that Cuban withdrawal from Angola would be a fine starting point for a Namibia settlement.

During mid-May, Secretary of State Alexander Haig held a meeting in Washington with his South African counterpart, Foreign Minister Roelof F. Botha. Afterward, Haig reported progress had been achieved. *The New York Times,* always a stern critic of the Reagan administration, was not persuaded. It announced in an editorial that Haig and his associates were "overly sanguine by half."[75] *The New York Times* felt that the Reagan administration was not being sufficiently severe in its dealings with South Africa. Instead it was asking significant sacrifices from black Africa—sacrifices that the newspaper doubted would occur. As a result, the United States would open itself to significant criticism from communist nations and black Africa.

At the start of June, the old Washington nemesis of news leaks became an important issue in the African-affairs area, especially in Namibia. Position papers were leaked to the press by Randall Robinson, the director of TransAfrica, a private lobbying group against apartheid. These papers seemed to indicate that, although on one hand the United States was strongly urging compromise by all sides in the Namibia situation, on the other it held out a definite carrot to South Africa that diplomatic relations with it would improve if it were willing to settle on Namibia. Many observers were afraid that this quid pro quo would, substantially slow down a move away from the apartheid regime in Namibia.[76]

During June 1981, Deputy Secretary of State William P. Clark, accompanied by the now finally confirmed Assistant Secretary of State for Africa Chester A. Crocker, went to South Africa for further talks on Namibia. Upon his return from South Africa and Namibia, Mr. Clark said that South Africa had made commitments to the United States on steps it would take to end the impasse.[77] Conversely, and consistent with the prior statement, Assistant Secretary of State Crocker testified before the House of Representatives Subcommittee on Africa that U.S. patience with South Africa had its limits. If peace prospects seemed dim, he intimated that his government would withdraw its services as negotiator.[78]

The Organization of African Unity interpreted the Crocker remarks as an open invitation to South Africa to cause further disruption in attempts to preserve the political status quo. Sam Nujoma, the SWAPO head, charged the United States with "entering into an unholy alliance with South Africa" and with "cruel and unusual manipulation" of the Namibian people.[79] President Daniel Arap Moi of Kenya, the new chairman of the Organization of African Unity, seconded the Nujoma comments.

On the last day of its conference, the Organization of African Unity unanimously adopted a resolution denouncing "the unholy alliance between Washington and Pretoria.[80] A U.S. State Department spokesperson rejected the charge and reiterated that the United States was not linked with South Africa. He stressed that the United States remained interested in Namibia peace only as a negotiator desiring peace in southern Africa.[81]

Surprisingly, Robert Mugabe was one of the few voices of moderation in the savage attack launched against the Reagan administration. He advocated that peace attempts on the part of the five Western nations continue. South Africa, during July 1981, clearly stepped up its attacks in Namibia and southern Angola in order to present the best possible bargaining position should they one day be forced to the table again. Secretary of State Alexander Haig and the foreign ministers of the four other Western nations involved—the United Kingdom, France, West Germany, and Canada—met at Ottawa on July 21 and 22, 1981, while the chiefs of state of their nations were also meeting. They agreed to keep up diplomatic efforts to bring abut peace in Namibia. Nevertheless, Mark MacGuigan, Canada's secretary of state for external affairs, was quoted as saying he was not optimistic about an early solution. Sixty-six years after South Africa, at the United Kingdom's invitation, marched into Namibia, it still showed little real inclination to leave of its own accord.[82]

Recent Namibian Happenings

The Negotiators Squabble

By late July 1981, fissures in the Western five-power united front became clear. It was now over three months since the U.S. initiative on Namibia had been approved at a Rome meeting and adopted as a unanimous Western five-power position. Especially in light of mounting world criticism of U.S. actions in Southern Africa in general and in Namibia in particular, the other four Western powers sought to detach themselves from the close linkages with the United States. West Germany, through Foreign Minister Hans Dietrich Ganscher, moved to go beyond the Rome agreement and proposed that statement-of-principles negotiations be started between the South African government and internal and external Namibian political groupings.[83]

On August 24, 1981, the Namibian situation took a turn for the worse. The South African militia mounted a major new assault into southern Angola from staging points in northern Namibia. South African tanks and armored personnel carriers moved from sixty-two to ninety-three miles into Angola. South African Major General Charles Floyd said, "Terror against the local population in Namibia cannot be tolerated and it is unavoidable that the terrorists will be pursued and the bases from which they operate wiped out."[84]

The latest action taken by the South Africans caused added problems for the U.S. government. It felt obliged to break ranks with its Namibia settlement partners when the UN Security Council moved to condemn the South African attack into Angola. The United States vetoed the resolution even though language leading to demands that UN members cut off trade with South Africa or impose mandatory sanctions against South Africa had been removed. The hope was that the United States, the United Kingdom, and France would support the resolution or, at the very least, would choose to abstain rather than veto. In the cases of the United Kingdom, who abstained, and France, who joined the majority, the opponents of South Africa at the UN were successful. Only the United States went it alone on the theory that the South African attacks could not be taken in isolation but must be viewed as a response to guerrilla raids into Namibia from Angola. The Uganda delegate, Olara Otunna, an outspoken Third World nations advocate, called the U.S. position very sad and one that would lead the world to conclude incorrectly that Angola had attacked South Africa and not the reverse as did actually occur. The Russian delegate, Rikhard S. Ovinnikov, agreed and accused the United States of "pandering" to the South African government.[85]

Angola, speaking for itself, used the U.S. veto as a reason for threatening that it might ask assistance from its allies in expelling South African troops from its soil. The reference to allies of Angola obviously included the USSR and Cuba. The legal justification for the potential invitation was Article 51 of the UN charter. By its provisions, countries have the right to take individual and collective self-defense when they are under attack and when the Security Council has not yet acted. Many critics of the United States were quick to point out that on the one hand it had joined in the unanimous Security Council resolution in June 1981 condemning Israel's bombing of the nuclear reactors in Iraq. On the other hand, it should be reported that the United States had refused to support Security Council action against Israel for the July 1981 Beirut, Lebanon, bombings. The critics felt that the one condemnation of Israel activity aside, the United States was protecting Israel and South Africa in a manner that it would not do for other nations.

By the end of the week of the attack, South African forces had begun to disengage. Its 45,000 troops began to return to Namibia. Over 450 SWAPO and Angolan troops originally were listed as being killed in the fighting. It was estimated that losses between SWAPO and Angolan troops were divided equally. South Africa said ten of its soldiers had died. This Angolan incursion differed from the large-scale 1975 battles because in the earlier attacks, South African troops fought mostly Cuban soldiers. The South African government was delighted by its capture of a Soviet noncommissioned officer in the raids. It also claimed to have killed two Soviet lieutenant colonels in the battles. South African radio and television stations, both government controlled, mounted a propaganda barrage, emphasizing the Soviet threat to Southern Africa and mocking Soviet government claims that it had only technical advisors and not military personnel in Angola.[86]

On September 3, 1981, perhaps partially to defuse mounting worldwide criticism of a perceived U.S. political tilt toward South Africa, Secretary of State Haig claimed during an interview that progress had been achieved on negotiating a withdrawal by South Africa from Namibia. "We are not where we want to be yet. But we are farther ahead on where we want to be," said the Reagan administration official.[87] On closer examination, it seemed that Mr. Haig based his optimistic appraisal on what, at best, would be a modest accomplishment. Haig's words, when stripped of rhetoric, could be reduced to a claim that South African attitudes on Namibia again were turning toward reasonableness. No one can doubt that South African attitudes had hardened unquestionably and become more obstructionist in the time since South Africa had rejected UN Security Council Resolution 435 of 1978 after previously agreeing to abide by its terms. Mr. Haig felt South Africa would accept once again Resolution 435 as a basis for peace-settlement negotiations. Thus, they would return to square one and begin the peace process at the point where it was at the time the resolution was passed: 1978.

Given that South African troops had been marching through southern Angola, literally within hours before the Haig press conference, it is not surprising that many observers and commentators were quick to disagree with the U.S. secretary of state.[88] These people wondered how South Africa's launching of the most serious military assault into Angola in over five years could be squared by Haig with his opinion that the Namibia peace-settlement situation was getting better. Onlookers suggested that, in fact, the South African actions were calculated shrewdly to exascerbate the situation to a point where settlement was impossible. To prove the point, as evidence that South Africa was trying to make other nations so mad that they would refuse to deal with South Africa, reference was made to the September 4 action of the UN General Assembly, in which it refused to allow the South African delegate to take part in the debate on the Namibia question.[89] As had occurred constantly since 1974, the vote to eject South Africa from the chamber easily carried. The few nations that thought expulsion played into

South Africa's hands by increasing the efficiency of its Namibia stalling tactics were outvoted, and their voice was drowned out by the blood-curdling condemnations of South African conduct.

Looked at from afar, it would seem hard to agree with Mr. Haig's opinion that better days were coming. South Africa appeared to be in the process of establishing a true buffer zone in northern Namibia.[90] If successful, the need for giving up the southern part of the region probably would be less clear to the Pretoria government. In addition, the aggressive South African strike into Angola was popular with the white population in South Africa. When this raid is combined with recent harsh moves to remove black and colored people living without permission in Capetown, the two moves in concert could send a message that the government in Pretoria had no intention of rolling over and playing dead in the face of unfavorable world reaction to their policies.

South Africa Remains Obstinate

To emphasize its spirit of independence, South Africa continued with its plan to turn over day-to-day control of Namibia affairs to an internal-settlement-supporting multiracial government led by Dirk F. Mudge. Under this South African–initiated plan that was set up in defiance of UN Resolution 435, only constitutional matters, military defense, and foreign affairs would remain under the purview of South African Administrator General Danie Hough.[91] France and West Germany, in particular, among the five Western powers, were opposed strongly to the South African–initiated plan and in private believed that the soft U.S. attitude in dealing with the Pretoria government had led to the independent South African attitude and the increase of tensions between the five potential peace seekers.

The UN General Assembly continued to demand that South Africa be punished for its activities in Namibia. On September 14, 1981, by a vote of 117 to 0, with 25 abstentions, South Africa was condemned and a promise to arm rebel fighters in Namibia was passed. Since the General Assembly has no power to pass binding resolutions, the exercise was only window dressing. It did, nonetheless, serve to isolate the five Western peace-seeking nations and their allies, all of whom abstained on the resolution. They were criticized heavily by the Third World and Communist-bloc nations. Such a clear division pleased the Soviet delegate, Oleg A. Troyanovsky, who loudly criticized Western interference in a Namibia settlement.[92]

The governments in Washington, D.C., and Pretoria ignored the worldwide expressions of disapproval and kept negotiating. U.S. and South African spokespersons made parallel pronouncements proclaiming significant progress was being achieved in bringing an end to the Namibian deadlock. Assistant Secretary of State Crocker, speaking two days after the General Assembly vote, told the House Foreign Affairs Subcommittee on Africa that he expected a turnaround and breakthrough by early 1982. He said South Africa would accept unconditionally the terms of the 1978 resolution as a peace formula and would permit UN peacekeeping forces to enter Namibia. Crocker also said that South Africa had given assurances that a settlement agreement would predate the working out of constitution details.[93]

South African Ambassador to the United States Donald B. Sole was in public agreement with Crocker and stated that the South African and U.S. governments had reached a Namibia agreement. Sole, however, was quick to add, "I don't want to overemphasize or underemphasize the difficulties that lie ahead.[94]

As if to emphasize the conditional nature of any South African change of heart, the Pretoria government chose this moment to revise its count of those killed in the twelve-day Angola incursion. The figure was raised from 500 to 1,000. In addition, the South African government disclosed that it had seized $214 million worth of military equipment, totaling 3,000 tons of military weapons. Among the cache were 13 Soviet-made T34 and PT76 tanks, 100 SAM7 missile launchers, and 300 vehicles.[95] *Newsweek* concluded that, "As last week's attack on Angola demonstrated, Pretoria is still living with its position as an international pariah."[96] Such an assessment was in direct contradiction to the U.S.-South African song of optimism.

On September 25, 1981, after consultation with South Africa and black African nations, the five Western peacemaking nations announced at the UN that they had developed a three-year independence timetable starting in 1982. The five nations, in independent briefings, admitted that much still could go wrong.[97]

The negotiations continued, and the shaky movement toward a power turnover staggered along at the end of 1981. In mid-November of that year, Sam Nujoma gave a boost to peace hopes while addressing 150,000 SWAPO supporters at a rally held in Lusaka, Zambia. The group's leader stated, "We have agreed to safeguard the interests of the minorities in Namibia because they are going to become citizens of Namibia."[98]

The momentum toward settlement gathered speed shortly thereafter when eight important African nations—Kenya, Nigeria, Zimbabwe, Tanzania, Mozambique, Zambia, Malawi, and Angola—joined with SWAPO to approve formally the steps being taken toward Namibian independence. Soon thereafter, however, Angola denied that it was necessarily in agreement with the Western peace initiatives. This statement emphasized how tenuous was the movement in the direction of peace.[99]

New Overtures Toward Peace

In early December 1981, the United States moved to stabilize its relationship
with the MPLA-directed government of Angola. It would seem that a settlement of the long-running internal strife in southern Angola would be a pre-
requisite to a stable, independent Namibia.[100] First, Uniao Nacional para a
Independencia Total de Angola (UNITA) leader Jonas Savimbi was
brought to Washington for talks with Secretary of State Haig and other foreign-policy decision makers. Simultaneously, the president of the interna-
tionally recognized MPLA government in Angola, Jose Eduardos dos Santos, indicated he would also be willing to start discussions with the United
States. The master plan from the Angolan government's point of view
would seem to be that if the United States dropped its covert support of
Savimbi and persuaded South Africa to withdraw overt support of Savimbi,
then Angola would work actively for peace on Western nations' terms in
Namibia. Once southern Angola was stabilized through a combination of
Namibian independence and civil-war cessation between the MPLA and
UNITA, the need for Cuban troops would vanish. Once the Cubans were
gone, the last obstacle to U.S. diplomatic recognition of Angola would disappear. In such an instance, U.S. corporate involvement in Angola would
increase markedly. The Angolan economy that had been decimated by the
Portuguese scorched-earth disengagement policy and the long-running
MPLA-UNITA-Frente Nacional de Libertacao de Angola (FNLA) civil war
would be helped significantly. An Angola that was in economic synchroni-
zation with Washington might serve to weaken substantially Soviet influence in southern Africa. Such a Pollyannaish solution to U.S. difficulties is
admittedly remote, but Haig and Crocker must be complimented for their
attempts in this direction.

U.S. policymakers must have taken satisfaction in the December 16,
1981, statement by Angola's Ambassador to Portugal Adriano Sebastiao.
Speaking in an official capacity, he said his government would be willing to
hold talks with UNITA rebel leaders Jonas Savimbi "as long as he remains
an Angolan citizen and cuts his ties with South Africa." Such a concilia-
tory-sounding comment would have been unthinkable until a few months
before.[101]

As 1981 drew to a close, UN diplomats remained cautiously optimistic
about Namibia peace prospects. Phase one of the negotiated settlement
called for an agreement to be reached concerning the need for the upcoming
constitution to include a multiparty political system, an independent judici-
ary, a bill of rights, white minority, and private-property protection. In
addition, there must be constitutional ratification by a two-thirds vote of
the still-to-be-formed Namibian national legislature. Skeptics felt South
Africa had left itself an out by being so quick to agree to broad language

concerning goals to be contained in the enabling legislation for the new nation. When specifics were reached on such touchy subjects as what is, for example, "adequate protection of white minority rights," difficulties inevitably would occur. The Rhodesian Civil War lasted an extra eighteen months while this question was being disputed. Should South Africa be displeased at the way the question was being resolved, even late into the peace process, Pretoria still retained enough political and military power to wreck the movement toward majority rule.

The second step of the peace process will be to involve the UN directly in supervising free elections in Namibia. A UN force would be brought in to carry out this function. South Africa is very distrustful of the impartiality of any such group since UN condemnation of South Africa and official support of SWAPO has been proclaimed on a variety of occasions. Whether those black and white Namibian citizens who had supported an internal settlement would receive fair treatment under a UN peace plan is problematic and a definite obstacle to an orderly transition process.

Under these circumstances, it is questionable if the hoped-for election time will be achieved. Many have felt all along that the projected phase-two completion date of March or April 1982 was hopelessly overoptimistic. Whenever the free elections are held, it is then planned that a complete handover of power to the new government and concurrent withdrawal of South African and UN forces would occur one year after the election. This would be the third and final phase of the Namibia peace plan.[102] If the whole process is completed in April 1983, as hoped, South Africa would then finish its occupation of Namibia a mere sixty-eight years after it had commenced. As was expected, later events made it certain that the occupation will continue through its sixty-ninth year and beyond.

The Role of Angola becomes Important

During mid-January 1982, the move to solidify the Angolan part of the Namibian peace settlement continued to pick up speed. Initiatives in this regard were so marked that one could be excused for forgetting that a normalization of relations with Angola was an interest subsidiary to placing the black majority in control in the neighboring nation: Namibia. In mid-January 1982, Chester A. Crocker and Angolan Prime Minister Paulo Jorge held a two-day meeting in Paris. The discussions were wide ranging but certainly included Namibia, U.S. attitudes toward South Africa, diplomatic relations between the United States and Angola, and most certainly, the withdrawal of Cuban military forces from Angola.[103]

A week later, the Soviets moved to salvage their standing with the Angolan government. A new ten-year economic-cooperation agreement was signed between the two nations. In addition, agreement was reached on a series of a five-year technical, economic, and trade accords. Soviet Premier Nikolai Tikhonov took the occasion to attack Western peace initiatives on Namibia as being a "broad plot of international imperialism."[104] In answering remarks, Lucio Lara, the national secretary of the MPLA, emphasized that his government had invited the Cuban troops into Angola and that they would stay for as long as the Angolan government felt necessary. Such comments by Tikhonov and Lara seemed to indicate that reconciliation between the United States and Angola, to say nothing of South Africa and Angola, would be difficult to accomplish.

During mid-March 1982, South Africa again launched a major raid in southern Angola. Those who had been predicting a swift settlement in Namibia once again were forced to admit that South African words and their actions were in fundamental contradiction. The South African Defence Force claimed that at least 201 black guerrillas active in the Namibian war were killed. South African losses were listed as three dead. The surprise raid occurred fourteen miles within Angolan territory. A large number of military stores, mostly Soviet in origin, also were captured.[105]

The renewed assaults into southern Angola by the South African Defence Force prompted a new set of peacemaking initiatives by the five-nation Western contact group. In early April 1982, U.S. Assistant Secretary of State Crocker and Jean Ausseil of France led a delegation to Luanda, Angola, to talk to leaders of that nation and of SWAPO. Afterward, the delegation flew to South Africa for further talks. The purpose of the meetings was to settle completely all remaining differences concerning the first phase of negotiations: a proportional-representation voting plan for electing a government in Namibia. South Africa had agreed in principle to the phase-one-provisions, but SWAPO and the front-line states still expressed reservations. Negotiators feared that South Africa would then have reservations to any modifications proposed by the other side, leaving more delay a distinct possibility. Crocker and Ausseil hoped to tie together all phase-one loose ends and proceed to phase-two negotiations. At this point it would be hoped to reach agreement on procedures for conducting voting under UN supervision. The negotiators also hoped to obtain SWAPO and front-line states agreement to constitutional principles drawn up by the Western contact group.[106]

Peace Hopes Fade Again

At times, the five-nation Western contact group must have felt as if their task, bringing peace to Namibia, was one of the most thankless in the world. Such an occasion must have taken place in early April 1982 when even their cosponsors, the UN, disregarded their advice. The question was whether to appoint a new UN commissioner for Namibia to replace Martti Ahtisaari, a Finn. The negotiators were afraid to give any participant a new chance to declare itself dissatisfied and interrupt negotiations. The recently installed UN Secretary Javier Perez de Cuellar disregarded their advice to leave the post vacant and selected a vocal Third World sympathizer, Brajesh Chandra Mishra of India. The mutterings of dissatisfaction from Pretoria could be heard as far away as New York.[107]

For the first time in over a year, SWAPO took to the offensive in a marked manner during mid-April 1982. One hundred guerrilla troops operating 130 miles into Namibia were responsible for the deaths of nine South African troops and four civilians. SWAPO losses were estimated at nineteen. The raid served warning that South Africa never could expect total peace within Namibia no matter how diligently it attempted to clean out border areas in southern Angola.[108] The latest SWAPO attacks came as a new census reported that only 71,530 of the total Namibian population of 1,035,000 people were now white. Previously, more than 100,000 white people had lived in the region.[109] Even in Pretoria, it would seem the handwriting must be on the wall. As if to emphasize the point, and that well may have been the purpose of his request, President Kenneth Kaunda of Zambia held a meeting with Prime Minister Botha that took place in a trailer astride the Botswana-South Africa border on April 30, 1982. Conditions much duplicated the Kaunda-Vorster discussions at Victoria Falls in 1975 concerning the fate of Rhodesia/Zimbabwe. This time Kaunda's topic was South-West Africa/Namibia.[110]

On June 11, 1982, the *Washington Post* carried the headline, "State Is Optimistic on Namibia Pact." Somehow it all sounded so familiar. Chester Crocker was headed back to the UN to work on phase two, the implementation phase. Left unemphasized was that phase one remained uncompleted. Undaunted, a high U.S. government official, unidentified otherwise, observed, "If things move according to the timetable we have in mind, it is foreseeable that we could within the next several months be in a position where the parties can agree upon a date for implementation and that date could be within the next few months as well."[111]

Some critics of the U.S. role in the negotiations were less optimistic. They noted that a U.S. desire for all Cuban troops to leave Angola as a part of the Namibia settlement seemed to be hardening into a demand. In the view of these observers finding a Namibia settlement was difficult enough without tacking on the removal of 18,000 Cuban Communists to the precedent conditions. Not surprisingly in their view, Prime Minister Botha seized the opportunity offered by the new U.S. bargaining tack. Speaking in Oshivello, Namibia, on June 17, 1982, Botha stated, "South Africa is unwilling to complete all the phases of the Western plan unless the Cubans leave Angola."[112]

Expelling Cubans from Angola

As months passed, the Namibian crisis continued to be unresolved. However, the U.S. State Department managed to remain cheerful. Witness, for example, *The New York Times* headline of July 14, 1982: "U.S. Reports Progress in Namibia Talks."[113] In early September, Prime Minister Botha stated South Africa not leave Namibia until there was an "unequivocal agreement" on the withdrawal of Cuban troops from Angola.[114] Later that month, in the same unhelpful mood, Botha hinted that his government might displace the interim Namibian regime of Dirk F. Mudge.[115] Added confusion and delay would result from any such move.

As a counterbalance to the South African position, U.S. Secretary of State George P. Schultz flew to New York to meet with Angolan Foreign Minister Paolo Jorge at the United Nations. During a subsequent press briefing, Jorge denied that Angola had shifted its position and said that it was none of the business of the United States whether or not Angola retained Cuban troops in its country. He did express hope, however, that peace would come to Namibia during 1983.[116] A few days later, during a trip to Zimbabwe, Angolan President Jose Eduardo dos Santos contradicted his foreign minister and expressed extreme pessimism. According to dos Santos, the United States was totally responsible for the lack of settlement in Namibia.[117]

During the following month, November 1982, South Africa continued its raids into Angola. The mood of Angola's leaders could not have improved when they discovered that Vice President George Bush had stated in Nairobi that a Cuban pullout from Angola was the key to a negotiated settlement in Namibia.[118] Long forgotten, apparently, were the many denials by Crocker and others in the Reagan administration that peace in Namibia and Cuban troops in Angola were linked inexorably.

South Africa stepped into a diplomatic negotiating role during late December 1982. South African Foreign Minister Roelof F. Botha, known familiarly as "Pik," traveled to Washington for meetings with Schultz, Crocker and other high Reagan administration officials.[119] Predictably, Botha told these American officials that United States had a real chance of affecting the international settlement in Namibia.[120] Less predictably, in mid-December, Botha held discussions with Angolan leaders on the Namibian question. The meetings took place in the Cape Verde Islands. If South Africa and Angola could come to an understanding the chances for a settlement in Namibia would improve notably.[121]

Even as the world started to hope that peace was attainable in Namibia, South Africa moved quickly to cast a shadow over these feelings of optimism. Under heavy pressure from South Africa, Mudge resigned as head of Namibia's interim government on January 10, 1983.[122] He gave as reasons the mishandling of affairs by the South African government and his inability to work in harmony with Danie Hough, the South African administrator-general for the territory. For the moment, at least, South Africa resumed direct rule, dissolving the National Assembly.[123] Such disheartening news neutralized any progress that might be seen in the continuance of talks between governmental delegations from South Africa and Angola.

Notes

1. John H. Wellington, *South West Africa and Its Human Issues* (Oxford: Oxford University Press, 1967), pp. 1-3.

2. United Nations, Economic and Social Council, *The Activities of Transnational Corporations in the Industrial Mining and Military Sectors of Southern Africa,* Commission on Transnational Corporations, E/C 10/51, March 1979.

3. T.R.H. Davenport, *South Africa: A Modern History* (London: Macmillan, 1977).

4. J. Goldblatt, *History of South West Africa from the Beginning of the Nineteenth Century* (Johannesburg: Juta Press, 1971).

5. Heinz Gerhard Hubrich and Heinz Melber, *Namibia—Geschichte und Gegenwart zur Frage der Dekolonisation einer Siedlerkolonie* (Bonn: Informationsstelle sudliches Afrika e.V., Wissenschaffliche Reihe 17, 1977).

6. H. Vedder, "The German Occupation of 1883-1914." In *The Cambridge History of the British Empire* (Cambridge: Cambridge University Press, vol. 8, 1936).

7. Ibid.

8. Goldblatt, *History of South West Africa from the Beginning of the Nineteenth Century,* p. 131.

9. Letter of Jan Smuts to M.C. Gillett, January 25, 1919. In *Selections from the Smuts Papers.* William K. Hancock, Jean van der Poel, eds. (Cambridge: Cambridge University Press, vol. 4, 1966), pp. 55-56.

10. League of Nations, *Covenant* (League of Nations Publications Series VI A, Mandates, 1945), pp. 18-21.

11. Permanent Mandates Commission of the League of Nations. *Mandate for Southwest Africa* (Articles 1-7). December 17, 1920.

12. Ruth First, *South West Africa* (Baltimore: Penguin, 1963), pp. 87-116.

13. United Nations, *Yearbook of the United Nations* (New York: United Nations Publications Office, 1946).

14. United Nations, General Assembly, *Resolution 65 (1),* December 14, 1946.

15. United Nations, General Assembly, 4th sess. Fourth committee, *Annex to the Summary Records of Meetings of 1949* (Doc. A/929), pp. 7–80.

16. First, *South West Africa,* p. 183.

17. Union of South Africa, *House of Assembly Debates,* vol. 66, col. 1275, February, 17, 1949.

18. United Nations, General Assembly, *Resolution 337 (IV),* December, 1949.

19. United Nations, General Assembly, *Resolution 338 (IV),* December, 1949.

20. United Nations, *International Court of Justice Reports* 128, July 11, 1950, pp. 131–144.

21. Ibid. pp. 157–159.

22. United Nations, General Assembly, *Resolution 449A (V),* 1950.

23. United Nations, General Assembly, *Resolution 749A (VIII),* 1953.

24. United Nations, General Assembly, *Resolution 1143 (XII),* 1957.

25. United Nations, General Assembly, 13th sess. *Annexes* (A/3900), agenda item 39, 1958, pp. 9–10.

26. United Nations, General Assembly, *Resolution 1243 (XIII),* 1958.

27. United Nations, General Assembly, 13th sess. (Suppl. no. 12, A/3906), 1958, pp. 28–29.

28. United Nations, General Assembly, *Resolution 1565 (XV),* 1960.

29. United Nations, "South-West Africa Cases, Preliminary Objections," *International Court of Justice Reports,* 1962, pp. 328–347.

30. United Nations, *International Court of Justice Reports* 6 (1966), pp. 17–51.

31. Richard A. Falk, "South-West Africa Cases: An Appraisal," *International Organizations* 21 (1967), pp. 13–14.

32. United Nations, General Assembly, *Resolution 2145 (XXI),* October 27, 1966.

33. United Nations, General Assembly, *Resolution 2145 (XXI),* sec. 6, October 27, 1966.

34. United Nations, Security Council, *Resolution 264 (XXIV),* March 20, 1969.

35. United Nations, *International Court of Justice Reports,* 1971, p. 21.

36. United Nations, *International Court of Justice Reports,* 1971, pp. 220–320.

37. *State* v. *Tuhadeleni,* et. al., "Address to Court of Toivo Herman Ja Toivo." In *The South-West Africa/Namibia Dispute,* John Dugard, ed. (Berkeley: University of California Press, 1973).

38. R.W. Johnson, *How Long Will South Africa Survive?* (New York: Oxford University Press, 1977).

39. *Namibia—The Last Colony,* Reginald H. Green, Kimmo Kiljunen, Marja-Liisa Kiljunen, eds. (London: Longman, 1981).; *Oxford History of South Africa,* Monica Wilson, Leonard Thompson, eds. (New York: Oxford University Press, 1969).

40. Anthony Lewis, "Reckoning in Namibia," *The New York Times,* January 9, 1978.

41. Milton R. Benjamin, "Vance to Attend Crucial Talks on Namibia," *Washington Post,* January 28, 1978.

42. David Anable, "Parley on Namibia Stalled," *Christian Science Monitor,* February 13, 1978.

43. John F. Burns, "Black Leader Shot to Death in Southwest Africa," *The New York Times,* March 28, 1978.

44. John F. Burns, "South African Force Crosses into Namibia," *The New York Times,* May 5, 1978; and Dusko Dodei, "U.N. Condemns Raid in Angola," *Washington Post,* May 7, 1978.

45. Martha Honey, "Nyerere Assails West over Zaire, Supports Soviets," *Washington Post,* June 7, 1978; David B. Ottaway, "Namibia Militants Agree to New Talks," *Washington Post,* June 12, 1978.

46. John F. Burns, "South Africa Bars Change in Namibia Plan," *The New York Times,* July 9, 1978.

47. Kathleen Teltsch, "Namibia Guerrillas Accept West's Plan on Future of Area," *The New York Times,* July 13, 1978.

48. Editorial, "Success in Namibia," *Washington Post,* July 16, 1978.

49. Editorial, "New Namibia Prospects," *Washington Star,* July 16, 1978.

50. Kathleen Teltsch, "South African Hints at Confrontation in U.N. over Namibia," *The New York Times,* July 18, 1978.

51. "South Africa Backs U.N. on Transition in Namibia," *Baltimore Sun,* August 1, 1978. See also, United Nations, Security Council, *Resolution 431 (XXXIII),* July 27, 1978.

52. Editorial, "The Walvis Bay Issue," *Baltimore Sun,* July 30, 1978.

53. Caryle Murphy, "Namibians Greet Arrival of U.N. Transition Team, *Washington Post,* August 22, 1978.

54. "7,500 Man U.N. Force Proposed for Namibia," *Washington Star,* August 30, 1978.

55. "Breakaway SWAPO Man to Return, *Sunday Times of London,* August 20, 1978.

56. John M. Goshko, "Namibia Plan Rejected," *Washington Post,* September 21, 1978; "South Africa Postpones Vote in Namibia by Two Weeks," *Baltimore Sun,* September 27, 1978.

57. Jim Hoagland, "Vance Plans Trip to South Africa on Namibia," *Washington Post,* October 6, 1978.

58. Anthony Lewis, "Southern Africa's Last Chance," *Washington*

Star, October 5, 1978; Jim Hoagland, "SWAPO Rejects Proposal for New Namibia Talks," *Washington Post,* October 25, 1978.

59. Reuter News Service, "Namibian Assembly Opens with New Vote Prime Issue," *The New York Times,* December 21, 1978.

60. Jay Ross, "West's Plan for Namibia Seen Back on Track," *Washington Post,* December 28, 1978.

61. "Botha on Namibia: Bucking for U.N. Vote," *Christian Science Monitor,* January 29, 1979.

62. Caryle Murphy, "U.N. Cease Fire Plan Threatened in Namibia," *Washington Post,* March 2, 1979; Louis Wiznitzer, "South Africa Scuttles U.N. Plan for Namibia, *Christian Science Monitor,* May 10, 1979.

63. Caryle Murphy, "New Administrator Named for Namibia, Apparently to Head Off White Unrest," *Washington Post,* August 2, 1979.

64. Cord Meyer, "Breakthrough in Namibia," *Washington Star,* August 10, 1979.

65. Associated Press, "South Africa Says It Killed 200 in Angola," *Baltimore Sun,* June 14, 1980.

66. Editorial, "Catching up with Namibia," *The New York Times,* July 24, 1980.

67. Louis Wiznitzer, "South Africa Agrees to U.N. Namibia Plan," *Christian Science Monitor,* October 31, 1980.

68. Caryle Murphy, "South Africa Guerrillas Set Namibia Talks," *Washington Post,* December 27, 1980.

69. Joseph Lelyveld, "Namibia Conference Convenes in Geneva," *The New York Times,* January 9, 1981.

70. Joseph Lelyveld, "Namibia Parley Fails to Achieve Accord on Truce," *The New York Times,* January 14, 1981.

71. Editorial, "The Namibia Failure," *The New York Times,* January 14, 1981.

72. Anthony Lewis, "Angolans Say Cubans Leave When Namibia Free," *The New York Times,* January 23, 1981.

73. John M. Goshko, "Allies Accept New Plan on Namibia," *Washington Post,* May 8, 1981.

74. Michael Berlin, "Western Nations Veto Sanctions against South Africa," *Washington Post,* May 1, 1981.

75. Editorial, "A No Win Policy on Namibia," *The New York Times,* May 11, 1981.

76. Karen Elliott House, "Haig Is Probing News Leak from Office of Nominee for U.S. African Affairs Post," *Wall Street Journal,* June 4, 1981.

77. "U.S. Official Plans Trip to South Africa for Talk on Namibian

Independence," *Baltimore Sun,* June 6, 1981; Joseph Lelyveld, U.S. Gets South African Commitment on Namibia," *The New York Times,* June 14, 1981.

78. Juan de Onis, "U.S. May Disengage from Namibia Talks, Aide Says," *The New York Times,* June 18, 1981; "U.S. to Press for Accord on Namibia," *Washington Star,* June 21, 1981.

79. Jay Ross, "African Leaders Criticize U.S. Stand on Namibia at O.A.U. Summit," *Washington Post,* June 25, 1981.

80. Pranay B. Gupte, "Africans Condemn U.S. for Collusion on Namibian Plans," *The New York Times,* June 28, 1981.

81. John M. Goshko, "U.S. Calls Black African Charges Distortion of Namibian Policy," *Washington Post,* July 1, 1981.

82. Henry Ginger, "5 Nations Press Namibia Action," *The New York Times,* July 23, 1981.

83. Bradley Graham, "West Germany Offers Initiative on Namibia," *Washington Post,* July 30, 1981.

84. "Angola Reports South Africa Attack," *Los Angeles Times,* August 26, 1981.

85. Bernard D. Nossiter, "A U.N. Rebuke to South Africans Vetoed as U.S. Splits with Allies," *The New York Times,* September 1, 1981; "The Namibia Trap," *Wall Street Journal,* September 2, 1981.

86. Reuter News Service, "Angola Threatens to Ask Its Allies to Help Fight the South Africans," *The New York Times,* September 2, 1981; Joseph Lelyveld, "South Africa Says a Withdrawal from Angolan Areas Has Begun," *The New York Times,* August 29, 1981; Caryle Murphy, "South Africa Says Angola Bore Heavy Losses," *Washington Post,* August 30, 1981.

87. Bernard Gwertzman, "Haig Says U.S. Makes Progress in Namibia Talks," *The New York Times,* September 5, 1981.

88. Bernard D. Nossiter, "South Africans Are Ejected from U.N. Namibia Parley," *The New York Times,* September 5, 1981.

89. Ibid.

90. Jay Ross, "South Africa Said to Be Seeking a Buffer Zone for Namibia," *Washington Post,* September 5, 1981.

91. Antero Pietila, "Amid Pressure, Pretoria Transfers Power to Regime," *Baltimore Sun,* September 4, 1981.

92. Bernard D. Nossiter, "U.N. Votes to Isolate South Africa over Namibia," *The New York Times,* September 15, 1981.

93. Barbara Crossette, "Pretoria's Hand in Shadowy Conflict," *The New York Times,* September 17, 1981.

94. David Lamb, "South African Reports Accord with U.S. on

Namibia Plan," *Los Angeles Times,* September 12, 1981.

95. Caryle Murphy, "South Africa: 1,000 Slain in Angola," *Washington Post,* September 15, 1981.

96. Kim Rogal et al., "An Assault on Angola," *Newsweek,* September 7, 1981.

97. "Timetable Is Set for Namibia Pact," *The New York Times,* September 25, 1981.

98. "Namibia Rebels Agree to Back Whites' Rights," *The New York Times,* November 20, 1981.

99. Caryle Murphy, "8 African Nations Agree on Namibia," *Washington Post,* November 21, 1981.

100. "Angola Denies Namibia Accord," *Washington Post,* November 22, 1981.

101. United Press International, "Angola Reported Ready to Talk with Rebel," *The New York Times,* December 17, 1981.

102. Paul Van Slambrouck, Louis Wiznitser, "Namibia: Toughest Round of Independence Talks Ahead," *Christian Science Monitor,* December 16, 1981.

103. Bernard Gwertzman, "U.S. Official Meets with Angolan; Door Open to New Talks," *The New York Times,* January 19, 1982.

104. Dusko Doder, "Soviets, Angolans Strengthen Ties, Discuss Namibia," *Washington Post,* January 22, 1982.

105. Allister Sparks, "South African Troops Raid Guerrilla Base in Angola," *Washington Post,* March 17, 1982.

106. "Western Officials Preparing for New Namibian Dialogue," *Washington Post,* April 1, 1982.

107. "Namibia and the United Nations: Cross Fire," *The Economist,* April 3, 1982.

108. Allister Sparks, "Namibian Rebels Battle South Africans in Biggest Assault," *Washington Post,* April 22, 1982; Joseph Lelyveld, "Namibian Guerrillas Make Deepest Raid in More Than a Year," *The New York Times,* April 17, 1982.

109. Antero Pietila, "Whites Fall Back in Namibia Census," *Baltimore Sun,* April 3, 1982.

110. Joseph Lelyveld, "South African-Zambian Meeting Set," *The New York Times,* April 30, 1982; Allister Sparks, "South Africa, Zambia Leaders Conduct Rare Dialogue," *Washington Post,* May 7, 1982.

111. Jay Ross, "State Is Optimistic on Namibia Pact," *Washington Post,* June 11, 1982.

112. Bernard Weinraub, "United States Officials Hopeful on Namibia Talks," *The New York Times,* June 14, 1982.

113. Bernard Weinraub, "United States Reports Progress in Namibia Talks," *The New York Times,* July 14, 1982.

114. "Botha Says Accord on Cubans Must Precede Namibia Pact," *Washington Post,* September 15, 1982.

115. Joseph Lelyveld, "South Africa Appears Eager to Oust Namibian Regime," *The New York Times,* September 25, 1982.

116. Richard M. Weintraub, "U.S., Angola Officials Meet for Talks on Namibia, Cuban Military Presence," *Washington Post,* October 6, 1982.

117. Jay Ross, "Angolan Expresses Pessimism on State of Namibia Talks," *Washington Post,* October 16, 1982.

118. Mary Anne Fitzgerald, "U.S. Insists on Cuban Pullout, Bush Tells Africans," *Washington Post,* November 20, 1982.

119. "South Africa Official, Schultz to Meet for Talks in D.C.," *Baltimore Sun,* November 24, 1982.

120. Richard M. Weintraub, "South African Sees Real Chance for U.S. to Solve Namibia Independence Issue," *Washington Post,* November 27, 1982.

121. Allister Sparks, "South Africa, Angola Meet on Issue of Cuban Troops," *Washington Post,* December 9, 1982.

122. "Mudge to Quit as Namibia's Interim Leader," *Washington Post,* January 11, 1983.

123. Joseph Lelyveld, "Namibia Loses Governing Role to South Africa," *The New York Times,* January 19, 1983.

5 The International Outlaw

The inability of the world community to hobble the apartheid system in South Africa should stand as an object lesson. International pressure has definite limits in being able to alter the internal policies of a defiant nation. Two important multinational organizations, the UN on a universal level and the Organization of African Unity on a regional level, have tried and failed to make the South African government change its racial policies in a significant manner; modify them, perhaps, but not alter them radically. This chapter examines arms-embargo attempts launched against South Africa and the minimum success achieved, as well as South Africa's nuclear-arms capacity.

Embargo Attempts against South Africa

The 1977 Mandatory Arms Embargo

The 1977 mandatory arms embargo enacted by the UN against South Africa was the culmination of twenty-plus years of UN efforts to eradicate apartheid and force the South African government to give equal treatment to its nonwhite citizens. The embargo enacted on November 4, 1977,[1] would have been stronger if five industrial nations had not vetoed proposals to expand the embargo to all commercial dealings of any kind with South Africa. Four days earlier, the United States, the United Kingdom, France, Canada, and West Germany had joined together to block wording that would have enacted a full-scale commercial boycott. The United Kingdom, for example, had $7 billion of investment in South Africa at the time of the action, and its government cast its veto in response to the wishes of its corporations threatened by the total-boycott proposal.[2] Similar reasoning motivated the United States in its veto actions. The watered-down resolution that eventually passed the UN did not even strike out current armament-licensing arrangements. As a result, the corporations that had sold arms in the past to South Africa still had an opportunity to profit from their actions.[3]

On December 9, 1977, the UN Security Council unanimously voted to set up a watchdog committee to administer effectively the mandatory arms embargo against South Africa.[4] Then, in mid-December 1977, the General Assembly adopted fourteen resolutions condemning South Africa and its apartheid system. This was three more than the number of resolutions the General Assembly passed on the subject in 1976.[5] The UN-attempted move toward all-out opposition to South Africa at the end of 1977 was complemented by various resolutions adopted by the Organization of African Unity and individual diplomatic actions taken by some of the more-important black African nations. At the end of May 1978, Liberia, Senegal, and the Ivory Coast called for the U.S. government to take the lead in retaliatory economic actions aimed at convincing South Africa to change its racial policy.[6]

The mandatory arms embargo adopted by the UN in November 1977 had to be a severe blow to South Africa.[7] True, the Pretoria regime had taken effective action to build its own arms-production facilities in its country, and it possessed the money to purchase military supplies on the black market and also retained rights to existing licensing arrangements. However, in public, no one who was a member of the UN could admit to be selling arms to the Pretoria regime. This shunning of South Africa even included Israel. Soon after the embargo was enacted, Israel announced that it would conduct its relations with South Africa on a legal basis alone and would not violate the Security Council resolution. Many people did not believe that Israel would abandon South Africa. Without doubt, however, armaments dealings between the nations would become more covert and, thus, by definition, more expensive.[8]

South Africa Defies the Embargo

South Africa for its part spewed defiance. The UN was criticized in the harshest of terms. Economic Affairs Minister Chris Heunis warned foreign companies doing business in South Africa that it might order them to produce militarily usable materials, presumably under the existing armaments licenses that South Africa was able to retain. Justice Minister Jimmy Kruger, backing his colleague Heunis, accused President Carter of applying double standards by supporting and not vetoing an arms embargo at the UN.[9]

Although many of the statements made by Heunis, Botha, and Kruger could be dismissed as defiant propaganda, the substantive message behind their remarks was clear. Many European and U.S. corporations depend more on South Africa than South Africa depends on them. If these corporations wish to stay in the country and coin profits, they might be called upon to assist South African military defense in a more-overt manner.[10]

In early January 1978, Nigeria, beginning to understand the power that its position as a major oil exporter now gave it, started to agitate in the Security Council for stronger actions to be taken against Rhodesia and South Africa. Nigeria noted with dismay that the United States, the United Kingdom, France, West Germany and Canada had abstained on a General Assembly vote calling for an arms embargo, even though the motion was only advisory in nature. At the same time, the Nigerians did note and encourage the Western nations to continue their peacekeeping attempts in Namibia. Western nations were quick to observe that the embargo being proposed against oil shipments to South Africa was counterproductive to the Namibia actions.[11]

Since no matter what they did neither South Africa nor Israel would receive approval for their actions from the UN, they kept their dealings on a bilateral level, out in the open. At times it seemed that their talks about the need for added commercial trade between the two nations was so provocative in nature that its main purpose had to be to wave a red flag in front of the UN.[12] Both nations talked of the need for scientific cooperation between their countries and stated that regular exchange of scientists must take place. Observers read this item as primarily affecting scientists involved in nuclear- and military-armaments research. Similar statements made by Israel and South Africa concerning the need for more civilian-aviation contacts between both countries was greeted in the same skeptical manner by outside observers. Israel and South Africa clearly were striving to obtain a balance in their trade. Israel's exports in all categories to South Africa had declined from $34.7 million in 1975 to $26.7 million in 1976 to $20.6 million during the first eleven months of 1977 before the embargo started.

In contrast, South African exports to Israel had increased from $40.2 million in 1975 to $45.2 million in 1976 to $48.7 million in the first eleven months of 1977. The major Israeli exports to South Africa were electronic goods, machinery, and textiles.[13] Then Foreign Minister of Israel Moshe Dayan reacted angrily to worldwide criticisms of his country's dealings with South Africa. He was particularly perturbed at statements condemning this practice made by U.S. President Jimmy Carter. Said Dayan, "It is not the business of the President of the United States whom we have for friends so long as we are within the law."[14]

In April 1978, Canada, a country that has been quick to criticize South Africa for it apartheid actions, announced a code of conduct for all of its companies operating in South Africa. The regulations were not backed up with sanctions for noncompliance by Canadian companies, and as a result, Canada's code could be looked on more as exhortatory than mandatory. The standard demands usually found in such codes were contained—for example, equal pay should be given for equal work from employees in South Africa; wages should be at least 50 percent above the subsistence level; all black trade unions, whether registered or not, should have bargaining rights; blacks should be trained for job promotion; working, eating, and other facilities should be integrated to the fullest extent possible; and annual reports showing compliance should be filed with the government, although no measures were taken to punish those corporations that did not. If Canada had wanted to take truly strict steps against South Africa, it could have ended commonwealth tariff preferences for South African goods exported to Canada, and it also would have have halted tax benefits for Canadian companies operating in Namibia. Neither action occurred, although the Canadian government promised to follow all developments closely.[15]

In June 1978, the foreign ministers of the nine European Economic Community member nations agreed to postpone any new economic sanctions against South Africa for fear these actions could upset efforts to arrange a peaceful transition to black rule in Namibia.[16] A few months later, and perhaps not unrelated, given West Germany's leading role in dictating European Economic Community policy, Alcatel and Siemen's AG of West Germany announced that South Africa had awarded them a $20 million contract to improve telephone equipment and service in South Africa.[17]

UN Opposition to South Africa

In the wake of the UN mandatory arms embargo, many nations of the Third World and the Soviet bloc again called for a mandatory oil embargo against South Africa. All doing so realized that the large industrial nations of the world probably would not take such a step and also that should a mandatory embargo take place, the black neighboring nations to South Africa would find their own economies affected in an equally drastic manner. Sure that their demands for an embargo extension would not be accepted, they sat back and took as much propaganda profit as possible.[18]

As the calls for further pressure on South Africa echoed through the halls of the UN and the Organization of African Unity, an occasional disparate viewpoint was heard—for example, the attorney general of Kenya, Charles Njonjo, stated in an August 1978 television interview in Nairobi that his opinion was that every African nation should have an ambassador in South Africa. In his viewpoint, diplomatic feelers rather than economic punishment were the way to convince South Africa to change. It is safe to say that such a viewpoint was not popular with many of his colleagues.[19]

In late August 1978, the UN held another of its seemingly endless number of conferences concerning the situation in South Africa. This one, entitled the United Nations Anti-Racism Conference, took place in Geneva. In its final session, the delegates passed a twenty-six-point declaration condemning the developing relations between South Africa and Israel and warned against nuclear cooperation between the two countries. Neither the United States nor Israel was present at the conference; their boycott was a protest against the 1975 General Assembly resolution that had equated racism with Zionism. South Africa also had boycotted the conference, and the nine members of the European Economic Community, along with Australia, New Zealand, and Canada, walked out when the final resolution was being considered.[20]

The five Western contact nations attempted a Namibia settlement between South Africa and SWAPO during October 1978. Their intervention was not greeted with approval by many of the more-militant UN members. They were bothered that the proposed agreement seemed to allow South Africa to escape the threat of economic sanctions against their own country, and in fact, many of these nations feared that an eventual South African surrender of Namibia might be the only satisfaction demanded by the five Western powers. In such a case, apartheid could hold sway indefinitely within South Africa.[21]

During 1979, South Africa, in effect, was forced to cope with the oil embargo that the UN had failed to arrange. Iran, after the revolution deposing the shah, cut off supplies and forced South Africa to buy on the spot market and to engage in bartering arrangements that would bring it the oil necessary to operate the economy. Prices for petroleum products rose and Pretoria, as counteraction, moved to increase its investment in the Sasol complexes that would turn the nation's abundant coal supply to oil. Because gold prices were rising as oil supplies were falling, South Africa was able at great cost to weather the worst of the oil disruption storm.[22] Despite all predictions to the contrary, South Africa has shown an ability to subsist without a steady supply of foreign oil. Their success in this undertaking must have sent a message to the countries of the UN and, most particularly, the countries of the Organization of African Unity that the inherent strengths of South Africa would carry it through many crises capable of bringing down less strongly entrenched governments.[23]

During 1979–1980, UN activity aimed against South Africa continued but took up fewer of the headlines. The world faced many other problems: from continuing difficulties in economic relationships between the developed and the developing world, to the takeover in Afghanistan to the Iranian hostage crisis and the Iran-Iraq war. The coming to power of a black government in Zimbabwe gave hope that the Namibia crisis might be settled before long. It was not realistic to expect similar success as to the South African political situation. After all, the white rebel nation in Rhodesia, with limited resources, managed fifteen years of defiance. It is not surprising that even with worldwide disapproval, South Africa is able to continue its own course for a significantly longer number of years.

In July 1980, the Organization of African Unity took the lead from the UN and vowed, at the end of a four-day summit meeting in Freetown, Sierra Leone, to place the most effective pressure possible against South Africa. The organization instructed the foreign ministers of Sierra Leone, Algeria, Nigeria, and Angola to participate in the September 30, 1980, UN Security Council meeting and to press oil-embargo and other sanctions against South Africa.[24] Organization Secretary General Edem Kodjo noted South Africa imported 99 percent of its oil, which represents 20 percent of its energy needs. "The country would be very vulnerable to an effective international embargo. Oil sanctions probably represent the most effective form of external pressure that could be exerted, even though South Africa has been building up a strategic stockpile of oil for over a decade and has made strenuous efforts to reduce its oil consumption."[25]

In the wake of the Geneva conference failure, at the end of 1980 and the start of 1981, to solve the Namibian crisis, the Japanese government urged the General Assembly to consider imposing sanctions on South Africa if its attitude on the protectorate question continued. Japanese Ambassador Masahiro Nisibori stated, "If the intransigent attitude of South Africa results in the failure of the international community's efforts, the international community will have no alternative but to consider further measures to insure South Africa's compliance."[26] Soviet Ambassador Rickhard S. Ovinnikov supported this statement.

The UN Keeps up the Pressure

In the wake of further stalling by South Africa on Namibia and the continued failure of the five Western nations to effect a power transfer, the UN again moved toward mandatory sanctions against South Africa. At the end of April 1981, the five Western contact nations were afraid that imposition of mandatory sanctions would thwart further their efforts in Namibia. As a result, the US, France, Canada, West Germany, and the United Kingdom attempted to politick to keep the mandatory-economic-sanctions issue from ever officially coming to a vote. The African nations were unhappy with a compromise suggestion made by the delegate from Ireland, Noel Dorr, the president of the Security Council. Dorr's proposal strongly urged all states concerned to use every means to facilitate the implementation of Resolution 435, which was aimed at bringing peace to Namibia.[27]

Despite Mr. Dorr's intervention, the full-scale economic-sanctions matter did come to a vote on May 1, 1981. The United States, the United Kingdom, and France vetoed four Security Council resolutions that had called for mandatory sanctions against South Africa for its failure to grant independence to Namibia. The United States and France said they would observe the 1977 embargo but did not vote for the imposition of a new embargo because they feared that Namibia settlement possibilities would be harmed by taking action against South Africa at this time.[28]

The discord between the Western nations—most particularly, the United States—and the African nations became stronger in late June 1981. The Organization of African Unity unanimously accused the Reagan administration of sinister moves to circumvent the efforts made by the United Nations to achieve a settlement in Namibia.[29] The United States condemned the action taken by the Organization of African Unity, but it is clear that Western peace-settlement actions in Namibia are causing an ideological split among the nations in the world as how to deal with the larger problem of ending the apartheid regime in South Africa.

The June 1981 OAU condemnation of U.S. support for South Africa was echoed during September of the same year to the full UN. The United States split from its allies and was the only negative vote to a Security Council resolution that would have condemned South Africa for its massive military raid into southern Angola during late August 1981. The U.S. veto defeated the resolution. Thirteen had voted in favor, and the United Kingdom had abstained. The U.S. reasoning for its veto was that it feared that if the resolution had been enacted, South Africa would have been presented with a further reason for stalling on the Namibia question.[30] It was clear to all that if the Reagan administration would not stand for a verbal condemnation against South Africa, it stood to reason that it would never permit a more-stringent boycott to be enacted than was presently in effect.

South African Armaments before the Embargo

Preparing for the Embargo

As well experienced and equipped as the South African military forces undeniably are at the present time, this strategic situation would have become even better but for the 1977 UN arms embargo. Since this worldwide prohibition against selling arms to the Republic of South Africa went into effect, the South Africans have been thrown back upon sanction-breaking purchases and increased local production to fulfill requirements. These forced steps have obliged the Pretoria government to make major outlays of time, effort, and most important, money that from the South African military perspective could have been better utilized by open free-market purchases of arms in the international market. The situation, however, would have been far graver if advanced preparations had not been made. These steps are detailed in this section.

South Africa had received ample warnings of the possibility of an international arms embargo. An earlier UN arms embargo against South Africa, enacted in 1963–1964, had for the most part failed,[31] but as political relations between the Republic of South Africa and the UN worsened, it was clear that the world organization would try again.

France, Italy, the United Kingdom, and to a lesser degree, the United States had been notable in ignoring the earlier armaments embargo. The U.S. Arms Control and Disarmament Agency estimated that South Africa purchased about $360 million in foreign arms between 1965 and 1974. France was charged with selling perhaps $225 million of this amount to South Africa.[32]

At the time of the 1977 mandatory arms embargo, South Africa possessed a 38,000-member standing army, backed by 13,000 ready reserves; 100 tanks, most of which were built in the United Kingdom; a commando organization; a well-furnished air force; and a navy that included six former British Royal Navy destroyers and frigates, five French-built submarines, and six Israeli-made Rashef gunboats with Gabriel missiles.[33]

At the time of the 1977 arms embargo, South Africa was spending about $1.9 billion annually on defense, 18 percent of a total budget that was 21.3 percent higher than the 1976 budget. It was estimated that $2.3 billion would be spent on defense in 1978 and that South Africa had spent $137 million on foreign arms purchases in 1975. It was also estimated that this figure rose to between $200 million and $300 million in 1977 prior to the embargo.[34]

In the period before the embargo, France acted in a manner consistent with its arms-selling profile of being an energetic supplier to any nation or group with sufficient available cash. France built the Koeberg nuclear power plant near Capetown for $1.2 billion. Perhaps it is not proper to consider this a military sale, but its atomic-energy uses certainly could be military, as South Africa and France were both well aware. Most South African helicopters, alouettes, and super frelons and many of their missiles, submarines, Mirages, and Impala fighter jets were manufactured in South Africa with Agosta-class submarines (two) and with type-A 69 frigates (two). Also in 1976 France sold Exocets missiles in an unknown quantity to the Republic of South Africa.[35] These same-type missiles were used with great effect in spring 1982 by the Argentine Air Force in destroying British warships during the Falkland Islands conflict.

The South African air force possessed 578 military aircraft at the time of the 1977 embargo. At least 178 of these, more than one-third of the total, were partially or totally of U.S. origin. Some of these planes—specifically, some F86 Sabre fighters and C130 Hercules transports—had been delivered before the 1963 executive order by the president of the United States ordering that the UN optional arms embargo be observed by the U.S. government. Thus, these sales could not be counted as sanctions busting. Since that time, fifteen Lockheed L100s, seven Sweringen Merlin IV transports, and twelve or more Cessna model 185 skywagons have been ordered and delivered.[36]

In addition to those planes built in the United States and sold to South Africa before 1977, a group of U.S.-designed and -powered planes, assembled elsewhere, also reached South Africa. These included nineteen Piaggio P166 patrol planes, forty AM-3C Bosbok utility craft, and forty C-4M Kudic liaison planes. The Lockheed L100, which is almost an exact replica of the C130 Hercules cargo plane flown by the U.S. Air Force, can carry 43,000 pounds of cargo or ninety-two combat troops for distances of up to 2,500 miles. Except for increased range and payload capabilities, some added electronics, and a paratroop door, differences between the two planes are minimal.[37]

The characteristics of the Sweringen Merlin IV are similar. It is powered by two turbo-prop engines and is capable of carrying fifteen to twenty passengers or up to 5,000 pounds of cargo for several hundred miles. It also would classify as a civilian plane, even though Chile and Oman have used it for military purposes. In like manner to the Lockheed L100 being an exact replica of the military C130 Hercules cargo plane, the Cessna model 185 skywagon can have both military and civilian uses. The military version is called the U17 and has taken an active-support role in border patrols in the United States. Both versions are capable of transporting up to six people for 1,000 miles and are powered by a single 300-horsepower engine.[38]

Those investigating possible arms sales to South Africa have focused upon another group of transactions that might, or might not, have been intended for military utilization purposes.[39] Guaranteed loans by the United States Export-Import Bank for sales to, ostensibly, civil buyers of Beechcraft model 55 planes and Baron model 58 planes to be used in South Africa have been questioned. The T141A Cochese is a military version of the Baron model 58 plane. The Cochese is used widely as a military-trainer plane in the United States, Spain, and Turkey.

Similarly, during May 1976, a United States Export-Import Bank discount loan of $163,000 to South African buyers was used to finance the sale of two Helio aircraft model 295 supercourier planes that also had been used throughout the world for military missions. Export-Import Bank funding for planes intended, in theory, for civilian use in South Africa also included the Beechcraft Bonanza A36, a single-engine utility plane that was used by the shah's air force in Iran and also by military in Mexico and Spain. Other civilian planes destined for South Africa and financed by Export-Import Bank loans included Cessna Executives, a plane that is very close to the model 185 skywagon used in Vietnam; Golden Eagles; Conquests; and Citations. In addition, purchases were noted of Piper Supercubs and the Mitsubichi MU, a two-turn turbo-prop STOL Transport produced in San Angelo, Texas, by Mitsubichi International.

During the 1963–1977 period, the United States assisted South Africa in installing a military-communications-and-intelligence system near the Simonstown naval base, close by the junctures of the Indian and Atlantic Oceans. The United States also sold about $27 million worth of spare parts to the South African government for pre-1963-sold C130 transport planes.

During the 1970s, especially in the years before the UN arms embargo came into effect, South Africa also purchased armaments extensively and wisely from industrialized nations other than the United States and France. In 1976, South Africa purchased two Reshelf fast patrol boats equipped with guided missiles and other models of such fast boats from Israel. In 1974, South Africa purchased fifty-four Tigercat surface-to-air missiles and forty-one Centurion tanks from Jordan. In 1971, three HS125 light transport planes and three WASP helicopters were obtained from the United Kingdom. Also in 1971, Aermacchi AM 3Cs were bought from Italy, and six Corvettes with surface-to-surface missiles were purchased from Portugal.[40]

In addition to the foreign purchases made in anticipation of the UN mandatory 1977 arms embargo, South Africa had been at work producing armaments at home as well. Since the early 1960s, it had become self-sufficient in the production of rifles, tear gas, ammunition, and field guns up to 90 millimeters. South Africa had also developed its own armored personnel carriers for internal usage, the 18-ton Ratel that could be equipped with either a machine gun or a 20-millimeter gun. It also possessed long experience in manufacturing the Eland armored car, a version of the French Panhard AML. Under license from Italy, South Africa had been making the Impala trainer and ground-attack jets, a version of the Italian Aermacchi MB326 trainer that was manufactured locally and that contained a sublicensed Rolls Royce Viper engine.[41]

South African Armaments after the Embargo

South Africa Scrambles and Survives

When the UN mandatory arms embargo finally came into effect in 1977, its wording displeased many African nations. They had hoped to have South Africa officially declared a threat to international peace. If they had been successful, sanctions agreements with terms far stricter than a mere arms-sale embargo would have followed as a matter of course. Instead, the plea-bargained agreement with the Western world was such that it was agreed for the first time that arms sales to South Africa were a threat to the maintenance of international peace and security. As a result, it was declared that a full arms embargo against South Africa was proper under Chapter 7 of the UN charter. All sales of armaments by UN members and any new licensing agreement or new technology needed to carry out current licensing agreements was banned. African nations failed in an attempt to have current South African licenses revoked.

As a result of the UN arms embargo, sophisticated weapons such as the Mirage I jet fighter still could be produced in South Africa on license from France. In the same manner, South African–designed and –manufactured— with French assistance—Cactus Crotale surface-to-air missiles also continued to be assembled. The licensing concession was a major boon to South Africa. It also could be assured that UN member Israel and non-UN members Taiwan and South Korea undoubtedly would defy all embargoes and still sell armaments to South Africa.

A further note of encouragement to the South African spirits was that the distinction between military and civilian usage of equipment remained as vague in the minds of corporate arms dealers as ever. An example of one such transaction was the sale of Boeing Jumbo 747 jets to South Africa. These monstrously large planes were used for civilian purposes in most of the world, but in South Africa they were immediately employed to ferry troops to Angola from military staging points in Namibia.[42]

One sanctions-breaking deal was uncovered by the British Broadcasting Company television program, "Panorama." A West German ship called the *Tugelaland* turned out to be leased on open charter to the wholly owned, subsidiary of the South African state-owned arms subsidiary Armscor. The *Tugelaland* had sailed to the Caribbean island of Antigua and had been loaded with expertly designed long-range shells that had been shipped to Antigua by Space Research Corporation, an arms manufacturer headquartered on the Canada-Vermont border, that owned a small research facility on Antigua. The loaded vessel then set sail for South Africa.

Transactions like this one have allowed South Africa to buy in recent years an estimated 40,000 special long-range 155-millimeter shells and a substantial but unknown quantity of guns, radar, and support equipment. These long-range shells counteract Soviet-made 122-millimeter long-barrel cannons that the Cubans had employed successfully in Angola.[43]

Space Research Corporation has been in constant trouble with the U.S. and Canadian governments over its manufacture and shipment of arms to South Africa. On March 25, 1980, Space Research Corporation (which had undergone a name change and had become Sabre Industries Inc.) and two of its principal officers pleaded guilty to shipping the ultra-long-range artillery shell casings and other military weapons involved in the Antigua incident to South Africa. The sanctions-breaking operation was undertaken without receiving an export license from the State Department office of Munitions Control. This was a violation of federal law for which the firm and its principal scientist Gerald Viebold, and chief operations officer Rodgers L. Gregory could have received, but did not, prison sentences.

The Canadian government also acted against Space Research Corporation because the company's headquarters spanned the U.S.-Canada border and was located in both nations. During August 1980, Space Research Corporation of Quebec was fined $55,000 by a Canadian court for violating the UN arms-sale embargo. The company pleaded guilty to selling at least 33,000 Howitzer shells and parts to the Republic of South Africa between October 1976 and September 1978. The false export certificates filed in Canada named Spain, Antigua, and Barbados as the supposed destinations of the shells.[44]

In a similar arms-embargo-violation action, a Johannesburg gun dealer was indicted during November 1978 for smuggling $350,000 worth of firearms and ammunition from Chicago's O'Hare Airport to Johannesburg in shipments labeled as playground equipment and underwater-breathing devices.[45]

Another large U.S. corporation, the Olin Corporation, one of the leading U.S. manufacturers of firearms, was indicted on March 14, 1978, for conspiring illegally to ship arms to South Africa and for filing twenty fraudulent statements with the U.S. State Department as to the eventual destination of the goods. Olin was charged with falsifying export documents on 3,200 firearms and 20 million rounds of ammunition. These goods supposedly were shipped to the Canary Islands, Greece, Austria, and Mozambique. The conglomerate Olin owns Winchester Rifle Corporation, whose sales are $289 million a year. Winchester salesmen, acting on their own, were charged with making the offending deal. The indictment was the first felony charge made by the U.S. government for violating the 1963 U.S. arms embargo.[46]

Many corporations in all countries, the United States included, wished to continue the lucrative arms sales to South Africa after the institution of the 1977 UN mandatory arms-sales embargo. Unlike those who chose to break sanctions directly, a number of other corporations sought to find legal methods of selling arms. Immediately after the embargo came into place, heavy pressure was placed upon the U.S. State Department to permit civilian-aircraft sales to South Africa. Six Cessna planes, valued at about $500,000, were sold during December 1977 for crop-dusting purposes. It was announced that forty-four other planes targeted for the same purpose soon would be sold.[47] The State Department was subjected to heavy criticism for allowing the sales, since the planes could be used for military purposes. In response, the department said that only if it could be shown that the parts or planes would be used directly or indirectly for military purposes by the South African government would the sales be banned. In all other cases, export permits would be granted or denied based solely on the merits of the individual case in question.[48]

Encouraged by their initial success in obtaining export licenses for sales to South Africa, some U.S. corporations increased lobbying efforts with the

U.S. Congress and the Executive Branch. Their hope was to expand the definition of permitted civilian-purpose sales. By December 1978, many U.S. manufacturers were agitating openly against what they considered to be more-stringent-than-necessary application of the arms-sale embargo by the U.S. government. In these complaints, specific reference was made to the Department of Commerce's February 1978 ban against any sale of a product or technology that might be used by South Africa's police or armed forces. The U.S. government justified this regulation by pointing out that given the integrated nature of South African society, it was hard to guarantee South African affiliates would not resell purchased products directly or indirectly to the police or military. Unimpressed by this reasoning, General Tire and Rubber Company claimed that it had lost over $1 million in after-tax profits in the first year of the embargo because of the ban. General Tire pointed out that it possessed less than a 25 percent interest in its South African affiliate and that less than 1 percent of total sales went to the Republic of South Africa military or police. Because it was no longer able to receive General Tire technology, the South African affiliate of the company proceeded to sign a six-to-ten-year contract with General Tire and Rubber's West German competition. Representative John Sieberling of Ohio pressed hard for commerce- and state-regulation changes to benefit General Tire and Rubber Company and Goodyear International Corporation, which also possessed a wholly owned South African subsidiary.[49]

The South African Weapons Position Improves

An August 1980 published update on South African military supplies contains little new of note.[50] Given the restrictions under which its government has been operating, its military strength is most respectable. However, it is less well equipped than otherwise would be the case. A question must exist whether or not South Africa can afford less than the best of military weapons given the size and potential destructive power available to its enemies. In the report, emphasis was placed on South Africa's ability to build for itself advanced aircraft parts including engines, armaments, and avionics. South Africa also is capable of building its own helicopters, armored-vehicle chassis and engines, and even a version of laminar armor. It can construct patrol-boat hulls, though not their engines or armaments. Thanks to licensing arrangements, on-the-spot construction of the French Mirage aircraft, the Miacchi jet-training aircraft, French Panhard armored cars, Israeli missile boats, and French Crotele surface-to-air and air-to-air missiles also can, and does, take place in South Africa. Also, South Africa can construct French-licensed artillery pieces, infantry weapons, and a wide range of ammunition.

A report of the International Institute for Strategic Studies in London concerning the military balance for 1980–1981 shows that South Africa still is moving forward in arms production and purchase.[51] For the first time in several years, Sherman tanks were found to be part of the South African arsenal. These have been long obsolete in most armies but can be modernized with new guns and engines for use for self-propelled artillery, as is happening in South Africa. South Africa was credited with possessing twenty-five new Agosta-Bell 205 multipurpose utility helicopters. This vehicle is a licensed South African–built Italian version of the U.S. Air Force Bell UH-1 David UH-1F helicopter used in the Vietnam War. It can carry a pilot and fourteen passengers and also serves for troop or equipment transport, tactical support, casualty evacuation, and rescue missions.

In the strike-craft category, South Africa, in 1980–1981, has purchased three more Minister-class fast-attack craft and has six more on order. In 1979–1980, its government possessed only three Minister-class fast-attack craft. In addition, the South African navy has acquired six single-missile Dvora-class crafts built in Israel.[52]

In 1978,[53] the Republic of South Africa possessed almost no heavy mortars, but two years later its supply consisted of two hundred heavy mortars of 120 millimeters each. As to artillery, in addition to standing supplies of 88-millimeter (twenty-five pounders), 140-millimeter (5.5 inch), and G5 155-millimeter guns, South Africa now possessed fifteen M7105 self-propelled guns and forty of the 155-millimeter towed and fifty self-propelled M109A1 Howitzers. No indication as to which nation sold these artillery pieces to the South African army is contained, but the U.S. is thought to be the only nation with these pieces in service. The M109A1 Howitzer has an eighteen-kilometer range and has been in production since 1970. Earlier versions were used elsewhere in the world.

In 1978, the Republic of South Africa possessed 287 Saracen armed personnel carriers and locally developed Ratel infantry fighting vehicles. By 1980–1981, they have the same 287 Saracen carriers but now have 1,000 Ratel infantry fighting vehicles, all locally produced.

Defense spending in South Africa remained high and constant during the 1970s. In real rand amounts, the outlay did increase notably because rising gold prices served to make far more money available to the Pretoria government than otherwise would have been the case.

Armscor

The South African para-statal (that is, state-owned) business, Armscor (the armaments production and development corporation), is largely responsible for the respectable showing in arms acquisition attained recently by South Africa. In similar embargo circumstances, few nations would have performed more efficiently.[54] Armscor was established in 1968 as an antidote to the arms embargoes sure to come. Armscor procures, develops, and manufactures products required by defense forces for economic and strategic reasons. The nine manufacturing subsidiaries of Armscor and the numerous service subsidiaries with which it contracts employ in excess of 20,000 people. Along with purchasing from other nations, contracting to private industry in its own country, and producing itself the weapons that fall in the cracks, Armscor is an effective vehicle for evading an arms embargo.[55]

Armscor continues to be a potent vehicle for South Africa's military preparedness. Between 1968 and 1978, its allocation of government funds rose from R32 million a year to R979 million a year. In the 1980 budget, the amount of government funds allocated to Armscor was estimated at R1.2 billion. In addition, Armscor was scheduled to raise an additional R100 million on domestic capital markets during the second half of 1980. The number of people working for Armscor has risen steadily. Present estimates are that it employs closer to 23,000 than the often quoted figure of 20,000 workers. Armscor trades with six hundred local companies in South Africa in addition to what it produces itself or buys abroad.[56]

In the past few years South Africa has become a net exporter of arms, and it is alleged that South African arms were captured by liberation units in the Spanish Sahara War from Moroccan troops who had possessed them. It also seems clear that Armscor has served as a middleman in arms transactions with UNITA in Angola and has sold to Jonas Savimbi's forces many weapons produced in South Africa. In like manner, rumors persist that Armscor owns a well-concealed 20 percent share in Space Research Corporation, the clandestine shell shipper located on the Canada-U.S. border.[57]

There is no doubt that Armscor is trying to improve relations with Taiwan and Israel. If Armscor is able to work out a deal so that cruise missiles can be employed, it would give South Africa a potent new weapon. Israel has a stockpile of two hundred or more nuclear bombs and can deliver warheads to attack its Arab enemies or even parts of the USSR. South Africa would like very much to get its hands on such a weapon so it could possess a similar capability to keep its unfriendly neighbors at bay. Cruise missiles are highly effective surface-to-air nuclear deterrents.[58] Recent discussions on the cruise missile are in keeping with the statement made in Parliament in early February 1979 by Prime Minister Botha to the effect that South Africa has made a major technology breakthrough that has enabled it to become independent of imports both as to air-to-air and air-to-ground missiles. If true, these cruise weapons would replace weapons of this nature sold to South Africa by France and Israel before, and perhaps after, the embargo.[59]

South Africa Increases Its Weapons Supply

Immediately before Christmas 1980, the role of Israel as a possible large-scale arms supplier of South Africa was brought into sharp focus. South African Finance Minister Owen Horwood went to Israel to sign a wide-ranging economic agreement with that similarly isolated nation. Nothing about military arms sales was mentioned, but most observers found it difficult to conceive that such wide-ranging dealings would not contain a hidden military protocol.

In the open portion of the South African–Israel agreement, Israel was extended $165 million of trade credits over three years. South Africa also agreed to extend its investment in Israel from $50 to $60 million. Promises for future negotiations on the sale of South African coal to Israel also were contained.

In the past few years, Israel has produced significant quantities of advanced weapons including the Kfir fighter-bomber and has sold them with rising frequency to Latin American governments. Mexico is the latest country in the long line of nations interested in Kfir purchase. Such transactions have become easier since the United States has lifted its contractual prohibition on Israel's selling of weapons made with U.S. components to selected third-party nation buyers. It would be relatively easy for Israel to sell the Kfir fighter-bomber to one of the approved nations in Latin America and then to protest innocence if resale to South Africa occurs. Such a transaction would free Israel from a direct, unilateral violation of the UN arms embargo.[60]

In addition to making purchases abroad, South Africa has been working hurriedly at home to improve its weapons supply. As years have passed, South Africa's position as a significant armed producer has become assured. It can be considered along with India, Israel, Taiwan, Brazil, and Argentina as being among the leading developing-country arms suppliers. Chile, Israel, Taiwan, and Paraguay purchase South African weapons as do some of the black African nations that some day might fight the Pretoria government. Of course, the South African military is the largest purchaser of locally produced arms by far. All the standard light weapons and ammunition are, as expected, by now, produced in South Africa.[61]

South Africa has profited from the pre-1977 arms-ban-licensing agreements. The Pretoria government has improved the components of these foreign-designed weapons so that they closely resemble the best available weapons anywhere in the world in categories such as fighter planes, surface-to-surface missiles, personnel carriers, and trainer planes. Only one newly designed South African weapon, the long-range, high-speed armored personnel carrier, has reached the world market. It is called the Ratel, possesses a 900-mile range, and has been widely accepted in the world's arms trade.[62]

    South Africa also has smuggled up-to-date component parts of military equipment from other nations to fit weapons the local arms industry has constructed partially on its own. A South African air-to-air missile that is similar to the U.S. sidewinder is suspected of being guided by U.S. computers. In a variant of this tactic, it is charged that India has smuggled tanks into South Africa. On site, they have been altered slightly before being introduced into Namibian combat. Israel is suspected of sending naval fast-attack craft that are altered similarly in South Africa.[63]

    The South African desire to be fully armed against all possible military adversaries was underlined when the 1981-1982 governmental budget was published. Military spending would be increased by 40 percent. The amount to be spent was $2.75 billion in contrast with the $1.97 billion estimated spent in 1980-1981.[64] In the current climate of wars, near wars, and armed insurrections, South Africa is sure to continue purchasing and producing more weapons.

The Reagan Administration's Attitude

The willingness of the Reagan administration to treat South Africa in a less-condemnatory fashion produced benefits for the South African military. The U.S. Commerce Department, with the concurrence of the State Department, loosened restrictions on nonmilitary sales to South Africa during February 1982. In the future, it would be possible for U.S. corporations to sell personal computers, calculators, personal communications equipment, and if no potential military use is contemplated, chemical and industrial equipment. Critics were quick to point out that computers are easily adaptable to many sophisticated military uses. The chairman of the Subcommittee on Africa in the House of Representatives, Howard Wolpe of Michigan, termed the new policy a very tragic mistake. The Organization of African Unity was quick to add its condemnation.[65]

    U.S. corporations jumped into the breach with great speed and determination. Requests were made and granted for a Sperry Univac 1182 computer to be sold to a subsidiary of Armscor. An IBM 4341 computer and a Data General MV/8000 were sold to Barlow Rand, a conglomerate closely affiliated with Armscor. A second Data General MV/8000 was sold to a branch of the Scientific and Industrial Research Council that was responsible for radar and defense-communications development in South Africa.

    One most definitely would have to be in a nonquestioning mood to accept assurances that these computers were not intended for military usage purposes. In the case of the Sperry Univac 1182 computer sale to Atlas Aircraft, one of the reasons for approving the sale advanced by the Commerce Department was that it had discovered the computer already had arrived in

South Africa and that the U.S. government was being faced with a fait accompli.[66] In the light of reasoning of this nature, it is easy to understand why critics of military sales to South Africa felt that the Reagan administration was willing to permit these sales any time a reasonable excuse for doing so presented itself.

The request for permission to make nonmilitary sales came with increasing rapidity and for increasingly sophisticated and strategic material. Control Data wished to sell a Cyber 170/750 computer to the Scientific Council of the South African government, and Beach Aircraft and Piper Aircraft wanted to sell small aircraft as air ambulances. Assurances by South Africa that these goods would not be used for military purposes converted few doubters even when on-site inspection rights were written into the contract.[67]

During the final months of 1982, South Africa adopted an increasingly aggressive posture concerning its arms capacity. In order to combat inflation running at 15 percent annually and to obtain funds to purchase sophisticated weapons on the world market, Armscor held public showings of weapons it had for sale. Its star attraction was the G-6 mobile artillery unit. Its six-wheel chassis permits maneuverings at speeds in excess of sixty miles per hour in open terrain and at satisfactory speeds in more cluttered areas. A 155-millimeter howitzer can be mounted on top and it is claimed that tactical nuclear weapons also could be utilized. A range in excess of twenty-five miles is promised.[68] Defense Minister Magnus Malan was quoted as saying, "We hope it will find a place in the arsenal of friendly countries."[69] Argentina, Chile, Paraguay, Taiwan and perhaps some black African nations—purchasing clandestinely—would appear to be the desired clientele.[70]

At the beginning of 1983, Armscor had reason to be satisfied with its performance over the past five years. From its status as a threatened, underarmed nation at the end of 1977, South Africa now has succeeded in becoming largely self-sufficient in armament production. Both its air force and navy are considered as being close to state-of-the-art at the present time.[71] Only in the missile area is the arms embargo still having a markedly adverse effect. The nuclear capacity of South Africa is clouded in secrecy. As a result, the possibility exists that even in this area South Africa has made enormous progress. Whether or not South Africa is producing nuclear weapons at present, no nation in the world would find it an insignificant foe.[72]

South African Nuclear Capability

Trouble with the UN

All estimates of South African military ability to fight a war with success would change if it were able to manufacture atomic weapons in its own country. The question would then become: Would South Africa use such awesome destructive power in their own defense? To many, the answer is, unquestionably, yes. As a result of this fear on the part of the world community concerning the use South Africa would make of atomic weapons, the UN mandatory arms embargo of 1977 dealt directly with this question. When the embargo was passed on November 4, 1977, the Security Council voted unanimously to place an immediate, permanent, and binding embargo on the sale of arms to South Africa.[73] A further declaration stated that any added acquisition of arms by South Africa posed a threat to international peace and security.[74] The resolution continued to specify that all UN members were prohibited from cooperating with the Republic of South Africa in helping it to develop nuclear-weapons capabilities.[75]

The United States, the United Kingdom, and France, earlier in the UN deliberations, as mentioned previously, had vetoed stronger proposals as being overboard. These proposals would have required all countries to desist from providing any form of direct or indirect assistance to the South African government in its military buildup.[76] A similar proposal would have prohibited any cooperation with the current racist regime in South Africa in nuclear development of any type.[77] U.S. officials, in giving reasons for not agreeing with this wording, stated that such restrictions would prevent the United States from exerting diplomatic pressure on the Republic of South Africa to sign the nuclear-nonproliferation agreement. If South Africa would sign the agreement, the Pretoria regime would be bound to observe international safeguards for the nuclear facilities that it was certain one day to construct. The United States preferred to leave open for later discussion the question of assisting South Africa in developing nuclear power for purely peaceful purposes.[78]

Nuclear cooperation between the United States and South Africa had begun in 1957. During the 1960s, the United States had supplied nuclear fuel from the U.S.-built reactor, the Safari I. In 1973 the Nixon administration agreed to provide nuclear fuel for the projected twin power reactors at Koeberg.[79]

In the wake of the 1977 UN arms embargo, South Africa feared that the United States would renege on its agreement to supply enrichment material for the Koeberg plant. It thought, not without reason, that the United States might claim the Koeberg nuclear plant would be used for military purposes.[80] South Africa decided instead to build its own commercial uranium-enrichment plant for nuclear fuel. The Pretoria government promoted a $410 million contract to the Murray and Roberts corporate group. The awarding agency was the South African Uranium Enrichment Corporation. The enrichment factory was to be built close to the pilot nuclear plant at Valindaba, northwest of Johannesburg. A subsidiary of the Murray and Roberts group had constructed this plant in 1975. The government-owned electricity-supply company, Escon, took rapid steps to be able to provide the 2,000 to 3,000 megawatts of electricity that the new enrichment plant would need. This supply would be assured by constructing two new coal-fueled power-plant stations, to be constructed between 1978 and 1982.[81]

The South African government realized, after the imposition of the UN arms embargo, that its nuclear fate was not in its own hands. It could no longer count on contracted-for amounts of slightly enriched (3 percent) uranium hexaflouride, and as a result, it must undertake the massive financial sacrifices necessary to become self-sufficient in nuclear power.[82] Another strong motivation for South Africa to undertake the drive to nuclear self-sufficiency was provided when, during 1977, the United States failed to deliver the contracted-for fifty-seven pounds of highly enriched weapons-grade uranium destined for the Safari I nuclear-research reactor at Valindaba.[83]

South Africa Goes Atomic-Bomb Shopping

During February 1978, South Africa increased negotiations with France for nuclear assistance. This move was made even though France also had voted for the arms and nuclear embargo against South Africa at the Security Council. Nonetheless, South African technicians destined to run the $960 million power station at Koeberg were sent to France for training. France had built the Koeberg plant with two pressurized water reactors, each with an electrical output of 922 megawatts. France had stressed that the Koeberg plant would be used for peaceful nuclear uses alone. The Koeberg plant would need an estimated 850 tons of nuclear fuel to start up and another 240 tons a year to run.[84]

When Minister of Mines Fanie Botha announced the details of the project for uranium enrichment, the form it took was far more modest than had been originally planned. It was to use the aerodynamic process of isotope separation that had been pioneered by the Republic of South Africa in 1961.[85] Thoughts of a 5,000-ton-a-year-producing plant that would be able to export surplus production and obtain over $200 million a year in foreign exchange had long since been shelved. Plans for the accompanying Valindaba plant were changed from the ambitious plans at the time of building a power project to building a full-time relatively small enrichment plant that would produce perhaps 250 tons a year of enriched uranium, hardly enough to supply South Africa let alone to bring in foreign exchange. The estimated cost of the uranium-enrichment plant was $1.2 billion, when first conceived in 1975, but already by 1978, with inflation, the cost had jumped to $2.3 billion.[86]

The Carter administration kept to its policy of noncooperation with South Africa. By the end of November 1978, the United States returned two large sums of money sent by South Africa to purchase nuclear fuel. First, the Department of Energy, obeying an export-license ban on fuel to South Africa, returned $391,000 that had been sent to U.S. Nuclear of Oakridge, Tennessee. This company experienced financial difficulty, and in liquidating its assets, it turned the order over to the Department of Energy, which quickly canceled the contract. The second transaction involved $660,000, the value of the unburned content of uranium fuel used in the Safari I reactor. Usually, the United States either rebought the used fuel or took it back as credit for future sales. This time, the United States told South Africa to keep the money.[87]

On December 5, 1979, South Africa was barred from participating at the International Atomic Energy Commission's New Delhi conference by a vote of forty-nine to twenty-four. Most nonaligned, Eastern-bloc, and developing nations voted against South Africa's participation, and only the industrialized nations, including the United States, voted in favor. The South African representative, J.W.L. De Villiers, termed the action as being "patently illegal, blatantly unconstitutional, politically-motivated and as sowing the seeds of destruction of the international agency."[88]

Gerald C. Smith, the U.S.-delegation head, predicted the banning action would undermine nonproliferation efforts and would allow South Africa to justify its continued refusal to sign the nuclear-arms-nonproliferation treaty. As a result, South Africa would be free to proceed as it wished in the nuclear field and to operate without supervision.[89] South Africa continued to refuse to sign, claiming, perhaps not without reason, that other nations would steal the secret nuclear-enrichment process it has developed. South Africa also pointed out that nuclear powers such as France, India, and China as well as nonnuclear powers such as Israel, Argentina, and Brazil have also refused to sign the nonproliferation treaty.[90]

By the end of September 1980, the South African Uranium Enrichment Corporation was speaking with optimism concerning the modified-centrifuge process it had perfected for making uranium-enriched fuel, both for use at the Koeberg plant for peaceful purposes and also for nuclear-weapons uses. South African sources say that uranium is being gasified. Then the gas is spun in a large drum so the molecules of uranium can be separated and filtered out from the gas mixture. Even with significant progress toward nuclear self-sufficiency having been taken, great concern about the cost involved remains. This is especially true since South Africa is so coal rich that many observers believe that South Africa should develop military uses for nuclear power before it sets up civilian energy uses.[91]

Weapons Research Continues

Indications are growing that South Africa has taken significant steps in military-related nuclear-weapons research. Columnist Jack Anderson reported that South Africa has perfected a "split-nozzle gaseous diffusion system" that performs the key nuclear-bomb step of extracting uranium-235 from uranium ore in a more-traditional gaseous-diffusion method employed by the United States. In addition, Anderson reported that the United States also is concerned that South Africa will share its nuclear resources with Israel and Taiwan, two other world pariahs. Sophisticated military nuclear capacity in the hands of any of these nations would increase significantly the number of world trouble spots and regional conflicts.[92]

With the Koeberg power plants due to come on line during 1982 and 1983, South Africa was well aware by 1978-level costs alone that it stood to lose R1.56 million, or $1.3 million, per day of plant idleness. It was estimated that a home-produced South African enriched-uranium supply would not be ready until the end of 1983 at the earliest, and even then South Africa was faced with the task of finding a country willing to process the 3 percent enriched uranium hexaflouride into fuel elements that can be fitted into the power-plant reactors. If South Africa could not convince the United States to supply the element, then its best hope appeared to be in convincing the French and Belgians to permit the Eurofuel Company to do so.[93] Since French interest built the Koeberg plant, it would seem to have been in their best interest to assure its operation. In this regard, a blow was struck to South Africa when Francois Mitterand, a friend neither of nuclear power nor of South Africa, defeated Giscard d'Estaing in the 1981 French presidential election.

During the Carter administration, the U.S. government saw potential nuclear military uses by South Africa lurking in the nation's every action. Not only was the 3 percent nuclear-enriched fuel denied to South Africa, but also the United States would not let it purchase highly enriched nuclear fuel, 93 percent weapons grade, destined for the U.S.-made small research reactor at Valindaba. At present, this reactor, which South Africa claims is used only for atomic-energy research in medicine and geology, is operating at 12 percent of capacity. As with the 3 percent enriched fuel, the 97 percent enriched fuel also could be produced in South Africa if necessary, but only at massive cost in terms of money, time, effort, and diversification from other priorities. The Reagan administration's much-talked-about tilt toward South Africa would become a reality if steps should be taken to sell the needed nuclear fuel to South Africa.[94]

On September 22, 1979, what was probably a low-yield nuclear explosion of 2.5 to 3 kilotons was detected near South Africa by a U.S. Vela surveillance satellite.[95] If it was a nuclear explosion, its force was equivalent to one-quarter the power of the Hiroshima bomb, and such an action by South Africa would have violated what President Carter claimed had been a pledge made to him by Prime Minister Vorster that Pretoria had no plans to explode nuclear devices for any purpose and that the Kalahari Desert test site was not to be used for nuclear purposes. However, there was no indication that this explosion took place in the Kalahari Desert or indeed any-where in South Africa.

South Africa denied it had detonated any nuclear device and suggested that a nuclear-explosion accident might have occurred aboard a Soviet Echo II–class nuclear submarine since a number of them had been sighted about that time off the strategic passage around the Cape of Good Hope. The Carter administration quickly rejected this theory. The atom-bomb-blast question fizzled into inconclusion, although some analysts felt certain the South African navy had launched a nuclear rocket from one of its ships. Few people doubt, however, that the Pretoria government could at this point, alone or in conjunction with Israel, detonate an atom bomb if it so desired.[96]

Recent Developments

The change of administrations in the United States from Carter to Reagan afforded a new opportunity for South Africa to attempt to obtain the needed enriched nuclear fuel to power the Koeberg nuclear reactors. South African Foreign Affairs Minister Roelof F. Botha flew to Washington for a May 14, 1981, meeting on this subject with Secretary of State Alexander Haig and Assistant Secretary of State for Africa Chester Crocker.[97] The startup date for Koeberg was scheduled to be March 1982. Although the pilot uranium-enrichment plant at Valindaba was able to produce small quantities of fuel that has been enriched with 45-percent uranium-235, there was no possibility that it could produce sufficient quantities of the needed 3 percent enriched fuel. Botha hoped he could persuade the United States to provide this fuel without the necessity for South Africa to sign the nuclear-nonproliferation pact and submit to the required inspections. It was unlikely the U.S. would agree to requests of this nature as long as South Africa retained possession of Namibia.

In early November 1981, the situation changed in a dramatic fashion. Framatone, one of the three French companies engaged in the Koeberg nuclear-power-plant construction, announced that the enriched fuel needed by South Africa would be loaded into fuel rods for shipment from the Framatone plant to Capetown.[98] The U.S. State Department was furious that the French government of President Mitterrand had issued an export license for this purpose. No one seemed to know which nation had supplied the fuel to be placed in the rods. What was clear was that France had helped South Africa to pull a fast one on its enemies. South Africa could now begin to provide nuclear power for energy-related usage and solve its energy problems to a large degree without needing to surrender on Namibia or to sign the nuclear-nonproliferation pact.[99]

The opponents of South Africa continued their detective work. Eventually, they solved the puzzle concerning the source of the enriched uranium for the two nuclear plants that are expected to generate eventually 2 million kilowatts of electricity. To the fury of U.S. liberals, two corporations from their country were involved intimately in the transaction as middlemen and, what was worse from their point of view, participated without seemingly violating U.S. criminal law.

Edlow International of Washington, D.C., and SWUCO, Inc., of Rockville, Maryland, bought excess uranium that had not been utilized in Belgium or Switzerland and turned it over to a pair of uranium-enriching companies. Most of the end product was shipped to Capetown for use at the Koeberg nuclear-power plant, but to add a touch of irony to the confusing proceedings, the South African Electric Supply Commission could not resist adding that it had purchased more uranium than it needed and that it would sell the excess to the United States for enrichment so that it could be resold to Japan as an end-product user.[100]

Perhaps in acknowledgment of reality, the U.S. government gave indications during late May 1982 that it would loosen its restrictions on nuclear-related sales to South Africa. Now that South Africa unquestionably possessed enriched uranium of the proper grade, supply deprivation was no longer the question at issue. The focus had changed, and the question now to be posed was whether or not South Africa would put the Koeberg reactors to military uses, something it had vowed not to do.[101]

A letter sent to the chairman of the Senate Governmental Affairs Subcommittee, Charles Percy of Illinois, by Secretary of Commerce Malcolm Baldridge signaled a change in U.S. governmental policy on nuclear sales to South Africa. Baldridge mentioned that the Reagan administration has adopted a more-flexible policy with respect to approval of exports of dual-use commodities and other material and equipment that have nuclear-related uses in areas such as health and safety activities. Thus, it would appear that the U.S. government still would not cooperate with the South African government for any project that was perceived as military in nature. Critics charged that South Africa could hide such usage by claiming that the purchases would be used for health and safety purposes. Once on home soil, other uses easily could be substituted.[102]

Whatever the use might be in any one particular case, the trend clearly was toward closer nuclear cooperation between the United States and South Africa even though South Africa had made no move to sign the nuclear nonproliferation pact or to permit on-site inspection of its nuclear facilities. Licenses for the sale of vibration test equipment and for multichannel analyzers and computers requested by South Africa on the questionable assumption that they would not be used for military purposes had been granted quietly by the U.S. government.[103] Alarm had been raised in some quarters by another pending South African nuclear-equipment application. This time, the request was for 95 grams of helium 3 that, under proper conditions, could be used to make tritium, a radioactive form of hydrogen with three times more mass for its atoms than those found in ordinary hydrogen atoms. Tritium is used in thermonuclear bombs. It would seem hard to envision that such a request could be granted on a dual-usage theory.[104] Twenty-odd years of attempts to make South Africa an international outlaw thus seemed to be on the brink of total failure.

During September 1982, the Reagan administration gave indications that it would further ease its policies on the sale of sophisticated metallurgical equipment to South Africa. The Commerce Department urged the White House to permit export of the equipment, even though it could be used as a critical component in manufacturing atomic weapons. The item in question was a large, hot isostatic press.[105] South Africa claimed it would be used to manufacture tungsten-carbide drill bits for oil rigs. Opponents of South Africa were uneasy, understandably, about these developments. Throughout the world, the United States was subjected to harsh criticism for its activities. It was pointed out that only one other nation, Sweden, also produced an isostatic press.[106] In its case, there was no question of selling such a press to South Africa. Therefore, unless the United States did so, no one would.

As the five years examined in this book come to an end, it still remains unclear whether South Africa possesses nuclear military capability at present. This same question was unanswered at the end of 1977. Perhaps South Africa is no better off in nuclear weaponry than it was five years ago; but perhaps South Africa possessed nuclear military capabilities five years ago. Some day soon, if not now, South Africa will be a nuclear military power. Such a reality must worry all opponents of the Pretoria regime.

Notes

1. United Nations, Security Council, *Resolution 418 (XXXII)*, November 4, 1977.

2. "U.N. Bans Arms for South Africa," *Baltimore Sun,* November 5, 1977.

3. Kathleen Teltsch, "Black Nations Urge U.N. to Adopt Economic Curbs on South Africa," *The New York Times,* November 15, 1977.

4. United Nations, Security Council, *Resolution 421 (XXXII)*, December 9, 1977.

5. "14 U.N. Resolutions Condemn Apartheid," *Washington Star,* December 15, 1977; United Nations, General Assembly, *Resolution 32/105 (XXXII),* December 14, 1977.

6. See M. Zenovich, "Foredoomed Regime," *Soviet Military Review,* 11, November, 1978, pp. 54-55.

7. See "Will the Arms Embargo Leave South Africa Defenseless?" *Government Executive,* 10, April, 1978, pp. 29-33.

8. Quentin Peel, "Israel and South Africa in Top Level Trade Talks," *Financial Times,* February 6, 1978; William E. Farrell, "Israeli Tours South Africa as Arms Trade Furor Grows," *The New York Times,* February 10, 1978.

9. Richard R. Leger, "Defiant Afrikaners: South Africans Say Pressure Stiffens Their Resolve," *Wall Street Journal,* November 14, 1977.

10. Quentin Peel, "South African Economic Policy Warnings," *Financial Times,* December 7, 1977.

11. Kathleen Teltsch, "Nigeria Seeks New Curb on Rhodesia, South Africa," *The New York Times,* January 10, 1978.

12. "Israel to Adhere to South Africa Arms Embargo," *Washington Post,* November 8, 1977.

13. See Major Gerald J. Keller, "Israeli—South African Trade: An Analysis of Recent Developments," *Naval War College Review,* 30, Spring, 1978, pp. 74-80.

14. Farrell, "Israeli Tours South Africa."

15. See Marjorie Hope, Jim Young, *South African Churches in a Revolutionary Situation* (New York: Orbis Books, 1981); Desaix Myers, et al., *U.S. Business in South Africa* (Bloomington: Indiana University Press, 1980).

16. "Common Market Defers Action on South Africa," *The New York Times,* June 13, 1978.

17. "Cheap Producers Aren't Cheating," *The Economist,* September 16, 1978.

18. Richard E. Bissell, "Stability and Security in Southern Africa," *International Security Review,* 6, Summer, 1981, pp. 173-188.

19. Agence France Presse, "Ties with South Africa Urged on African Nations," *Washington Post,* August 10, 1978.

20. Reuter News Service, "Israel, South Africa in UN Fire," *Christian Science Monitor,* August 28, 1978.

21. See Richard Dale, "Political, Economic and Security Changes in Botswana, Namibia, and South Africa, 1966-1979," *Parameters* 9, September 1979, pp. 56-69.

22. See Melvin A. Conant, Charles K. Ebinger, "Tremors in World Oil: The Consequences of Iran," *International Security Review* 5, Spring 1980, pp. 27-42.

23. See James D. Hessman, "Simonstown, SASOL and Soweto," *Sea Power* 24, August, 1980, pp. 50-55.

24. Guy Arnold, "OAU Summit: Turning Point for Africa?," *Christian Science Monitor,* July 27, 1979.

25. Carey Winfrey, "OAU's Unity Loses Appeal," *The New York Times,* July 23, 1979.

26. South African Institute of Race Relations, *Survey of Race Relations in South Africa,* (Johannesburg: South African Institute of Race Relations, 1981).

27. Bernard D. Nossiter, "U.N. Council Given Plan to Avert Clash on South African Sanctions," *The New York Times,* April 30, 1981.

28. Michael J. Berlin, "Western Nations Veto Sanctions against South Africa," *Washington Post,* May 1, 1981.

29. Jay Ross, "African Leaders Criticize U.S. Stand on Namibia at O.A.U. Summit," *Washington Post,* June 25, 1981.

30. Bernard Nossiter, "A United Nations Rebuke to South Africans Vetoed as United States Splits with Allies," *The New York Times,* September 1, 1981; David B. Ottaway, "Arms Embargo Comes Too Late to Affect South Africa," *Washington Post,* October 28, 1977; "U.N. Bars Arms for South Africa," *Baltimore Sun,* November 5, 1977.

31. See Charles Latour, "South Africa: NATO's Unwelcome Ally," *NATO's Fifteen Nations,* 21, June-July, 1976, pp. 58–64.

32. See Arms Control and Disarmament Agency, *World Military Expenditures and Arms Transfers: 1970–1979* (Washington: ACDA, 1982); Ruth Leger Sivard, *World Military and Social Expenditures: 1981* (Leesburg, Virginia: World Priorities Press, 1981).

33. See Trevor N. Dupuy, Grace P. Hayes, John A.C. Andrews, *The Almanac of World Military Power* (San Rafael, California: Presido Press, 1980. 4th ed.).

34. See Stockholm International Peace Research Institute, *World Armaments and Disarmament: SIPRI 1978 Yearbook* (London: Taylor and Francis. 197 p.).

35. Ibid.

36. See *Jane's All the World's Aircraft: 1978–1979,* John W.R. Taylor, ed. (London: Jane's Yearbooks, 1978).

37. Ibid.

38. See *The Rand McNally Encyclopedia of Military Aircraft,* Enzo Angelucci, ed. (Chicago: Rand McNally, 1980).

39. See Dupuy, Hayes, Andrews, *The Almanac of World Military Power,* 4th ed.

40. See "Will the Arms Embargo Leave South Africa Defenseless?" *Government Executive* 10, April 1978, p. 29.

41. Martin Dickson, "Well-Armed against Its Sea of Troubles," *Financial Times,* October 28, 1977; Michael T. Klare, Eric Prokosch, "How the United States Is Helping Equip South Africa's Military," *Baltimore Sun,* February 19, 1978.

42. David Anabel, "What Arms Mean to South Africa," *Christian Science Monitor,* November 4, 1977.

43. Fred Emery, "Shipment of Long-Range Shells to South Africa through Antigua Alleged in BBC Panorama Report," *London Times,* November 6, 1978; David C. Martin, John Walcott, "Smuggling Arms to South Africa," *Washington Post,* August 5, 1979.

44. Associated Press, "Vermont Firm Guilty in Shipping Arms to South Africa," *Washington Post,* March 26, 1980; Reuter News Service, "Company in Quebec Fined for South Africa Arms Sales," *The New York Times,* August 15, 1980.

45. "South African Gun Dealer Charged with Smuggling," *Christian Science Monitor,* November 20, 1978.

46. Robert E. Tomasson, "Olin Indicated on Arms to South Africa," *The New York Times,* March 15, 1978.

47. United Press International, "Sale of US Civilian Aircraft to South Africa Is Supported," *Washington Post,* December 15, 1977.

48. Katherine Teltsch, "South African Deal on Planes Criticized," *The New York Times,* December 19, 1977.

49. Graham Hove, "Ban on Arms to Pretoria Worrying US Businesses," *The New York Times,* December 21, 1978.

50. "South African Weapons," *Cape Times,* October 6, 1980.

51. See International Institute for Strategic Studies, *The Military Balance: 1980–1981* (London: International Institute for Strategic Studies, 1981).

52. Ibid.

53. Ibid.

54. Dickson, "Well Armed against Its Sea of Troubles."

55. *South Africa 1980–1981/Official Yearbook of the Republic of South Africa* (Ferrierasdorp, Johannesburg: Chris Van Rensburg, 1980), p. 286.

56. Beacon Simon, Simon Henderson, "South Africa Gears Itself for War," *Financial Times,* August 22, 1980.

57. Peter Durisch, "Unraveling a Secret Arms Deal," *The Observer,* May 17, 1981.

58. Jack Anderson, "Three Nations to Begin Cruise Missile Project," *Washington Post,* December 8, 1980.

59. "South African Missiles," *Washington Post,* February 9, 1979.

60. "Israel and South Africa: Need Unites," *The Economist,* December 20, 1980.

61. Caryle Murphy, "Embargo Spurs South Africa to Build Weapons Industry," *Washington Post,* July 7, 1981.

62. D. Ryazantsev, "Armoured Personnel Carriers," *Soviet Military Review* 5, May 1980, pp. 43–44.

63. Murphy, "Embargo Spurs South Africa to Build Weapons Industry."

64. "Arms Budget in South Africa is Being Raised by 40 Percent," *The New York Times,* August 12, 1981.

65. William Chapman, John M. Goshko, "U.S. Lifts Curbs on Certain Sales to South Africa," *Washington Post,* February 27, 1982.

66. Ibid.

67. Reed Kramer, "Proposed Aircrafts Sales to South Africa Tests New United States Trade Policy," *Washington Post,* March 16, 1982.

68. Paul Van Slambrouck, "South Africa Selling Weapons Developed under Arms Embargo," *Christian Science Monitor,* September 13, 1982.

69. Bernard Simon, "Pretoria Aims for Sales to Foreign Arsenals," *Financial Times,* September 14, 1982.

70. Allister Sparks, "South Africa Promotes Sale of Modern Arms," *Washington Post,* September 27, 1982.

71. Joseph Lelyveld, "South Africa Tries to Sell Its Arms," *The New York Times,* December 5, 1982.

72. See James Hansen, "High Strategic Stakes in Southern Africa," *National Defence* 66, May–June 1982 (pt. 1), pp. 42–46; 67, July–August 1982 (pt. 2), pp. 42–46.

73. United Nations, Security Council, *Resolution 418 (XXXII),* November 4, 1977.

74. Ibid.

75. Ibid.

76. Milton R. Benjamin, "Arms Ban on South Africa Remains Stalled in UN," *Washington Post,* November 2, 1977.

77. David Anable, "What Arms Ban Means to South Africa," *Christian Science Monitor,* November 4, 1977.

78. Ibid.

79. "Koeberg Nuclear Plan Contracts," *State Department Bulletin,* December, 1973.

80. Richard Burt, "U.S. Tells South Africa to Accept Atomic Curbs or Face Fuel Cutoffs," *The New York Times,* December 20, 1977.

81. David Fishlock, Richard Ralph, "South Africa Goes Ahead with Nuclear Fuel Plant Plans," *Financial Times,* December 23, 1977.

82. Caryle Murphy, "South Africa to Act Soon on Disputed Iranian Plant," *Washington Post,* January 15, 1978.

83. Burt, "U.S. Tells South Africa to Accept Atomic Curbs or Face Fuel Cutoffs."

84. Herve Florentia, "South Africa Sends Aid Team to France," *Christian Science Monitor,* February 15, 1978.

85. "Unenriched But Rich," *The Economist,* February 25, 1978.

86. Milton R. Benjamin, "South Africa's Pilot Enrichment Plant," *Washington Post,* December 5, 1978.

87. Graham Hove, "U.S. Returns South Africa Funds," *The New York Times,* November 13, 1978.

88. Michael T. Kaufman, "Nuclear Parley Bars South Africa," *The New York Times,* December 6, 1979.

89. Ibid.

90. Gary Thatcher, "South Africa Indicates Nuclear Weapon Capability," *Christian Science Monitor,* September 30, 1980.

91. Ibid.

92. Jack Anderson, "South Africa's Secret Uranium Process," *Washington Post,* September 15, 1980.

93. Caryle Murphy, "Embargo Slows South African Atom Plants," *Washington Post,* September 12, 1980.

94. Ibid.

95. "U.S. Finds Sign of Nuclear Blast off South Africa," *Baltimore Sun,* October 26, 1979.

96. Caryle Murphy, "South African Navy Probes A-Blast Report," *Washington Post,* October 28, 1979.

97. "Pretoria in New Moves to Get U.S. Nuclear Fuel," *Atomic Energy Digest,* July 3, 1981.

98. Caryle Murphy, "South Africa Skirts U.S. Efforts to Bar Nuclear Fuel Supply," *Washington Post,* November 13, 1981.

99. "OAU Assails Aid to South Africa," *Washington Post,* March 1, 1982.

100. Thomas O'Toole, "United States Firms Help South Africa Get Uranium," *Washington Post,* April 13, 1982.

101. Judith Miller, "United States Easing Policy on Nuclear Sales to South Africa," *The New York Times,* May 19, 1982.

102. Ibid.

103. Richard M. Weintraub, "Policy Clash Develops on Shock Batons," *Washington Post,* September 24, 1982.

104. Ibid.

105. Milton R. Benjamin, "Administration Reconsidering South Africa Equipment Ban," *Washington Post,* September 15, 1982.

106. Ibid.

6

The South African Economy

Overview

The Republic of South Africa, as a public-relations measure, often takes pains to describe itself as a developing, Third World nation. As far as the nonwhite population is concerned, such a description is accurate; for the white population, it is not. The number of wealthy whites and the sophistication of the industrial sector compare favorably with any. Such a statement cannot be made without paying attention to the significant number of poor-white urban (mostly English speaking) and rural-farmer (mostly Afrikaans speaking) citizens. This group provides much of the pressure that motivates the government to keep the apartheid system in full vigor.

This chapter examines the Westernized, developed economy of South Africa. Because of the important, utterly crucial role gold plays, heavy emphasis is placed on developments in this sector. Should the South African economy fall into a prolonged economic slump, discord that leads to significant political change or revolution might follow. Should economic conditions be favorable, the pressure to change the political system that satisfies the white population will lessen.

During the five years under study, the South African economy took on a definite hills-and-valleys profile. The sum total is that the economy averaged out somewhere in the middle. As a result, some changes occurred in the political system from 1977 to 1982; but far less than would need to occur to insure peaceful political evolution in South Africa.

The Economy in 1977

As the period following the problems in Soweto began to take shape, the economy of South Africa took a nose-dive. As far as business people were concerned, 1977 could not be described as a glowing year. Manufacturing, construction, and retail trade outlets reported the worst year in recent history. Profits in all sectors of the economy, almost without exception, were less than in 1976. Bankruptcies reached their highest point in history—more than 2,000 in one single year. Auto sales fell 16 percent.

In the primary industries the overall financial picture was more encouraging since mining and agricultural profits remained reasonably strong. As always, gold was the leading money maker in the economy. At the end of 1977, the world market price was in excess of $170 a troy ounce as opposed to $121 a troy ounce at the end of 1976. The South African gold industry yield for 1977 was said to be $3.2 billion. In 1976, the yield had been less than $2.7 billion. This rosy picture for gold was somewhat offset by the continuing outflow of capital from South Africa that had been fueled by the investor panic after the Soweto riots and the Steven Biko death. During the first nine months of 1977, the cash outflow from South Africa was $1.1 billion.[1]

The Johannesburg stock market reflected the uneasy attitude held by both domestic and foreign investors. The economy already had absorbed the shock of the Biko death by late December 1977, and the market had returned to the 210 industrial-index point on the Rand Daily Mail scale. The highest point of the year had been 211.2, after an early-year low of 169.1. Observers felt that institutional stocks must lead any 1978 rise in prices that might occur and that foreign investment in South Africa would be selective at best, concentrating in special areas such as gold, diamonds, platinum, and antimony.[2]

Many people believe that as the DeBeers corporation goes, so goes the nation. If so, those predicting at the end of 1977 that the South African economy still was in respectable shape had a reference point for their belief. During that year, the DeBeers central selling organization, which dominates the diamond industry, reported record sales of over $2 billion for gems and industrial diamonds. This figure constituted a 33 percent rise over 1976 sales. DeBeers also announced plans to increase diamond production by 13 percent, or by 1.36 million carats in 1977.[3]

During 1977, the amount realized for South African iron and coal exports was ten times higher than that recorded in 1975. Gains in both coal and iron exports were due in large part to two new harbors completed in 1976. These harbors were located at Saldanha, situated on the Cape province's underpopulated west coast and Richards Bay, located in the province of Natal. One long-term difficulty foreseen with Richards Bay was that Chief Buthelezi claimed that it should become part of an independent Kwazulu. It has been projected that both South African ports will expand in size in a few years.[4]

The uranium business also had been booming in South Africa before 1978. Uranium-production foreign-exchange earnings of $170 million in 1977 placed this product in the same respectable export-profit category as copper, wool, and deciduous fruits. Uranium exports, nonetheless, still fell well behind diamonds, sugar, and maize in the South African–export arsenal, to say nothing, of course, of gold. South African economic experts felt, with justification, that a rise in world demand and sales price for uranium could make this commodity competitive with diamonds as the second-largest export source for South Africa. Because South Africa had refused to sign the nuclear-nonproliferation treaty, it was free to sell uranium to any potential buyer. France, not coincidentally, which in 1977 was importing 60 percent of the Republic of South Africa's uranium output, also was a non-signer of the nuclear-nonproliferation treaty.

Almost all of South Africa's uranium is produced as a gold by-product. As a result, recovery costs are lower than in competing uranium-producing countries such as Canada, Australia, and Greenland. Adding to the competitive strength of South Africa has been its fully developed infrastructure—thanks to its gold production. This linkage factor allows South Africa to support the uranium industry in a more-refined manner than is possible in competing countries.[5]

When making his own appraisal of the economy at the end of 1977, Prime Minister Vorster also saw a picture with mixed elements. A politically shrewd person, he was confident enough of the eventual outcome to predict that the recession that had plagued South Africa almost continually since the third quarter of 1974 was finally on the wane. He could not make any such statement, though, without pinpointing some continuing causes of worry. In the third quarter of 1977, as compared with the previous quarter, the balance-of-payments surplus for South Africa decreased from R1.27 billion to R32 million—a drop of almost R1 billion in three months. Deciding to take firm steps, the prime minister and his economic advisory council chose to pump prime the economy. Extra spending to assist the non-white races in the country was authorized to the tune of R250 million. In addition, permission was given to blacks to receive loans from building societies and to take out hire-purchase agreements to buy automobiles. Not coincidentally, white-owned business would also profit from the additional credit being made available to black consumers.

The Economy Improves

At the end of March 1978, Minister of Finance Owen Horwood introduced a record $11.3 billion budget. $1.7 billion were destined for defense, 6 percent lower than in the 1977 budget. Special credits, however, could raise the defense spending another 14 percent if put to use. The $2.89 annual tax paid by all black men to the government was canceled due to the availability of funds from other sources. Bulwarking these actions was the high amount of taxes obtained by the South African government from fast-rising profits being earned by gold-producing corporations.[6]

Many stock brokers on international exchanges were impressed with the future of South African gold stocks. During April 1978, the respected analyst Elliot Janeway suggested investment in South African companies engaged in gold mining.[7] He was pleased by their 15 percent yield at a time when bonds were returning 9 percent on their investment. Janeway also was influenced by the dramatic rise in the price of sales for uranium as a gold by-product.

By the end of 1978, gold had risen $50 a troy ounce to a price of $225 a troy ounce. Observers considered the weakness of the U.S. dollar at the time as mainly responsible for the rise in gold prices. In 1978, the thirty-five active gold mines in the Republic of South Africa had produced 750 tons of gold—50 percent of the world production. During this year alone, South African gold had earned more than $4.1 billion, a figure up more than $1 billion over the record set in 1977. The 1978 gold earnings led to a positive growth rate for South Africa that year of 2.5 percent. This was a strong figure when the major difficulties experienced by the economy were taken into account. It was predicted that the gold rate would boost the economic growth rate another 3 percent in 1979, even though oil-import prices again would take a huge leap. In the wake of the 1976 Soweto riots, the gold boom experienced by South Africa made the difference between a slide into a catastrophic depression and the event that did occur—namely, a medium-range decline soon to turn around.[8]

Responses to Economic Challenges

The Lack of Oil

Gold's role as the salvation of the South African economy continued throughout 1978. In some ways it was a false savior because the enormous damage being done to the South African economy by rising imported-oil prices was not appreciated. The 700 tons of gold mined in 1978 in South Africa were expected to net $6 billion in income, double the $3 billion oil bill for that year. The government stepped up oil-exploration operations during 1978, raiding the gold-surplus money account to pay for further drilling.

The lack of a steady oil supply always has been one of the main Achilles heels for the South African economy. Without oil, the nation is forced to resort to purchases on the spot market or to carry through a coal-to-oil substitution plan like Sasol. As long as the shah was in power in Iran, he was most willing to sell oil to South Africa. By the start of 1979, however, the Iran crisis was building to a point that made South Africa nervous about its crude-oil supply. Pretoria feared the cutoff for a protracted period of their main supply source. In order to raise funds to build an oil stockpile, the Pretoria government announced a raise in gasoline prices of 18¢ to $1.59

a gallon. The government wanted the excess cash for a stabilization fund in case the government of the shah fell and the successor refused to sell oil to the apartheid-supporting regime. However, Kuwait and Saudi Arabia had been for some time surreptitiously buying foodstuff and building materials from South Africa and Venezuela, another OPEC member, also trades with South Africa.[9] Based on these precedents, it seems likely that any of these nations might surreptitiously replace Iran as the main oil supplier to South Africa.

South Africa had been a constant friend of Iran since the days of World War II, when the shah's father Reza Shah Pahlevi, came to South Africa in exile. He died there and his body was returned to Iran. A statue and museum in Johannesburg are dedicated in his honor. This historical occurrence was one reason it was suspected incorrectly as it turned out, that when the shah was driven from Iran he might be able to find a home in South Africa. In another set of international-political circumstances, such reasoning might have been correct.

In the middle East, Iran had been the largest importer from the Republic of South Africa. For years it had been buying cars, mobile homes, and citrus fruits from South Africa. In return, South Africa was importing at the time of the cutoff 430,000 barrels a day of oil because it had no internal oil. As large as this figure is, it should be remembered about 75 percent of South Africa's energy requirements are met by coal and hydroelectric power. Sasol, in 1978, was providing 5 percent of energy supplies for the country.[10] Iran, under its new Ayatollah Kohmenhi government, intended to cut off oil supplies to Israel along with those to South Africa.

During 1979, South Africa gave evidence that its economy still could function despite an oil embargo enacted by major producers. South Africa had to pay 60 percent in excess of published crude-oil prices in order to obtain its supply. Because of the favorable earnings of the gold industry, the country was able to do so and, as a result, to outbid the United States for available supplies of crude oil. The competition between the two oil-dependent nations contributed to the rise in prices that all nonproducing countries were forced to pay for oil. Some doubt existed as to who was supplying oil to South Africa after Iran stopped doing so. Best guesses were that it was one of the Arab emirates such as Dubai or Abu Dhabi or, possibly, Bahrain.[11]

South African attempts to obtain oil were unable to keep pace with the rise in prices. During June 1979, it was necessary for the government to raise gasoline prices another 36 percent to a base price of $2.44 a gallon. Economic observers heard rumors that South Africa was being forced to pay $50 a barrel on the spot market, double the going price, in order to obtain oil. The government denied this and said that part of the raise in prices of gasoline would go to finance Sasol construction. It now cost $51.70 to fill a large automobile's gas tank and $26 to fill that of a Volkswagen.[12] The price of other petroleum products, from aviation fuel to lubricants, jumped in a similar manner. The price of kerosene increased by 45 percent. Since most blacks were forced to use kerosene for heating and cooking, this rise that they could ill afford hurt them far more than the rise in the price of gasoline to propel automobiles they did not own.

The reduction in oil supplies and their expanding costs produced more than just personal inconvenience. Business that could not absorb higher costs caused by the rise in oil prices were forced to go out of business. The oil pinch came at a time when an 8 percent annual growth rate was needed in South Africa to absorb the 250,000 new job-seeking blacks coming into the job market each year. A higher rate of growth than 8 percent a year would be needed to start reducing the unemployment figure of 1.5 million blacks presently in the job market.[13]

The Sasol Project

One strategy employed by the South African government to combat oil-supply difficulties is to increase their monetary subsidy in the coal-to-oil conversion process known as Sasol. The para-statal Sasol is more formally denominated as the South African Coal, Oil and Gas Corporation, Limited. The huge deposits of coal in South Africa are attractive to economic planners in the country. Since dedicated searches for oil have failed, the utilization of coal as a base for petroleum-fuel products has long been envisioned. The deteriorating political situation has spurred on government interest in the project.

The first Sasol oil-conversion plant was built in the early 1950s, fifty miles south of Johannesburg at Sasolburg. The plant started operations in 1955. The second Sasol plant, Sasol Two, is located ninety miles east of Johannesburg, along with its new town, Secunda. An article in *The New York Times* in September 1979 stated that Sasol One currently was producing about 5 percent of South Africa's energy needs and that Sasol Two would be ten times larger than Sasol One and would occupy an area one-mile wide by one and one-half miles long. Sasol Two started producing oil from coal during March 1980, with full production scheduled for 1982. The Sasol Two plant took over the land of fourteen farms and requires for production about 40,000 tons of coal per day. It possesses a coal stockpile the area of sixty football fields. Twenty-five thousand people were employed in the construction of Sasol Two alone.[14]

Government planners assumed that Sasol would produce 50 percent of South Africa's transport fuels by the early 1980s. Sasol Three is being built adjacent to Sasol Two and will be virtually identical. The U.S. corporation

Fluor is the contractor for Sasol Two and Sasol Three. When all three Sasol plants are operating at full capacity, it is estimated that about 75,000 barrels a day of petroleum-fuel products will be produced. This is a significant percentage of South Africa's motor-fuel needs.[15]

In the Sasol conversion process, coal is gasified to produce a reactive synthesis gas, which is then converted into a liquid fuel. The process also produces, as by-products, fertilizer chemicals, creosote, and a wide variety of waxes. It emits some air pollutant but no waste water. The Sasol One process claimed up to a 60 percent thermal-efficiency rate.[16]

In fiscal year 1978, Sasol sales exceeded $1 billion, with profits of $140 million. As a result, Sasol decided to offer $600 million in shares to private investors on the Johannesburg stock exchange. This offering took place during July 1979, the month in which the gold price rose to the then-stratospheric heights of $300 a troy ounce.[17] In addition to promises eventually to fill half of South Africa's oil needs, the prospective Sasol investors were told that most of the feed stock for petrochemicals for South Africa would be provided by Sasol as well. A 12 percent return on investment to shareholders was predicted.[18]

Freeing the Rand

Coal-to-oil conversion has been, by no means, the only major challenge facing South African economic planners. As early as August 1978, South Africa was experiencing an economic crisis caused when the value of the U.S. dollar plunged contemporaneously with a sudden, strong surge in the market price of South African gold. The South African rand had been tied traditionally with the U.S. dollar in a formal, official manner. As a result, when the U.S. dollar fell in value, it would always take more South African rands to pay any debt South Africa owed in rands to a third country. In the period from August 1977 through August 1978, the U.S. dollar dropped 25 percent in value in relation to the other five major world currencies. In this period, the market price of gold rose $143.30 a troy ounce to a high of $216.75 a troy ounce on the London exchange.[19]

The South African government decided to act. During late January 1979, it announced steps to free the rand from the U.S. dollar. The alternative would be to engineer a managed float. South African currency had been pegged to the dollar at the rate of R1.10 to $1.00 since the late 1975 South African devaluation of 18.5 percent. The announcement of the managed float made by Foreign Minister Horwood coincided with the DeKock commission report release that urged a complete overhaul of the South African–economy monetary policy.[20] South Africa hoped to obtain more investment capital and to strengthen foreign investments by better management of its economy. The Pretoria government hoped new currency rules would attract foreign investors, who had been alienated in the past by profit-repatriation restrictions that had given the South African Reserve Bank a potential total veto. Loosened rules in this regard and a freer exchange-rate policy were intended to increase worldwide participation in the South African economy.

The innovative exchange-rate policy enacted in January 1979 was an attempt by the government to address the double weakness of the South African economy. Its currency essentially is undervalued on current account but overvalued on capital account. The limited two-tier exchange rate was an attempt to entice foreign investors. The government committed itself to the concept of more-frequent parity changes and promised to move toward an eventual true two-tier exchange rate for foreign nonresident financial transactions.

At the same time, the Pretoria government ignored the DeKock Commission recommendations that the financial-rand market be opened to residents. The South African Reserve Bank insisted on its prerogative to quote indicative rates and to hold on to revenues generated by gold-bullion sales. The government did, however, promise to examine the practicality of allowing at least a portion of Krugerrand and diamond foreign-exchange revenues to be processed through the banks. The same promise was made for overseas borrowing by public corporations and local authorities.[21]

The South African government simultaneously changed the system of government forward-exchange-rate cover. As a result, it made foreign credit for South African importers 3 percent more attractive than before and wiped out benefits from obtaining cheaper South African credit. In addition, the Republic of South Africa moved to limit foreign borrowing by public corporations since it was found to be a most expensive method of strengthening the capital account. Public corporations under the new legislation would have to bear the cost of any depreciation of the dollar against the Swiss franc or the Deutsch mark. Thus, South African public corporations, for the most part, would be forced to stop borrowing against these two strong European economies.[22]

Economic Optimism

The Price of Gold Rises

By November 1979, the gold-price explosion had affected the South African economy most advantageously. The price for the mineral had stabilized for the moment at $385 a troy ounce, a rise of $160 a troy ounce since the start of 1979. The one-day high price for gold in London during 1979 had been $437 a troy ounce, quite a change from the officially frozen $35-a-troy-ounce price in effect as late as 1971. In making this economic gain, the Republic of South Africa had benefited from the soaring gold prices, the weak dollar, political uncertainty, and inflation.[23]

During late 1979, the South African government began to spend the money in its possession due to taxation on gold profits. Minister of Finance Owen Horwood announced a new plan to stimulate the economy by placing more than $360 million into social projects and other forms of financial assistance. $192 million were destined to repay personal-loan levies. The elderly were to receive a $31 million bonus, and $78 million was to be spent on food subsidies, mostly to keep down bread prices for blacks. By stimulating the private economy, the South African government hoped to raise the 3 percent growth rate caused by the energy crisis.[24]

Although gold and silver are not the controlling factor on their own in the economy of the Republic of South Africa at the start of the 1980s as they were in the past, the late-1979-early-1980 prosperity was most clearly linked to their good showing. In 1978, the mining sector of the economy accounted for 13.6 percent of South Africa's gross national product (GNP). Gold was the leader with 9 percent of the GNP. Each year, the thirty-six active mines in the Transvaal and the Orange Free State produce about 700 metric tons of gold, around 60 percent of the non-Communist-world output. This percentage estimate drops to about 50 percent if sales of gold by the U.S. Treasury and the International Monetary Fund are computed in the figure. At an estimated average price for the year 1979 of nearly $285 a troy ounce, gold would account for about 43% of export earnings, a 26.5 percent rise in the 1978 gold-export-earnings percentage. Profits of such a magnitude placed South African export-earning percentage in third place in the world behind only Japan and West Germany. Export earnings of this size would allow South Africa to offset inflation, political risk, an oil cutoff, and capital-funds withdrawal all at once.[25]

As 1980 approached, wishful thinking concerning the price for gold abounded. Economists spoke of expecting an average gold-bullion price for 1980 of $500 a troy ounce and said that such an amount could push the expected real growth rates for the South African economy for 1980 to 6.8 percent, a significant rise over the previously hoped-for 5 percent rate. Should the average price of gold reach $600 a troy ounce for the year 1980, it was presumed that the average growth rate for South Africa would increase to 8 percent a year. The mining companies poured enormous amounts of their windfall profits into structural improvements, inflating the total fixed investment of the country by an added 4 to 5 percent. Gold-mine taxes and lease payments to the government had reached the stupendous figure of $1.9 billion for the first three months of 1980, about 85 percent higher an amount than the estimate for this period found in the 1979 budget. A gold price above $400 a troy ounce for the entire year of 1980 would hand the government an added $2.9 billion in extra income during the year 1980–1981.[26]

Everyone inside and outside the South African government devoted him- or herself to planning how best to spend the added revenue provided by the increase in gold prices. At least $915 million was set aside to finance tax cuts and similar fiscal-assistance measures. It was presumed that lower company and personal taxes also would be charged. The top marginal tax rate was scheduled to be reduced. Civil-service salaries would be increased, a step aiding far more whites than blacks, as would increases in old-age pensions.

The emphasis upon the prosperity brought about by worldwide gold-price increases tended at times to obscure the point that the success stories in the mineral industries in South Africa extended beyond gold.[27] For example, platinum exports for 1980 were estimated to be in the neighborhood of $1.2 billion, almost three times the 1978 rate. Anglo-American is developing two new coal fields to supply the new Sasol power stations. General Mining is developing a new mine, joined with the Coalbase Petrochemical plant in the northern Transvaal. Maize and sugar exports were rising, and the rand had risen 6 percent against the dollar during 1979 to a figure of $1.22 per rand. The discrepancy between the rand and the dollar would have been even greater if the South African Reserve Bank had not kept a brake on the upward surge of the rand. A laissez faire attitude on its part would have hurt exporters badly. As 1980 started, the only dark cloud on the South African economic horizon that could not be washed away completely by rising gold prices was the continuing inflation rate. In a strong economy, manufacturers and merchants were taking advantage of firm demand to raise their prices. For example, fertilizer cost in 1979 rose 17 percent, and postal rates and transport charges also were due to rise. The 1979 inflation rate in South Africa was 14 percent and due to become higher during 1980.

Industrial Expansion Plans

Early in 1980, taking advantage of the optimistic conditions then holding in the South African economy, two major private South African corporations, General Mining and Sentrachem, a large chemical corporation, announced they were looking to start their own coal-to-oil plants. They intended to use higher-grade coal and different liquification processes than those used in Sasol's gasification process. Such private initiative was encouraged strongly by the South African government.[28]

Even though, by the beginning of 1980, many opponents of the South African system were willing to claim that it would collapse of its own weight in future years, the message had not yet been received by the large corporations operating in South Africa. As the local economy boomed, all across the economy expansion plans were made.[29] One of the leaders in pouring new funds into the South African business projects was the huge mining conglomerate, Anglo-American. At its Western Deep Levels mine it started a new shaft system at a projected cost of $886.6 million. The completion date was to be 1992. A new shaft was installed at its President Brand mine at a cost of $155 million. This new gold project had a 1986 completion date. At two other Anglo-American mines, new gold shafts for added mining were started. These were at the South African Lands mine and at the Erfdeel Dankbaarheid gold mine. The total cost of Anglo-American expansion at all its mines was estimated in the range of $1.5 billion.

Other mining companies also announced expansion plans. For example, the DeBeer corporation could extend its diamond mines at an added cost of $155 million. The Amcoal Genmin-Rand mines intended to open new coal mines for the added needs of the power stations coming on line. The cost was estimated at more than $1.25 billion. Gold Fields of South Africa announced plans to expand its mines at Doornfontein and Libanon, at an estimated cost of $125 million. Gold Fields also announced less-specific plans to add to their gold mines at North Driefontein. With the possible exception of the last announced project, all the projects in this group were to be completed in 1981.

Impala Platinum announced plans to expand its mines and refinery capacity at a cost of $155 million, with a 1982 completion date. Rustenburg Platinum would expand its nickel and copper refineries at a cost in excess of $69 million, with a 1981 completion date. Anglovall, at a cost of $43 million, would reopen its rand leases. Taken as a sector of the economy, it is clear that mining was booming. Expansion plans for the industry as a whole exceeded $4 billion.

In the energy field, General Mining Corporation and Sentrachem announced a joint oil and uranium expansion plan to cost $1.24 billion. The completion date was not given. On its own, Sentrachem announced plans to establish an ethanol plant at a cost of $744 million. The African Explosives and Chemical Industries (AECI) intended to expand its plant producing methanol, monoethylene glycol, and polyol at a cost of $558 million.

The electricity-supply commission intended to expand its thermal- and nuclear-power station system at an estimated cost of $13.64 billion, with a 1980 completion date. Sasol will add to its coal-to-oil conversion plant and its collieries at an estimated expansion cost of $7.733 billion, with a 1984 completion date. The Uranium Enrichment Corporation will build a new uranium-enrichment plant, but details are unknown. Projected additions to the energy sector of the economy are estimated to exceed $25 billion.

In conjunction with expensive expansions in the mining and energy industries, corporations in other business sectors also stepped into the breach and concentrated upon import replacements. Operating as they are in a most unstable economy fraught with perils from economic sanctions and other external politically motivated repressive acts, South African business concerns moved to become as self-reliant as possible. In this effort, they were encouraged with financial and administrative assistance from the South African government.

In 1980, National Process Industries intended to establish a hydrogen-peroxide plant at a cost of $3.72 million, and Armscor would purchase supplementary defense material at a cost of $37.2 million. Other projects, announced with a 1981 completion date included Styrochem's polystyrene plant expansion at a cost of $14.88 million; South African Nylon Spinners, Incorporated would expand its nylon and polyester plants at a cost of $49.6 million; Southern Cross Steel Corporation would build a stainless-steel rolling mill at a cost in excess of $157 million, and Volkswagen would build a new engine plant and make other additions at a cost in excess of $57 million.

Projects announced with a 1982 completion date in the import-replacement sector of the economy included Sentrachem's synthetic-rubber-carbide plant at a cost in excess of $202 million and AECI's low-density polyethylene plant at a cost of $186 million.

Projects with a 1983 completion date included General Mining and Zahnrad-Fabriken's joint effort to build a gear-box-and-steering plant at a cost of $149 million, the Industrial Development Corporation's plan to build a diesel-engine plant at a cost in excess of $380 million, and Toyota's plan to build extensions to comply with local-contents rules at a cost of nearly $50 million.

A project with a 1985 completion date was announced by Hoechst Industries. Construction would begin on fiber-plant expansions and other projects at a projected cost of $186 million. New projects announced in the import-replacement sector of the economy totaled close to $1.5 billion.

In the miscellaneous sector of the economy, added money for facility expansion was being invested in a manner that was anything but minimal. The Fedmis Corporation announced a new phosphoric-acid plant, with a 1980 completion date and a cost in excess of $21 million. Projects with a 1981 completion date included Highveld Steel plans to build prereduction kilns and an oxygen plant at a cost in excess of $45 million. South African Board Mills boxcard-plant extensions were announced at a cost of nearly $30 million. A group of supermarkets—Checkers, OK Bazaar, and Pick 'n Pay—added to their holdings at an announced cost in excess of $372 million.

Projects with a later completion date included South African Broadcasting Company's intended second television channel at a cost in excess of $92 million with a 1982 completion date; the Black Affairs authorities electrification of Soweto at a cost of nearly $190 million with a 1984 completion date; Sappel's timber, paper, and pulp expansions at a cost of $682 million with a 1985 completion date; DeBeers Corporation additions to their industrial-diamond-manufacturing capacity at a cost in excess of $161 million with a 1985 completion date; and the post-office system's telephone-network expansion at a cost of $4.96 billion with a long-away 1995 completion date.

The total cost for industrial-sector expansion as of 1980 was estimated at between $35 billion and $50 billion. Clearly, such a commitment would not be made by corporations thinking that their time left in South Africa was limited. It must be remembered, however, that political upheaval could cause alteration or cancellation of plans at any moment. The history of the South African economy in the years shortly after Sharpeville and Soweto provided strong lessons of this historical tendency by investors to panic in the face of adversity.

The Oppenheimer Empire

The overall strength and diversity of the South African economy is exemplified by corporate giants like the Anglo-American Corporation. During March 1980, *Business Week* carried a long article on Anglo-American and its president, Harry F. Oppenheimer.[30] For the Anglo-American fiscal year that ended on March 31, 1980, this corporation's earnings had jumped 50 percent to $350 million. The success was due to great leaps in gold and diamond prices. Unconsolidated group profits were $700 million, more than a 40 percent profit jump. Abroad overall, the corporation did less well. Nonetheless, the Phillips Brothers Corporation, a division of Engelhard Minerals and Chemical Corporation, did as well as other oil companies and turned in its share of profits. In 1977, Anglo-American shut down a $260 million joint-venture copper and cobalt project in Zaire and a mine in Mauritania.

Oppenheimer's Anglo-American Corporation, through its companies in Botswana, is developing a copper-nickel deposit and a rich new diamond lode. Anglo-American also has sizable copper holdings in Zambia, even after Kenneth Kaunda nationalized the industry. It also has a nut-processing plant in Mozambique, and it is astonishing, given Tanzania's socialist slant, that Oppenheimer sits on the board of directors of the state-owned and -operated Diamond Mining Corporation.

The Oppenheimer empire, by control percentage and market value in millions of dollars, is totally staggering. E. Oppenheimer and Son directly owns 8.2 percent of Anglo-American Corporation of South Africa. This company has a market value of $3.6 billion. Anglo-American Corporation in turn owns 4 percent of DeBeers Consolidated Mines, with a market value of $1.3 billion, and is a diamond-mining-and-marketing corporation that itself holds 26 percent of shares in DeBeers Consolidated Mines. Anglo-American Corporation of South Africa also owns 48 percent of the Anglo-American Gold Investment Company with a market value of $2.3 billion as well as 49 percent of Anglo-American Coal Mining Corporation, which has a market value of $674 million. It also owns 44 percent of Anglo-American Industrial Corporation, with a market value of $675 million. Anglo-American Industrial Corporation is a steel, machinery, food, auto, and chemical operation. One of its other owners is DeBeers, which possesses 12 percent of the shares in the same company.

The Anglo-American Corporation of South Africa also owns 100 percent of Anglo-American Insurance Company, an operation with a market value of $695 million, and 49 percent of Anglo-American Properties, a real-estate corporation with a market value of $31 million. DeBeers owns 19 percent of the shares of Anglo-American Properties.

Anglo-American Corporation of South Africa holds portfolio investments including 41 percent of Johannesburg Consolidated Investments, a mining and industrial corporation. Another substantial investment of Anglo-American is in Rustenburg Platinum Holdings. As of March 1980, Anglo-American possessed 24 percent of the shares of this important conglomerate. It also holds an 8 percent share in Barlow Rand, an industrial conglomerate.

Anglo-American controls 32 percent of the Minerals and Resources Corporation of Bermuda, another large holding company, and 36 percent of the shares of Charter Consolidated Company of Great Britain, still another large holding company. Not to be outdone, Charter Consolidated holds 15 percent of the shares of the Minerals and Resources Corporation of Bermuda.

The Minerals and Resources Corporation of Bermuda, in its own name as of March 1980, possessed substantial holdings in the following corporations: 29 percent of the shares in Engelhard Minerals and Chemicals; 50 percent of the shares in Anglo-American Corporation of Canada, a Canadian corporation that owned 28 percent of the shares of Francana Oil and Gas Company of Canada; and 45 percent of the shares of the Hudson Bay Mining and Smelting Corporation of Canada.

The Minerals and Resources Corporation also owns 50 percent of the shares of the Inspiration Consolidated Copper Corporation of the United States; 43 percent of the shares of Trend Exploration Corporation of the United States and Indonesia; 47 percent of Anglo-American Corporation of Zimbabwe, a corporation involving minerals, timber, and agriculture; 49 percent of the shares of Zambia Copper Investment Corporation; 20 percent of the shares of Anglo-American do Brasil; and 30 percent of the shares of Australian Anglo-American Corporation.

Charter Consolidated Company of Great Britain, as of March 1980, owned 28 percent of Johnson Matthey and Company of the United Kingdom, 26 percent of the Selection Trust of the United Kingdom, and 4 percent of the Rio Tinto Zinc of the United Kingdom. It also owned 14 percent of Tara Exploration and Development Corporation of Ireland, 29 percent of the Malaysia Mining Corporation, and 50 percent of Beralt Tin and Wolfram Corporation in Portugal.

Gold at Its Zenith

During the middle of January 1980, gold reached the incredible price of $850 a troy ounce and settled at $812 for a one-day COMEX high. As a result, both the commercial rand (used within the country) and the financial rand (used outside the country) soared to new highs. Within a year of its institution, the financial rand had risen from a value of 68¢ when gold was selling at $240 a troy ounce in February 1979 to its January 1980 rate of $1.10, when gold was selling at $812 a troy ounce. The commercial rand, which is government controlled with strictness, was selling in January 1980 at the rate of $1.22 per R1, with the predictions of eventual stabilization at a sum priced between $1.25 and $1.30 per rand.[31]

Each time the price of gold rose $10 a troy ounce on world markets, South African gold producers made an added $2 million. Sixty-seven percent of increased revenue would go to the South African government in revenues. Much of this tax income could be described fairly as being used to keep the apartheid system going. In 1979 the Republic of South Africa produced 703 metric tons of gold, 51 percent of the gold in world markets, and returned $7.3 billion to corporations in the Republic of South Africa government. On January 21, 1980 gold peaked at $825 a troy ounce. The recent modern low was $103 a troy ounce, reported in September 1976. The 1979 average was $305 a troy ounce. Gold deposits lie in an arc stretching from a point 100 miles south of Johannesburg all the way to the Orange Free State. There are now 38 working mines in the country where there used to be 120, and unless major new deposits are found, profitable mining will end within fifty years. All the gold mines since 3900 B.C. are estimated to have produced 116,000 metric tons.[32]

In the rush to compile statistics comparing gold production in South Africa from one month or year to another, sight often can be lost of the fact that enormous amounts of work go into mining gold. An average single bar of gold contains 58 pounds of gold and consumes a half day's output by 8,000 laborers. It is necessary to blast 3.5 tons of rock in order to obtain one ounce of gold, or 3,248 tons (that is, 649,600 pounds) of rock in order to obtain one gold bar. The cost of producing gold varies from $128 to $545 a troy ounce. Break-even figures in the South African gold industry during

1980 were calculated at $214 a troy ounce. In 1980, 90 million metric tons of ore were mined to obtain 675 tons of gold, the lowest Republic of South Africa total in twenty years but roughly half of world production. Injury figures in the gold-mining industry are staggering. Between 1970 and 1979, 5,455 miners were killed. Of this total, 5,189 of these men were black.[33]

At the end of March 1980, Finance Minister Owen Horwood made good on his promise of a budget to benefit the people if gold prices remained high. Recent government revenues had been $14.5 billion, 20 percent more than expected. Under the new government plan, income taxes were cut by 23 percent for those with salaries in excess of $25,000 per year and 48 percent on salaries between $6,250 and $25,000 per year. People earning $2,500 or less a year would owe nothing under the new scheme, a benefit for most blacks. Low-interest loans and subsidies to the tune of $175 million were provided to assist black living standards. Blacks also received promises of larger tax deductions than whites in the future and a promise of larger pay raises than would be given to whites. The import surcharge was eliminated—a step that probably hurt blacks more than any raises helped them since it would reduce the number of new jobs to be created in South Africa. The government did, however, increase subsidies on basic food commodities and gave a bonus equal to one month's pay to all civil servants, in addition to granting them a substantial pay increase.[34]

The boom in gold prices had to stop somewhere, and by mid-April 1980, it was clear that although favorable conditions would continue, runaway prosperity was probably at an end. The surge in the Johannesburg stock market had reached at least a temporary hiatus. The Federal Reserve Bank in the United States hiked U.S. interest rates significantly, triggering a drop in the gold price in South Africa. The South African economy slumped alongside the fall in gold prices.[35]

Despite temporary setbacks, proofs of the continued viability of the South African gold market and its long-term beneficial effect on the economy kept coming forth during 1980. During July 1980, Anglo-American combined three existing mines with a proposed new mine in order to make this Orange Free State holding, called Western Holdings, the largest one in South Africa. When linked together, this group would have a potential milling rate of 9.1 million troy tons per year. The current leader had been Vaal Reefs at 8.2 million troy tons per year.[36]

Even with the new investments in gold mining showing that large corporations believed in the long-term future of South Africa and their own part in it, when September 1980 began the price of gold and of shares in gold mines continued to stagnate. Uncontrolled jumps and plunges became the rule of the day; the gold price for the most part stayed above $600 a troy ounce, but the *Financial Times* Gold Mine Index rose and fell thirty points in a week, and stock brokerage firms changed their gold-stock buy orders to hold status and even to outright sell recommendations.[37] As gold shares in the Republic of South Africa were sold, the value of the financial rand in which the shares would be redeemed would also suffer. As the financial rand was placed under pressure, a spiraling move again lowering the gold-share prices was certain to occur. The loss of investment capital would hurt the large mining conglomerates at a time when added cash was needed to pay for rising mining costs and the bills due and owing for projects undertaken during the more-favorable financial climate of the past year.

When the totals for 1980 were computed, South African gold output had fallen 4 percent to approximately 21.7 million troy ounces from the high figure of 22.6 million troy ounces mined in 1979. The Chamber of Mines attributed the fall in production to the continued exploitation of lower-grade ore bodies in the wake of the 1979 gold boom. It estimated that gold would remain at a production figure ranging between 21.5 million and 21.7 million troy ounces in 1981, if bullion prices stayed at $550 a troy ounce. Production would drop to about 21.4 million troy ounces if gold rose to an average price of $650 a troy ounce. From 1982 onward, production is due to rise because expansion begun by the gold-mining companies in 1979 will have come to fruition.[38]

Even with the slight financial dropoff as 1980 returns for the full business spectrum became known, it was clear that South Africa had performed in an outstanding economic manner. With gold resting in the $600-a-troy-ounce category, it would be hard for it to perform otherwise. Gold earned $5 billion more in profit during 1980 than in 1975. For the first time in three decades, it appeared that South African gold-export earnings would exceed the total of all other export earnings combined. Overall private-sector investment in 1980 rose 24 percent over the previous year. As of the end of 1980, it appeared that there would be a 5 percent growth rate for 1981. The irony of the situation is that even with a strong performance of this nature, the result is not sufficient to keep up with the needed 300,000 more jobs a year that must be found to match the number of nonwhite employees entering the labor force each year. Joseph Lelyveld, writing in *The New York Times,* stated that the lack of skilled workers is debilitating modern South African society.[39] As a result, the government is in a quandary. On the one hand, it must expand the economy in order to find work for unemployed nonwhites. On the other hand, it is severely constrained from expanding because of the lack of skilled labor. The only alternative is to train more blacks. By doing so, it would risk stirring up their resentment at their lack of political freedom. Either power sharing or revolution would be the eventual outcome, neither of which is acceptable to the Pretoria regime.

The Economy Weakens

The Economic Pace Slackens

South African exports to the rest of Africa have been booming ever since 1978, the year in which the South African government authorized the Credit Guarantee Insurance Corporation to extend full insurance cover to all South African exports to purchasers in these other nations. Previously, only sales of capital goods had been so protected.

The South African government claimed that trade with the rest of Africa constitutes 10 percent of all nongold exports. This trade within Africa has reached $1.4 billion a year according to the South African government. If these figures are accurate, they represent an increase of 52 percent in the total amount of such trade in 1980 as compared with the previous year, 1979. The 1979 trade with the rest of Africa rose an even more impressive 74 percent from its 1978 level.[40] Food sales, especially of maize and wheat, led South African exports to the rest of Africa. Such deals especially infuriate critics of the South African government since they come as many blacks in the homelands, especially in the Ciskei and Kwazulu, have been suffering from malnutrition. During 1980, forty-seven of the fifty-three other countries on the continent purchased food from South Africa.[41]

So much discussion occurs about oil, gold, and diamonds and their place in the South African economy that the important role played by its agricultural industry is often forgotten. South Africa is a large exporter to neighboring black African countries less blessed with fertile soil. In addition, it provides sustenance farming for its own millions of impoverished inhabitants. As a result, droughts are a most serious setback when they occur.

During the middle of 1980, a severe drought took place in the Kwazulu area of the country. Starvation among the black citizens was rampant. The possibility also occurred that the country's favorable food-surplus and agriculture-export position would change drastically for the worse. The problems in Kwazulu were not experienced in the rest of the country. The South African Department of Agriculture in Pretoria estimated for 1980 a record 11.5 million ton corn crop, a 25 percent increase over the previous year's harvest. Peanut, soybean, and sunflower-seed crops also were expected to be more plentiful than in 1979.

On the deficit side, however, it appeared that wheat would need to be imported for the first time in the recent past. The last time this had been necessary was in 1970. It was expected that the 1980 crop would come in at 1.5 million tons of wheat as opposed to 2.5 million tons the year before. Sugar crops for 1980 were estimated to total 1.85 million tons, a significant drop from the 1979 total of 2.29 million tons. As usual, the poor of the country would be the biggest losers.[42] At the time, blacks were earning less than 15 percent of the salaries of whites. With essential-foodstuff prices rising due to supply scarcity, nonwhites were least able to afford the added demands on their pocketbooks. The white desire to retain one of the world's most leisured lifestyles continued, unabated.[43]

During January 1981, the South African economy started to weaken in one area well familiar to other industrialized economies, especially the United States—namely, interest rates began to rise. The South African government, until that time, had been controlling the amount that could be charged on mortgages. Unable to keep the economy in check with such rigid regulations in force, the government withdrew its restraining hand. As a result, the building societies suffered, and investors transferred their accounts to banks.[44]

In the wake of mounting inflation, increasing labor troubles, and a drop-off in the price of gold on the world market, the Federated Chamber of Industries, the largest organization of South African businesses, issued a set of guidelines during January 1981. The long-range implications of their recommendations were many. For the first time, a system of cooperation with black unions was urged upon the white moguls of the country. The chamber stressed that the approach should be flexible and pragmatic. The members were warned not to depend upon the cumbersome government procedures to solve their industrial problems for them. Such an accommodating approach to black unions would weaken the parallel union structure or the white-only unions that hold forth in many industries. In the long run, a corporation that truly determined to seek good relations with the rising numbers of black workers might bring the nation to equality faster than any step the government could take. Until the end of 1980, the Federated Chamber of Industries had advised its member companies consistently not to deal with black unions that are not registered with the Pretoria government. It would seem that now the chamber was encouraging such independent action, and some corporations were quick to follow the lead suggested.[45]

Even though the picture for the South African economy was mixed, there were some bright spots. It is ironic that one such area was South African trade with the rest of Africa. At the same time as political relations between the two groups worsened, the need of the black countries in Africa to expand their economies forced them to look southward and to trade with the Pretoria government and the South African corporations. In 1980, South African industrial and agricultural exports to the rest of black Africa rose by 52 percent. This strong gain occurred after an even more-impressive 74 percent rise had taken place in 1979. As a result of expanding export markets in the rest of Africa as 1981 started, 10 percent of all South African nongold exports were shipped to other nations on the continent. In 1976, 3 percent of such exports went to the rest of Africa. South African imports from its own continent are far smaller and in 1980 were estimated at $350 million.[46]

As the first quarter of 1981 passed, it became clear that the 8 percent real growth in gross domestic product that had taken place in 1980 would not be repeated in the new year. The first hint of this situation came during the last quarter of 1980, when it was announced that based on that quarter's statistics, the annual inflation rate in South Africa was running at a 22 percent per annum rate.[47] As a result, it was expected that economic growth in the country during 1981 would drop to the 4 to 5 percent level. For the total year 1980, inflation had risen at a rate of almost 14 pecent per annum. It was announced that if current trends continued, the inflation rate would average around 20 percent in 1981.[48] As a result of this inflation factor, if gold did not average $500 a troy ounce in 1981, the balance-of-payments deficit could be in the $2 billion range. In 1975, the balance-of-payments deficit in the same $2 billion range had forced an 18 percent rand devaluation from which the country did not soon recover.[49]

The Economy Loses Direction

By the middle of 1981, the definite findings of the DeKock report on the South African economy still were being awaited by the Pretoria government and the business people in South Africa. Rumors were rife that the report, when finally published, would argue for a sharp drop in government involvement in the economy. It was assumed a heavy emphasis on free trade in private industry would be advanced as the best way for South Africa to retain its economic position during the 1980s. Two large groups, the agricultural sector and the discount houses, were expected to complain bitterly should a withdrawal of government protection be suggested. Both industries were heavily subsidized, and their competition was regulated and restricted. It was also known that the DeKock Commission would advocate a change in the current two-tiered rand system. In its interim report published in 1978, the commission had observed:

> A unitary exchange rate, under which an independent and flexible rand finds its own level in well-developed and competitive spot and forward foreign exchange markets in South Africa subject to Reserve Bank intervention or management by means of purchases and sales of foreign exchange (mainly U.S. dollars), but with no exchange control over nonresidents and only limited control over residents is advocated.[50]

The South African government, in the light of the interim recommendation, made some moves in the direction of a unitary currency system. It allowed overseas companies to borrow more money in South Africa by permitting them to invest in South African unit trusts by using the financial rand. Regulations were eased to facilitate this investment by foreign corporations wishing to do so. Some U.K. insurance companies were quick to sell their holdings to South African companies or to trade them on the Johannesburg stock exchange.

Many observers felt that if South Africa had acted decisively when gold was selling at $850 a troy ounce and the discount rate between the two rands was a mere 10 percent, it could have merged the two currencies to its profit. Unfortunately for Pretoria, it failed to do so when it had the opportunity.[51]

The stagnation that developed in the South African economy served to expose some ironies with an amusing side. In the sphere of politics, the South African government found it necessary to adopt an anti-Communist posture that was so extreme that it borders upon caricature. In this manner, it hoped to win the support of Western nations and to soften cries that it adopt a multiracial posture in governance. Simultaneously, the Pretoria regime found it necessary to institute a highly centralized economy. Behind this rigid control structure has been a fear that if profits earned in South Africa could be shipped from the country with impunity, many white business magnates would invest abroad rather than at home. In such an event, the South African economy would slump and political unrest would no doubt increase.

By choosing a centrally controlled economy that leans heavily on parastatals, exchange controls, and central-bank-indicated interest rates, another whole set of economic problems came into being that would not have occurred if South Africa (which so firmly proclaims itself to be a Western-style democracy) had permitted its economy to function as a genuine, Western-style free-market. At root, the reluctance of the South African government to adopt a free-market system seems to indicate that it believes many of its more-affluent citizens lack confidence in the correctness of government policies and the long-term outlook for a successful resolution of problems in South Africa. A deep-seated distrust is being displayed by keeping such a rigid lock on the economy. It must be believed in Pretoria that if people had the opportunity, they would position their assets elsewhere.

Adding to the irony of the current political-economic situation in South Africa is the reality of its ever-increasing trade exposure with black Africa. Even though the other nations on the continent truly abhor apartheid, their own shaky economies have desperate need of goods that only South Africa can supply within feasible shipping distance at less-than-prohibitive costs. Such commerce lessens the economic pressure upon the South African government and allows it more freedom to continue its present political orientation. Although their black African trading partners are aware of this result, in the current situation they see few alternatives but to continue to trade with South Africa.

The Picture Turns Gloomy

By the end of 1981 it was clear that the long-deferred economic slump finally had trapped South Africa in its grip. The gold-led recovery that had been in effect since 1978 had run its course. Analysts expected a prolonged downturn. The growth of the gross domestic product for 1981 would be in the 4 percent range, and its was expected that for 1982 it would be at best half this amount. Since the spectacular 8.1 percent gross domestic product growth in 1980 barely had been able to keep pace with the need for jobs among the rising black population, it was clear that government efforts to lighten the burden of the nonwhite population were again failing.[52]

Some analysts thought that the economic situation in South Africa was even grimmer than the government would admit. They point out that for the first time in five years South Africa would be running a current-accounts deficit—a huge one at that, in the range of R4 billion.[53] The predicted deficit in current accounts for 1982 has been estimated to be about $2.76 billion. Skeptics say that the estimated 2 percent rise in the gross domestic product predicted for 1982 and the estimated current-account deficit for 1982 of $2.76 billion are predictions slanted heavily in the favor of the government. To reach these still-dubious goals, it would be necessary that gold sell for the year 1982 at an average price of $460 a troy ounce. Many doubted this gold price figure could be reached, however.

To back up their warnings, gloom-seeing analysts pointed out that each drop of $10 in the price of gold caused a loss of $220 million in foreign-exchange earnings. At the time that 2 percent gross domestic product rises and $2.76 billion current-account deficits were being forecast for 1982, gold was selling at $430 a troy ounce.[54] Even at that relatively strong price, bank interest rates had climbed to 16 percent, and the inflation rate would remain above 15 percent for 1981. The rand had lost 23 percent of value against the U.S. dollar during the year, and the money supply had increased alarmingly. Should the average gold price for 1982 level off in the $300–$325 a troy ounce range, as well could happen, the economic carnage would be terrible.

As 1982 began, it must have been difficult for South African government and business officials to remember the glory days of less than two years before when gold reached the price of $850 a troy ounce in London and an even more-astronomical $875 a troy ounce in New York. By the end of 1980, the price had fallen by more than 40 percent to its year-end closing figure of $602 a troy ounce. The precipitous decline continued throughout

1981. The closing price on December 31, 1981, was $400.50 a troy ounce, a further price drop of 33.5 percent in one year's time.[55] The bottom was nowhere in sight.

Why did gold prices drop so quickly and definitively? The reasons are myriad. Without doubt, it had been overpriced at the end of 1979 and at the start of 1980. The grip of OPEC weakened. Middle Eastern money that had flown toward gold during previous world crisis tended to do so less often than in the past. The South African inability to control its own economy was also a factor since it was obliged to sell more than otherwise would have been the case. One other element came into play to the surprise of many. The USSR markedly increased its gold sales, further depleting the world price of the precious metal.[56]

The Soviets have been forced to pour enormous sums of money into propping up the regime in Poland, supporting the invasion in Afghanistan, refurbishing their imposing supply of nuclear weapons, and searching the world market for grain to purchase in the wake of its third successive domestic grain failure. In 1981, it is estimated that the USSR purchased 14 million tons of U.S. grain alone, at a cost of approximately $2.5 billion. At the start of 1982, Soviet hard-currency reserves were reported to be at their lowest level in more than two years.[57] It was estimated that the USSR was in debt to European banks for an amount in excess of $15 billion and that no repayments to reduce the debt had been made during 1981. Under such circumstances, it is not surprising that their sale and swaps of gold had increased to a marked degree. Experts claimed that the USSR had sold nearly 250 metric tons of gold in 1981, a figure that more than tripled the 80 metric tons of gold it had sold in 1980.[58]

Given South Africa's and the USSR's position as twin giants in the minerals field, it is not surprising that some observers feel that collusion occurs. Given the political antipathy the Soviets feel toward South Africa and vice versa, such a gold selling combine is unlikely. There is some evidence, however, that both nations keep each other informed of their forthcoming moves as to platinum and chrome sales.[59]

By March 1982, everyone in South Africa understood that hard days had arrived, economically speaking. For the first time in history, the value of the South African rand had fallen below that of the U.S. dollar. DeBeers missed a dividend for the first time in thirty years. The price of gold dropped to $300-a-troy-ounce level. The Standard Bank Investment Corporation was predicting that if the price of gold averaged $350 a troy ounce for the year 1982, the current-accounts payment deficit would rise to $4.58 billion. Such dire warnings were in sharp contrast to earlier predictions that the economic situation would start to ease. The result of all this doom-saying was that in late March 1982, the government issued a projected budget for the forthcoming fiscal year that sharply cut government spending. The racial discord that surely would follow such a move had yet to be felt.[60]

Diamonds, Platinum and Coal

The slippage accompanying gold transactions was paralleled in the diamond sector.[61] The DeBeers Consolidated Mines Ltd. had controlled the world gem-diamond market for so long and so profitably that it was hard to conceive hard days arriving in this sector as well. No question existed, however, that prices had fallen. A one-carat D-flawless stone, the top of the line, that had sold for $63,000 in March 1980 was being quoted at $42,000 fifteen months later.[62] Similarly, a one-carat FVVS2 diamond, a middle-quality investment, that had been selling for $17,000 in March 1980 was being quoted at $10,000 fifteen months later. Since DeBeers controlled 80 percent of world diamond sales, the corporation's loss of income was easy to understand. DeBeers disclosed that diamond sales were $1.5 billion less in 1981 than they had been in 1980, constituting a 46 percent drop.

Chinks in the DeBeers armor began to appear. First, Israel starting holding back diamonds for speculation purposes rather than giving them to DeBeers to sell. Then, Zaire ended a fourteen-year exclusive selling arrangement with the DeBeers selling arm. Finally, Australia began making noises to the effect that it would not use DeBeers to market diamonds recently discovered near Lake Argyle, Australia. Minerals professionals tend to discount the impact of these three seemingly catastrophic events. The skepticism comes from a profound sense of respect. DeBeers, through its own holdings, its tentacles interlocking with other profit-making corporations, and its vast experience in manipulating the diamond market to make the highest profits for itself and its clients, remains as strong a corporate enterprise as exists anywhere. In addition, experts in the field say that Israeli holdings are comparatively small in number and that Zaire business and government people will probably discover that DeBeers will top the best black-market price and, as a result, will sell to DeBeers anyway. The Australian diamonds are of unproven quality.

Harry Oppenheimer, the head of the DeBeers/Anglo-American empire, tried to put a bright face on the South African diamond industry's economic downturn. "I am perhaps the only person in our organization who can remember times more difficult than our present ones."[63] The sinking price and the consequent withholding of diamonds for sale by DeBeers weakened the economy of South Africa at a time when it needed all the tax revenue it could obtain. Less appreciated was that Botswana and Namibia also have massive diamond holdings. Their citizens have desperate need of the revenues obtained by the DeBeers sales. The lowered price and supply cutbacks were crippling. Because of the white overlord image of DeBeers, nonwhites in all three countries tend to blame the South African government when difficulties are experienced with DeBeers. Some irony exists in this situation. The loudly proclaimed, if not always observed, liberalism of Oppenheimer often strikes the South African government as being unhelpful agitation and rabble rousing. The involvement of Oppenheimer in the Buthelezi scheme for a united Natal-Kwazulu is one example of his actions that annoy the government.[64]

The downturn in profits in the gold and diamond industries has also occurred in the area of platinum. South Africa produces 51 percent of the world platinum group of metals. The price has fallen from around $722 an ounce in September 1980 to around $390 an ounce fifteen months later. A reduction in automobile sales in the United States and loosening regulations concerning the need for catalytic converters has been blamed for the platinum-price downturn.[65]

The one continuing, and even increasing, bright-light mineral in the South African economic picture is coal. By 1980 figures, South Africa is the fourth-largest coal exporter in the world. It trails the United States by a three-to-one margin and also exports less than Australia or Poland. It does lead the USSR, Canada, and West Germany in exports of coal by a significant amount. The expansion of the shipping terminal at Richards Bay has caused South Africa to talk of doubling exports in the near future. Even though the world price of coal appears to have stabilized, it would seem that coal could provide a significant boost to the overall economy.[66] Coal also serves as the base for added Sasol coal-to-oil development.

A Period of Economic Stagnation

When all is said and done, any discussion of the South African economy and its continued viability must return to gold. This one commodity is so vital to the financial well-being of South Africa that, traditionally, success is assured when gold is prospering; no matter what is happening in the rest of the economy and vice versa. Such a simplistic statement remains, for the most part, correct. What has changed, however, is the gold-market price at which gold sales insure economic success for South Africa. This success figure, whatever it may be, has risen enormously. The reason for this situation has to do with the worldwide economic recession that has affected every nation adversely in the last few years. Because the overall situation in South Africa and everywhere else is grave, economically speaking, the price any one commodity that seeks to be a life saver must attain rises proportionately.

The laboring state of the South African economy during the middle part of 1982 happened even though gold climbed back in price from quotations in the $300-a-troy-ounce range to quotations in the $450-or-better-a-troy-ounce range. One would suspect that such an increase in revenue would spur the South African economy. So far, and for the foreseeable future, the gold-price rise has not been sufficient to accomplish this. Too many negative elements are present. Inflationary trends persist throughout the economy, yet signs of disinflation are strongly present and also serve to negate the effects of the gold-price rise, especially since the value of the commercial rand had fallen to distressing lows.

Lurking behind the failure of the $450 gold price to inject life into the South African economy is the growing realization that little gold, relatively speaking, is changing hands. For the most part, the transactions in question are paper transactions. The amount of gold being sold is quite small. The volatility is attributable to speculation, especially in the gold-futures market. At a time when less gold is being produced in South Africa, the amount received as tax revenue in Pretoria is declining. The total effect of this situation is that the South African economy continues to labor and stagnate. Even if the government wished to pour massive amounts of funds into improving nonwhite living conditions (and no indications exist that the government wishes to do so), the needed capital is not available. Given world economic conditions, little hope exists that South Africa will again be able to find available funds of this amount. If it had taken advantage of opportunities during early 1980, perhaps the situation now would be different. Unfortunately for the well-being of the nonwhite population, such is not the case. The history of South Africa is a history of missed opportunities. Failure to profit from economic success in 1979–1980 is merely one more example of a lost opportunity. The future will reveal the bad consequences of this error.

Hopeful Signs

During the last months of 1982, the price of gold inched determinedly upward. By early September, an increase of 70 percent over quotations made in early June had been noted. Local observers were less encouraged this time than they had been in the past when gold prices were on the rise.[67] Expenditures by the South African government were still outstripping revenues by a considerable amount. The government had been forced to raise the general sales tax from 5 to 6 percent in order to compensate for the shortfall.[68] Rising gold prices tended to benefit the citizenry as a whole less than it did the major mining houses.

Gold is sold on the world market for U.S. dollars. The price of gold rose at the same time that the U.S. dollar was rising quickly in value on world exchanges. As a result, each dollar was worth far more rand than was previously the case. Even though gold was selling in the $500-a-troy-ounce range during September 1982, the mining houses obtained only as many rand for an equal quantity of gold to be sold as had been the case in January 1980, when gold sold at the $800-a-troy-ounce range and when the United States dollar was weak on world exchanges.[69]

Many analysts believed that gold price rise would be short lived.[70] Particular mention was made of the recent International Monetary Fund decision to make more loans available to debtor nations. It was feared that worldwide inflation would occur. Investors agreeing with this line of thinking would seek safe, shortterm asset havens such as gold. In the long term, however, a downturn adjustment appeared certain.[71]

On October 4, 1982, South Africa applied for a $1.7 billion loan from the International Monetary Fund (IMF).[72] Finance Minister Owen Horwood cited the worsening balance of payments situation as the reason for the application. Left unsaid was the implicit admission that South Africa's attempt to raise cash by gold swaps with French, Swiss and West German banks during the last year had not remedied the shortfall.

The South African loan application contained two separate parts: $689 million from the compensatory financing facility and $394 million for a standby arrangement.[73] The General Assembly of the United Nations, human rights groups and many Democratic members of the U.S. Congress were opposed unalterably. The position of the U.S. Treasury was that technical and economic reasons for opposing the loan did not exist. As a result, South Africa as an IMF member was entitled to have its loan application approved. On November 3, 1982 the IMF voted in favor of the loan.[74] Insiders stated that Saudi Arabia was the most vociferous opponent of the loan; but its opinion did not prevail.[75]

As significant a sum as $1.7 billion may be in real terms, it accounts for less than 10 percent of public-spending amounts in South Africa for any recent year. The true import of the IMF loan lies in its demonstration that South Africa is a supple, multifaceted financial enterprise able to use all available financial tools with skill in order to bolster its lagging economy.

At the start of 1983, the South African economy was a leaner, slicker, more efficient entity than it had been five years previously. Personal income-tax rates, government spending and parastatal investment have all been lowered. The rate of real economic growth, which had been mired at a zero-growth rate in 1977, has risen to the 5 to 8 percent level in recent years. Sad as the economic plight of nonwhites remains, it cannot be denied that housing expenditures, wages for workers and the amount spent on education have risen for nonwhites in a dramatic fashion since 1977.[76] Although not healthy, at present, the South African economy is not in its death throes, either. Should the apartheid regime one day fall, it will not be the weight of its economy that will bring it to ruin.

Notes

1. Quentin Peel, "South African Economic Policy Warnings, *Financial Times,* December 7, 1977; John F. Burns, "South Africa: Weakening of the Foundation," *The New York Times International Economic Survey,* February 5, 1978.

2. "South Africa," *The Economist,* December 24, 1977.

3. "South African Diamonds Bring Renewed Income," *Washington Post,* January 11, 1978.

4. "Japan's Two South African Ports," *The Economist,* February 25, 1978.

5. "Unenriched But Rich," *The Economist,* February 25, 1978.

6. "South African Budget," *Washington Post,* March 30, 1978.

7. Eliot Janeway, "On Gold Stocks," *Washington Star,* April 27, 1978.

8. John F. Burns, "South Africa: Gold Keeps the Books in Balance," *The New York Times International Economic Survey,* February 4, 1979.

9. Reuter News Service, "South African Oil Output to Grow," *Washington Post,* February 23, 1979.

10. Jack Foisie, "South Africa Is Hit Hard by Iranian Oil Shortage," *Washington Post,* January 18, 1979.

11. Craig Howard, "South Africa Outbids United States for Arab Oil," *Journal of Commerce,* March 26, 1979.

12. Gary Thatcher, "Filling VW in South Africa: $26," *Christian Science Monitor,* June 12, 1979.

13. John F. Burns, "South Africa: Plunged into Oil Crisis, Seeks Way to Cope," *The New York Times,* July 13, 1979.

14. John F. Burns, "South African Oil Plan May Be Hard to Sell," *The New York Times,* September 5, 1979.

15. Jack Foisie, "South Africa Holds Lead in Making Oil from Coal," *Los Angeles Times,* July 30, 1979; Richard Gibbs, "Sasol's Multi-Million Dollar Baby," *Management,* January 1977.

16. Jan C. Hoogendoorn, "Gas from Coal for the Synthesis of Hydrocarbons," paper presented at Institution of Gas Engineers, 112th Annual General Meeting, 1975.

17. Stephen Mulholland, "South Africa's Synfuel Program," *Wall Street Journal,* July 23, 1979; "South African Oil Plan May Be Hard to Sell."

18. "Processing State Assets," *The Economist,* August 4, 1979.

19. South Africa Gains on Gold, Loses on Dollar," *Baltimore Sun,* August 17, 1978.

20. "Rand Freed from the Dollar," *The New York Times,* January 25, 1979.

21. "South Africa's Two Tier Future," *The Economist,* January 27, 1979.

22. Ibid.

23. John F. Burns, "Chamber of Mines Sets 13% Rise for 1979," *The New York Times,* November 14, 1979.

24. "South Africa Planning 300 million R. Infusion to Boost Economy, *Financial Times,* September 19, 1979.

25. "Golden Opinions," *The Economist,* January 19, 1980.

26. Ibid.

27. Ibid.

28. Robert Parker, "South Africa Steps up Coal to Oil Production," *Washington Star,* February 18, 1980.

29. "South Africa's Investment Boom," *The Economist,* March 8, 1980.

30. "Anglo-American's Golden Windfall," *Business Week,* March 17, 1980.

31. "South African Rand Rides Boom in Gold, Which Touches $850 Mark in New York," *Wall Street Journal,* January 21, 1980.

32. Jack Foisie, "Midas Touches South Africa as Gold Price Surges," *Los Angeles Times,* February 17, 1980.

33. Joseph Lelyveld, "South African Gold Boom Has Diverse Implications," *The New York Times,* June 7, 1981.

34. "South Africa Cuts Income Tax Because of Rise in Price of Gold," *The New York Times,* March 27, 1980.

35. "South Africa," *The Economist,* April 12, 1980.

36. "South African Mines," *The Economist,* July 19, 1980.

37. "South African Gold Market Seesaws," *Washington Star,* September 1, 1980.

38. "Gold Production Falls by 4% in South Africa," *Wall Street Journal,* January 28, 1981.

39. Joseph Lelyveld, "South Africa's Golden Glow Marks Deeper Problems," *The New York Times,* February 8, 1981.

40. "Southern Africa Trade in the Black," *The Economist,* May 16, 1981.

41. Ibid.

42. "South Africa Scorched by Drought and Fears of Famine," *The New York Times,* August 17, 1980.

43. Adam Hochschild, "Enlightened Despotism," *Harper's,* January 1981.

44. "Pampered No More," *The Economist,* January 24, 1981.

45. "Employers Decide Black Is Beautiful," *The Economist,* January 24, 1981.

46. "South African Trade in the Black."

47. Smith Hempstone, "Who Won Isn't Full Story of South African Election," *Washington Star,* May 6, 1981.

48. "The Economic Reckoning after the Election Boom," *Financial Times,* May 1, 1981.

49. Ibid.

50. "South African Money Market Still Has to Come of Age," *The Economist,* June 6, 1981.

51. Ibid.

52. J.D.F. Jones, "South Africa Waits Its Turn for Recession," *Financial Times,* November 12, 1981.

53. "South Africa Eases Interest Rate Limits; Prime Rises to 18%," *Wall Street Journal,* February 18, 1982.

54. "South African Gold Output," *New York Times,* January 28, 1982.

55. Ibid.

56. "Drop in Gold Prices Laid to Rise in Sales by Soviet, South Africa," *Baltimore Sun,* January 7, 1981.

57. Ibid.

58. Ibid.

59. Caryle Murphy, "South Africa and Soviet Union: Odd Pair on Minerals Markets," *Washington Post,* August 4, 1981.

60. Allister Sparks, "South Africa Cuts Spending as Gold Profits Plunge," *Washington Post,* March 27, 1982.

61. "The Veldskoen Pinches as the Gold Price Falls," *The Economist,* March 27, 1982.

62. "Zaire Sells Diamonds to European Dealers, Ending Exclusive DeBeers Arrangements," *Wall Street Journal,* June 3, 1981; and William Branigan, "Diamonds Dazzle Conceals Bitter Fight," *Los Angeles Times,* December 5, 1981.

63. "DeBeers Says That It Can Survive Woes without Having to Cut Diamond Prices," *Wall Street Journal,* May 11, 1982.

64. Ibid.

65. Allister Sparks, "South Africa's Precious Minerals Turn to Lead," *Washington Post,* January 17, 1982.

66. Joseph Lelyveld, "Coal's Surge as a South African Export," *The New York Times,* March 24, 1982.

67. Paul Van Slambrouck, "South Africa Not Enchanted by Glitter of Gold Hike," *Christian Science Monitor,* September 8, 1982.

68. Bernard Simon, "Gold Price Rise Fails to Brighten South Africa Outlook," *Financial Times,* August 25, 1982.

69. Allister Sparks, "South Africa Seeks Loan from IMF of $1.0 Billion," *Washington Post,* October 5, 1982.

70. J.D.F. Jones, "Why South Africa Has Turned to the IMF," *Financial Times,* October 6, 1982.

71. Hobart Rowan, "IMF, World Bank Meetings Conclude on Uneasy Note," *Washington Post,* September 10, 1982.

72. $1.1 Billion Loan to South Africa Reportedly to Get IMF Approval *The New York Times,* October 15, 1982.

73. Clyde H. Farnsworth, "IMF Loan to Pretoria Is Voted," *The New York Times,* November 4, 1982.

74. Ibid.

75. Raymond Bonner, "Economic Opposition on Loan to South Africa," *The New York Times,* January 13, 1983.

76. Thomas J. Bray, "South Africa: Growth and Political Reform," *Wall Street Journal,* September 9, 1982.

7

Simmering African Hot Spots

This chapter examines in detail the continent-wide climate of instability that endures in Africa outside of the Republic of South Africa. The direct effect on South Africa from any potential blowup elsewhere is hard to determine in advance. It is clear, however, that all instances of instability on the African continent lead to a climate in which the long-term stability of South Africa is threatened. The seven situations that could lead to potential difficulties of an unspecified future nature for South Africa are: (1) The Ethiopian situation, (2) the situation in and around Angola, (3) the Zimbabwe situation, (4) the southern Africa region, (5) the Libyan situation, (6) the role of France in Africa, and (7) the Indian Ocean situation. The role of the United States in relation to South Africa receives treatment in chapter 8.

The Soviet Penetration of Ethiopia

Ethiopia Takes an Ally

Soviet military assistance to Ethiopia has been massive.[1] During a three-year period beginning in late 1977, a sum in excess of $1.5 billion was spent for this purpose.[2] Fifteen percent of the USSR's total air-transport fleet was involved in this military-support operation. Sea lanes were jammed with freighters headed for the same destination.[3] At the outset the Ethiopian Air Force received MIG 21s, MIG 23s, and SU fighter-bombers. Later on, attack helicopters and MIG 24s were added to the Ethiopian weapon supply.[4]

With a traditional per capita income of less than $200 per year, Ethiopia remains one of the poorest countries in the world. It never will be able to repay the funds advanced by the USSR. This continued financial dependence must be considered along with the loss of physical control over its own destiny that has occurred. Ethiopia has paid a high price for Soviet support and Cuban troops. Nonetheless, without this assistance, the Ogaden, Eritrea, and perhaps Habre Provinces would have fallen to forces opposed to the central government in Addis Ababa.

Cuban troop strength in Ethiopia has ranged between 10,000 and

18,000 soldiers. An estimated 3,000 Soviet military advisors served in the Ethiopian campaign at the height of the Eritrean and Ogaden conflicts.[5] Two Soviet destroyers regularly shelled Eritrean forces from the waters near Massawa.[6] The Soviet air-transport fleet consistently and without permission violated Pakistani air space in order to deliver military supplies to Ethiopia.[7] Finally, it should be kept in mind that this activity occurred while the SALT II (Strategic Arms Limitation Talks) were taking place.

Even though Soviet and Cuban intervention in Ethiopia has kept the Mengistu government in power, the country's three simultaneous wars continue. Liberation forces hostile to the central government are still in the fields in Eritrea, the Ogaden, and in the northern provinces. In all three cases, thanks to Soviet and Cuban assistance, the Addis Ababa government remains clearly in the lead.[8]

Ethiopia has attained a clear advantage over Somalia in the Ogaden struggle. In 1981, Ethiopia found itself better situated than at any time during the past century. The Ogaden struggle had started in 1877 when Italy and the United Kingdom drew up boundaries that placed many ethnic Somalians within Ethiopian territory. When Somalia became independent in 1960, a further opportunity to settle the dispute occurred. Again, there was failure. The new nation of Somalia was created by unifying the former British Somaliland protectorate and the UN trust territory of Somalia. In the ensuing years, occasional fighting broke out. This struggle led to all-out war in 1977. Somalia invaded the Ogaden in order to support the independence claims of the Western Somalia Liberation Front (WSLF) against the Addis Ababa government. In the next six months, regular Somalian troops and WSLF guerrilla forces occupied 90 percent of the Ogaden. However, in 1978, 68,000 Ethiopian soldiers, aided by 7,000 Soviet-equipped Cuban soldiers, routed Somalian forces in heavy fighting. Since then, Somalian resistance within Ethiopia has been restricted to occasional guerrilla fighting.[9]

To the northeast in Eritrea province, the seaport stronghold of Massawa was lost by rebel forces. They were forced to flee to the mountains as a result. Since then, Eritrean rebel forces have spent almost as much time in fighting each other as they have in fighting the Ethiopian Army—with or without Soviet and Cuban assistance.

As if wars in the Ogaden and Eritrea were not enough to keep the Ethiopians and their allies occupied, two other liberation groups have appeared to mount challenges to the national government forces. The Tigre People's Liberation Front claims to control 80 percent of Tigre Province north of Addis Ababa. The rebels claim that 40,000 national troops are engaged in fighting in Tigre Province. In a similar development, another group of dissidents has started the Oromo Liberation Front among the Galla ethnic group. Rebels of all four groups—those in Eritrea, Ogaden, Tigre, and Galla—hope to become united in their common struggle against the national government and their Soviet and Cuban supporters.[10]

Ethiopia Consolidates Its Gains

At the end of 1980, the Ethiopian national government of Lt. Colonel Mengistu Haile Mariam made a series of diplomatic moves that weakened two of its main enemies, Somalia and the Eritrean rebels. First, Mengistu and Kenya President Daniel Arap Moi agreed to coordinate their activities in the struggle against Somalia. Almost simultaneously, Ethiopia and Sudan agreed to cooperate. The Eritrean rebels had been using the Sudan as an easy escape point from the Ethiopian force's challenge. Since the three nations involved—Kenya, Somalia, and the Sudan—are recipients of U.S. aid, and because Somalia and Kenya have granted U.S. ships access rights to local naval bases, the Ethiopian diplomatic initiative was watched with concern in Washington.[11]

During July 1981, the Mengistu government was the recipient of a surprisingly uncritical article in *Newsweek*.[12] Foregoing discussion of the hundreds of thousands of people that have been murdered, the reporter portrayed Mengistu as being less than totally under the spell of the Soviets. It was suggested that he was in the process of diverting his revolutions toward a more-Western orientation. Such wishful thinking is highly unlikely. The USSR does not deposit close to $2 billion in a country without expecting a high rate of return and without the best of geopolitical reasons for making such an expenditure. As is discussed, Ethiopia is situated ideally as a control point for Soviet influence throughout the Red Sea–Indian Ocean–Persian Gulf water route, to say nothing of posing as a land-based threat to Western-leaning nations in the region such as Egypt, Saudi Arabia, Sudan, and Kenya.[13]

Soviet military analyst Dimitri Simes has made a pertinent observation in this regard:

> The Soviets as yet have been cautious about overthrowing legitimate governments in Africa. They got involved in a struggle between rival factions in Angola and conflicting government in the Horn, but have not used dissident groups or hostile neighbors to remove pro-Western regimes. In Egypt, the Sudan, Somalia, and earlier in Ghana, the Soviet Union, despite strong displeasure, did not resist orders by local governments to withdraw its personnel. However, it is unclear what Moscow would do if it were told to leave a country where the Kremlin in addition to advisors, technicians, and a handful of pilots, could rely on Cuban combat units. Furthermore, African governments serving as hosts to Moscow and Havana, particularly those that do not enjoy, as for instance in Ethiopia and Angola, a strong control over their population and territory, would be naturally inhibited in challenging the Kremlin by the knowledge that their very survival may depend on Soviet good graces.[14]

Few analysts of the Horn of Africa situation have gone beyond a simplistic explanation of the goals for Soviet activity in Ethiopia. The phrase

'Out of Somalia and into Ethiopia' appears to exhaust the scope of most analysis. Such reasoning makes much of the tempestuousness of spirit among Somalian leaders and, at times, almost appears to take the Siad Barre government to task for not keeping its bargain with the Soviets. Some analysts seem to suggest that if the Somalians had been faithful to their agreements, the Soviets would not have masterminded the takeover of Ethiopia.[15] Such one-at-a-time reasoning is as incorrect in this instance as it was when it was supposed that the USSR would not supply arms to both India and Pakistan during their 1971 war. The same statement can be made for the belief that the Soviets would not be working to dominate the southern African sea lanes simultaneously with establishing domination over the Persian Gulf–Indian Ocean–Red Sea sea route.

Concerning the Horn of Africa, it is far more likely that the USSR would have desired to supply both Ethiopia and Somalia with their weapons, to train and lead their troops in the Ogaden fighting, and to use the strategic position of both nations to influence and perhaps control neighboring countries such as Kenya, Uganda, Sudan, Djibouti, and even Egypt.[16] When the USSR linked up with Ethiopia upon being expelled from the southern part of the Horn in Somalia, it turned its sights eastward at the same time and toiled fervently in an attempt to increase its presence and influence with the island nations located in the Indian Ocean. This theme is examined shortly.

Disruptions Continue

The confusing morass of small-scale wars plaguing the Horn of Africa added one more to its membership list during mid-1981. Not only did the Ogaden region house the WSLF as it had for many years but also, now there was a second guerrilla group operating in this area: the Somali Salvation Front (SSF). To complete this confusion, the SSF possessed a totally different objective than that of the WSLF. As discussed earlier, the WSLF is dedicated to freeing the Ogaden from Ethiopian central government control; not so with the SSF. This group is intent on overthrowing the Somali government of President Siad Barre and is cooperating with a similar group attempting Siad Barre's overthrow from neighboring Southern Yemen, across the Gulf of Aden from Somalia.

Not all observers were convinced that the members of the SSF were truly Somalians. Some felt they could be Ethiopians in liaison with the Addis Ababa government, and others wondered whether they might be Libyan troops allied to Kaddafi. In all, there are estimated to be 1,000 to 2,000 well-supplied military troops of the SSF located in the Ogaden near Diredawa, Harar, and Wardair. It is incontrovertible that the mischievous Kaddafi had been the arms supplier and that the original manufacturer of these weapons had been the USSR.[17]

The situation worsened in late August 1981 when Somalia ordered the Libyan diplomatic mission closed in its capital, Mogadishu. It also withdrew its own diplomatic representation from Tripoli, the capital of Libya. Somalia charged that Kaddafi had been guilty of endangering the unity and independence of the Somali Republic by his recent signing of friendship and cooperation treaties with Ethiopia and Southern Yemen. Both nations are longtime enemies of the Siad Barre regime in Somalia.[18]

During September 1981, President Siad Barre of Somalia displayed the sort of political legerdemain that had enabled him to stay in power since 1969. He sent out political feelers toward arranging better relations with Kenya. By so doing he followed by almost a year similar moves in this direction made by Ethiopian leader Colonel Mengistu. Siad Barre, by his efforts to forge a new alliance, proved once again that instability is the only stable element in Horn of Africa politics. The United States announced through its State Department that it was pleased Somalia was taking steps to ease tensions with one of its neighbors.[19] Since Somalia has become a client state of the United States, the Reagan administration has a definite stake in protecting the Siad Barre government. Another element in the equation is that the amount of weapons being provided by the Soviets to Ethiopia is so vast and expensive that all countermoves by the U.S. government are destined to be inadequate, surely, but also extremely expensive. The closer to living in a state of peace with the neighboring states in the region Somalia can manage to come, the less expensive will be the U.S. military-hardware bill for supplying the Siad Barre government.

During November 1981, in the wake of the Sadat assassination, the United States announced plans to carry out a test of the U.S. rapid-deployment force of 4,000 troops in Egypt, Somalia, Sudan, and Oman. The Ethiopian government reacted with fury and claimed the United States was encouraging aggression by Somalia and endangering the safety of Ethiopia. The foreign ministers of Ethiopia, Libya, and Southern Yemen vowed to make a formal protest to the UN concerning U.S. actions. Protests also were to be filed with the Organization of African Unity, the Arab League, and the Nonaligned Movement.[20]

The confused picture concerning U.S.-Ethiopian relations took another, puzzling twist during January 1982. The U.S. State Department made the judgment that affairs in Ethiopia had stabilized to a point that citizens of that country who had been allowed to stay in the United States on a year-to-year emergency basis should be sent home. The State Department decided it was no longer necessary to presuppose that the life of any expatriate Ethiopian would be in immediate danger by a forced return home. In the future, only those Ethiopians resident in the United States on an emergency basis who could prove they were on a Mengistu government wanted list or that they were a relative of a well-known political figure in Ethiopia would be allowed to stay on in the United States.[21]

Columnists commentating on the policy shift drew blood it would seem. Chester Crocker, the assistant secretary of state directly involved, took to the "Letters to the Editor" column in *The New York Times* to defend the new policy.[22] He pointed out that conditions in Ethiopia had stabilized to a point where the Mengistu government would be treated in a manner similar to a group of other harsh dictatorships with which the United States did not agree. Many observers did not agree and felt that a harsher standard was being applied in the Africa bureau than was the case for dealing with refugees from eastern Europe, to name but one other region with unpopular dictatorships. At the start of 1982, 2,400 Ethiopians resident in the United States received notice that their voluntary-departure status that had kept them resident in the United States had been canceled. Many other of the estimated 25,000 to 40,000 Ethiopians legally resident in the United States on a temporary basis were in fear of also being asked to leave.[23]

The timing of the Ethiopian-expulsion policy was baffling since it came as diplomatic relations between the United States and Ethiopia were at their worst. Speaking on October 2, 1981, U.S. Ambassador to the UN Jeane Kirkpatrick condemned the savagery of the Mengistu government and pointed out that during the five-year repressive Red Terror that ended in 1978, at least 5,000 Ethiopians were killed and 30,000 citizens were imprisoned. Kirkpatrick claimed that weekly arrests of 300 to 400 enemies of the people were continuing.[24] When political conditions of this type are added to the climate created by the coordination of foreign policy currently being practiced by Ethiopia, Libya, and Southern Yemen, the aims of the U.S. State Department move become clouded at best.

The Horn during 1982

The twenty-year Eritrean Province War heated up again during February 1982. The Ethiopian government launched an offensive in the northern part of the beleaguered province at places near the Sudanese border. Heavy damage was inflicted. A spokesperson for the Eritrean Peoples Liberation Front, speaking in New York, claimed that government troops employed napalm bombs, nerve gas, and cluster bombs in the attack.[25] The charge was also made that 400 Soviet military advisors had accompanied 90,000 Ethiopian troops into the battle. The Ethiopians were said to be employing Soviet-produced MIG 21 and MIG 23 jets, Soviet MI 24 helicopters, Libyan-supplied transport planes, and U.S. F5 fighters. The pilots were said to be, for the most part, Soviet-trained members of the Southern Yemen Air Force.[26]

The central government in Addis Ababa announced that it never would employ chemical weapons against its own people. Colonel Mengistu emphasized his position by stepping up his previously announced campaign of economic development for Eritrea called Operation Red Star. Despite continuing warfare between the Mengistu government and a wide range of opponents including the Somalian government and a variety of liberation forces in Eritrea, Habre, and Oromo Provinces, the Ethiopian leader seems to be succeeding in portraying his government in a more-favorable light before the world community than previously had been possible. Ethiopia continued to receive significant aid from Sweden and Norway each year even though official persecution continued against the Oromo Province–based Mekane Yesus Church that was much favored in Scandinavia.

In similar fashion, Ethiopia received a $173 million line of credit from France to improve the rail line between Addis Ababa and the Indian Ocean port in Djibouti. This assistance undertaken by the Mitterand government once it came into power contradicted earlier Socialist party positions. In the past, it had suggested that Eritrea, a former Italian colony that had been joined to Ethiopia by the UN as an autonomous federation in 1952 and formally annexed in 1962, should be given its freedom.[27]

During July 1982, the U.S. government backtracked. It announced that the Ethiopians who were to be sent home could remain in the United States. This belated realization that a reign of terror still existed in Ethiopia seemed to slow the trend that had been developing toward accepting it as a normal member of the community of world nations.[28]

Also in July 1982 the Somali-Ethiopia conflict again escalated. At first, the conditions of battle were unclear. It was not certain if Ethiopian regular troops were joining with the SSF—or, as it is sometimes called, The Somali Democratic Salvation Front (SDSF)—in the attack against the Somalian government of President Siad Barre.[29] Within a week it became clear that Somalia was being attacked by a joint venture. Ethiopian regulars were very much in the middle of the attack. The fighting was the worst that had occurred in five years.

In reaction to changing circumstances, the United States significantly increased its military support to the Somalian government. In the past, the United States had been reluctant to supply the Siad Barre government with the massive amount of weapons that it had always desired and now was destined to receive. It had been a long-standing fear that all arms obtained by the Somalian government would be used to restart the Ogaden War. Now that the other side had taken the first step, the main reason the U.S. government had been practicing restraint was wiped out. Traditionally Kenya and Sudan had been worried about Somalia renewing the conflict with Ethiopia but even they were alarmed by the new Ethiopian initiative and agreed with the United States intent to supply arms to Somalia.[30]

The United States had to be extremely concerned by the weak condition of the Somalian government.[31] Any successor government surely would be less sympathetic to Washington than the current government in Somalia has been since 1977. Should Ethiopian troops march through southeastern Somalia and seize or isolate the Indian Ocean port of Mogadishu, the U.S. Horn of Africa strategy would be affected in the most adverse of manners.[32]

As 1982 drew to an end, the Horn of Africa stood in no better shape than five years earlier.[33] The Soviets and Cubans still directed an aggressive Ethiopian military presence. Free access to the Indian Ocean by Western ships remains in peril, and matters have not changed for the better. In the next section, the situation in Angola is examined, revealing the same dismal picture.

Angola and Its Neighbors

A Government in Search of an Identity

The situation that has developed in Ethiopia has a parallel farther south-ward on the continent in Angola. The similarities are striking. Both nations are militantly socialist and non-Western in their governmental orientation. In each case, the predecessor system had been Western oriented. It is true that Ethiopia and Angola continue to trade with Western nations, but such activity is more a matter of necessity than choice. Concentration on trade statistics with the West obscures the reality that political penetration by the USSR and its allies grants the ability to influence economic moves in any direction desired. The economies of Ethiopia and Angola are so weak that neither nation could at this point participate profitably in Comecon, neither from their own point of view nor from that of the USSR. As a result, it is in the best interest of the USSR to allow, and even encourage, Angola and Ethiopia to improve their short-term commercial ties with the West. Such activity is advisable if for no other reason than to lessen the need for Soviet financial aid to these beleaguered economies. The USSR is having enough problems in shoring up the weak economies of longtime partners such as Poland and Cuba without adding more of an economic burden than neces-sary on the African continent.

A number of U.S. corporations, many of them in the petroleum indus-try, have been strong advocates of expanded trade with Angola. Usually, the argument is made that Angolans are pragmatic people who do not let their Marxist ideology interfere with their economic best interests. As a result, Western nations are presented with a new market in an oil-rich country. Those wishing to deal with Angola do not feel that politics should interfere with business.[34] Such corporate leaders are fond of citing the example of Cuban troops defending U.S. oil rigs in Cabinda Province. Such reasoning ignores the fact that Soviet political penetration in Angola is so complete that compliance with Moscow's dictates is assured, all self-serving statements of U.S. businesses to the contrary.[35]

As Angola seeks to repair its war-torn economy, it is faced with massive internal and external problems. Safe to say, even if the economic picture improves, the country will not be stabilized until the related external problem of UNITA and Namibia is solved. A SWAPO-controlled Namibia would serve to sandwich the ephemeral forces of Jonas Savimbi between two most unpalatable pieces of bread: the Soviet-and-Cuban-supported Angolan army to the north and a Namibia that would have strong Soviet support and a significant Cuban presence to the south. Since the Republic of South Africa would be driven on to the defensive by such a turn of events, it would be unlikely that the UNITA dissidents would long survive without the help of the Pretoria regime.

A liberated, stable Angola that had banished UNITA and had seen a SWAPO-controlled government take over Namibia would then be free to dominate its region of Africa. If the Angolans chose to play a role as a Soviet puppet, they could cause havoc by serving as a lightning rod for attacks aimed at overthrowing the apartheid regime in Pretoria. In any such anti-Western scenario, the mineral wealth of Zaire's Shaba Province would probably be the first stop. Its copper and cobalt holdings could again lure Katanga irregulars and perhaps this time Angolan regular troops as well. Both the Western world and South Africa would be threatened by any such mineral-wealth takeover. Soviet control or even influence over the distribution of the copper and cobalt resources of Shaba, Zaire, and of the mines in neighboring Zambia is almost too horrible for Western strategic planners to contemplate.

If the Angolans, with or without Soviet and Cuban help, did take the Shaba Province, Zaire's economy, and no doubt its governmental structure, would disintegrate. A locally based Marxist government with links to Luanda would serve just as well as a direct Angolan conquest. Once Shaba had fallen from the Western path, it must be assumed that Kenneth Kaunda's shaky government in Zambia soon would follow. At such time, the cards would topple one after the other. There would be an anti-Western circle starting in Namibia, continuing in Angola, Zaire, Zambia, and Mozambique. Under such circumstances, certainly not Malawi and probably not even Zimbabwe could withstand the anti-Western influences that would be set loose upon southern Africa and against the apartheid government in Pretoria.

Soviet Influence in Southern Africa

Pieces of the puzzle are starting to fall into place. At the start of 1980, a most disturbing $100 million arms deal was arranged between the USSR and Zambia. This agreement provides Kenneth Kaunda's government with a dozen MIG 21 fighter planes and a vast supply of military hardware.[36] Less than coincidental, perhaps, that the United States provided Zambia with gifts of food worth $100 million during the years from 1977–1979. Zambia's newfound discovery of the USSR's usefulness has thrown into doubt Kaunda's longtime inclination to depend upon the People's Republic of China for Communist-nation assistance.

Soviet influence in Mozambique also has been mounting. Soviet naval forces appeared near Mozambique's Indian Ocean ports during February 1981 in order to support the Samora Machel government against further attack from the Republic of South Africa. On land, Mozambique has made comparable moves that are anti–United States in character and, thus, by extension, pro–socialist bloc. During the beginning of March 1981, Mozambique broke what had been a trend toward better relations with the United States. The Machel government expelled four U.S. embassy officials for alleged Central Intelligence Agency (CIA) spying. A U.S. businessman and a visiting U.S. university professor were arrested in the same incident. The U.S. State Department denied with vehemence the correctness of the charges and blamed Cuban advisors in Mozambique for starting the trouble.[37] The U.S. government interrupted talks that had begun concerning the giving of economic aid to Mozambique. The purpose of the interruption was to protest the steps taken by the Machel government. As could be expected, the anti-Western bloc of nations criticized the United States for insensitivity to the disadvantaged people of the Third World. All rhetoric aside, Western influence in Mozambique today is not strong. Mozambique and Angola are two of the few Third World nations that have refused to join in trading pacts, called Lome Convention pacts, with the European Economic Community. Instead, Mozambique and Angola trade frequently with the USSR and other Communist countries.[38]

At some time, South Africa's military and political presence in Namibia will have to end. When that occurs, the encirclement action against South Africa will be close to complete. A strong anti-Western (or at least pro-socialist) group of nations will be free to threaten South Africa. Sam Nujoma's SWAPO forces are fully supplied with Soviet land mines, automatic rifles, and armored vehicles.[39] In addition, the assembled mass of Communist and nonaligned nations provides the loudest of vocal support for SWAPO in the assemblies of the world. In the case of Namibia, the prize to be won is most certainly worth the price the USSR will have to pay in order to have their way. Namibia's mineral resources include uranium, gold, diamonds, zinc, and copper. Adding to the riches up for grabs, the South African–constructed and –operated deep-water port facility at Walvis Bay has enormous commercial and strategic value and potential. The long-term external outlook for South Africa on the African continent could not be worse.

Stability in Angola

The move toward peace in Namibia that continued during the last half of 1981 and the first half of 1982 kept the focus on Angola as an important factor in all southern African strategic calculations. The long-held position of the U.S. government has been that the Angolan government must expel its resident Cuban troops before this former Portuguese colony can be recognized on a diplomatic level. In July 1981, this U.S. position gave signs of softening when the first U.S. Export-Import Bank loan to Angola since independence in 1974 was granted. The bank pledged $85 million to develop Angolan oil fields being operated in a joint venture by a Gulf Oil subsidiary and Sonamgol, the Angolan parastatal.[40]

The major South African assault into Angola at the end of August 1981 exacerbated relations between Angola and the United States.[41] Although it could be assumed that the U.S. government played a part in having South Africa limit the invasion to a duration of one week, the subsequent U.S. veto at the Security Council that frustrated attempts to censure South Africa for its invasion won the United States few friends or plaudits.[42] As the only nation vetoing the proposal (the United Kingdom abstained), worldwide condemnation was heaped upon the Reagan administration. In such circumstances, subsequent avowal of continuing close cooperation made by Angola and the USSR had to be expected. The sting may have been relieved somewhat by the favorable news concerning a Namibia peace time-table that was announced at the UN on September 24, 1981.[43] Angola pro-nounced itself to be satisfied, in general, with the steps toward peace, but a virtually simultaneous U.S. Senate action repealing the Clark Amendment must have caused the Angolan government to change its mind. This mea-sure removed the prohibition against the U.S. government sending military aid to forces trying to overthrow the MPLA government in Angola. The Reagan administration had lobbied heavily for the repeal of the Clark Amendment on general principles. It stressed that military aid to Jonas Savimbi and UNITA was not being contemplated at that moment but that the U.S. government felt it must be free to do so should the need arise. The Angola government could not be expected to appreciate the fine points of such reasoning.[44]

During December 1981 and January 1982, fervent efforts were made by the U.S. State Department to shore up relations with both the central government in Luanda and the UNITA rebels. Haig and Crocker invited Savimbi to Washington for talks. Rather conveniently, once the meetings had concluded, Savimbi claimed a breakthrough had taken place.[45] It was clear that the U.S. assistant secretary of state for Africa was offering a pacified Jonas Savimbi and a South African turnover in Namibia as trading inducements for the expulsion of Cuban troops as a return concession by the Angolans in subsequent talks to be held in Paris with the Luanda government.[46] In such circumstances, U.S. diplomatic recognition of Angola then would follow. It was understandable that the Angolan government would be skeptical as to whether Savimbi and his UNITA forces ever would join a coalition government in Angola. In equal measure, it was unclear whether or not a Namibian settlement would take hold. In both cases, South Africa was the major fly in the ointment. As long as South Africa perceived that it was to its advantage to prevent majority rule in Namibia, the odds were high it would frustrate negotiations and continue to encourage Savimbi to keep southern Angola in a state of turmoil. The possibility for Crocker's succeeding in normalizing U.S.-Angola relations seemed tied irretrievably to his success in convincing South Africa that it is not in its best interests to continue in encouraging ferment in the Namibia–southern Angola region. Few would envy the U.S. diplomat in his task.

In the wake of U.S. attempts to normalize relationships with Angola, the U.S. State Department was encouraged by a recently scheduled upcoming exchange of foreign prisoners to take place between MPLA and UNITA forces. Planned for February 7, 1982, at Kinshasa, Zaire, two American mercenaries and two Russians were involved.[47] The Angola government, at the same time that it was taking the first step toward peace with Savimbi and UNITA, did not neglect the opportunity in late January 1982 to strengthen its already tight ties with the USSR. The two nations signed a new ten-year economic pact and a new five-year trade, economic, and technical cooperation accord. More significant, Lucio Lara, secretary general of the MPLA, took the occasion of the pact signing in Moscow to state that the retention of Cuban troops in Angola was an internal matter separate from negotiations for peace in Namibia.[48]

Angola during 1982

The first half of 1982 was marked by continued U.S. corporate pressure aimed at convincing their government to recognize the MPLA government in Angola. David Rockefeller, the retired chairman of the Chase Manhattan Bank, was the leading advocate for this position. Speaking in March, at the end of a trip to southern Africa, he advanced his theory that the presence of

Cuban troops and Soviet advisors in Angola had no significant effect upon the ability of U.S. corporations to transact business in that country. His remarks had particular reference to the banking and petroleum fields.[49]

Angola, following the example of Ethiopia, has tried to broaden its international economic and diplomatic contacts in recent years. Both nations remain snugly within the Soviet-influence sphere, but the economic advantages to better relations with the West have become clear to both nations. Angola has been particularly active in broadening its political base. For example, the U.S. consulting firm Arthur D. Little was employed to give economic-planning advice; diplomatic relations were instituted with Senegal; the Portuguese foreign minister was invited for an official visit; negotiations were opened again with Zaire over their border disputes; a $15 million line of credit was opened with Macao, the last Portuguese colony; an official Angolan delegation visited the Canton international trade fair in the People's Republic of China; and political discussions continued with U.S. Assistant Secretary of State Chester A. Crocker.[50]

The South African government, as could be expected, continued to give the Angolan government serious cause for concern. Military incursions continued to be launched during the first half of 1982 from South African military bases in Namibia into the southern part of Angola. In one such raid that took place in mid-March 1982, Pretoria claimed that 201 SWAPO guerrillas were killed in southern Angola. In such an atmosphere of strife and discord, it is not surprising that Angola continued to desire the support provided by their Cuban and Soviet allies. Angola continued these alliances even though its economic and foreign-exchange situations were desperate and the foreign-exchange assistance that could be provided by the West would not be available until Angola loosened it ties with the Eastern bloc of nations.

The U.S. State Department remained firm in its demand that Angola send home their Cuban and Soviet troops and advisors before diplomatic relations could be established. Such a rigid position has allowed South Africa to tag along on U.S. coattails and to refuse to disengage in Namibia before the Soviets and Cubans leave Angola. It would seem that Botha had managed the tactical coup of being able to control both the timing of a Namibian solution and of U.S. diplomatic recognition of Angola.[51]

Sensing the disadvantage of their situation, but apparently powerless to react effectively, the Angolans during the middle of 1982 appeared to take steps to strengthen their ties with the Eastern bloc. New trade and military-assistance pacts were negotiated with the Soviets, and perhaps more important, a July 1982 cabinet shakeup led to the dismissal of a group of ministers whose ties to Moscow were not considered to be sufficiently firm.[52]

During the last months of 1982 and the first few months of 1983, Angola found itself squarely in the middle of the political and military unrest in southern Africa. First, South Africa maneuvered the United States into linking a Cuban troop withdrawal from Angola with a South African peace settlement in Namibia.[53] Then South Africa followed this initiative with an even more skilled diplomatic move. Foreign Minister Botha offered to hold wide-ranging diplomatic meetings with the Angolan government.[54] In both cases, the Angolan government appeared to have more to lose than to gain should the talks fall apart. The two situations demand separate study.

Once Vice President Bush had made it clear that a Cuban troop withdrawal was intrinsically linked with a Namibian peace settlement in U.S. thinking, the Angolans found themselves on the defensive. In the eyes of the Third World, Angola would be looked upon as an appeaser if it agreed. Even if peace came to Namibia without a simultaneous troop withdrawal from Angola, many would think that Angola had nonetheless capitulated to Western imperialism. Critics would be certain that Cuban troops would leave in a short time and that their continuance on Angolan soil was a face-saving mechanism to be ended at the first feasible moment. Those thinking in this manner could well be correct. The U.S. would seem to have placed the Angolan government in an awkward position.[55]

At the same time, if the Cuban troops remained, the South Africans would have found a reason for extending their occupation in Namibia (and continuing their military forays into Angola). In either event, the Angolans would be the losers.

The South African attempts to negotiate a wide-ranging bilateral arrangement with Angola placed the MPLA government in an equally difficult position. Since South Africa was attacking Angolan territory at the same time as it was funding the internal UNITA guerrilla campaign of Jonas Savimbi, it seemed imperative for the Luanda government to negotiate with the Pretoria government. The danger was that no matter what happened, the Angolan government risked added complications. If the two governments failed to reach an agreement, the South Africans would have still another reason for prolonging their Namibian occupation. Should the South Africans adopt the Bush-Crocker posture and link an unconditional troop withdrawal from Angola with a Namibian settlement, an agreement between Luanda and Pretoria would be most unlikely. It seemed the South Africans unquestionably held the upper hand.[56]

In the unlikely event that the South Africans and Angolans might be able to agree upon a wide-ranging peace treaty, problems would still remain for the Angolan government. It appears almost inconceivable that any agreement with which the Botha government would be content, could satisfy Sam Nujoma and SWAPO. By a chain reaction, the OAU and the rest of the Third World nations would be equally dissatisfied. Angola would be heavily criticized in such circumstances and its leadership role among the nations of southern Africa would be threatened seriously. Hard days lie ahead for the MPLA government in Luanda, no matter what happens.

Zimbabwe

The First Days of the New Nation

If this new nation, formed from the wreckage of Rhodesia, follows its neighbors by embracing Soviet influence and desires, one day in the future South Africa could be faced with a solid, wide-ranging, powerful front of opposition from outside its borders. In the first two years since Zimbabwe's independence, the amount of overt Soviet domination in the new country is in question. There are indications that the country's president, Robert Mugabe, wishes to be nonaligned in the true sense of the word. If so, he will be one of the very few African leaders who have been able to separate internal Marxist-socialism from external dependence upon the will of the USSR. Mugabe may be successful in retaining such a distinction if he is able to keep his political and military dependence upon the USSR separate from the pressures that influence his day-to-day running of Zimbabwe. In this regard, it might be remembered that Comecon membership for Zimbabwe might not be a bad idea, either for Mugabe's nation or for the USSR and its trade partners. The ease with which Zimbabwe entered the rolls of the African, Caribbean and Pacific (ACP) developing countries as a Lomé Convention signatory could be duplicated in dealings with the USSR.[57] Zimbabwe would not be a destitute stepsister to the USSR in economic matters as Ethiopia and Angola have been.

Neither Mozambique nor Angola has accepted the increasingly persistent invitations of the European Economic Community for them to join as ACP members of the Lomé Convention. Should Mugabe decide to take his nation out of the Lomé Convention and make a full commitment to Comecon, the balance-of-trade power and the Soviet influence in southern Africa would shift in a significant manner.

Looking at the results of the first two years of an independent Zimbabwe, it is clear that some type of Marxist-Leninist perspective will prevail as the government's dominant political philosophy. Nonetheless, it must be admitted that the swing in this direction has been less sudden and less radical than most Western observers had expected.

Even Ian Smith was motivated to volunteer that conditions in independent Zimbabwe were not as he had thought they might be. In case anyone might have assumed that the former prime minister of Rhodesia was mellowing, he did hasten to add that "he found a number of Mr. Mugabe's ministers to be moving in the opposite direction."[58] He thought they were provocative and that they went out of their way to humiliate and insult white people, an action obviously upsetting to those of them who hope to stay in Zimbabwe. It should be mentioned that not all analysts agree that the disappearance of whites from Zimbabwe and the adoption of an anti-Western pro-Soviet stance by the Mugabe government will necessarily go hand-in-hand, although the odds in that direction are strong.

Robert Mugabe has demonstrated a strong grasp of the art of the possible in national leadership. Nonetheless, events have cast doubt on his ability, or anyone's ability for that matter, to keep the ship of state on a steady course in the new nation. Mugabe's hold on power is tenuous, and hotter heads could combine to oust him at any time. These insurgents would be sure to erase any doubts still existing as to whether Marxist-Leninist philosophy would prevail in Zimbabwe or whether whites would be able to stay in the country. In the event of a Mugabe overthrow from the left, one more African state most certainly would come under Soviet domination. Even with Mugabe in control, the result could well be the same.

Largely because of Robert Mugabe's smoothly presented politicking for massive U.S. aid from the Carter administration during his fall 1980 visit to Washington, it was widely assumed that Moscow had suffered a setback in Zimbabwe. Such wishful thinking flies in the face of the long-proven African tendency to accept aid from any and all donors while simultaneously being far slower to let their political persuasions be affected by the beneficence of the donor. Especially in the deprived areas of the Third World, this independent cast of mind may not be the worst of attitudes for struggling regimes to adopt. The move of the Carter administration, supported and confirmed by the Reagan administration, to dispense $85 million a year of aid for three years in Zimbabwe must be evaluated in this light. It well could be possible that U.S. analysts overrate the effect this donation will have on Mugabe's thinking concerning the major-power confrontation between the United States and the USSR.

While taking a two-week tour of Asia during 1981 that included visits to China, Japan, India, and Pakistan, Mugabe made statements that illustrated his continuing intention to stay independent and nonaligned on an international level. He refused to support the Reagan administration attempts to bring about independence in Namibia along with a simultaneous withdrawal of Cuban troops from Angola. Mugabe stated that he hoped the United States would not drift from the UN's position. He gave the opinion that the South Africans are not in Namibia because the Cubans are in Angola. He followed by stating, "If that is the logic being employed in Washington, then Zimbabwe should give a logic lesson to the American administration."[9] Mugabe says Zimbabwe cannot accept that the solution black African nations are seeking for Namibia should depend on withdrawal of the Cubans from Angola. That is a different matter, he concluded. During the same May 1981 trip to Asia, Mugabe also strongly condemned the Soviet invasion of Afghanistan. He compared it with South Africa's incursions into Angola and Mozambique and said the Soviet action was utterly wrong.

During the early days of Zimbabwe's independence, some Western analysts placed great emphasis on Prime Minister Mugabe's lethargy in recognizing the USSR's ambassador to the new nation. Those impressed by this move assumed it meant a Western swing was taking place in Mugabe's thinking. So far, this conclusion remains unsubstantiated. It is more likely that Mugabe was slow to recognize the USSR as a method of chiding the Soviets for supporting the Joshua Nkomo forces rather than his own during the war for independence. In addition, Mugabe, by his slowdown tactics, was serving notice that he would not follow slavishly in the path dictated by Moscow, if he was able to do otherwise. During the war, much of Mugabe's outside support had come from the People's Republic of China.

Another reason for Mugabe's cautious attitude toward the USSR could well have been that it permitted him to lull Western nations to sleep. He could be confident in the belief that their short span of attention would lead them to forget Zimbabwe after a year or two. Such Western inattention would allow him to implement whatever political philosophy he chose to pursue.

Zimbabwe Moves toward Becoming a One-Party State

As the months pass by, it is becoming certain that, all talk of one-man-one-vote aside, Zimbabwe was becoming a one-party-rule socialist dictatorship. During February 1981, Joshua Nkomo's mostly Matabele tribal forces were defeated in two serious clashes that threaten to replace the recently ended black-against-white civil war with one of a black-against-black variety. 300 people were killed and 100 more left homeless in skirmishes between various armed groups in the Bulawayo area. With the help of white troops left over from Ian Smith's Rhodesian army, Mugabe was able to quell the rebellion and install order. It seems unlikely that forces loyal to Nkomo will be able to defeat the national army in future armed skirmishes.[60]

Another event that shook the fledgling nation during early days of independence concerned the activities of Edgar Tekere, a strong threat to Mugabe's unchallenged place of overall leadership. Tekere had been a guerrilla leader of great courage. However, he seemed to have difficulty in realizing that the war was over. While serving as chairman of Zimbabwe African National Union-Patriotic Front (ZANU-PF) and as minister of manpower, planning, and development in the Mugabe government, he was a strong advocate of extracting revenge against white people on the losing side. Mugabe was having extreme trouble in keeping the leader of the national political party under control. However, a surprising event caused most observers to forget Tekere as an aspirant for Mugabe's throne.

Tekere was acquitted, in a highly publicized trial, for the August 1980 murder of a white farmer near Salisbury on a technicality, one that was the height of irony. During the days of the Rhodesian government, Ian Smith had pushed through Parliament a law exonerating cabinet members and members of Parliament for criminal activity taken in the pursuit of preserving peace and justice. The law had not been repealed, and Tekere was allowed to go free as a result.

Once the celebration within ZANU-PF had run its course upon Tekere's acquittal, Mugabe moved quickly to remove his friend and associate from the political limelight and, most probably, away from the seat of all authority. Tekere was dismissed as minister for manpower, planning, and development. This government move also must have weakened Tekere's power within Mugabe's majority political party, ZANU-PF. Some months thereafter, Mugabe removed him from this post as well. Edgar Tekere remains nonetheless a powerful political figure, and alone, or in conjunction with other black supremacists such as Rex Nhongo, Hert Ushewokunze, or Eddison Zvobgo, an overthrow of Mugabe and a lurch toward the USSR is never beyond reasonable conjecture.[61]

At the same time as Edgar Tekere was dismissed from the government, Joshua Nkomo, the so-called Father of the Revolution, was demoted from the minister of home affairs post in which he controlled the nation's police, to a largely ceremonial post of minister without portfolio. Clearly, Nkomo was humiliated by the move, but he had little choice other than to accept.[62]

In addition to pushing aside Nkomo and Tekere, Prime Minister Mugabe has moved to eradicate what little was left of freedom of press in the communications industry of Zimbabwe. The government forced the South African–based Argus publishing group to sell their Zimbabwe newspapers including the prestigious *Zimbabwe Herald, Sunday Mail* and the *Bulawayo Chronical*. ZANU-PF has taken over control of these papers and most probably will administer them in much the same one-party-state manner as it now does the radio and television of the nation. In such a climate, subtle agitation toward confiscation of some white farmland easily can be justified and promoted. For the first time in the history of this troubled land, it has been noted that it is necessary on occasion to bribe government officials in order to receive necessary permits. It similarly may be necessary to hire the services of party faithfuls in order to obtain many contracts. In addition, during February 1981, Zimbabwe granted full diplomatic recognition to the USSR. The period of chiding the Soviets for their lack of support during the independence war would seem to have ended.

The political maneuverings in the new nation of Zimbabwe captured the headlines, but in reality, the restoration of the economy was the most pressing priority. Roger Riddell, a liberal British economist who had attached himself to the Mugabe forces during the war, became the leading planner for economic change. Riddell, who had studied in Rhodesia during the years that he was a Jesuit, possessed great experience in studying the existence of poverty in Rhodesia. As a result of the Riddell Commission proposals, the Mugabe government moved to double, triple, and in some cases, raise even higher the minimum wage for various sectors of the economy. The basic strategy was eventually to place the whole economy on a wage-earning basis, end subsistence farming, and terminate the many preferences that whites had built in to the Rhodesian economy for themselves. Whether or not whites would choose to remain in the new Zimbabwe was to be up to them. At least in the short run, it appeared Mugabe would not discriminate against whites. Since they no longer would receive a preference, it was questionable how many would remain in a colorless society in which they would be a small numerical minority—150,000 to 175,000—in a population of 9 million.[63]

During May 1981, the Mugabe government succeeded in disarming all former guerrillas. Groups of well-armed guerrillas had presented a continuing problem. There was not room for all of these fighters in the new Zimbabwe army, yet at the same time, the government owed them a great deal: independence would not have been obtained without their assistance. Sitting idly for many months, it was inevitable many would turn to criminal activity or, in the case of Joshua Nkomo's supporters, military attempts to overthrow the Robert Mugabe government.[64]

Zimbabwe continued on its path toward eradicating all traces of its past. Corporate and individual taxes were raised significantly. Affluent whites were the main targets of the new laws. Making the situation worse from their point of view was the Mugabe government decision to tighten currency-exchange regulations making it extremely hard for those leaving the country to take their assets, even their personal possessions, with them.

No one step, however, brought home the fact that the situation in Zimbabwe had changed irreversibly with more force than the arrival of 100 North Korean advisers to train a brigade of Zimbabwean army troops.[65] It must be remembered that during the civil war, the Ian Smith government had emphasized its pro-Western anti-Communist roots with every bit as much force as took place habitually in South Africa. Ian Smith had been a fighter pilot in the United Kingdom during World War II and had been shot down and badly scarred. Even though most of the white population in Rhodesia/Zimbabwe felt they had been betrayed by the United Kingdom during the years of UDI, Western roots were sufficiently strong that they must have been disgusted and frightened by such a manifestation of nonalignment or, perhaps, Marxist leanings in the Mugabe government. Hopes of a black-governed, Western-style democracy appeared to be fading.

By late October 1981, Prime Minister Mugabe was discussing openly the possibility of a one-party state for Zimbabwe. Speaking at the southern-border town of Plumtree, he stated, "There are only two parties left. [Bishop Abel] Muzorewa, [James] Chikerema and [Ndabaningi] Sithole have fallen by the wayside. They do not matter any more."[66] Mugabe allowed that a one-party state would not be formed if the people did not wish it. Given the heavy concentration of power now found in his hands and his predilection to rule without the interference of Joshua Nkomo, it appeared to be a matter of time alone before a one-party Marxist-oriented state would rule supreme in Zimbabwe. Long forgotten, it would seem, were U.S. and British assurances to all that a Western-style democracy would flourish in the new nation.

Mugabe and Nkomo Feud

The rickety alliance between Robert Mugabe and Joshua Nkomo finally ended on February 17, 1982. Twenty-two months of national-unity government drew to a close. Mugabe dismissed Nkomo and accused him of plotting to overthrow the government. Mugabe disclosed that a supply of Soviet-made weapons had been found on a farm owned by a holding company controlled by Nkomo. "We feel cheated," said Mr. Mugabe. "Those we have trusted as partners turn out to be deceitful persons."[67] Joshua Nkomo, for his part, claimed that Mugabe had instituted a reign of terror.

Some observers assumed that Nkomo would soon be arrested, with a widely publicized political trial to follow. However, they proved to be incorrect. The Mugabe government did not wish to allow its opponent to don the robes of a martyr. Strong steps, nonetheless were taken. Enough arms to conduct a small war were confiscated, and many businesses associated with Nkomo and his followers were closed. In addition, some of his followers were detained under emergency legislation still in effect from the time of the war. Although Prime Minister Mugabe could not establish a one-party state for at least seven years according to the terms of the Lancaster House Peace Treaty, he had arrived at the next best solution. His only serious power rival had been stripped of all power. In many ways, it was sad to see a man like Nkomo, who had devoted three decades to bringing black rule to Zimbabwe, forced to stand mute on the sidelines so soon after independence and the establishment of black rule.

Two weeks later, Robert Mugabe turned his attention to the mining industry. Enabling legislation was passed to give the government control of the marketing of all minerals extracted in Zimbabwe. Those looking on the bright side pointed out that no indications existed that the government would move to use this power and, in effect, to nationalize the profitable $600-million-a-year industry. British, U.S., and South African corporations, heavily invested in minerals in Zimbabwe, remained extremely worried. Their fears were transmitted quickly to other multinational corporations doing business, or thinking of doing business, in Zimbabwe. Such investor panic did untold harm to the economy of the war-ravished, fledgling nation. When the Minerals Mining Act was coupled with the move toward the Marxist model of a one-party state, many became worried that South Africa would feel threatened and contemplate actions to cause further trouble for Robert Mugabe.[68]

The difficulties within Zimbabwe continued. After an encouraging start, the economy began to waver seriously. All the expected pitfalls began to be encountered. The infrastructure was weak; foreign currency was lacking; skilled white technicians were leaving the country before local replacements could be trained; and the foreign-investment climate was clouded by fears of expropriation and revolution.

In 1981, the inflation rate was 14 percent, almost double the 7.3 percent rate in 1980. Strict currency and price controls had to be enacted after the trade deficit skyrocketed to $126 million in 1981 after recording an impressive surplus of $92 million in 1980. Exports fell to their lowest level since 1970. Imports were at their highest level since 1974. The current-account deficit rose to a figure in excess of $500 million.[69] Mining production fell by 5.1 percent after a rise of 31.8 percent in 1980. The mineral-profit decline recorded in 1981 was the first that had taken place in twenty years. More disturbing, it came as asbestos prices were rising on the world market. This gain did not offset market softness in the prices of gold, silver, copper, and nickel.[70]

In such a volatile climate, it is not surprising that an assassination attempt was made upon the prime minister. It failed, but it well may not be the last such attempt. The attack took place on June 24, 1982. Predictably, supporters of Nkomo were blamed.[71] Matters in Zimbabwe seemed to be deteriorating daily. One did not need to have acute hearing to be able to detect white South Africans saying, We told you so.

As months passed, the situation deteriorated, if one defines the move to a Mugabe-led dictatorship as deterioration. The homeless placed heavy demands on the government for land.[72] Both whites and members of the Nkomo faction were disturbed by the redistribution methods employed. It was difficult for the Prime Minister to preach reconciliation in such an atmosphere.[73] Matabele-tribe supporters of Joshua Nkomo became increasingly alienated. The government charged many of Nkomo's supporters, including two famous liberation fighters, Lookout Masuku and Dumiso

Dabengwa, with treason.[74] With reason, Nkomo feared he might be next. Heavy fighting between government troops loyal to Mugabe and former freedom fighters loyal to Nkomo broke out in early 1983 in the Bulawayo area. More than 150 people were killed in the skirmishing, and the sad days of killing in Rhodesia–Zimbabwe appeared to be returning.[75] By the end of February 1983, it seemed Nkomo was left with two options: Flee or be arrested. As this book heads to print, March 1983, he has chosen to flee.

Regional Solidarity in Southern Africa

A Region of Weakness

As important as Angola and Zimbabwe are as independent factors in southern African political and economic projections, they both also hold vast potential as future regional leaders. For the present, the Angolans are so deeply involved in their own problems that regional leadership, or even active participation, cannot be contemplated seriously. The story could be different in Zimbabwe, but as discussed, the situation within Zimbabwe seems to be deteriorating, and with this deterioration, the chance to assume regional leadership is fading.

As long as the black nations of southern Africa drift rudderless the Pretoria government is most able and willing to dominate the region and to prefer its own interests to that of its black-governed neighboring nations. Four of the nine nations in the region are already closely and disadvantageously tied to the South African government. These nations are Botswana, Lesotho, and Swaziland, often called the BLS nations, and the tiny nation of Malawi. Economic realities promote the continuation of the status quo. Of the other five black nations in the area, Tanzania is far enough away geographically from South Africa so as to be less directly involved. Problems in Zambia and Mozambique are at least as serious, however, as those in Angola and Zimbabwe. The sum total is that South Africa remains the unchallenged regional leader.

The southern African nations surrounding South Africa appear doomed to pass the next few years in a state of perpetual instability. Such a condition further aggravates the natural weaknesses caused by their gravely inferior economic and political situation when compared with that of South Africa. Even if their white-skinned adversary headquartered in Pretoria sat back and did nothing to stir added discord in the region, nations such as Zambia, Zimbabwe, Angola, and Mozambique will contend with economic and political instability of major proportions in the next few years. Should South Africa choose to hinder economic or political progress in a major way, it could cause many problems even if no direct political steps were taken to bring down the government of the nation in question.

Zambia is one example of a vulnerable southern African economy. The day can be seen when its mining industry no longer will be the main foreign-exchange provider for this landlocked economy. Estimates are that within twenty years the copper and cobalt reserves of Zambia will be reduced seriously.[76] It will be necessary for agriculture and industry to take up the slack.

The first twenty years of an independent Zambia do not offer much hope for quick progress toward building the nonmining portions of the Lusaka government's economy. Even a prosperous 1981 corn crop could not hide the enormous weakness of the foreign-exchange picture in Zambia. Payment arrears on overseas purchases rest at a sum in excess of $600 million. Repayment demands require an average of two years for fulfillment. Zambia hopes the International Monetary Fund will provide $950 million to assist its hard-pressed economy. Unfortunately, most of this money is, of necessity, destined to rectify the payment imbalance rather than to improve the agricultural and industrial infrastructure. As a result, favorable crop years like 1981 will not provide the impetus toward economic advancement that otherwise would be the case. When bad crop years occur, such as happened to Zambian corn in 1979 and 1980, South Africa can charge almost any price it wishes for the corn surplus it has available for sale. If it wished, South Africa could exploit the economic situation in Zambia and push the population toward revolt.[77]

The economy of Mozambique is also quite feeble. The erratic political course traced by Samora Machel has not helped in this regard. The U.S. government has provided minimal assistance at best. Only in cases like the starvation conditions found in the wake of the 1981 droughts and floods would Washington permit grain to be shipped to Mozambique. The Marxist-oriented government has been notedly anti–United States as, for example, when it expelled several U.S. diplomats in March 1981 for being undercover CIA agents. Without U.S. food assistance, Mozambique also must turn in the direction of South Africa—a fact not lost on the Pretoria government when it deals on a political basis with Machel and his ministers. The external debt of Mozambique resembles that of Zambia. It is estimated to be between $600 and $800 million while the overall balance-of-payment deficit stands at $250 million. External investment that could occur in oil, minerals, and light industry have not taken place because of excessive political risk. The same constraints exist as to development aid that otherwise might be forthcoming.[78]

The Search for Acceptable Ports

Mozambique possesses the port potential to establish itself as a respectable regional trade entity, one not overly dependent upon South Africa. In reality, however, neither Beira nor Maputo has become the fulcrum of southern

African black nations' trade that had been hoped.[79] Beira, for example, two years after the end of the Rhodesia/Zimbabwe civil war, was still shipping less than half of the freight tonnage it did ten years ago. Such failure has subverted the most ambitious dreams of the Southern African Development Coordination Conference (SADCC). This group of nine black-ruled nations was still acting upon the euphoria produced by the ending of white rule in Rhodesia. SADCC, formed in 1979, adopted the premise that Beira, Maputo, and the smaller port at Nacala, all located in Mozambique, possessed the potential to provide the member nations with an alternative to shipping their goods through South African ports. A black African outlet to the Indian Ocean would be the first step toward breaking South African domination of the continent's southern perimeter.

Evaluated three years later, the Mozambique port option appears to be a failure. As a result, the converse is also true. South Africa has succeeded in retaining its position of economic domination in relation to the nine nation members of SADCC: Angola, Botswana, Lesotho, Malawi, Mozambique, Swaziland, Tanzania, Zambia, and Zimbabwe. This statement has particular validity in terms of the six landlocked members of the SADCC: Botswana, Lesotho, Malawi, Swaziland, Zambia, and Zimbabwe. They must find external-port outlets for their goods. Since political and economic conditions in Angola and Tanzania remain highly tenuous, Luanda and Dar Es Salaam possess limited major-port potential for the region. As a result, ports in Mozambique or South Africa are the only viable alternatives. If Mozambique cannot provide a port shipping solution, then the only answer is the unpalatable one of continued dealing with South Africa.

Why has the Mozambique-port alternative plan failed? The answer contains the usual elements associated with hurried development: weak infrastructure, poor planning, overtaxed facilities, corruption, pilferage, and the like. In addition, three other elements have been present. First a brushfire civil war conducted by the Mozambique resistance movement has shaken regional confidence in the stability of the Machel government. Persistent acts of destruction at the ports and on the railroad lines in Mozambique have caused potential customers to continue shipping via South African ports.

The Samora Machel government has charged that the South African government is supplying their guerrilla opponents so that they will wreck the Mozambique economy. Such charges are difficult to prove, and the South African government has denied their truth vociferously. It is certain, however, that South Africa is supplying UNITA guerrilla forces in Angola and that these Jonas Savimbi–directed troops are disrupting the Angolan economy to the eventual profits of South African business. A similar South African strategy is not unlikely as to Mozambique.

The second added element accounting for the failure of the Mozambique-port alternative concerns the depth of South African penetration of the decision-making levels in the Mozambique government. Secrecy shrouds this situation on both sides. Machel and his supporters do not wish to admit that their white opponents in South Africa still control many corporations and government functions in their socialistic-tending nation. Such a state of affairs will change slowly. South African and Portuguese economic domination of colonial Mozambique may be on the wane today, but it still has not evaporated. Even the Mozambique ports still are directed by South African functionaries. The Mozambique government, for its part, will not discuss the subject of lingering colonialism. Its justification for allowing South African participation must be that the faltering Mozambique economy needs specialized outside help and that people who have spent all their life in southern Africa, such as white business people and government functionaries, are inherently better equipped to provide this assistance than would be any Soviet, Cuban, or East German volunteer, no matter how well motivated ideologically such a person might be.

The South Africans still affiliated with Mozambique by governmental or commercial ties operate in the same netherworld as French citizens who play a similar, equally well-remunerated, role in their former colonies in Africa. In both cases the developed nation in question has implanted its tentacles deeply. France still has a large say in the dealings of its former colonies even though a near quarter-century has passed since independence. No one should be surprised that South African and Portuguese interests still are well protected in neighboring Mozambique, all Marxist rhetoric to the contrary notwithstanding. Any movement toward massive port expansion in Mozambique would not be appreciated in South Africa and, thus, in the short run, is unlikely to occur.

The third reason for the slowdown in Mozambique port usage is harder to explain but is nonetheless equally verifiable. Zimbabwe has been slow to switch port business from South Africa to its ideologically compatible black neighbor, Mozambique. A group of reasons, all perhaps with partial validity, can be advanced for this slower-than-anticipated business switch. The first and no doubt the most valid reason is that old habits die hard. Especially during the long civil war, Rhodesian commerce had been routed exclusively southward to Durban, Capetown, and other South African ports. To the extent whites remain in charge of shipping details in newly independent Zimbabwe, such trade-routing patterns still hold.

The second reason is that the black government and newly installed black business leaders in Zimbabwe also, less expectedly, have been following the lead of their predecessors. Fear of disruption and inefficiency at ports in Mozambique must be the main motivator for continuing usage of South African ports. The postwar Zimbabwe economy is fragile enough without adding shipping difficulties to its problem list.

The third reason is that there is a competitive factor involved in keeping trade away from the ports in Mozambique. Robert Mugabe is dedicating full effort to establishing Zimbabwe as the commercial giant of the SADCC group. Overly heavy shipping dependence on Mozambique would not well serve such ambitions.

Tensions between South Africa and Zimbabwe

In Zimbabwe itself, relations with South Africa have been careening along a wavering path. As months passed by, the Pretoria government displayed growing impatience with anti–South African rhetoric emanating from Salisbury. On most occasions, the Botha government suffered the abuse in silence. However, it did feel constrained to remind Zimbabwe that it still held massive economic leverage it could instantly apply against the new nation whenever it so wished. Over 90 percent of exports and imports from and to Zimbabwe pass through South African ports, a fact that Pretoria is not unwilling to call to the attention of the Mugabe government on occasion.[80]

During 1981, South Africa took time to define the ground rules of its relationship with Zimbabwe. A firm hand was applied by Prime Minister Botha. In March 1981, the South African government announced the forthcoming end of preferential bilateral trade agreements favoring Zimbabwe. Then, in a follow-up step, white Zimbabweans were obliged to obtain visas for each entry into South Africa. This move was aimed unquestionably at business travelers, many of whom had been virtual commercial commuters between Salisbury and Bulawayo on one end and Johannesburg on the other. The resultant slowdown was highly inconvenient and hampered business transactions especially since telephone communications can be uncertain anywhere in southern Africa, even within the city limits of Johannesburg.

During July 1981, the South African government increased economic pressure by withdrawing permission for Zimbabwe to continue using twenty-six locomotives that had been on loan from South Africa. The hard-pressed Zimbabwe transport system could ill afford the added pressure placed upon it by this obstructionist move. Shortly after the locomotive-transport withdrawal, the diesel-oil supply inside Zimbabwe dropped to a three-day supply. This disruption was due to be alleviated since a Beira-Salisbury oil pipeline was scheduled for reopening during 1982. It had been closed during the early days of the Rhodesian civil war. In addition, newly purchased U.S. locomotives would arrive eventually—returning the overall trade situation to approximately the same unsatisfactory place it had been when the South African locomotive withdrawal had started.

South Africa continued to insist quietly but firmly that Zimbabwe tone down the rhetoric. Without doubt, the Botha government was still smarting at the insult handed to it by Prime Minister Mugabe when he had led Zimbabwe to sever diplomatic relations with South Africa. When the locomotive issue arose, South Africa demanded that the Zimbabwe government, and not private business in the country, must request the extension of the transport leases. Such a need for official contact at government levels would be humiliating to Zimbabwe since it had proclaimed it would have nothing more to do with the government of South Africa. Given the current circumstances, massive pride swallowing appeared to be in order. As if to emphasize the point, South Africa chose this moment to announce that it had loaned twelve locomotives through government channels to Zaire and Botswana in recent months. Zimbabwe appeared to have little choice but to fall in line as well.[81]

As 1982 began, backstage negotiations on relations between South Africa and Zimbabwe gathered speed. Observers were certain that U.S. Assistant Secretary of State Chester A. Crocker was playing an important role in this activity. It appeared that Crocker and other Western-nation intermediators were afraid that a South African economic freeze out of Zimbabwe might tip the scales in sending the newly formed nation into the anti-Western, pro-socialist camp. Pressure was placed on the Botha government to be more reasonable.[82] Threats by Robert Mugabe to end "the minerals ripoff," as he termed it, by nationalizing the country's substantial natural resources were seen as an attempted counterattack on his part, aimed at forcing Western nations to persuade South Africa to ease the economic pressure it was applying.[83] Mugabe demonstrated great shrewdness by allowing mineral corporations working in Zimbabwe to shoulder the main burden of the politicking on this point. Anglo-American, Rio-Tinto, Lonrho, Turner, Union Carbide, and Newmont Mining are well capable of having their point of view considered in world capitals such as Washington, D.C., London, and Pretoria.

On his own behalf, Robert Mugabe was equally as vocal. He accused South Africa of training 5,000 to 6,000 black guerrillas who eventually would filter into Zimbabwe in order to cause destruction as a prelude to a coup attempt. Explosions and arms-cache robberies that took place within Zimbabwe during early 1982 were blamed on Pretoria, a charge quickly and scornfully rebutted by the white-controlled government to the south.[84]

The situation prevailing in Malawi, Botswana, Lesotho, and Swaziland is equally depressing. Especially in the case of the BLS nations, their economic inferiority is guaranteed by the terms of the Southern African Customs Union Agreement with South Africa. As long as this agreement remains in effect, hopes for a powerful grouping of the nine black nations in the area most probably will fail to be realized. Originally instituted in 1889 as an agreement between the Cape Colony and the then independent Orange Free State, from the beginning the customs union was planned to encompass other regions. In 1910, after the foundation of the republic, the BLS territories became signatories of the second part. The successor agreement, the Customs Union Agreement of 1970, between South Africa and the BLS countries significantly raised, by 42 percent, the amount of tariff duties retained by the BLS countries. Unfortunately, these three small nations have been kept in a state of dependence, both economic and political, upon South Africa. Not only do the BLS economies fail when their own nations come upon hard times, but also the BLS economies fail when the South African economy falls upon hard times. Either way, the BLS countries are the losers. Regional solidarity is difficult, perhaps impossible, to achieve in such an economic atmosphere.

By the end of 1982, it had become clear to all that South Africa was actively working against its neighbors' attempts to join together in cooperative efforts. The evidence of interference and destabilization efforts being launched from Pretoria was overwhelming. First, the chief of the South African Defense Force, General Constand Viljoen, was forced to admit that three white soldiers killed in Zimbabwe on August 18, 1982, had been members of his force. He stated they had entered the territory of Zimbabwe without permission in an attempt to free some political dissidents believed to be held in the southern part of the country. Seventeen white soldiers, all former members of the Rhodesian army, took part in the unauthorized attack.[85]

On December 9, 1982, saboteurs attacked a fuel pipeline outside Beira, Mozambique. Fires erupted that burned all day. As a result, all oil deliveries to Zimbabwe were made impossible, and within two weeks, oil and gas supplies in Zimbabwe evaporated. Shortages as serious as any encountered during the Rhodesian war were the immediate result. A guerrilla organization, the Mozambique National Resistance claimed credit. The Samora Machel government blamed South Africa and claimed that it was supporting destabilization in Mozambique and in the rest of southern Africa.[86]

The evidence would seem to support the destabilization charge. In addition to the armed incursion into Zimbabwe, and the probable involvement in the destruction of the Beira-to-Zimbabwe pipeline, South Africa has, in recent months, launched armed attacks into Angola and Lesotho, threatened Swaziland and, at the least, turned a blind eye to the activities of South-African-led white mercenaries attempting a takeover in the Seychelles. In the light of such activities, many doubt that South Africa desires to bring peace to Namibia or racial equality and freedom to its own land.

Kaddafi's Libya

A Violent Past

Libya is the third Soviet helpmate. The erratic Colonel Muammar Kaddafi is willing to start wars of destabilization aimed at trans-Arabic solidarity on every occasion possible. Since taking control of his oil-rich country in 1969, Kaddafi has pursued one expansionistic scheme after another.[87] A year-by-year accounting of his exploits demonstrates that the colonel has been a busy man.

In 1970, he proposed a federation with his neighbor, the Sudan, and gave aid and training for members of the Palestine Liberation Organization (PLO). This PLO support has continued until the present day. In 1971, he proposed mergers with both Egypt and Syria and supported a plot against King Muhammad Hassan II of Morocco. In 1973, he proposed a merger with Egypt.

1974 was a particularly busy year for Kaddafi. He authored an unsuccessful plot to assassinate Anwar Sadat of Egypt. He also proposed a merger with Tunisia and attempted to assassinate President Jaafar Nimeiry of Sudan. His attempts to overthrow the current government in Sudan have continued until the present.

In 1975, he agreed to a short-lived and unsuccessful alliance with Algeria and started financing the production of an Islamic nuclear bomb in Pakistan. This unsuccessful project continued through 1978. During the same year, he also began his support of the Polisario rebels in the western Sahara. In like manner, support to these highly successful rebels has continued until the present. During 1978 he attempted to annex territory in mineral-rich Niger. In the following year, 1979, his forces fought border skirmishes with Egyptian military forces. In the Horn of Africa he withdrew his support from the Eritrean Liberation Front and gave it to the Addis Ababa government of Mengistu Haile Mariam.

During 1979, Colonel Kaddafi sustained his most marked military defeat to date: He attempted to preserve Idi Amin as dictator in Uganda. In 1980, his forces interfered with the election of President Milton Obote. In the Gambia he trained local insurgents. Once again he proposed a merger with Syria. In 1981 he encouraged tribal conflict in Ghana, dispatched Libyan volunteers to aid the PLO, and attempted to have the president of Somalia, Muhammad Siad Barre, overthrown.

Kaddafi Moves into Chad

Kaddafi's other moves pale in comparison with his 1980–1981 large-scale intervention in the civil war in Chad. Before most observers realized what had happened, Kaddafi's Libya had achieved a blatant, audacious, and immensely successful conquest of a strife-torn neighboring country. Kaddafi's virtual annexation of Chad was a total repudiation of the Organization of African Unity. He made it clear for all to see that its long-held principle of promoting territorial integrity and regional unity on the African continent could be evaded with impunity.

The implications of a permanent Kaddafi takeover in Chad would be enormous. First, as stated, any Organization of African Unity hopes for permanent promulgation of the principles of territorial integrity and noninterference in the internal affairs of other organization members would be destroyed. In an intemperate editorial, the *Washington Post* compared the Libyan colonel to Hitler. It also said that "Colonel Kaddafi's outlawry is only matched by other nations' tolerance of it."[88]

Second, Libya has served notice to all other countries in the region that they had better beware. When Chad and Libya are taken together as a pivot base from which aggressive activities could emanate, the number of nations immediately threatened is huge. The following nations have borders touching Libya, Chad, or both: Tunisia (Libya), Egypt (Libya), Sudan (Libya and Chad), Central African Republic (Chad), Cameroon (Chad), Nigeria (Chad), Niger (Chad and Libya), and Algeria (Libya).

Among the group of nations that border on Libya and/or Chad, the weakest militarily speaking would be Sudan, the Central African Republic, Niger, and Tunisia. Without large foreign-power support, none of these nations could withstand attack from Libya. Niger is the most likely target of the four. Tunisia is the least likely target, and the Sudan and Central African Republic fall in the middle.

Niger is poverty stricken, poorly run, militarily weak, and blessed with large though declining quantities of uranium. Its appeal to Kaddafi is understandable, especially since he has decided to make self-production of an atom bomb one of his nation's top priorities. On a strategic level, control of Niger would add significantly to the number of border states that then would be threatened seriously by Libya. Niger borders upon Mali, Upper Volta, and Benin. Algeria and Nigeria already possess touching borders with Libya and Chad respectively, but a Libyan-controlled Niger would exascerbate the situation.

Extending the falling-dominoes theory slightly further, a Libyan-controlled Niger also would give access to the borders of the virtually deserted country that is Mali, and Mali lies at the doorway to a plethora of west African nations that list the Atlantic Ocean as their westwardmost boundary. No less than eight coastal nations border on Mali: Mauritania, Senegal, Gambia, Guinea Bissau, Guinea, Sierra Leone, Liberia, and the Ivory Coast. If Upper Volta's bordering nations are included in the list, the number of common borders with the Ivory Coast expands, and Togo and Benin are added to the common-border list.

The three other nations sharing common borders with Libya and Chad that have been identified as being particularly vulnerable also have common boundaries with many other countries: the Central African Republic, Sudan, and Tunisia. The Central African Republic shares common borders with the Sudan, Zaire, and the People's Republic of the Congo in addition, of course, to Chad. Sudan, long sharing borders with Libya and Chad, also holds space contiguous to the Central African Republic, Zaire, Uganda, Kenya, and Ethiopia. Tunisia, the smallest of the Mahgreb nations (Algeria, Morocco and Tunisia), is situated on the Mediterranean Sea and finds itself sandwiched between Libya and Algeria.

Since the French invasion during September 1979, there is a question of whether the Central African Republic should be considered on its own as an independent nation or as a colony of France. If it can be assumed that it is a weak independent nation, then of the three nations being considered the Central African Republic seems to be the most inviting prospect for invasion by Libya. If Kaddafi were able to seize this country, it would give him easy access to the incalculable untapped riches of Zaire and, at the same time, would place Libya within easy access of tiny Gabon's massive oil holdings through the passageway provided by the strategic geographic location of the People's Republic of the Congo.

At least until the time of the French-orchestrated deposition of Jean Bedel Bokassa, Bokassa the First, as emperor of the Central African Empire in 1979, it was quite possible that Libya would be able to establish a dominant presence in the poverty-stricken kingdom. Thanks to the swift action of Valery Giscard d'Estaing on September 30, 1979, this worrisome possibility was no longer as likely. At the time the French military arrived in Bangui, thirty-seven Libyan soldiers were stationed in the capital, engaged in the training of police officers for the empire. Without doubt, the French had feared that more Libyan troops were on the way. No one can doubt that the massacre of over one hundred school children directed by Bokassa was the main event motivating France's military actions, but at the same time, the threat posed by Kaddafi cannot be forgotten. With Zaire beckoning a mile away across the drought-emptied Ubangi River, it must be assumed that the land-hungry colonel was well aware of the possible spoils that would be so easily within his grasp.

The Sudan always has exerted an overwhelming attraction for the Libyan leader. His fascination is understandable since the combination of Libyan and Sudanese territory would bring a massive land area under his domination. More-balanced observers might be scared by the poverty and refugee problems to be inherited by Sudanese takeover. Kaddafi, however, as has been documented time and again, is by no means pragmatic. The Libyan colonel views the Sudan as an essential step in his Pan African-Islamic Foundation. In this assumption he is correct. If the territory of the Sudan and the territory of Chad were bound to Libya in a permanent manner, the nation of Colonel Kaddafi would be in control of a large portion of the upper half of the continent.

A Libya-Chad-Sudan axis would weaken significantly the power base currently enjoyed by Algeria and Ethiopia. Libyan control of the Sudan would place both Kenya and Zaire within Kaddafi's easy grasp and would allow the settling of old scores with the Obote-Nyerere combination of Ugandan-Tanzanian neighbors. Taken in all, there is much to interest Libya in the Sudan. As a result, Egypt also has been considering a merger with Sudan in order to thwart Libyan plans.

When Tunisia is compared in the same manner, it would appear to be a far less-pleasing takeover prospect for Kaddafi. Libya already has a substantial opening of its own on the Mediterranean Sea. As a result, Tunisia is not necessary for that purpose, and from a political point of view, any such takeover would threaten Algeria and perhaps mobilize it into action. The Islamic nation of Algeria is more valuable to Kaddafi as a friend than as an enemy, especially since the two nations have cooperated in backing the Polisario front in its highly successful western Sahara liberation war.

Moves to Counteract Kaddafi

Geopolitical discussions must include possible countering moves. On one hand, the African and European nations with strong interests on the African continent cannot be expected to stand aside and allow Libya to march wherever it wishes. On the other hand, the Soviets cannot be expected to ignore such a splendid opportunity to encourage and support anti- Western African destabilization.

It is probably an exaggeration to hold, as some observers do, that Colonel Kaddafi is a closest Soviet surrogate and jumps to Moscow's tune as much as do the leaders of Ethiopia, Cuba, and East Germany. Those who hold such a theory probably are confusing socialism with radical, theocratic absolutism. Political philosophy aside, strategic planning makes strange bedfellows, and at the current time, both the USSR and Libya see an advantage to mutual cooperation and support. As a result, those who view Colonel Kaddafi as a destabilizing menace are checkmated by those who applaud an unstable situation as a laudable transition period leading to effective, radical, political change on all parts of the African continent.

A consensus emerged that Libyan adventurism in Africa must be checked. Among the nations that made their views felt were widely diverse political forces such as Nigeria, the Ivory Coast, Senegal, Algeria, Egypt, France, the U.S., and lest they be forgotten, the Republic of South Africa. Only a Kaddafi could bring this disparate group together. In the aftermath of the Libyan move into Chad, the *Christian Science Monitor* carried an article by Tom Gilroy. In his opinion, the Libyan army was so strong thanks to its supply of sophisticated Soviet weapons that no black nation on the continent would be able to defeat it in battle. He saw France as the only possible counterweight but assumed that it no longer wished to be the gendarme of Africa. As a result, Gilroy concluded, "the Libyan agitation will probably get worse."[89]

The outlines of Mr. Gilroy's conclusions are, of course, correct. It may be, however, that he overestimates Libyan military prowess and underrates that of the other major African powers, especially if they were acting with American and French help in consort under the banner of Organization of African Unity. The one significant inter-African skirmish in which Libya has engaged did not turn out in its favor. Tanzanian forces supporting the anti-Amin forces in Uganda experienced little difficulty in routing Colonel Kaddafi's troops. Three factors involved in the Ugandan conflict must be kept in mind since they make lesson-drawing appraisals of Libyan military performance difficult to make. First, Libyan forces were less copiously supplied with Soviet military equipment during the Ugandan war than currently is the case. Second, supply lines between Uganda and Libya were not contiguous or easily accessible. Third, Amin had brutalized his country to a point at which no one, except his closest henchmen, would support him. A Libyan military force fighting today on its own behalf to secure territory for its own usage might perform with more success. If the Chad situation is any indication, the number of Soviet weapons available for such a foray would be awesome.

Even without assistance from Europe or the United States, some of the African nations threatened by Libya possess sufficiently strong military forces to make an invasion of Libya costly and its eventual success less than certain. Egypt must prevent any Libyan merger or consolidation with the Sudan. Algeria finds itself in the same position in relation to Tunisia. Senegal, the Ivory Coast, and Nigeria would be less-than-negligible adversaries if their states or those of close neighbors were attacked. It is unlikely that they would stand by or allow a Libyan takeover without attempting a contradicting response.

The Response to Libyan Aggression

The move to combat Libyan aggression picked up speed during July 1981. Assistant Secretary of State Crocker stated the United States would increase military aid to nations that stand up to Libya. His goal was to prevent another merger like the one that took place in Chad and, perhaps, to arm countries willing to contest the takeover in Chad. The first concrete step under this program encompassed a sale of fifty-four M60A tanks to Tunisia to aid it in defending itself against a possible Libyan attack. The January 1980 Libyan-backed guerrilla attack on Gafsa, Tunisia, was cited as the justifying precedent for the sale.[90] The same rationale could apply to reinforcing the Somali government of Siad Barre against the Libyan-supported SSF.[91]

Relations between the U.S. and Libya reached an all-time low when U.S. fighters shot down two Soviet-built SU22 fighter planes over the Gulf of Sidra. The U.S. fleet was attempting to use the Mediterranean Sea near Libya for maneuvers. The strong reaction to the Libyan challenge was sent as a warning to Kaddafi that his aggressive conduct would not be tolerated further without counteracting force being applied.[92]

During late September 1981, diplomatic moves made behind the scene to force the extraction of Libya from Chad became intense. Jean-Pierre Cot, President Francois Mitterrand's minister of economic cooperation and development, visited Washington to discuss the role France would play in ending the conflict. Presumably, Mr. Cot reported on the results of his recent discussions held in Paris with President Goukouni Waddei of Chad. Having used Kaddafi's soldiers to rout the anti-Goukouni forces of former Chadian Prime Minister Hissene Habre, the president of Chad would now like to direct the country himself. Getting rid of Kaddafi was beyond his unaided capabilities. Since France had been responsible for maintaining some state of independence and stability in Chad since independence in 1960, it seemed logical for the Mitterrand government to take the lead in restoring order. Good intentions notwithstanding, France clearly did not wish to resume its role as full-time francophone—African police officer. Nonetheless, the commercial interests of France in Africa dictated that Colonel Kaddafi must not be allowed to wander the length and breadth of the continent causing destruction at will. As a result, France, by necessity, was drawn toward cooperation with two of its largest African potential commercial competitors, Nigeria and the U.S. All had large amounts of money to lose if Kaddafi remained an overwhelming political risk factor in any potential business dealing anywhere on the African continent.[93]

As if regional security were not sufficiently shaky, matters in the upper part of the African continent took a decided turn for the worse. First, President Anwar Sadat, a significant obstacle to future progress for Kaddafi expansionism, was assassinated in Cairo. At the same time, in a seemingly unrelated move, President Jaafar Nimeiry of Sudan, Egypt's strongest ally and defense partner, announced that an attempted coup against his government had been detected and quashed. In a week-long police action, it is estimated that between 5,600 and 8,000 illegal immigrants and plot suspects were apprehended. Kaddafi was charged by the Sudanese government with being behind the plot, an allegation the Libyan government did nothing to discourage. If Sudan could be added to the list of nations dominated by Kaddafi, his dreams of supreme power in the upper half of Africa would be well on the way to completion.[94] Under the circumstances, it seemed inevitable that the Reagan administration would feel obliged to support Sudan the way it had Egypt and, recently Somalia. The quicksand appeared to have a deeper bottom than previously thought.[95]

By the start of November 1981, it was clear that France indeed had decided to insert itself once again into Chadian affairs. By so doing, it also chose to take sides by favoring forces loyal to Goukouni over those loyal to Habre. Such a selection could not be expected to meet with total U.S. approval. Habre, after being driven from the Ndjamena area, had fled toward Sudan and had arranged a working agreement with the Nimeiry government. Given the U.S. predilection for supporting the Sudan against possible Libyan takeover, it is understandable that the U.S. government would support forces in the Chad civil war opposed to the group that had invited Kaddafi into Chad in the first place.[96]

At the Cancun conference in October 1981, devoted to Third World development, President Mitterrand of France called for a peacekeeping force to bring order to Chad. Senegal, Kenya, Nigeria, and Egypt quickly agreed to take part, if asked. A similar call made by the Organization of African Unity at their June 1981 meeting in Nairobi, Kenya, had not received any positive responses.[97]

Kaddafi Withdraws from Chad

The always-unpredictable Colonel Kaddafi unexpectedly began to issue recall summonses for the estimated 9,000 Libyan troops stationed in Chad. Observers were nonplussed and found it hard to believe that Kaddafi would surrender occupied territory in such a seemingly casual manner. Surprising or not, such a withdrawal was precisely what took place. Slumping prices for oil sales caused even the abundantly wealthy Libyans to think of the costs sure to come from continued occupation of Chad.

Nigeria requested U.S. air support for the Chad peacekeeping contingent. Other nations that the Organization of African Unity, with French tutoring, decided should take part in the Chad peacekeeping mission along with Nigeria were Senegal, Zaire, Benin, and Gabon—all French-speaking African nations.

The United States, to no one's surprise, acceded to the Nigerian request. After all, given the perceived U.S. tilt toward South Africa, it was rare that the Reagan administration and the Nigerian government were in agreement on any major issue. Only a disruptive force like Kaddafi could bring these two nations to ideological agreement. The U.S. commitment to the Organization of African Unity's peacekeeping effort included $10 to $12 million worth of air transport, food, and supplies.[98]

The Libyan commander in Chad, Colonel Radwan Saleh, predicted that the Libyan withdrawal would lead quickly to a renewal of hostilities and tribal fighting in and around Ndjamena. The current foreign minister in Chad, Ahmat Acyl, a man with his own private army, was quick to agree with Saleh. This open split with President Goukouni Waddei forecast even more trouble for Chad and demonstrated it was an oversimplification to think of limiting the Chad conflict to a battle between forces loyal to Goukouni or to Habre.[99]

The *Washington Post* felt that the U.S. government should follow up the advantage obtained by the Libyan departure from Chad. It suggested the United States should cut back purchases of Libyan oil and call all Americans home from Libya—two steps later taken by the Reagan administration.[100]

The Economist decreed that Colonel Kaddafi had to be stopped and decided there could be no legal or moral objection to participating in the ouster of a man who has broken so many international rules. Although *The Economist* understood and evidently sympathized with the desires of Egypt and Sudan to mount a military campaign against Libya, the British journal seemed skeptical of success chances. It suggested as an alternative that internal Libyan dissent fueled by an external oil boycott be encouraged.[101] Perhaps those within Libya opposed to Kaddafi would save outside powers the trouble of removing him.

In early January 1982, as an attempt to add to the stability of his country and also, not incidentally, to isolate his internal enemies, President Goukouni Waddei of Chad traveled to Khartoum to reach a settlement with Sudan President Jaffar Nimeiry. At the end, Nimeiry announced he would no longer support former Foreign Minister Habre, and Goukouni pledged to keep his independence from Libya and, presumably then, to allow the Sudan to forget about the threat of a possible united Libya-Chad attack along the wide expanse of their borders.[102]

Back in Ndjamena, however, President Goukouni's hold on power was as shaky as ever. Forces of former Prime Minister Habre were infiltrating closer to Ndjamena as February 1982 started. Only three African nations had fulfilled their peacekeeping obligations: Senegal, Zaire, and Nigeria. Organization of African Unity funds for the peacekeeping mission began to evaporate. Once again, Chad seemed to be slipping back into virtual anarchy and perhaps a Libyan return to assume power. In mid-February, the situation became even more serious when France announced it would not ship any more arms to the Goukouni government and urged he negotiate with all rival factions in the Chad civil war.[103]

Habre Returns to Ndjamena

During the first half of 1982, it became clear that Habre forces were staging a successful comeback. The Organization of African Unity peacekeeping force that always had been partial to the Goukouni side found itself unable to keep order or to move the parties toward settlement. Intense international pressure was placed upon Colonel Kaddafi in order to discourage him from again entering Chad to support Goukouni.[104] The U.S. government participated quietly in this effort. During March 1982, the United States had banned all oil imports from Libya and had ordered all Americans to leave the country.[105] These steps were taken because the U.S. government believed that Kaddafi had been involved in a plot aimed at killing hundreds of Americans living in the Sudan. Because of the complete lack of diplomatic contact between Washington and Tripoli, France took the diplomatic lead in forcing Libya to honor its promise to stay out of the Chadian civil war.

On June 7, 1982, the capital of Ndjamena fell to the Habre forces. Eighteen months had passed since their expulsion by Goukouni and Kaddafi.[106] This time, Kaddafi refused the last-minute pleas of Goukouni for assistance.[107] All African nations in the region breathed a collective deep breath of relief. Perhaps, finally, Colonel Kaddafi was beginning to realize that territorial integrity was a principle in African diplomacy that even he could not violate with impunity.

As soon as Habre secured control of Ndjamena, he set to work to stabilize his regime. Conciliatory talks were held both with Goukouni and with southern Chadian leader General Kamougue. No one expected any breakthroughs and none occurred. In the tense climate, true elections were an impossibility. The set of circumstances that has for so long produced coups and countercoups in Chad still seemed to be in vogue.[108]

In succeeding months, however, the situation in Chad stabilized in a surprising fashion. The main catalyst was the flight from the country into Cameroon of the southern military leader, General Abdelkader Kamougue. As a result, for the first time in memory, no military opposition to the central government was active within Chad.[109]

Habre seized the opportunity to preach peace and reconciliation with both his own people and with his neighbors, even Libya.[110] It would be overly optimistic, by half, to think that conditions in Chad will improve markedly in the short run. The memories of death and misery go too deep for this to happen. Progress can be seen, nonetheless. Perhaps other areas of Africa will be able to assume the unenviable role of being potential hotspots in the near future.

France's Role in Africa

French Influence in Postindependence Africa

In the wake of the great success of the European economic community and the implementation of the Lomé Conventions on the one hand, France's control of the economies of its former colonies weakened slightly. On the other hand, until Kaddafi's move into Chad, no African nation had dared to challenge France's self-appointed gendarme role in its former colonies. For two decades France had shown a willingness to intervene militarily on the African continent whenever it felt that destabilization was occurring within its sphere of influence. It is not surprising that France's interest in the matter took precedence before any consideration of how a move would affect the nation involved. Never people to lack self-confidence in their rectitude, French presidents and prime ministers were totally at ease in equating what would be good for France in Africa with what would be good for Africa itself.

During the first half of the 1960s, as independence overtook its former colonies, France acted often to reestablish order, to quell military uprisings, to thwart attempted coups, and to mediate in tribal wars. Among the nations in which its presence was felt during this period were Cameroon, Congo Brazzaville, Chad, Niger, Mauritania, and Gabon.

In the second half of the 1960s and the first half of the 1970s, France, during the last days of the de Gaulle government and during the Pompidou government, adopted a low-level military presence in Africa. It did support Bokassa in the Central African Republic in 1967, and it supported the Tombalbaye regime in Chad between 1968 and 1971. France's main activity during this period was what in a later year was termed by the Swedish International Peace Research Institute (SIPRI) as "France adheres to its traditionally pragmatic policy of selling as much as possible whenever possible."[111]

It would seem that France did not find the slightest contradiction in equipping eighteen former French colonies in black Africa, Biafran rebels in Nigeria, and the military forces of the Republic of South Africa at the same time. If at some future point the Republic of South Africa and black Africa come to a stage of all-out conventional warfare, both sides will owe a large share of their death-dealing capacity to the longtime willingness of French corporations to arm any and all nations willing and able to pay the sales price demanded. To illustrate, in 1978 France was the third-largest arms exporter to other nations of the world. Its sales of $2.2 trillion (1975 U.S.-dollar value) accounted for 11 percent of world arms exports. Only the United States and the USSR exported more arms. In 1978, Africa, as usual, was one of France's largest arms customers. Dollar amounts are difficult to obtain, but according to the definitive *SIPRI Yearbook* for 1979, France in the preceding year sold arms to Cameroon, the Central African Empire, Chad, Djibouti, Egypt (enormous amounts, some financed by Saudi

Arabia), Gabon, Guinea Bissau, the Ivory Coast, Kenya, Libya (enormous amounts), Morocco (enormous amounts), Mauritania, Malawi, Nigeria (large), Saudi Arabia (staggering amounts, some distributed in Africa), Senegal, South Africa, Syria, Togo, Tunisia, and Zaire (large amounts).[112]

France as Power Broker

As Africa became a chessboard for active major power manipulation during the latter half of the 1970s, France resumed its role as power broker and military intervener on the African continent. From 1974 onward, France raised its support level in Chad in a largely unsuccessful attempt to end the long civil war in that country and to support the pro-Western southern Chadian forces of General Felix Malloum. France shored up the Mauritanian government in 1977 and intervened massively in Zaire to thwart the Katangan gendarme (so-called) invasion of Shaba. In 1978 French troops once again returned to Shaba to restore peace, to keep Mobotu's territory and pocketbook intact, and not coincidental or unimportant, to keep France's supply lines to Shaba Province's copper and cobalt open and functioning smoothly.

On September 30, 1979, France took its boldest postcolonial-period step in Africa and, in one lightning move—in less than one hour's time—carried out one of the most imperialistic seizures of African territory and power to be found in the history of the African continent during the last two decades. To complete this wondrous event, criticism of the conquest on a worldwide level was muted to the point of inaudibility. The event to which reference is being made is, of course, the French-military-engineered and -effectuated deposal of Jean Bedel Bokassa as the Central African Empire's first, and undoubtedly only, emperor. Two divisions of French troops replaced Bokassa with their chosen successor, his cousin, David Dacko. With massive French assistance, Dacko consolidated power, suppressed opposition, returned the nation to republic status, and protected France's heavy corporate investment in the abundant natural resources of the Central African Republic/Empire. In 1980, France supported the Tunisian government in its successful attempts at preventing Algerian-and-Libyan-supporting rebels of Tunisian nationality from overthrowing that nation's French-oriented government.

The number of French interventions that have taken place in African struggles has led to a natural inclination to forget about the times France has chosen not to intervene, in and of itself, as much a power determinant factor as if it had chosen to take part. In early independence times in francophone Africa, France allowed events to run their unhindered course in Togo in 1963 after President Olympio's assassination, in Congo Brazzaville during 1963 when it could have saved the regime of the ardent francophile Abbe Fulbert Youlon,[113] in Dahomey (now Benin) in 1963 upon President

Hubert Maga's resignation, in Niger in 1974 upon President Hamani Diori's regime being overthrown, in Chad in 1975 when President Francis Tombalbaye was assassinated, in Mauritania in 1978 upon the overthrow of President Ould Daddah, and in Upper Volta in 1980 when President Abou Kakar Lamizana was overthrown.

Even when taken together as a group and considered as one entity, France's failure to act in these government crises pales into noninterference insignificance when compared with its decision to permit Colonel Kaddafi's forces to sweep southward and to annex, or at the very least to dominate, Chad. For the first time, France's guiding-hand authority in Africa had been challenged and successfully contravened. Kaddafi gambled that France's desire to be done once and for all with its supervisory role—both potential and actual—in Chad and its need to be supplied with Libyan crude oil would in the end prove persuasive in counseling a noninterference reaction. The colonel was correct. In the wake of African howls at Kaddafi's aggressive actions in Chad, France tightened its hold on the defense perimeter encircling Chad by adding to its troop strength in the Central African Republic. However, the damage had been done and the lesson expounded for the world to see and absorb. The day of France's unquestioned ability to enforce its will upon the African continent had ended.

French prestige and domination potential on the African continent may be at a modern-time low, but this former colonial power still possesses strong forces that could serve at some future point to check the forces of Kaddafi or of other Soviet surrogates operating in Africa. The number of French military personnel on duty in Africa keeps changing. Since 1980, great fluctuation has occurred in Chad, on Reunion Island, and in the Central African Republic. Continentwide best estimates of French-troop strength would fall in the range of 15,000 people. France states that it has twenty-two military-training missions in Africa and agreements with six nations to defend them against any outside attack. French naval vessels are found at bases on five islands situated off the east African coast. Its strength in the Indian Ocean is comparable to that of the United States and the USSR.

Forty-five hundred French troops have been stationed in strategically important Djibouti, situated against the Gulf of Aden and the opening to the Red Sea. In addition, troop strength fluctuating between 2,000 and 5,000 strong has been based on Reunion Island. Across the continent in west Africa, Senegal retains its close military links with France. As long ago as the Napoleonic Wars, Senegalese soldiers served in the French army. Today, 1,300 French troops are stationed in Senegal. Relatively insignificant numbers of French troops are scattered throughout the rest of French-speaking Africa, including representations in Zaire, Burundi, and on Mayotte Island, a Comoro Islands chain breakaway. With these troop concentrations in Africa, it must be remembered in today's airborne world that the question is not where they are stationed but rather how long it will take them, or troops stationed in southern France at Marseilles, to fly to the new hot spot on the continent, wherever it might be.[114]

The election of Francois Mitterrand in France in April 1980 has thrown the traditional African policies of that country into question. French activity in Africa should be less imperialistic in the future. Mitterrand had condemned the Giscard d'Estaing invasion of the Central African Empire. The new socialist government may be more frigid to South Africa and willing to deal with the rest of Africa on a mature, equal-to-equal basis than in the past.[115] It could be that the Mitterrand government will seek stability on the African continent that aids Africa as much as it aids France. The irony is that if France slows down the reactionary leftist forces at move on the African continent, the biggest beneficiary will be the reactionary rightest government of the Republic of South Africa, unintended though that result might be from Mitterrand's point of view.

The Mitterrand Regime

Claude Cheysson was appointed foreign minister in the Mitterrand government. Even before he took over his new position, Cheysson publicly pledged to support African liberation movements and back economic sanctions against South Africa. Whether or not he would carry through his determination when practicalities crowded out rhetoric remained to be seen.[116] As if to emphasize the point, the first step taken by Cheysson was to supervise the change in name of his ministry to the ministry of external affairs.

Despite the socialistic bent of the new Mitterrand government, observers did not expect France to alter the traditional trade relationship that the more-capitalistic-oriented governments of de Gaulle, Pompidou, and Giscard d'Estaing had nurtured so lovingly and carefully. As Mitterrand and Cheysson turned to the imposing difficulties of managing their economy, they could not be displeased that 12 percent of their country's total trade was conducted with Africa and that the three most successful of their former African colonies—the Ivory Coast, Gabon, and Cameroon—still purchase between one-half and two-thirds of their imports from France. Less encouraging to observers is that these prosperous nations are among the very few of the nineteen former French colonies in Africa for which it can be alleged without fear of contradiction that living standards clearly are improved over what they were in 1960, at independence time.[117]

Differences in approach between France and the United States on methods of development assistance for Africa have grown in recent years.[118] The Reagan administration has been emphasizing open-marketplace bilateral trade as the best approach. To the contrary, France, under Mitterrand, has supported increases in developed-nation donor aid in order to strengthen the developing-world economies. In like manner, close attention to remarks of Mr. Cheysson could lead to the assumption that France would be willing to support treaties and cartels aimed at raising mineral prices that would bring added revenue to the economies of developing nations.[119]

The political role played by France on African questions during 1981 and 1982 for the most part was couched in softness. France parted from the United States on the need for vetoing the UN resolutions condemning South Africa's late August 1981 attack into Angola. Even though France joined the condemning-vote group, it did not criticize the United States in public. Even more interesting, when the Namibia peace timetable was announced by the five-nation Western contact group in late September 1981, France did not try to grab the limelight but stood back and allowed Secretary of State Haig to take credit as the main architect of the movement toward peace. In equal measure, France permitted another change of government in the Central African Republic without becoming involved. Unlike the September 1979 overthrow of Jean Bedel Bokassa and his replacement by David Dacko, which France orchestrated, this time it raised not a hand as a military combine led by General Andre Kolingba assumed power on September 1, 1981.

France Opposes Libya

France has been reserving the largest share of its recent African attention for Colonial Kaddafi. The Mitterrand government stiffened its attitude toward Libya as months went on. In July 1981, the newly installed Mitterrand government weathered heavy international criticism when it carried through on arms-sales commitments made to Libya by the Giscard d'Estaing government. The Mitterrand government permitted the transfer of hundreds of millions of dollars worth of military equipment, for the most part naval vessels and fighter planes. These sales were carried out even though Libyan military forces remained in Chad at the time. Many African nations including all of the French-speaking nations were appalled by the action of the Mitterrand government and made their opposition to the sales clear to the French government. After all, what would stop the Libyan government from using these weapons not only in Libya or in Chad but also in an attack against one of the neighboring countries?

In the light of francophone-African unhappiness at the French arms sales to Libya, President Goukouni of Chad probably received a warmer reception in Paris than otherwise would have been the case when he asked for help in expelling Kaddafi's forces from his land. After all, Goukouni had extended the occupation invitation to Libya in the first place. The Giscard d'Estaing administration had severed France's long-standing support of whatever government was in power in Chad during 1980, largely because it was unhappy with the Muslim religion observing Goukouni's close relations with Kaddafi. For the most part, France, after taking its forces out of the country, previously had maintained neutrality between the Goukouni-Habre forces in their never-ending battles and feuds. Now, in October 1981, France began to embrace the Goukouni side of the dispute in an attempt to remove Libya from Chad. By so doing, the Mitterrand government flew in the face of U.S. wishes and encouraged the United States to shift its support from the Sudanese-supporting Habre to the Libyan-supporting Goukouni. This political maneuvering was done in Chad behind the scenes, and France defined its renewed interest in a limited manner by refusing to resume its longtime role as constable.[121]

A side effect of the new French backstage role in Africa was that its "up front, everyone be damned," arms-sales policy was open to more criticism than in the past. At the start of 1982, France was fielding barbs for recent arms sales to Egypt and Ethiopia in Africa and to Nicaragua in Central America. These three places were potential trouble spots. Egypt has been faced with the need to combat possible Libyan attacks against itself or its ally, Sudan. Ethiopia, now an ally of Libya, has been involved in endless civil wars and skirmishes with Somalia; Nicaragua far away in Central America was also a potential war location. By selling arms to the three nations, France made it clear that limits to its disinterested good offices still existed. Some observers thought the French arms-sale activity was spurred on by the loss of potential income from being forced to suspend future arms sales to Libya.[122] It also appeared that arms sales to Chad would be suspended.

Problems at Home

In France, the economic situation continued to deteriorate. The forced devaluation of the French franc dealt a terrible blow to the economies in Africa linked to the French currency because of their membership in the Central Franc Zone.[123] These nations that were former French colonies had no choice but to devalue their own currencies as well, regardless of whether or not the move was a help to the economy of the African nation in question. In such an economic context, relations with France understandably were quite strained. Some of the more-conservative African nations in the French bloc such as Senegal and the Ivory Coast also were displeased that France's socialist-oriented government seemed to be favoring ideologically compatible regimes in Algeria and Libya rather than themselves as traditionally had been the case. Morocco and Tunisia also felt this way and began increasingly to court the United States as an ally.

Although France was active in keeping Kaddafi from reentering the conflict in Chad, as Habre returned to Ndjamena in June 1982, the Parisian control of events on the African continent is not what it once was. A country experiencing economic and political turmoil at home is not in the strongest position to tell other nations how to act, even though the nations receiving the orders are former colonies of France.[124] Throughout Africa, it was feared that an economically ailing France would reduce its peace-keeping role on that continent.

France still intends to play a role of consequence on the African continent. French self-interest aside, even though the profits France has culled from Africa over the years have been enormous, the former colonies are in better condition to face the 1980s than they would have been if France had followed the English model of almost total disengagement from its former African colonies.[125] In a remote way, South Africa profits by the French willingness to continue playing a stabilizing-force role on the African continent. Stabler governments are prone to turning inward to address their nation's problems as their government's first priority. Less-stable governments looking for diversions tend to seek out exterior problems as a leading priority. The stable black governments also are opposed to the apartheid regime in South Africa, and in the long run, economic and political pressure of the type they are able to initiate will stand more chance of carrying the day and destroying apartheid than will underequipped military attacks against South Africa. Unfortunately, as long as France sees South Africa as a strong potential customer for French goods, it cannot be expected that France will take major steps to cooperate with African nations in trying to bring significant changes to South African life.

The Indian Ocean Islands

Soviet Interests in the Area

Present indications are that the USSR is concentrating on upgrading its presence and influence in the area located in or adjacent to the western portion of the Indian Ocean.[126] The base points in this planning maneuver appear to be a group of islands around the Persian Gulf–Gulf of Aden: the Seychelles Islands chain and Gan Island of the southern Maldives chain, both located in the Indian Ocean, and Sofala (near Beira) and Maputo, on the Indian Ocean coast of Mozambique in southern Africa.[127]

The combination of political ferment and economic anarchy that is taking place on two other, significantly larger, Indian Ocean islands, Madagascar and Mauritius, suggests that in the future, either one or both of them might increase contacts with the USSR and permit added usage of their naval bases by the Soviet navy.

The group of Soviet naval bases established in the Red Sea–Persian Gulf area have the utmost strategic impact. Their existence justifies the billions of dollars that the Soviets poured in to support anti-Western governments in Ethiopia and Southern Yemen. As a result, they have been able to put into operation a group of naval bases that is located at Socotra Island in the Gulf of Aden, at the port of Aden, at Perim Island in the Bab-el Mandeb Straits at the entrance to the Red Sea, and at Kebir Island in the Dahlak Archipelago. By such maneuverings, the Soviets have long overcome the losses suffered in 1977 when Somalia expelled them from the Indian Ocean ports of Mogadishu and Berbera.

Kebir Island is situated in the Red Sea within fifty miles of the important Eritrean-Province-situated, but Ethiopian-government-held, port of Massawa. From this strategic vantage point, Soviet naval forces control northward to the Suez Canal virtually unchallenged except for a small U.S. ship staging at Raz Benir, Egypt. Southward, Kebir Island allows the Soviets unchallenged access to the crucial Bab-el Mandeb Straits 250 miles away that control access to the Gulf of Aden, the Indian Ocean, and eventually, the Persian Gulf.

Kebir Island has been selected as the site of a major Soviet naval base if recent construction activity and the number of Soviet ships patrolling the area can be taken as an accurate indication. Sightings made by observers have included a Krivak-class destroyer, two guided-missile-class frigates, a troop cargo carrier, a Kresta-class cruiser, a nuclear submarine with eight missile tubes, and numerous support vessels. In addition to controlling the sea lanes, it should also be remembered that Dahlak Archipelago allows the Soviets to monitor and control activities in the Yemens and to pose a threat to Saudi Arabia while simultaneously forcing the Eritrean rebels in Ethiopia to deal with a hostile military presence at their backs at the same time as they must fight Ethiopian and Cuban forces on the land.

Not satisfied with the enormous tactical advantages obtained by the erection of their Kebir Island base in the Dahlak Archipelago, the Soviets also have been hard at work to improve their naval base on Perim Island; their naval base at Aden, South Yemen; and their base on Socotra Island, which is situated 120 miles off Africa's northeast tip, Cape Guardaful. Socotra Island also is located off the coast of South Yemen and strategically controls traffic to and from the oil-rich Persian Gulf and the nearby Gulf of Oman.

These Soviet nautical maneuverings portend hard days for the nations of the developing and developed world that covet access to the oil supplies of this region. Adding to the legitimate concerns posed by Soviet naval power in the Persian Gulf region is the fact that the Persian Gulf is also within 750 or fewer flying miles of two Soviet-controlled regions: Ethiopia and Afghanistan.[128] As a result, it must be stated realistically that the Straits of Hormuz are almost as totally under Soviet domination as are the Bab-el Mandeb Straits. Last-minute U.S. attempts to counter this Soviet influence by means of the Carter administration's fevered attempts to purchase access to antiquated naval bases in Oman, Kenya, and Somalia (the old Soviet base at Berbera), although better than no response at all, hardly rate as an adequate checkmate tc such as awesome power display.[129]

Given the clear strategic superiority that the USSR has amassed in the Horn of Africa-southwest Asia area, the focus for uninterrupted sea travel inevitably shifts southward toward the Indian Ocean-Cape of Good Hope-south Atlantic Ocean route to western Europe and the United States.

In some respects, the Cape of Good Hope route is the more vital of the two, regardless of the situation prevailing at any particular moment along the Red Sea-Suez Canal route, since this more-northern route cannot accommodate tanker tonnage in excess of 125,000 tons. Sixty percent of western Europe's oil requirements are transported along the Cape route, as are 20 percent of U.S. oil requirements and 90 percent of Japan's.[130] It should be noted also that 25 percent of Europe's food is transported via the Indian Ocean-Cape of Good Hope route. It is estimated that during the .1980s the Cape route will be used to transport 60 percent of U.S. oil supplies and 70 percent of all strategic supplies destined for Europe.

Most analysts of the Cape of Good Hope route spend surprisingly little time discussing either the approach or egress access from the Cape area. They ignore the potential danger of the Soviet military presence in the Indian Ocean—and its potential presence in the south Atlantic Ocean—that would result if SWAPO gained control of Walvis Bay.[131] Ignoring these factors seems shortsighted. It is true that the part of the route touching South Africa is crucial because of that nation's unstable political climate, but interference with shipping channels could come either before or after this portion of the voyage.[132] If the USSR should be successful in dominating the access and egress to waters surrounding the Republic of South Africa on the one hand, then the free world will find itself in a bind from which it is impossible to escape. On the other hand, even if the Soviets are not successful, the free world could find itself dependent upon the good auspices of South Africa to facilitate passage for that part of the voyage. Neither alternative is appetizing.[133]

The southern section of the Indian Ocean route to the Cape of Good Hope has been developing in a manner that should give pause to U.S. and South African strategic planners. Soviet naval activity in and around Mozambique has risen significantly, and many observers feel that the Soviets are intending to establish bases at Sofala and Maputo. Friendship agreements signed between the Soviets and Samora Machel's government in April 1977 and reinforced by added treaties signed in November 1980 are looked on with concern by some analysts.[134]

On January 30, 1981, as has been discussed elsewhere, the Republic of South Africa's commando force launched a surprise attack into Mozambique. The target was an ANC house located in Matola, a suburb of Maputo and forty miles inside Mozambique. Five members of this black South African opposition group and one Portuguese man caught in the crossfire were killed. This serious incursion into the territory of Mozambique was the first such action by South Africa. The excuse given by South Africa was that Mozambique had permitted the ANC to use its territory to launch raids against South Africa.[135]

As would be expected, the nations of the world were quick to condemn the South African action. Less noted was the action of the USSR. In the present context, since both the Indian Ocean and friendship treaties are involved, this involvement should be given full weight. In response to the Matola attack, the Soviets stationed armed warships in the Indian Ocean at points near Beira and Maputo. Soviet diplomats in the Mozambique capital, Maputo, were quoted by the Portuguese radio as saying that their country's purpose was to assist the local government if needed. Without doubt, the Soviets also wished to warn South Africa of the possible consequences of further attacks.[136]

The Soviet diplomats in Maputo cited the 1977 friendship treaties between Mozambique and the USSR as the justification for their nation's actions. Warning would seem to have been served that the USSR is willing to act offensively in the Indian Ocean region to carry out its political objectives. It might also be noted that South Africa did not repeat its incursion into Mozambique's territory to neutralize activities of the ANC. The recent Soviet activity in the Straits of Mozambique has led to the assumption that full use of Mozambique's two Indian Ocean ports at Sofala and Maputo by its fleet would not be far in the future.[137]

The Situation in the Seychelles and Maldives

The Seychelles Islands were granted independence by the United Kingdom on June 28, 1976. This stunningly beautiful but woefully underpopulated chain of ninety-two islands had been taken from France by the United Kingdom as a result of the French-English wars of 1810–1811. In the last few years, the government of the Seychelles Islands has moved to cut itself from its colonial path. Socialism has been grasped with ideological fervor. Since the 1977 coup that placed Albert Rene in power, socialism has been adopted as the controlling reality. Affirmative steps in many domains have started to make this ideological commitment also a practical reality. In such a climate, Soviet interest was inevitable, especially since the Seychelles Islands are situated in the middle of the oil-tanker route from the Persian Gulf to the Cape of Good Hope.[138] In earlier years, the USSR had maintained a limited tanking and refurbishing base in the Indian Ocean waters near the Seychelles. The advantages of a land-based naval staging were evident. If the Soviet presence could be expanded to include a missile base, the rest of the world would be most alarmed.

During 1980, some indications were present that the Soviets may have succeeded in obtaining permission to erect a naval or missile base in the Seychelles Islands. Since U.S. involvement in the Seychelles historically has been extremely light, it is not surprising that verification or denial of the reports by Washington was hard to obtain. During July 1980, when these reports of a Soviet missile base were at their strongest, the United States did not have an ambassador resident in the Seychelles. A junior official in charge of the U.S. consulate was taken on an airplane tour of the islands by officials of the local government. At the end of the trip, he proclaimed himself satisfied, at least for the public that no such Soviet military presence existed.[139]

The Seychelles Islands chain is located 1,150 miles to the east of Tanzania and, as cannot be repeated often enough, is located directly on the main Persian Gulf–Indian Ocean–Cape of Good Hope tanker route heading for western Europe and the United States. A Soviet naval base in the Seychelles would counter a U.S. naval base at Mombasa, Kenya, in a most effective manner. In addition, any such Soviet base would weaken significantly efforts of the U.S. government to checkmate Soviet bases in Aden and on Socotra Island by means of naval bases at Berberra, Somalia, and in Oman. When President Rene assumed power by a coup in 1978, he declared that he would not allow his country to be used as a power pawn in East-West struggles. Given recent events, one must wonder if this still is the case.[140]

The comic-opera coup attempt of November 25, 1981, only served to point up the vulnerability of the Seychelles Islands government. Most experienced observers were less surprised that forty-five white mercenaries tried to take over the country than they were that the coup attempt failed. Even if Mad Mike Hoare, the 61-year-old white South African group leader, and his fellow soldiers of fortune could not succeed, others might be able to do so.[141] On August 18, 1982, a group of mutineers from the army tried their luck at overthrowing the Rene government and were equally unsuccessful. Nonetheless, the instability in the region is unsettling for all superpowers— the United States and the USSR certainly, but also South Africa because of the vulnerable Cape route. This fear of hostile naval forces occupying the Seychelles or, at the least, using it as a military staging point led the Pretoria government to turn a blind eye toward preparations for the Hoare coup attempt that took place on South African soil.[142]

The Maldives Islands chain is also a strategically situated, underpopulated, Indian Ocean ministate that has shed its colonial links to the United Kingdom and chosen to embark on self-rule. Conforming to the pattern, Soviet interest in the new islands-chain nation became intense immediately thereafter. The Maldives are a grouping of 2,000 islands, of which perhaps 215 are inhabited. Total population of this nation that won its independence from the United Kingdom in July 1965 has reached 150,000 people. The Maldives slink their way southward for 550 miles through the Indian Ocean in the direction of the Chagos archipelago and, most specifically, in the direction of the burgeoning U.S. air and naval base at Diego Garcia.

Gan Island in the southern Maldives is less than 300 miles from Diego Garcia Island and is 700 miles southwest of Sri Lanka (Ceylon). Gan Island possesses both an accessible harbor and an unused 8,700-foot airplane runway complete with radar system and other electronic instruments that remain in good working order. These desirable facilities were abandoned by the United Kingdom in 1974 when it chose to abandon its status as rent-free tenant of the base. By the terms of the independence agreement, the United Kingdom could have used the island naval base until 1986.

The USSR sought to replace U.K. military and naval forces with its own. Fervent diplomatic attempts were made to conclude a treaty with the Maldives government. Negotiations dragged on for three years but were put to rest in 1977 when President Ibrahim Nasir rejected a $1-million-a-year Gan Island rental offer. The Soviets had vowed that their only interest in the island was to establish a base for their fishing fleet. Other observers were doubtful that the Soviets could bring themselves to pass up the military advantages of the island. President Nasir's refusal to enter into a lucrative rental for his financially hard-pressed homeland undoubtedly meant that he also had doubts about the Soviet motives and feared that a military installation also would be constructed and maintained once Soviet influence in the Maldives solidified.

The USSR is nothing if not persistent. During April 1980, the USSR and the Republic of the Maldives government, headed by President Maumoon Abdul Gayoom, finally signed a series of cultural and scientific agreements in order to assist the island chain's communications and tourism industries. Nothing was said in the agreement specifically about Gan Island, and indeed, the air field still lies fallow and the harbor undeveloped. Nonetheless the Soviets remain most interested. Since the U.S. build-up took place at Diego Garcia Island in the neighboring Chagos Archipelago, the USSR has erected a *cordon sanitaire* of submarines and guided-missile cruisers that successfully envelops the U.S. base. Only the distance to its own refurbishing bases has restricted the success of this Soviet action. If the Soviets do succeed in obtaining base rights at Gan Island, the effectiveness of their Diego Garcia encirclement and their general strategic position in the deep realms of the Indian Ocean would be improved substantially at minimum cost.[143]

The Situation in Madagascar and Mauritius

In the same conceptual manner that the Seychelles and Maldives can be paired, so for analytic purposes can be Mauritius and the Malagasy Republic (Madagascar). They are the two largest and most important islands in the western part of the Indian Ocean. Both have a long colonial background, with Mauritius having been a U.K. protectorate since being taken from France in 1811 and Madagascar having remained French until independence in 1960. Both nations, during the last few years, have turned markedly leftward and anticolonialist in their political orientation. As a result, neither the United Kingdom nor France was encouraged to continue a military presence on these islands even though postindependence agreements had provided for this eventuality. Both nations have become increasingly vocal in demanding that the Indian Ocean become an area of peace, free from large-scale major-power nuclear presence.[144] Many Western observers are fearful that since treaty obligations have ways of being interpreted in a variety of manners in different parts of the world, any such agreement might give a significant tactical advantage to the Soviets. Western nations, especially the United States, appear ready to resist such pacific calls and, as a result, be labeled as warmongers.[145]

In recent months the economic situation in both the Malagasy Republic and Mauritius has become increasingly grave. In 1979, the per capita income on Madagascar, the world's fourth-largest island, was $275 per year. The nation is broke largely due to the double burden of escalating oil costs and erratic world prices for the country's cash crops as import costs continue to soar. The story in Mauritius is similar. This land, located 750 miles off the east African coast, is dependent upon one crop, sugar. In this day of fluctuating sugar prices and increasing usage of sugar substitutes, the outlook for Mauritius is bad.

Given conditions in both the Malagasy Republic and on Mauritius, it is not surprising that President Lt. Commander Didier Ratsiraka on Madagascar and the octogenarian Prime Minister Sir Seewoosagur Ramgoolam of Mauritius were being subjected to pressures from the disaffected. Turns to the left are quite understandable in such circumstances, as is increased Soviet aid and interest in these island nations.[146]

On June 11, 1982, the long-expected change of government on the Isle of Mauritius finally took place. The Labor party of long-time Prime Minister Sir Seewoosagur Ramgoolam was defeated soundly in national elections

by the Mauritian militant movement led by Paul Berenger. In the wake of
the government turnover, the status of the U.S. air and naval base on Diego
Garcia Island again came to the forefront. Berenger listed as a first priority
of his new government expelling the Americans from the base and, as a cor-
relate, rallying the Indian Ocean littoral nations in a move to neutralize
militarily the Indian Ocean.[147]

Diego Garcia, a small island in the Chagos Archipelago, was purchased
by the United Kingdom from Prime Minister Ramgoolam's colonial administration before Mauritius obtained its independence from the United Kingdom in 1968.[148] The 1,400 residents of Diego Garcia were evicted summar-
ily, and the United Kingdom negotiated an agreement with the U.S. government for military-base rights. In subsequent years, Diego Garcia has
become the central staging point for U.S. naval and air power in the Indian
Ocean–Persian Gulf region.[149]

Over the years, socialist elements in Mauritius have become agitated
increasingly over the Ramgoolam giveaway of Diego Garcia.[150] During
March 1982, the U.K. government agreed to pay $7 million in reparation to
the dispossessed atoll residents.[151] These unfortunates now live in abject
poverty in the Mauritian capital, Saint Louis. If the British and their U.S.
associates thought such a move would appease their critics, they were sadly
mistaken. The payoff only served to call added attention to the situation.
Countries throughout the Indian Ocean littoral increased the insistence of
their demands that the U.S. use of Diego Garcia be ended and that the
United Kingdom cede title of the atoll to Mauritius.[152]

The United States Experiences Difficulties

By the middle of 1982, the strategic situation in the Indian Ocean region
could not have seemed bright to U.S. planners. This being so, by extension,
then, the South African government must have been equally as worried. A
supposedly neutralized Indian Ocean would make easy pickings for
increased Soviet influence and pressure. Free access to the Cape of Good
Hope sea route would be threatened by such a set of happenings.[153]

By August 1982, the U.S. strategy for obtaining access to naval bases in
Somalia, Kenya, Oman, and on Diego Garcia appeared threatened on all
fronts. Mauritius had launched an all-out diplomatic attack against U.S.
use of Diego Garcia, the pro-United States government of President Moi in
Kenya was forced to put down an air-force-led coup, and the pro-United
States government of President Barre in Somalia was threatened with overthrow by both Ethiopian and internal guerrilla forces.

Perhaps the most vulnerable and certainly the most important of all the
threatened U.S. allies in the region is Oman. Soviets and Cubans in Ethio-

pia and in Southern Yemen; hostile Iranian forces threatening Iraq and, by extension, Saudi Arabia, Kuwait, and Oman; and Arab pressure in the wake of Israel's invasion of Lebanon imperil the military-cooperation arrangements between the United States and Oman. South Africa must be as concerned by these unfavorable trends as the United States since their interests in a pinch are similar.

U.S. strategic interests in the Indian Ocean depend on a significant American presence. Since it remains untenable from a political perspective for the United States to cooperate overtly with South Africa, Diego Garcia is the only truly satisfactory alternative. Given the 2,500-mile-plus range of many U.S. weapons, southern Africa is as well covered from this small island in the Chagos archipelago as it would be from Simonstown, South Africa.[154] As the United States continues to build its capacity on this island, the leftward-leaning neighbors such as Madagascar, Mauritius and even India, increase demands that the United States leave Diego Garcia and that Great Britain return ownership to Mauritius.[155] The days ahead for the United States in the Indian Ocean appear troubled. Eventually, if only from self-preservation as it defines the term, the U.S. government may think again of closer strategic ties with South Africa.[156] It is hard to envision continent-wide stability being increased by any such trend.[157]

Notes

1. For an excellent discussion of the geopolitical situation in Ethiopia prior to the fall of the Selassie government, see Mesfin, Wolder-Mariam, "Ethiopia and the Indian Ocean." In *The Indian Ocean—It's Political, Economic and Military Importance,* Alvin J. Cottrell, R.M. Burrell, eds. (New York: Praeger, 1972), pp. 181–196.

2. Dusko Doder and Jay Ross, "Soviets, Cuba Double Ethiopian Force," *Washington Post,* December 17, 1977.

3. Vernon A. Gildrie, Jr., Henry S. Radsher, "U.S. Assured by Soviets on African War," *Washington Star,* February 10, 1978; Drew Middleton, "Pitfalls for a Soviet-Backed Ethiopian Offensive," *The New York Times,* February 9, 1978.

4. United Press International, "Soviets Funneling Attack Helicopters to Ethiopians," *Washington Star,* June 14, 1980; see Normal Polmar, Floyd D. Kennedy Jr., *Military Helicopters of the World,* (Annapolis: Naval Institute Press, 1981).

5. Henry S. Radsher, "Soviet General Leading Forces in Ethiopia," *Washington Star,* February 25, 1978; Gary D. Payton, "The Soviet-Ethiopian Liaison—Airlift and Beyond," *Air University Review,* December 1979, pp. 66–73.

6. Reuter News Service, "Eritreans Say Soviet Craft Join Port Battle," *Baltimore Sun*, January 18, 1978; A.M. Kashai, "The Eritrean Struggle in Historical Perspective," *Islamic Defense Review* 5 no. 3, 1980, pp. 7–13.

7. "Soviet Arms Airlift to Ethiopia Violates Air Space of Pakistan," *Aviation Week and Space Technology*, December 19, 1977; Steven David, "Realignment in the Horn: The Soviet Advantage," *International Security*, Fall 1979.

8. Douglas Watson, "The War That's Over in Ogaden Is Just Beginning for Guerrillas," *Baltimore Sun*, April 14, 1981.

9. Bernard Gwertzman, "U.S. Aides Frustrated over Soviet Gains in Ethiopia," *The New York Times*, December 29, 1977; Graham Hovey, "U.S. Charges Soviet Mounts Big Airlift to Ethiopian Army," *The New York Times*, December 14, 1977.

10. "Soviet-Backed Ethiopian Regime Faces Threat from Growing Guerrilla Activity," *Baltimore Sun*, December 18, 1980; Gayle Smith, "Ethiopian Dissidents Step up Guerrilla War in Northern Tigre Province," *Christian Science Monitor*, February 5, 1981.

11. Jay Ross, "Ethiopia's Anti-Somali Campaign Might Make Trouble for Reagan," *Washington Post*, December 28, 1980; Ross, "U.S. Clears Way for Military Aid to Somalia," *Washington Post*, January 17, 1981; Douglas Watson, "Somalia Turns Increasingly to New and Willing Friend: United States," *Baltimore Sun*, April 13, 1981.

12. Ray Wilkinson, "The Reign of Mengistu," *Newsweek*, July 6, 1981.

13. UPI, "Soviets Funneling Attack Helicopters."

14. D. K. Simes, "The Soviet Offensive in Africa." In *Implications of Soviet and Cuban Activities in Africa for U.S. Policy*, Michael A. Samuels et al., eds. (Washington, D.C.: Center for Strategic and International Studies of Georgetown University, 1979), p. 41.

15. Charles W. Corddry, "Soviet Effort in Ethiopia—A Test Run," *Baltimore Sun*, March 2, 1978.

16. William F. Buckley, Jr., "Somalia and Soviet Strategy," *Washington Star*, February 14, 1978.

17. Helen Winternitz, "Libya Assisting Guerrilla Group in Ethiopian Desert," *Baltimore Sun*, August 9, 1981.

18. "Somalis Shut Libya Mission," *The New York Times*, August 26, 1981.

19. John Worrall, "Kenya-Somalia: An African Hot Spot Coming Off the Boil," *Christian Science Monitor*, September 22, 1981.

20. Jay Ross, "Ethiopia Says U.S. Maneuvers Encourage Aggression by Somalia," *Washington Post*, November 19, 1981.

21. Anthony Lewis, "Hypocrisy Wins Again," *The New York Times*, January 4, 1982.

22. Chester A. Crocker, Letter, *The New York Times,* February 1, 1982. See also the three-part series on conditions in current-day Ethiopia by Helen Winternitz: "Ethiopia's Poor See Gain from Revolution, but Memory of 'Red Terror' Still Lingers," *Baltimore Sun,* August 30, 1981; "Ethiopia Turns Tentatively to West out of Need for Development Aid," *Baltimore Sun,* August 31, 1981; "Chairman Is More a 'Socialist Emperor' as He Leads Ethiopia in Troubled Times," *Baltimore Sun,* September 1, 1981.

23. Winston Williams, "Ethiopians in U.S. Fear Deportation," *The New York Times,* January 27, 1982.

24. Mary Thornton, "U.S. Pushing Ethiopians to Go Home," *Washington Post,* January 26, 1982.

25. "Ethiopia Said to Open Drive against Eritrea Rebels," *The New York Times,* February 21, 1982.

26. Ibid.

27. "Mengistu Launches Red Star Campaign in Eritrea," *Africa News,* February 8, 1982.

28. Joanne Omang, "Policy Change Will Let Exiled Ethiopians Stay in United States," *Washington Post,* July 9, 1982.

29. Alan Cowell, "Guerrilla Drive in Somalia Seen Part of a Proxy War," *The New York Times,* July 16, 1982; "Two New Fronts Opened, Somali Rebels Claim," *Washington Times,* July 16, 1982.

30. Richard Halloran, "U.S. Flying Arms to Somalis after Ethiopian Raids," *The New York Times,* July 25, 1982.

31. Ibid.

32. See, in general, the excellent article by Gerald A. Funk, "Some Observations on Strategic Realities and Ideological Red Herrings on the Horn of Africa," *CSIS Africa Notes,* July 1982.

33. Ibid.

34. "Companies Urge U.S. to Stay out of Angola, Decline Aid to Rebels," *Wall Street Journal,* March 27, 1981; Terrence Smith, "Some Companies Resist Policy on Angola, Libya," *The New York Times,* June 27, 1981.

35. Anthony Lewis, "Angola Says Cubans Leave When Namibia's Free," *The New York Times,* January 23, 1981; Jean Claude Pomonti, "Five Years of Angolan Independence," *The Guardian,* February 15 and 22, 1981.

36. John Borrell, "Zambia's Surprising Soviet Arms Deal," *Christian Science Monitor,* February 5, 1980.

37. Caryle Murphy, "U.S. Disputes Spy Allegations by Mozambique," *Washington Post,* March 6, 1981; Bernard Gwertzman, "U.S. Blames Cuba for Expulsion of Six Americans from Mozambique," *The New York Times,* March 5, 1981.

38. Jean Pierre Langellier, "Mozambique Five Years On," *The Guardian,* January 4 and 11, 1981.

39. See Frank J. Parker, "Peace Prospects in Namibia," Slater International Lecture at Wellesley College, Massachusetts, November 6, 1982; Parker, Letter to the editor, *The New York Times,* November 8, 1982.

40. Tracy Dahlby, "U.S. to Finance Oil Project in Marxist Angola," *Washington Post,* July 10, 1981.

41. Conditions in Angola at the time of the major South African assault at the end of August 1981 are well explained in a seven-part series carried in the *Washington Post* during the previous month. Richard Harwood, "Angola: A Distant War," *Washington Post,* July 19–25, 1981.

42. Bernard Nossiter, "A U.N. Rebuke to South Africans Vetoed as U.S. Splits with Allies," *The New York Times,* September 1, 1981.

43. "Timetable Is Set for Namibia Pact," *The New York Times,* September 25, 1981.

44. Steven V. Roberts, "Senate Votes to End Ban on Aid to Angolan Rebels," *The New York Times,* October 1, 1981; John A. Marcum, "The U.S. and Angola, Policy Choice," *Worldview,* August 1981.

45. "Savimbi Finishes U.S. Talks, Calls Them a 'Breakthrough'," *Washington Post,* December 11, 1981.

46. Michael Getler, "U.S. and Angola to Hold Two Day Talks in Paris," *Washington Post,* January 15, 1982.

47. Don Oberdorfer, "Prisoner Exchange Plan Reported between Angola and UNITA Rebels," *Washington Post,* January 22, 1982.

48. Dusko Doder, "Soviets, Angolans Strengthen Ties, Discuss Namibia," *Washington Post,* January 22, 1982.

49. Jay Ross, "David Rockefeller Cites Advantage to U.S. of Normal Ties with Angola," *Washington Post,* March 3, 1982.

50. Richard Timsen, "Portugal Tries to Help Angola Meet New Friends," *Christian Science Monitor,* March 10, 1982.

51. Allister Sparks, "South African Troops Raid Guerrilla Base in Angola," *Washington Post,* March 19, 1982; William Roberts, "Bureaucracy, Shortages Afflict Angola, Mozambique," *Christian Science Monitor,* May 3, 1982. See also "Angola: Some Economic Notes," *Africa Index,* April 15, 1982.

52. Michael Holman, "Angola Spells out Conditions for Withdrawal of Cuban Forces," *Financial Times,* July 9, 1982; "Angola Quietly Purges Its Nationalist Leaders," *The Guardian,* July 16, 1982.

53. Robert I. Rotberg, "Namibia and the Cuban Connection," *Christian Science Monitor,* November 9, 1982.

54. Allister Sparks, "South Africa, Angola Meet on Issue of Cuban Troops, *Washington Post,* December 9, 1982.

55. Anthony Lewis, "Namibia: No Dead End," *The New York*

Times, December 13, 1982.

56. Joseph Lelyveld, "Pretoria Pursuing Wide Angolan Pact," *The New York Times,* January 28, 1983.

57. *The European Community and Southern Africa* (Brussels: Commission of the European Communities, 1977) (166/77E).

58. Ian Smith, Associated Press interview, *Baltimore Sun,* March 15, 1981.

59. Jay Ross, "Mugabe Rejects U.S. Linkage of Issues," *Washington Post,* May 27, 1981.

60. James MacManus, "Zimbabwe Averts Civil War," *The Guardian,* February 22, 1981; "Bloodletting in Bulawayo," *Newsweek,* February 23, 1981.

61. For an earlier appraisal of Eddison Zvobgo, see R.W. Johnson, *How Long Will South Africa Survive?* (New York: Oxford University Press, 1977), p. 3.

62. Jay Ross, "Mugabe in Control," *Washington Post,* January 15, 1981; June Kronholz, "Mugabe Tries to Consolidate His Power by Move against Two Zimbabwe Ministers," *Wall Street Journal,* January 13, 1981.

63. Jay Ross, "Treading on a Tightrope," *Washington Post,* April 20, 1981.

64. Jay Ross, "Zimbabwe Says All Ex-Guerrillas Disarmed," *Washington Post,* May 20, 1981.

65. Jay Ross, "North Korea Advisers Arrive to Train Force in Zimbabwe," *Washington Post,* August 11, 1981.

66. Reuter News Service, "Zimbabwe Premier Details Ideas on One-Party State," *Los Angeles Times,* October 25, 1981.

67. Joseph Lelyveld, "Nkomo Ousted in Zimbabwe; Plot Is Charged," *The New York Times,* February 19, 1982.

68. John Borrell, "Mugabe to Sign a Zimbabwe Mining Bill That Lessens Economic Power of Whites," *Wall Street Journal,* March 3, 1982; "Zimbabwe Acting on Minerals," *The New York Times,* March 17, 1982.

69. "Price Controls in Zimbabwe as Inflation Worsens," *Financial Times,* May 5, 1982.

70. "Dismal Look to the Economy," *African Economic Digest,* April 9, 1982.

71. "Mugabe's Residence Attacked by Gunmen," *The New York Times,* June 25, 1982.

72. June Kronholz, "Zimbabwe Gives Land to Landless, But Can Economy Bear Costs," *Wall Street Journal,* September 10, 1982.

73. Margaret A. Novicki, "An Interview With Robert Mugabe," *Africa Report,* October 1982.

74. Paul Van Slambrouck, "Zimbabwe Treason Trial Seen as Signpost on Nation's Political Future," *Christian Science Monitor,* February 9, 1983.

75. "Split by Victory in Zimbabwe, Ex-Allies Wage a Bitter War," *The New York Times,* February 18, 1983.

76. Ronald Howard, Reuter News Service, "Zambia Banking on Corn to Aid Economy," *Los Angeles Times,* June 28, 1981.

77. Ibid.

78. Michael Holman, "Machel Secrecy Makes Foreign Investors Shy," *Financial Times,* February 1, 1982; Reuter News Service, "United States Shipping Wheat to Mozambique," *Baltimore Sun,* November 10, 1981.

79. Merril Stevenson, "Southern Africa's Bid to Shun Pretoria May Hinge on Ailing Mozambique Port," *Wall Street Journal,* December 30, 1981.

80. John Borrell, "South Africa's Railroads Bind African Economy," *Washington Star,* July 18, 1981.

81. Antero Pietila, "Tensions in Southern Africa Said to Imperil Stability," *Baltimore Sun,* September 14, 1981.

82. Allister Sparks, "South Africa to Open Talks with Zimbabwe on Renewing Trade Pact," *Washington Post,* January 8, 1982.

83. Tony Hawkins, "Mugabe Moves to End the Mining Rip-off," *Financial Times,* February 1, 1982.

84. "South Africa Involved in Destabilization, Says Mugabe," *Financial Times,* February 1, 1982.

85. Allister Sparks, "South Africa Admits 3 of Its Soldiers Were Killed in Zimbabwe," *Washington Post,* September 3, 1982.

86. Reuter News Service, "Mozambique Rebels Attack Depot Linked to Zimbabwe," *Washington Post,* December 10, 1982.

87. Editorial: "The Outlaw State," *Washington Post,* February 22, 1981.

88. Reuter News Service, "Libya Said to Use Soviet Pilots," *Baltimore Sun,* January 30, 1981.

89. Tom Gilroy, "Libyan Presence in Chad Gives Neighbors the Jitters," *Christian Science Monitor,* February 24, 1981.

90. United Press International, "U.S. Planning Increase in Aid to Countries that Resist Libya," *Washington Post,* July 9, 1981.

91. Helen Winternitz, "Libya Assisting Guerrilla Group in Ethiopian Desert," *Baltimore Sun,* August 9, 1981.

92. William Fulbright, "Another Gulf of Tonkin," *Washington Post,* August 23, 1981.

93. Geoffrey Godsell, "Big Power Interests Vie over Insecure African Borders," *Christian Science Monitor,* September 29, 1981; Alan Cowell, "Qaddafi Is New Chip in Horn of Africa Poker Game," *The New York Times,* September 21, 1981.

94. David B. Ottaway, "Sadat's Death Seen Heightening Concern for Sudan's Stability," *Washington Post,* October 8, 1981.

95. Pranay B. Gupte, "U.S. to Speed Arms," *The New York Times,* October 13, 1981; Louise Lief, "Sudan's Leader Predicts an Invasion by Libyans," *The New York Times,* October 13, 1981.

96. Pranay B. Gupte, "Ex-Chad Official, in Sudan, Reported to Plan War," *The New York Times,* October 19, 1981.

97. Edward Girardet, "France Stepping up Its Role in Chad to Support Waddei, Undercut Libya," *Christian Science Monitor,* October 29, 1981.

98. Don Oberdorfer, "U.S. Plans to Airlift Supplies to Africa Peace Force in Chad," *Washington Post,* November 19, 1981.

99. Alan Cowell, "Libyan Officer Sees a Renewal of War in Chad," *The New York Times,* November 11, 1981.

100. "Thinking about Libya," *Washington Post,* November 10, 1981.

101. "Ring around Qaddafi," *The Economist,* October 24, 1981.

102. Geoffrey Godsell, "Sudan, Chad Leaders Bury Feud to Shore up Their Positions at Home," *Christian Science Monitor,* January 15, 1982.

103. Alan Cowell, "African Force in Chad Seen Shifting Role," *The New York Times,* January 21, 1982; Jonathan C. Randall, "France Cuts off Supply of Arms to Chad's Ruler," *Washington Post,* February 19, 1982.

104. Mark Webster, "Fears about Libya Persist after Chad," *Financial Times,* December 17, 1981.

105. Michael Getler, Lou Cannon, "U.S. Bans Imports of Libyan Oil," *Washington Post,* March 11, 1982.

106. "Capital of Chad Reported to Fall," *The New York Times,* June 8, 1982.

107. Alan Cowell, "Chad Believed to Seek Closer Libya Ties," *The New York Times,* May 27, 1982.

108. "Habre in Peace Offer to Southern Chad," *Financial Times,* July 6, 1982.

109. Reuter News Service, "Southern Chad Leader Is Reported Toppled," *The New York Times,* September 6, 1982.

110. Leon Dash, "Chad, with Calm Restored, Reaps, Fruits of Stability," *Washington Post,* December 10, 1982.

111. Swedish International Peace Research Institute, *SIPRI Yearbook: 1979, World Armaments and Disarmaments* (Stockholm: Ginn and Russak, 1979), p. 180.

112. Ibid.

113. A reevaluation of the contribution of Abbe Fulbert Youlou to the development of independent Africa is long overdue, in this author's opinion. Given what has occurred in the last few years, some of the more-uncharitable remarks concerning his sanity might have to be revised. See Rene Gauze, *The Politics of Congo Brazzaville,* translated, edited and supple-

mented by Virginia Thompson, Richard Adloff (Stanford, Calif.: Hoover Institution Press, 1973). See also Jean-Michel Wagret, *Histoire et Sociologie Politiques de la Republique du Congo* (Paris: R. Pichon et R. Durand-Auzias, 1963).

114. Frank J. Parker, "France's Future in Africa," Working paper no. AD-60 (Chestnut Hill, Mass.: Management Institute, School of Management, Boston College, 1980). See also Parker, "Congo-Brazzaville Holds Little for U.S. to Cheer About," *Boston Sunday Globe,* August 21, 1977.

115. Henry Brandon, "France Eyes Third World through a New Minister," *Washington Star,* June 7, 1981.

116. Frank J. Prial, "France Supports New Measures against South Africa," *The New York Times,* May 27, 1981.

117. June Kronholz, "Staying On: The French in Africa, A Colonial Master Who Didn't Go," *Wall Street Journal,* July 22, 1981.

118. Bernard D. Nossiter, "France Breaks with U.S. on Third World Aid," *The New York Times,* September 24, 1981.

119. See, in general, Ellen Frey-Wouters, *The European Economic Community and the Third World,* (New York: Praeger Co., 1980).

120. Reuter News Service, "Central African Military Forms a Government," *The New York Times,* September 2, 1981.

121. Jim Hoagland, "France Outlines Tough Approach toward Qaddafi," *Washington Post,* October 2, 1981; and Girardet, "France Stepping Up Role in Chad."

122. Edward Girardet, "France Reaches Out to Third World as an Alternative to Super Powers," *Christian Science Monitor,* January 11, 1982.

123. Tom Gilroy, "Francophone Africa—Some Call It More Home than Paris," *Christian Science Monitor,* August 31, 1982.

124. Antero Pietila, "After Independence, Many Poor African Nations Are More Dependent Than Ever," *Los Angeles Times,* February 10, 1983.

125. Ibid.

126. Drew Middleton, "Soviets in Ethiopia: The Long View," *The New York Times,* January 3, 1978.

127. "New Soviet Anchorage Reported in Ethiopian Isles in the Red Sea," *The New York Times,* October 28, 1980.

128. Salamat Ali, "A Temptation That Was Too Strong to Resist," *Far Eastern Economic Review,* January 23, 1981. This article was one of a group of articles on Reagan and Afghanistan appearing in this issue. Taken as a whole, these articles provide a most helpful interpretation of the Afghanistan crisis.

129. Richard Burt, "Indian Ocean Lands Reported to Agree to U.S.

Use of Bases," *The New York Times,* February 15, 1980.

130. Louis H. Gann, "The Cape: The Other South Africa," *Baltimore Sun,* October 8, 1980.

131. See *The Indian Ocean in Global Politics,* Larry Bownan, Ian Clark, eds. (Boulder: Westview Press, 1981).

132. Gary Thatcher, "Safeguarding the Oil Lifeline around the Cape," *Christian Science Monitor,* December 17, 1980.

133. W.A.C. Adie, *Oil Politics and Seapower—The Indian Ocean Vortex,* Strategy Paper no. 24 (New York: Crane Russak, 1975); James H. Hayes, "Indian Ocean Geopolitics," Rand Corporation Paper Series 5325-1 (Santa Monica, January 1975).

134. Kenneth L. Adelman, "That Elusive Soviet Quagmire," *Wall Street Journal,* January 4, 1979.

135. Associated Press, "South African Force Attacks Rebels in Mozambique," *Baltimore Sun,* January 31, 1981.

136. Reuter News Service, "Soviet Ships Lying Off Mozambique," *Baltimore Sun,* February 20, 1981.

137. Ibid.

138. Drew Middleton, "Soviet Ships Reportedly Destined to Reinforce Indian Ocean Fleet," *The New York Times,* February 5, 1980.

139. Michael Getler, "Gulf Buildup Is Stretching U.S. Forces Around World," *Washington Post,* July 19, 1980.

140. Richard Halloran, "U.S. Sending New Force of Marines to Indian Ocean," *The New York Times,* July 17, 1980.

141. Allister Sparks, "Mercenaries Thwarted in Seychelles," *Washington Post,* November 27, 1981.

142. "Seychelles Rebellion Is Reported Quelled," *The New York Times,* August 19, 1982.

143. George C. Wilson, "Indian Ocean Bases Plan Hits Snag," *Washington Post,* August 28, 1980. See also Chester A. Crocker, "African Dimensions of Indian Ocean Policy," *Orbis,* Fall, 1976, pp. 637–667.

144. Caryle Murphy, "Under the Beauty of Madagascar Lie Economic Woes," *Washington Post,* March 8, 1981; Murphy, "Old and New Mix Easily in Tropical Lushness of Madagascar," *Washington Post,* March 14, 1981.

145. Caryle Murphy, "Single-Crop Economy in Mauritius Suffers as Worldwide Demand for Sugar Slumps," *Los Angeles Times,* April 15, 1981.

146. K.R. Singh, *The Indian Ocean* (Columbia, Missouri: South Asia Books, 1978), pp. 40–42.

147. Antero Pietila, "Opposition Sweeps Vote in Mauritius," *Baltimore Sun,* June 13, 1982.

148. *U.S. Department of State Bulletin* 56 (February 6, 1967):225.

149. Admiral Elmo R. Zumwald, "Strategic Importance of Indian Ocean," *Armed Forces Journal International,* April 1974, p. 28.

150. Richard Halloran, "U.S. Studying One Billion Dollar Expansion of Indian Ocean Base," *The New York Times,* April 6, 1980.

151. Colin Legum, "Mauritius Elections Could Shift Indian Ocean Political Balance," *Christian Science Monitor,* June 9, 1982.

152. "Digging In at Diego Garcia," *Time,* July 14, 1982.

153. "U.S. Announces Pact with Oman on Access to Air Bases and Port," *The New York Times,* June 6, 1980; Associated Press, "U.S. Expected to Seek B-52 Use of Indian Ocean Isle," *Washington Post,* March 4, 1981.

154. Richard Halloran, "Special U.S. Force for Mideast Is Expanding Swiftly," *The New York Times,* October 25, 1982.

155. "Second Chapter in the Red Book," *The Economist,* November 13, 1982.

156. William Clairborne, "Mauritius Seeks Change in Status of Diego Garcia," *Washington Post,* February 9, 1983.

157. See Frank J. Parker, "Indian Ocean Power Vacuum," research paper presented at Yale University Southern Africa Research Project, New Haven, Conn., January 19, 1983.

8

U.S. Government and Corporate Dealings with South Africa

During 1977–1982, U.S. government and corporate interests in relation to South Africa have taken a roller-coaster ride. Although the United States always has had diplomatic relations with African nations, not until Henry Kissinger's 1974 trip to Lusaka did events on the African continent become of primary interest to the U.S. government. It is ironic that Kissinger, in assuring his and his government's interests in bringing about majority rule to South Africa, Rhodesia and Namibia, repeated the long-defunct myth that white South Africans belonged in South Africa because they had reached the Cape of Good Hope area before the Bantu tribes had done so. This piece of propaganda is totally false but has been cleverly disseminated by white South Africans over the centuries. Mr. Kissinger did nothing to debunk the harmful myth.[1]

The building U.S. interest in bringing majority rule to Southern Africa that surfaced during Kissinger's reign as secretary of state in the Nixon and Ford administrations further escalated when the Carter administration came into power. UN Ambassador Andrew Young, his assistant Donald McHenry, Secretary of State Cyrus Vance, and Assistant Secretary of State for Africa Richard Moose were committed to ending minority rule on the southern part of the continent. As a result, U.S. corporate involvement in South Africa was examined with marked severity.

Recently, the climate has changed. First, while the Carter administration was still in office, the United States was less than successful in its peacemaking attempts in Zimbabwe and Namibia. Especially on the question of a Zimbabwe settlement, the Carter administration seemed incapable of achieving a meeting of the minds with the Thatcher government in the United Kingdom. As a result, Lord Carrington's skill in ending white rule in Zimbabwe brought great credit to his country and little to the United States. When peace finally arrives in Namibia, it is equally unlikely that the U.S. contribution will receive acclaim in the world.

The Reagan administration has shown a tendency to seek accommodation, not confrontation, with South Africa. Republican party philosophy does not favor forcing U.S. corporations to pass up money-making oppor-

tunities wherever found. It seems unlikely in the present climate that the
U.S. government will place heavy pressure on its corporations to divest in
South Africa. In the same fashion, private groups such as college students
and black activists seem to be switching their primary political emphasis
from obtaining majority rule in South Africa to preventing the Reagan administration from seriously cutting social programs within the United
States.

American Attitudes in 1977

In many ways, the end of 1977 was the high point of U.S. government and
private activity aimed at convincing South Africa to change its policies.
U.S. vote at the United Nations for mandatory arms-sales sanctions was a
strong warning to the South African government that it must change. Also,
it was an executive decision to promote sanctions that would deprive U.S.
corporations of overseas profits, even though such action would prove
unpopular and could damage the future election prospects of Carter and his
congressional supporters. Support for the U.S. action at the UN was
widespread in Congress. On October 31, 1977, the House of Representatives approved by a vote of 347 to 54 a resolution strongly denouncing the
government of South Africa for repressive measures against black and
white opponents of its apartheid policy.[2]
     Newspaper commentary concerning the U.S. action was for the most
part favorable but became cautious when the substantive questions of U.S.
trade with South Africa were reached. The *Washington Post* approved of
the Carter administration move to support mandatory arms-sales sanctions
against South Africa and the willingness of Congress to approve of this
move. The *Washington Post* also took note that the United States had
observed a voluntary ban on arms sales to South Africa since 1963. The
newspaper cautioned the administration to discuss fully any added boycott
measures under consideration with the U.S. public. Otherwise, the
necessary support for such actions might be lacking.[3] As so often seemed to
be the case, the *Washington Star* was less impressed with the liberal direction of the Carter administration foreign policy. The *Star* felt that the
United States was devoting overly marked attention to details of internal
South African politics. In the newspaper's view, this action was the logical
result of "our unctuous talk about human rights."[4] The newspaper warned
that a serious crisis, mixing ideology and race in dangerous proportions,
could take place.
     At the time of this controversy concerning further U.S. action to isolate
South Africa and dissuade it from its current path, many of the large U.S.
corporations adopted the lowest of profiles, hoping that the trend would

subside and that business could continue as usual. The Investment Responsibility Research Center (IRRC) estimated as of the end of 1977 that the United Kingdom had a figure of between $5 and $7 billion dollars invested in South African business and estimated U.S. investment at the time as $1.66 billion.[5] U.S. investment was spread through the economy, and even leaving apart the mineral companies, it represented the strongest indication of U.S. corporate interest in the country. About 70 percent of the South African computer market was controlled by U.S. companies. Half of this investment was held by IBM. At least forty-seven U.S. banks including the Bank of America and Chase Manhattan had loan portfolios in South Africa. The Commerce Department estimated that by the end of 1977 there was a total exposure of $2.2 billion. U.S. automobile manufacturers held a 23 percent share of the South African market, led by General Motors and Ford. U.S. oil firms controlled 43 percent of South Africa's petroleum refining. Mobil and Caltex were the two largest of these firms each selling more than $500 million worth of their products in South Africa in any one year. A group of other large firms had substantial holdings in South Africa, including Exxon, ITT, General Electric, Chrysler, Firestone, Goodyear, and 3M.[6]

Conditions for Doing Business in South Africa

On the political side, Andrew Young, the U.S. ambassador to the UN, continued his heavy criticism of South Africa. As would be expected, he supported the arms embargo. Rather surprisingly, at first glance at least, Young did not support a total economic boycott on trade with South Africa because he believed such a move lacking in efficacy. He stated that total boycotts force nations to become independent and self-sufficient. In the case of South Africa, this would mean the rest of the world would lose its hold on the Pretoria regime. If the South African government were free of outside constraints, apartheid never would end.[7]

U.S. firms doing business in South Africa began to examine practices involving employees in that country. By the end of 1977, fifty-four U.S. firms had signed a statement of principles developed by Reverend Leon Sullivan, a black from Philadelphia and General Motors director. These Sullivan principles required the signatories to work for a group of goals, among them instituting equal pay for equal work; ending segregation in cafeterias, working areas, and restrooms; developing training programs to prepare nonwhites for supervisory, administrative, technical, and clerical work; introducing fair employment practices for all workers with no job restrictions; increasing the number of nonwhites in supervisory jobs; and improving workers' lives outside the plant in housing, transportation, education, and health. Some of the largest U.S. corporations were slow to sign this statement of principles. Among those who did not immediately sign were General Electric, Johnson and Johnson, and ITT.[8]

Senator Richard Clark of Iowa, chairman of the Subcommittee of African Affairs of the Senate Foreign Relations Committee and soon to be a surprise loser in the 1978 senatorial election held in November of that year, was another leading force in demanding U.S. foreign investment in South Africa be curtailed. Clark, speaking early in 1978, suggested an end to Export-Import Bank insurance and loan guarantees to South Africa, the permanent withdrawal of the commerical attache to the U.S. Embassy in Pretoria, denial of U.S. tax credits to U.S. corporations for taxes paid to the South African government if that government continues to fail to act in ways consistent with U.S. policy, and withholding approval of private groups organizing in defense of U.S. corporate investment in South Africa unless they satisfactorily support corporate guidelines and fair employment practices laid down by the U.S. government. Clark stressed that he considered his recommendations quite mild and pointed out that they were virtually identical to policies that had been adopted by the Canadian government in December 1977. Clark offered the opinion that U.S. economic interests in South Africa have been pivotal in directly assisting the South African government and that U.S. corporations operating in South Africa have collectively made no significant impact on either relaxing apartheid or establishing company policies which would offer a limited, but nevertheless important model of multinational responsibility.[9]

Congressional concern was expressed that the Export-Import Bank and the International Monetary Fund were still making new loans to South African business. Representative Andrew McGuire of New Jersey, a leader of the new ad hoc congressional caucus on South Africa, stated, "We're saying that at the very least we can demur from using public funds and agencies to further encourage additional private investment, which cannot be defended either in terms of human rights or the long-term security of the investment community."[10] The Federal Reserve Bank pointed out that U.S. bank loans outstanding to South Africa declined in the first six months of 1977 to $2.2 billion from $2.24 billion in the previous six months. It is in this climate that continued in-bank short-term-insurance of trade credits has been criticized—in 1977, $86 million of such credits were granted to South Africa, which although less than the $116 million granted in 1976, was more than the $73 million granted in 1975 or the $26 million granted in 1973.[11]

Corporate Shareholders Become Uneasy

In addition to private pressure like that exerted by the Sullivan principles, individuals and groups as stockholders of corporations dealing with South

Africa used the vehicle of corporate-stockholder meetings to attempt to have their corporations either modify or end their business dealings in South Africa. One such corporation to feel this stockholder pressure was Citicorp, the holding company for Citibank of New York, the second-largest bank in the United States. Citicorp defended itself before its stockholders by stating that it would turn down direct loans to the South African government and to South African corporations. *Direct,* of course, was the key word.

At the same time, Citicorp found it necessary to defend itself against attack from congressional investigators. A report in the U.S. Senate said that Citicorp had participated in more than $760 million of loans to South Africa, mostly the government groups, from 1974–1976. It also was one of eleven U.S. banks that lent $2.2 billion to South African–government bodies and others at the beginning of 1977. Citicorp noted that it was an original signer of the Sullivan principles and that its management deplores apartheid. It did continue to state, nonetheless, that its opinion was that the withdrawal of international financing to South Africa probably would have disproportionately adverse effects upon the black community and other minority groups there.[12]

The issue of investment in South Africa became important on U.S. college campuses during the spring 1978 semester. On a direct level, students demanded that their colleges not hold investments in corporations doing business with South Africa or, at the very least, doing business in South Africa without signing the Sullivan principles. The demonstrations employed much of the same rhetoric and, on a lesser scale, the same tactics as used in protests against American participation in the Vietnam War. The success of the student protests against investment in South Africa was surprising. College after college took note of students' concern, and many pressured corporations in which they held investments to respond to their inquiries on the matter. The board of trustees of the University of Massachusetts at Amherst debated the issue in open session for an hour and a half before deciding to sell $600,000 in stock in twenty companies doing business in South Africa. The regents of the thirteen-unit University of Wisconsin system voted in February 1978 to sell $8 million of shares in sixteen corporations. The regents justified their action by stating that holding the stock violated a 1973 law forbidding investments by the university in companies that discriminate. Smith College, in early 1978, wrote four companies with operations in South Africa and asked what their policies were concerning the Sullivan principles. The response of the Firestone Tire and Rubber Company did not satisfy them, and the trustees voted to sell 42,014 shares of Firestone stock with a value of $680,000. The University of Michigan at Ann Arbor announced plans to cash in $38 million in stocks in companies with ties to South Africa, unless the companies were following the Sullivan principles. Clearly, Sullivan-principles compliance had become a middle-road easy out for some college boards of trustees. Others claimed that loss of needed income would result from the reshuffling of any portfolio. Vice-president-treasurer of Wesleyan University Richard W. Greene estimated that it would cost Wesleyan University $100,000 to trade its $36 million of stock in companies doing business in South Africa.[13]

During April 1978, a black congressman from Maryland, Parren J. Mitchell, unsuccessfully sought legislation barring credit guarantees by the U.S. Export-Import Bank for all transactions to South Africa. Congressman Mitchell stated that his motivation was his horror upon learning that the Maryland National Bank had applied for such guarantees to extend credit to its South African customer. Mitchell, the chairman of the congressional black caucus, said that he was disturbed by the bank's transaction because "it had seen fit to enter into a financial arrangement with a company from the avowed racist country of South Africa."[14]

The April 1978 meeting of the stockholders of J.P. Morgan Company, the holding company for the large New York bank Morgan Guaranty Trust, gave indications that despite the complaints of those shareholders seeking divestment in South Africa, the rank-and-file of this and most other large corporations were not as convinced of the urgency of the issue. Several church groups holding stocks in J.P. Morgan and Company placed before the rest of the shareholders a proposal that would order the bank to disclose all loans it had made to South Africa since 1970. The proposal went down to ignominious defeat—5.49 percent of the votes cast were in favor of the bank's disclosure to its stockholders. The management of the bank had opposed disclosure on the familiar grounds that it would violate client confidentiality and that the bank's position on continued loans to South Africa would be assessed on a case-by-case basis.[15]

Even though eleven U.S. banks had more than $2.2 billion in loans outstanding to South Africa at the beginning of 1977, as criticism of this activity mounted, the banks' responses would make one think that none still was actively participating in South Africa. Gabriel Hauge, the chairman of the Manufacturer's Hanover Corporation and a former economic advisor to President Eisenhower, stated that apartheid was "having a direct and growing negative impact on the risks involved in making loans to South Africa, its agencies and related entities."[16] He stated that because of such risk assessment, the Hanover Trust Company now was inactive in lending to South Africa. He declared to define exactly what he meant by inactive. A group of churches who held stock in the Manufacturer's Hanover had placed a proposal before the shareholders to ban loans to the South African government. This suggestion was defeated by 22.4 million votes against as opposed to 1.2 million votes in favor. A similar proposal at Citicorp was voted down overwhelmingly by its stockholders. Citicorp did state "it would regard tangible progress away from apartheid as a positive factor in its risk evaluation process."[17]

Bank America Corporation, the nation's largest bank, also received antiapartheid pressure from its stockholders during early 1978. The aim was to force the bank to discontinue loaning money both to the government and to private corporations in South Africa. A.W. Clausen, the bank president, refused to comply and pointed out that his bank's relative exposure in South Africa was so small that its elimination would not affect total profits to a notable degree. Clausen also affirmed the right of his bank or any U.S. bank to transact business anywhere in the world not prohibited by the U.S. government.[18] Such bravado statements did not help the British bank, Barclays. The Nigerian government removed all its funds from that bank's Nigeria operation and expelled one-third of its British employees in order to protest Barclays Bank dealings with South Africa.[19]

Diverse Opinions on Divestment Are Heard

The National Association for the Advancement of Colored People (NAACP), at its 1978 convention in Portland, Oregon, advocated that U.S. corporations pull out of South Africa and divert these investments to Botswana, Lesotho, and Swaziland.[20] The *Washington Star* termed this NAACP action as "quixotic."[21] The newspaper emphasized that U.S. investment in South Africa was less than one-third of the combined European Economic Community investment. The *Star* felt U.S. corporations could make a more-constructive contribution by investing responsibly and continuing to advocate for the South African government to modify its attitude.

Distinguished South African black newspaper editor, Percy Qobosa, began to make himself heard on this question of divestment. Since Qobosa was a longtime courageous advocate of liberty for blacks in South Africa and one of the world's finest examples of a dedicated Christian working for peace and racial harmony for all, his views on divestment received a wide hearing. Arguing as always with cogency, Qobosa pointed out that complete divestment would cause economic chaos. All-out racial war would seem a sure next step. Qobosa criticized those who from, as he phrased it, "8,000 miles away, say let the blood flow."[22] Qobosa did concede that in the long run, he still felt divestment was the better course because, of their own volition, whites in South Africa would never end the long-standing discriminatory system of apartheid. Speaking contemporaneously with Qobosa, colored political spokesperson Sonny Leon also called for total divestment. Forsaking the moderate tone of his black counterpart, Leon scathingly criticized U.S. citizens for profiting from the apartheid system in South Africa.[23]

The South African Council of Churches, during July 1978, passed what was for it a remarkably strong statement of disapproval concerning international investment in South Africa. It called on foreign corporations and foreign countries with financial holdings to "radically revise their investment policies."[24] This ecumenical body represents churches with a membership of 15 million people in South Africa. Commenting on the statement, black leader Bishop Desmond Tutu, who is the general secretary of the council, emphasized that it was not a full call for divestment in South Africa. He did not state, but it was true, that any such action could have brought criminal prosecution for sabotage and treason by the government.[25] Tutu also observed that immediate withdrawal of existing capital and loans by corporations already doing business in South Africa is almost impossible since South African law effectively blocks any large withdrawal of foreign funds. Bishop Tutu is correct in this appraisal. Although South African foreign-exchange regulations traditionally have permitted free repatriation of profits, they have not been as generous as to capital. A U.S. corporation wishing to leave would have to find a South African buyer, make a distress sale, and then would have to invest the proceeds for at least seven years in low-yield South African government securities, a rather Machiavellian arrangement defeating the purpose of divestment in the first place.

The then editor of *Fortune,* Herman Nickel (later to be U.S. ambassador to South Africa in the Reagan administration), argued that U.S. investment in South Africa was not large enough to cause the Pretoria regime to change its policies in order to retain it. Nickel argued that working within the South African system and placing subtle pressure on the government to modify its conduct was a more-effective change catalyst than preemptive withdrawal of U.S. investment. He also pointed out that most of the U.S. companies who pulled out had not been invested heavily in South Africa in the first place. He cited Polaroid as an example in this category and suggested that the company might have fallen into the temptation to give the withdrawal decision more of a moral gloss than the relatively minor business decision to cut adrift a troublesome small part of its business might have deserved.[26] Almost simultaneously with the Nickel article, an editorial in the *Wall Street Journal* advanced similar views.[27] As could be expected, many social-action and church groups disagreed with Nickel and the *Wall Street Journal.* Most vocal in this regard was the Interfaith Center on Corporate Responsibility (I.C.C.R.) of the National Council of Churches.[28]

The noted black U.S. diplomat, Franklin H. Williams, who has been ambassador to Ghana and then president of the Phelps-Stokes Fund, wrote a nuanced article advocating divestment. This piece appeared in the *Amsterdam News* of New York.[29] Williams pointed out that the large corporations have used a clever advertising campaign to explain why they should keep business in South Africa. Williams denied that economic growth in South Africa, depending heavily as it does upon foreign investment, changed conditions to the point where blacks benefit to a marked degree. He pointed out that most of the success was capital intensive and that the black population was producing more members at a time when, relatively speaking, there were fewer jobs for those entering the workforce. The high amount of disease among destitute blacks was cited as proof that foreign investment had not succeeded. Mr. Williams also made the point that until blacks had full labor-negotiating rights in South Africa, the Sullivan principles would not change the situation in any significant manner. Williams took the Carter administration to task for refusing to back up their rhetoric with action and for using the excuse that blacks really did not want divestment.

In May 1979, the IRRC published a report on the impact of the Sullivan principles.[30] The center found that the principles were successful in areas such as arranging for desegregating of work facilities and housing and training of black employees. However, in the more-important areas of advancement in executive-area positions, in union representation of workers, and in elimination of wage gaps between whites and blacks, little progress had been made. The IRRC report also pointed out that the Sullivan principles had not been successful in persuading the South African government to change its policies. The deputy director of IRRC, Desaix Myers, III, stated, "Many of the changes made to date are among the easiest to achieve."[31] Mr. Myers also said that poor education for blacks is the largest obstacle to be overcome in South Africa.

The Divestment Controversy Continues

Given the enormous disparity between U.S.-corporate activity in South Africa and that of the United Kingdom, one might wonder whether too much was being made of U.S. corporate activity and too little of its counterpart. During 1979, South Africa loosened restrictions on repatriation of profits and on restrictions against divestment. At the same time, it changed the financial-rand regulations to encourage foreign corporations to remain in South Africa. Some British firms did seize the opportunity to divest and sold to South African corporations. Legal and General Holding Company sold 70 percent of its stock to the Volkskas banking group. This sale of $24 million took Legal and General out of the insurance business in South Africa. In the same way, Cape Industries sold its asbestos-mining interest to Barlow Rand. The sale price was $33.6 million. Cape Industries was 67.3 percent owned by Charter Consolidated, a British company. Another British corporation, Commercial Union Assurance, sold 30 percent of its South African holdings to Gold Fields of South Africa. Commercial Union sold another 25 percent of its holdings on the open Johannesburg stock exchange. Together, it realized $10 million from its sales. In 1978 and 1979, British divestment in South Africa exceeded $240 million. Nonetheless, many large corporations such as Barclays Bank, Standard Chartered Bank, and Gold Fields of South Africa remained in South Africa, making profits with their local operation. Critics who advocated divestment could take courage in the fact that few new foreign corporations had come into South Africa in 1978 and 1979, the most notable being the Eveready Battery Company.[32]

During October 1979, longtime black union leader Lucy Mvubelo toured the United States, arguing for more foreign investment in South Africa rather than less. Mrs. Mvubelo hardly could be called an appeaser or supporter of the Pretoria government. In her many years as leader of the 24,000-member National Union of Clothing Workers, she had resisted courageously the actions of the Pretoria government and had demanded better treatment for her black coworkers. Mrs. Mvubelo told U.S. audiences that she considered it cruel for Americans to call for divestment in South Africa "when we are only now getting some sunshine in that very dark country of ours."[33] She advocated added U.S. investment since, in her view, it would force the Pretoria regime to educate more blacks and to improve their working conditions in order to satisfy the productivity demands of the foreign multinationals.

In line with continuing efforts by a small group of stockholders to force their corporations to disclose the extent of their dealings with South Africa, some of the largest U.S. corporations reluctantly made limited disclosures. In March 1980, for example, both General Motors and Ford Motor Company began to tell their stockholders about the extent of their holdings. Some other U.S. corporations were less willing to do so. One of the more reluctant was Black and Decker Manufacturing Company. A group of shareholders, at its January 1980 meeting, noticed and commented upon the absence of a statement about the firm's dealings in South Africa in the last two annual reports to shareholders. Management said that its dealings there were so minimal that it was not worth taking up the space.

Other U.S. corporations seemed to fall into this it's-no-big-deal sort of defense of their actions. Baltimore Air Coil Company, a wholly owned subsidiary of Merck and Company, noted that it has approximately seventy-five people, mostly black, working in a manufacturing plant near Capetown and stated that company income had not risen dramatically in the last few years. It pointed out that South African operations contributed significantly less than 1 percent of Merck's $2.2 billion sales in 1979. Another firm, Eastmet Corporation, a specialty-steel producer, stated it did buy chrome from the Republic of South Africa and said the amount it buys depends upon supply-and-demand factors. No dollar or tonnage would be given. The PHH Group, a vehicle-management and leasing operation, stated that less than 1 percent of its sales, about $300,000 worth, took place in South Africa in a year and that it did not feel necessary to divest. A Maryland seasoning producer that was part of McCormick and Company stated its company did $120,000 of business in South Africa in 1979 and also saw no reason to divest from this steady, but not growing, income source.[34]

During March 1981, another woman, as well known as Lucy Mvubelo in the South African civil-rights struggle, spoke in an opposite manner concerning Western investment. This was Mrs. Winnie Mandela, wife of imprisoned black nationalist Nelson Mandela. It must be remembered that a year had passed since Mrs. Mvubelo's statements and since the Reagan administration had taken over from the Carter administration. Mrs. Mandela, a strong critic of Reagan administration policies, asserted that Western investment in South Africa contributes to the continued enslavement of black workers. She stated, "America could do us a favor by just getting out of our way."[35] She said that instead the Reagan administration was more concerned about investments in South Africa than with the rights of the majority of South Africa's people.

Study Commission on U.S. Policy Recommendations

During May 1981, the question of U.S. relations with South Africa on both a governmental and corporate level were brought into sharp focus again when the Study Commission on U.S. Policy toward Southern Africa of the Foreign Policy Study Foundation, Inc., made its report. This private research group, under the chairmanship of Franklin A. Thomas, president of The Ford Foundation, issued a 456-page report entitled *South Africa: Time Running Out.*[36] The report made five major recommendations as to the U.S. government's objectives: (1) to make clear the fundamental and continuing opposition of the U.S. government and people to the system of apartheid, with particular emphasis on the exclusion of blacks from an effective share in power; (2) to promote genuine political power sharing in South Africa with a minimum of violence by systematically exerting influence on the South African government; (3) to support organizations inside South Africa working for change, to assist the development of black leadership, and to promote black welfare; (4) to assist the economic development of the other states in southern Africa, including the reduction of the imbalance in their economic relations with South Africa; and (5) to reduce the impact of stoppages of imports of key minerals from South Africa.

Dealing specifically with U.S. corporations, the study commission noted that U.S. corporations doing business in South Africa should not expand their operations and that those not already there should stay out. Those U.S. corporations already doing business in South Africa should commit a generous proportion of their corporate resources—determined in accordance with a specific social-development-expenditure standard—to improving the lives of black South Africans and should subscribe to and implement the Sullivan principles. Compliance with the principles should be monitored. These measures should be undertaken on a voluntary basis for the moment, and the government in Washington should endorse them as important parts of overall U.S. policy. Divestment and other economic sanctions are not recommended under current circumstances.[37]

The Crocker American Legion Speech

The moderate recommendations of the Study Commission on U.S. Policy Toward southern Africa were bypassed swiftly by events in southern Africa. On August 29, 1981, speaking before an American Legion convention in Honolulu, Assistant Secretary of State Crocker gave a major speech explaining what would be the policy tone of U.S. action with regard to South Africa during the Reagan administration:

> We have defined a new regional strategy, responsive to our national secu-rity, economic, commercial and political interests. That strategy is based on three basic realities of southern Africa. First, United States economic inter-ests in sub-Sahara Africa are heavily concentrated in the southern third of the continent. . . . The second reality is that southern Africa is an increas-ingly congested arena engulfed in global politics. . . . The third reality is that southern Africa is a highly complex arena which must be understood on its own regional merit if we are to succeed in our efforts. . . .
>
> The legally entrenched apartheid policies of South Africa are anathema to its African-ruled neighbors. They seek lessened dependence on South Africa and increased political pressures on it for domestic change. All par-ties are aware of the enormous price that will be exacted if the pressures in and around South Africa degenerate into destructive revolutionary vio-lence.[38]

Crocker went on to state the Reagan administration's perception of the current state of affairs in Angola and Namibia. He then sought to define the general tenor of U.S. relations with South Africa. This part of his speech was the most controversial and caused extensive comment and great con-cern in many nations of the world.

> It is clear that southern Africa contains within itself the seeds of growing violence. To ward off this possibility we must have a realistic strategy, one that assures our credibility as a regional partner. We cannot and will not permit our hands to be forced to align ourselves with one side or another in these disputes. Our task, together with our key allies, is to maintain com-munication with all parties—something we in the West are uniquely able to do—and to pursue our growing interest throughout the region. Only if we engage constructively in southern Africa as a whole can we play our proper

role in the search for negotiated solutions, peaceful change and expanding economic progress. In South Africa, the region's dominant country, it is not our task to choose between black and white. In this rich land of talented and diverse peoples, important Western economic, strategic, moral and political interests are at stake. We must avoid actions that aggravate the awesome challenges facing South Africans of all races. The Reagan administration has no intention of destabilizing South Africa in order to curry favor elsewhere. Neither will we align ourselves with apartheid policies that are abhorrent to our own multiracial democracy.

South Africa is an integral and important element of the global economic system, and it plays a significant economic role in its own region. We will not support the severing of those ties. It does not serve our interest to walk away from South Africa any more than it does to play down the seriousness of domestic and regional problems it faces. The Reagan administration recognizes that the future of southern Africa has not yet been written. It would be an act of political irresponsibility and moral cowardice to conduct ourselves as though it had been. We need policies that sustain those who would resist the siren call of violence and the blandishments of Moscow and its clients. The U.S. enjoys fruitful ties with most of the African states in this region—Zaire, Zimbabwe, Zambia, Botswana, Malawi, Lesotho, Swaziland and Tanzania. We seek to strengthen and expand these relationships through diplomatic efforts on the interrelated conflict in Namibia and Angola, through strong programs of foreign assistance and by fostering expanding trade and investment. The U.S. also seeks to build a more constructive relationship with South Africa—one based on shared interests, persuasion and improved communication. There is much ferment in South Africa today, centered on the question of how all South Africans can more fully share and participate in the economy and political process. We recognize that a measure of change is already underway in South Africa at such a time when many South Africans of all races, in and out of government, are seeking to move away from apartheid. It is our task to be supportive of this process so that proponents of reform and nonviolent change can gain and hold the initiative.[39]

South African Conduct Modifies Temporarily

The future direction of U.S. political dealings with South Africa, outlined by Crocker, did not satisfy many. Critics detected a displeasing level of softness. Subsequent statements by Haig and Crocker that seemed to promise a swift end to the Namibia conflict were interpreted by some critics as attempts to counter adverse reactions to the Crocker speech on relations with South Africa. Even if Namibian independence could be obtained, observers feared that such a settlement would serve to give South Africa an expended breathing space before efficient attacks against the apartheid-enforcing government in South Africa again could be mounted.

As 1982 began, the working relationship between the United States and

South Africa appeared to be continuing relatively smoothly. No dramatic breakthroughs were recorded, but some amelioration in official South African conduct could be noted. Three specific examples come to mind. In each case what was certainly the U.S. preference was honored, and it can be assumed that South Africa had kept this factor in mind when making the policy decision involved. The first instance concerned the continuation of the peace-settlement procedure in Namibia. Without the guiding hand of the United States, it could be presumed that once again a reason for breaking off Namibia peace negotiations would have occurred to the procrastination-inclined government in Pretoria. Instead, the world community was entitled to hope that the longer the protagonists kept negotiating, the more likely would be the possibility of a turnover to a majority-rule government.

Second, the South African decision to try all the white mercenaries involved in the November 1981 aborted coup in the Seychelles Islands was looked on with favor by the world community. The United States had made public its displeasure at the original Pretoria government decision to release forty of the forty-five involved and to content itself with trying only the sixty-one-year-old leader, Colonel Mike Hoare, and four others for kidnapping. The invaders had failed to advance beyond the Victoria International Airport in their coup attempt and had carried out their escape from the island chain by hijacking an Air India plane. At gunpoint, they forced the pilots to fly them to Durban, South Africa.[40] The United States had acted quickly and efficiently within diplomatic circles when it became clear that South Africa would be content to let off the mercenaries with, at most, a proverbial slap on the wrist. The U.S. State Department announced in public that it would hold South Africa to the terms of the 1970 Hague Convention of which it was a signatory. Under its terms, participants agreed to extradite or prosecute anyone involved in skyjacking. In 1978 at Bonn, seven major nations—the United States, the United Kingdom, France, Japan, West Germany, Italy, and Canada—agreed to end all links with countries that failed to observe the Hague Convention. South Africa was reminded officially by the United States of the terms of this Bonn sanctions agreement. After waiting a suitable period of time in order to save diplomatic face, South Africa capitulated and announceds on January 5, 1982, that it intended to rearrest and try for hijacking all forty-five coup-attempt participants.[41]

In the third example of the mood of relative reasonableness within the Pretoria government, in subsequent weeks, it appeared that South Africa was engaged in relaxing the level of economic pressure being applied against Zimbabwe. No longer did South Africa demand that totally new trade pacts be negotiated between the two nations. Instead, South Africa indicated a willingness to extend current pacts. By so doing, Zimbabwe was relieved from dealing with a thorny dilemma. When it had joined the Lomé Convention as a signatory, the Mugabe government had been forced as an entry condition to promise that it would not give more-favorable trading terms to any non–European Economic Community/ACP nation than it did to European-community trading-partner nations. Given South Africa's overwhelming trade domination in southern Africa, the Pretoria government is always able to compel more-favorable terms for itself when dealing with other southern African nations than these neighboring black-ruled nations would be willing or able to give to European Economic Community and other large trading-partner nations. By ending the agreements currently in force between itself and South Africa and by negotiating new arrangements, South Africa would have presented Zimbabwe with a true dilemma. If Zimbabwe was forced to extend to the European Economic Community the same terms as South Africa would be able to command, the Zimbabwe economy might fail. Conversely, if Zimbabwe refused to extend to the European Economic Community the same terms South Africa received, the Mugabe government would violate the Lomé Convention, risk being expelled from the ACP grouping, probably lose its trade-aid package from the European Economic Community, and again, for all practical purposes, go bankrupt. The one saving loophole in the Lomé Convention specifies that trade agreements in effect when a nation signed the Lomé Convention could be extended indefinitely. By becoming reasonable on this score and agreeing to extend rather than terminate present agreements and begin again with new ones, South Africa preserved its favorable trade position while simultaneously permitting Zimbabwe to benefit from its association with the European Economic Community. Behind-the-scenes U.S. negotiating was perceived as being the cause for the constructive change in the attitude of the Pretoria government.

The slight improvement in the southern African political climate attributable to the South African short-term move toward external reasonableness could not hide three disturbing factors of overriding importance. First, the apartheid system in South Africa progressed with little diminishment or hope of radical change. Second, the public announcements of optimism issued habitually by Washington at the smallest signs of South African reasonableness demonstrated just how far the situation would have to change before true racial harmony could come to southern Africa. If a truly important step forward like a valid peace settlement in Namibia ever did occur, it can be presumed that the Pretoria government will feel it had bought itself a U.S. guarantee of many months and years of freedom from external harassment. Third. U.S. corporations took advantage of the loosening in the amount of meaningful pressure the Reagan administration chose to apply against the Pretoria regime. Business between U.S. corporations and South African business interests began to flourish in a manner seldom seen before.

The United States Cooperates Commercially

In 1980, the United States became South Africa's leading export and import trade partner. The United Kingdom, the traditional leader, fell into third place. West Germany was second. Imports from the United States rose by 74 percent to $2.2 billion. Overall imports to South Africa, worldwide, were 47 percent higher during 1980 than they had been in 1979. The dollar total reached $16.4 billion, of which more than 13 percent came from the United States. The main goods exported to South Africa from the United States were airplanes, motor vehicles, chemicals, paper, base metals, and heavy machinery.[42]

Exports from South Africa to the United States took advantage of the weak dollar exchange rates to be found in 1980. As a result, exports from South Africa to the United States were 28 percent higher, overall, in 1980 than in 1979. Excluding gold, the percentage rise was 16 percent. Precious metals are the main export category of goods shipped from South Africa to the United States. As would be expected, sales are led by diamonds, chrome, manganese, platinum, and vanadium. The Krugerrand gold-piece phenomenon demands separate treatment and explains the reason gold exports to the United States are separated out for statistical purposes. The gold-piece-buying mania spoke more to U.S. displeasure with Carter administration policies that it did to any indications that perpetual purchase of gold pieces from South Africa would be a significant part of any habitual U.S. import purchase-pattern profile. Even when U.S. gold purchases from South Africa are included, it must be remembered that the United States currently imports three times as much in dollar value, predominately crude oil, from Nigeria than it does from South Africa.[43]

As the Reagan administration and the South African government moved closer together on policy matters, U.S. corporations followed the lead and began to expand their base of operations in deals with South Africa. One major example of this trend involved the South African subsidiary of the General Motors Corporation. The subsidiary received contracts from the Zimbabwe National Railways and South African Railways to build 111 diesel electric locomotives. The contracts were to be executed by the Canadian and U.S. branches of General Motors. The linking of U.S. and South African corporate interests in such a deal was explicit and obvious. The same could be observed as to a recent $250 million loan by Citibank to South Africa.[44]

During late October 1981, four U.S. nuclear-safety specialists visited South Africa. It was feared that the 1978 Carter administration ban on sales of nuclear fuel to South Africa that was to remain in effect until it signed the nuclear nonproliferation pact was in danger of being overturned. If South Africa's energy problems could be solved, its determination to continue current policies might strengthen. Widespread use of nuclear power was being urged as the key to economic success.[45]

In a political climate that stresses cooperation between the United States and South Africa, opponents of U.S. corporate involvement are thrown back upon devices like the Sullivan principles in hopes of reducing the manifest inequality existing between the economic position of whites and blacks in South Africa.

The Sullivan Report Findings

To read the recent reports of U.S. compliance with the guidelines set down by the Philadelphia clergyman for fair treatment of black South African workers, success apparently was occurring in improving the plight of South Africans working in U.S.-run businesses. Thirty U.S. corporations transacting business in South Africa in 1981 were rated as "making good progress." Forty-seven U.S. businesses were rated as "needing to become more active." Those observers professing to find encouragement in such statistics are quick to point out that the ratings qualifications have been raised substantially in the last year or so. As of October 1981, the date of the "Fifth Report on the Signatory Companies to the Sullivan Principles," concrete examples of compliance made relatively impressive reading.[46] Ninety-five percent of reporting units claimed all their facilities are desegregated; 96 percent of reporting units claimed to have common medical, pension, and insurance plans for all races; and nearly all reporting units professed to award equal pay for equal work and to be raising the salary of black workers at increasingly frequent intervals. The number of blacks in sales and supervisory positions has been rising. U.S. contributions to black South African economic development also have increased.

Critics of the Sullivan principles are less enthralled with the progress U.S. corporations have made in their level of ethical South African dealings. They point out that the consultant corporation employed to compile the report is doing just that—reporting, not monitoring. Critics of the Sullivan principles feel the distinction is vital. The corporations involved make their own report to the Arthur D. Little Company, the consulting reporter-supervisor.

Among all reporting units, in only nineteen cases do the companies involved allow outside verification of the accuracy of their conclusions. In these cases, the corporations employ the firm of chartered accountants hired to examine their books—not, perhaps, the most objective outside evaluator that could be imagined. The point is not so much that fabrication might take place but that an insider view of what is fair and equal could differ substantially from the definition used by an outsider. This discrepancy is most crucial if, as often occurs, the U.S. corporation chooses to employ an Afrikaner as head of the South African operation and, thus, by definition, the person responsible for evaluations to be reported for Sullivan-principles purposes.

U.S. corporate signers of the Sullivan principles have been less than enthralled with the pro-union bias of the requirements and the need to subscribe to the National African Federated Chamber of Commerce (NAFCOC), a black-run chamber of commerce in Johannesburg, to obtain full approval. A salary raise of 30 percent for workers in a South African subsidiary of a U.S. corporation could well be used by the unions dealing with the home plant in the United States as a precedent helpful in obtaining a higher wage increase in future contracts. Distinctions are quickly forgotten in such instances between the pitiful wage level at which the black in South Africa starts bargaining and the elevated wage level at which the U.S. counterpart performs the same function. The U.S. corporations subscribing to the Sullivan principles are not enamored of them under such circumstances.

In the same vein, U.S. corporations are bitterly unhappy at being compelled to pay $610 to join this black chamber of commerce. It is not the money but that they see no return for their money. The organization in question kept changing headquarters and addresses, did not have a telephone, accounted for funds sloppily, and left the post of executive director free for an extended period of time. The situation infuriated U.S. executives on a professional-competence level: the amount of money involved could not be said truthfully to be the issue. The lack of organization displayed by the NAFCOC bothered them out of all proportion to the true magnitude of the irritant involved. The issue did surface as a ready whipping boy for those U.S. corporations looking to minimize or ignore the Sullivan principles. Arguments that inefficiency and underdevelopment tend to go hand in hand were ignored by those in opposition to NAFCOC.

Ingersoll-Rand, a large industrial-machinery manufacturer, stands as an example of a U.S. corporation that will not sign the Sullivan principles even though it accomplished $47 million of sales in South Africa during 1980. The company proferred three main levels of arguments to justify its signature refusal. First, it said that its policies in South Africa already comply with the Sullivan principles in spirit. Second, Ingersoll-Rand expressed its reluctance to participate in a movement aimed at causing social and political revolution. Third, Ingersoll-Rand noted the Sullivan principles had been amplified and expanded twice since they were written in 1977. It characterized the principles as being "uncertain, complex and presenting a constantly moving target."[47]

As long as the Sullivan principles are kept in perspective and are treated in the manner they were intended originally—that is, as a reporting vehicle intended to indicate what progress had been made—they tend to work. If more is asked of the principles, they do not work. The opportunities for evasion are too great, and the legal difficulties of making the Sullivan principles mandatory among U.S. corporations should warn about the real limits possible for their effectiveness.

Commercial Linkages

Without strong government compulsion, from Washington, it is unlikely that voluntary U.S. corporate divestment, or even significant scaling down of trade with South Africa will occur. Over and above direct trade, two other forms of linkage have been developing. First, U.S. corporations have sponsored South African–run subsidiaries that are self-sufficient on day-to-day matters but that are answerable to the home office in the United States for overall policy. The September 1981 contract awarded to General Motors of South Africa for sixty main-line locomotives for Zimbabwe at a cost of $53 million and for fifty-one diesel locomotives for South Africa at a cost in excess of $21 million, to be built in the United States and Canada, indicates the interrelated nature of large commercial transactions in the business world of today.[48]

The second linkage, less appreciated but, perhaps in the long run, equally as important, is the fact that South African corporations have invested heavily in U.S. businesses. The Oppenheimer empire has been extremely active in this regard. Minorco, a totally owned Oppenheimer subsidiary, has been the vehicle employed for this purpose. It owns 27.2 percent of Phibro, a large commodities-trading firm in New York. Phibro is the sole owner of the New York investment house Salomon and Brothers. Phibro is a spin off from Englehard Mining and Chemicals Corporation, which owns many mining and petroleum subsidiaries. With 27.5 percent of the stock, Minorco is the largest holding of the renamed Englehard Co. Minorco. Consolidated Gold, another DeBeers-Oppenheimer holding, owns 22.4 percent of Newmont Mining, one of the world's largest copper producers. Newmont owns 27.5 percent of Peabody Coal Co., the largest coal company in the United States. The interlocking directorates involved in these and similar corporate holdings guarantee that constant pressure will be placed upon the U.S. Congress and Executive Branch to be reasonable in all dealings with South Africa.[49]

The moves of the Reagan administration to loosen requirements for export licenses for deals involving South Africa are the latest in a long line of hints that U.S. corporations will continue business as usual with South Africa, for the near-term future at least. Year by year, the roots of U.S.-South African relations go deeper and would be harder to dislodge if an administration not favoring business with South Africa returns to power in the White House.

The Situation Turns Bleak

United States relations with Africa took a marked turn for the worse during the last months of 1982. Black nations became convinced that the Reagan administration had abandoned the search for black liberation and freedom in South Africa. The reasons for reaching this conclusion were not always easy to pinpoint. No one action taken by the Reagan administration precipitated the downturn in continent-wide opinion. A group of events taken together caused the nations of black Africa to reach the opinion that the sympathies of the Reagan government were allied closely with the Botha regime. Continent leaders thought they detected a general trend toward favoring Pretoria. One major indication was the permission given by the U.S. government for the Autoclave Engineers Inc. of Erie, Pennsylvania, to sell large, hot isostatic presses to South Africa. The potential use of this equipment in atomic-weapons manufacture worried other African nations. From a human rights viewpoint, similar objections were made when the U.S. government permitted its corporations to sell electric shock police batons to the South African government. Little imagination needed to be employed to guess the use to which these devices would be put.

On the political–economic front, it was felt that the United States should have voted against and led the move to stop the $1.07 billion IMF loan to South Africa. U.S. government protests that South Africa was entitled to this loan under the rules of the organization fell upon deaf ears. In like manner, it was felt that the United States should have reacted in a public manner and punished South Africa for its attempts to destabilize its neighbors.[50] Examples of such attempts include the early-December South African army raid into Lesotho in which thirty-seven people were killed; the deaths of three South African soldiers slain by Zimbabwe troops within Zimbabwe territorial limits during late August; and support given by South Africa to UNITA forces in Angola, MLM forces in Mozambique, and perhaps to supporters of Nkomo or Muzorewa in Zimbabwe. In all of these cases, the black nations of Africa were angered by the silence of the Reagan administration. Without doubt, the black nations of Africa will become increasingly strident in their opposition to the emerging Botha-engineered power-sharing plan that excludes blacks. If the United States does not become vocal in its opposition it is certain that it will be criticized for its insensitivity.

All of the other objections to U.S. policy added together could not begin to equal the amount of opposition generated within black Africa by trends in the Reagan administration's efforts to bring peace to Namibia. Ironies abound. The goal of the United States is to persuade South Africa to grant freedom to the territory it has held for more than two-thirds of a decade. One would think black nations would appreciate the efforts expended by Washington in this regard. Such definitely is not the case, and criticism has been constant and scathing. Forgotten is the reality that the United States is only one of five negotiators that have failed.[51] In the eyes of many African nations, the United States is the only failure.

When Vice President Bush announced that a Cuban pullout from Angola must be linked with a South African pullout from Namibia, a new degree of gravity had been reached.[52] Speaking at a conference in Harare, Zimbabwe, on January 10, 1983, Prime Minister Robert Mugabe gave the United States a tongue lashing and termed the linked pullout plan blackmail.[53] Assistant Secretary of State Chester A. Crocker, the chief architect of the new policy, was present in the audience and a fellow conference participant. Mugabe charged the United States with impeding settlement attempts in Namibia. Understood was the allegation that the Reagan administration had clearly chosen to cast its lot with the apartheid regime in South Africa.

The five years under consideration in this book end with a full-circle change in attitudes on one level, and on another level they end in exactly the same spot as five years previously. In 1977, the Carter–Vance–Young triumvirate was perceived as being totally committed to bringing freedom and equality to all natives of South Africa. The 1983 Reagan administration triumverate of Regan, Shultz (his brief tenure has not eradicated unfavorable opinions held concerning his predecessor, Alexander Haig) and Crocker is thought of as favoring glacial progress, if any, toward freedom and equality for all in South Africa. Both perceptions are oversimplifications, as are all generalizations. What is neither an oversimplification or incorrect generalization is that significant progress toward solution of the racial problem in South Africa has not occurred between 1977 and 1982. Five more years have passed. Five years of lost opportunities.

Notes

1. Leonard P. Thompson, "Political Mythology and the Limits of Intellectualism," paper presented at the Yale University Southern African Research Project Workshop, New Haven, April 18, 1982.

2. Susanna McBee, "House Censures 'Repressive' South African Tactics," *Washington Post,* November 1, 1977.

3. Editorial, "Arms Embargo on South Africa," *Washington Post,* October 29, 1977.

4. Editorial, "Sanctions for South Africa?," *Washington Star,* October 27, 1977.

5. Robert A. Rosenblatt, "Race Bias in South Africa Eased by U.S. Firms," *Los Angeles Times,* December 29, 1977.

6. Ibid.

7. Dick Clark, "Against Financing Apartheid," *The New York Times,* February 21, 1978; "South Africa Investment Criticized," *Baltimore Sun,* January 26, 1978.

8. "First Report on the Signatory Companies to the Sullivan Principles" (Cambridge, Mass.: Arthur D. Little, April 1978).

9. Clark, "Against Financing Apartheid."

10. Ann Crittenden, "Role of Ex-Im Bank in South Africa Gets Growing Criticism," *The New York Times,* February 9, 1978.

11. Ibid.

12. "Citicorp, Citing Apartheid, Halts Loans to South African Government, State Firms," *Wall Street Journal,* March 13, 1978.

13. See, in general, the excellent pro-and-con articles on U.S. universities holding investments in South Africa by Robert I. Rotberg and William H. Wells, "Should U.S. Firms Do Business in South Africa?," *Christian Science Monitor,* July 5, 1978.

14. "Mitchell Seeks to Bar South African Credit Deals," *Baltimore Sun,* April 12, 1978.

15. Jack Egan, "Morgan Doesn't Deny a Report on South African Loan Moratorium," *Washington Post,* April 13, 1978.

16. "Citicorp, Citing Apartheid, Halts Loans."

17. Ibid.

18. "Bank America," *The New York Times,* March 23, 1978.

19. Ibid.

20. "NAACP, in Policy Shift, Asks Sanctions against South Africa," *The New York Times,* July 4, 1978.

21. Editorial: "South African Disinvestment," *Washington Star,* July 10, 1978.

22. "Qobosa, A Role for the U.S.," *Time,* April 17, 1978.

23. William Raspberry, "U.S. Investment: Does It Affect Apartheid?," *Washington Post,* May 1, 1978.

24. "South African Council of Churches Speak Out," *Southern Cross,* July 28, 1978.

25. Ibid.

26. Herman Nickel, "The Case for Doing Business in South Africa," *Fortune,* June 19, 1978.

27. Editorial, "Business in South Africa," *Wall Street Journal,* August 18, 1978.

28. Allan R. Nelson, letter to editor, "What IRRC Is All About," *Wall Street Journal,* August 29, 1978.

29. Franklin H. Williams, "U.S. Business: A Partner in Apartheid," *Amsterdam News,* October 21, 1978.

30. David Southerland, "U.S. Firms, Records in South Africa Faulted," *Christian Science Monitor,* May 31, 1979.

31. Ibid.

32. "Processing State Assets," *The Economist,* August 4, 1979; "Investment in South Africa: Two Way Traffic," *The Economist,* September 1, 1979.

33. William Raspberry, "Investing in the Fight against Apartheid," *Washington Post,* October 8, 1979.

34. "Loans to South Africa Opposed," *The Washington Post,* January 21, 1980; "Firms Divulging, Defending Their South African Dealings," *Baltimore Sun,* March 1, 1980.

35. Gary Thatcher, "Reagan No Friend of South African Blacks, Winnie Mandela," *Christian Science Monitor,* March 13, 1981.

36. Study Commission on U.S. Policy Toward Southern Africa, *South Africa: Time Running Out,* (Berkeley: University of California Press, 1980).

37. Ibid.

38. Address by Chester A. Crocker, to the U.S American Legion Convention, Honolulu, August 29, 1981.

39. Ibid.

40. "Pretoria Frees 39 in Seychelles Plot," *The New York Times,* December 3, 1981.

41. Allister Sparks, "South Africa, in Switch, Charges Mercenaries with Seizing Plane," *Washington Post,* January 6, 1982.

42. Antero Pietila, "U.S. Boosts Trade with South Africa," *Baltimore Sun,* July 14, 1981.

43. Ibid.

44. "General Motors, South Africa gets $74.2 Million Contract," *Wall Street Journal,* September 24, 1981; Charles Austin, "Business-Church Accord on South Africa Is Elusive," *The New York Times,* September 30, 1981.

45. Antero Pietila, "Four U.S. Nuclear Specialists Visiting South Africa," *Baltimore Sun,* October 22, 1981. Also see the excellent general appraisal of the situation by Thomas Karis, "Leaders in Waiting," *Washington Post,* December 31, 1981.

46. "Fifth Report on the Signatory Companies to the Sullivan Principles" (Cambridge, Mass.: Arthur D. Little, October, 1981).

47. South Africa Review Service, *Company Report: Ingersoll-Rand*

Co. (Washington, D.C.: Investor Responsibility Research Center, June 1981).

48. "G.M. South Africa Gets $74.2 Million Contract," *Wall Street Journal,* September 24, 1981.

49. Thomas W. Lippman, "A South African Empire Reaches to United States," *Washington Post,* April 11, 1982; and Lippman, "Minerals: South Africa Firm Extends Its Influence," *Los Angeles Times,* April 26, 1982.

50. Clyde H. Farnsworth, "I.M.F. Loan to Pretoria Is Voted," *The New York Times,* November 4, 1982.

51. Paul Van Slambrouck, "Bush Likely to Feel Sting of Black Africa's Anger at U.S." *Christian Science Monitor,* November 9, 1982.

52. Mary Anne Fitzgerald, "U.S. Insists on Cuban Pullout, Bush Tells Africans," *Washington Post,* November 20, 1982.

53. Jay Ross, "Mugabe Criticizes U.S. Policy in Africa," *Washington Post,* January 11, 1983.

Bibliography

Adam, Heribert. *Modernizing Racial Domination*. Berkeley: University of California Press, 1971.

Adam, Heribert; Giliomee, Herman. *Ethnic Power Mobilized: Can South Africa Change?* New Haven, Conn.: Yale University Press, 1979.

Adie, W.A.C. *Oil, Politics and Seapower: Indian Ocean Vortex*. New York: Crane Russack, 1975.

Africa Guide. Essex, England: World of Information, annual.

Albright, David E. *Communism in Africa*. Bloomington: Indiana University Press, 1980.

Alexander, Jonah, ed. *International Terrorism*. New York: Praeger, 1976.

Alverson, Hoyt. *Mind in the Heart of Darkness: Value and Self-Identity among the Tswana of Southern Africa*. New Haven, Conn.: Yale University Press, 1978.

Barber, James P. *South Africa's Foreign Policy, 1945-1970*. London: Oxford University Press, 1970.

Bissell, Richard E. *Apartheid and International Organizations*. Boulder, Colo.: Westview Press, 1977.

Bissell, Richard E.; Crocker, Chester A. *South Africa into the 1980s*. Boulder, Colo.: Westview Press, 1979.

Bouch, R.J., ed. *Infantry in South Africa 1652-1976*. Pretoria: South African Defence Force Documentation Service, 1977.

Brotz, Howard M. *The Politics of South Africa: Democracy and Racial Diversity*. London: Oxford University Press, 1977.

Carter, Gwendolen M.; O'Meara, Patrick, eds. *Southern Africa in Crisis*. Bloomington: Indiana University Press, 1977.

——. *Southern Africa: The Continuing Crisis*. Bloomington: Indiana University Press, 1979.

Cottrell, Alvin J. *The Persian Gulf States*. New York: Johns Hopkins University Press, 1980.

Crocker, Chester A. *South Africa's Defense Posture: Coping with Vulnerability*. Washington Papers no. 84. Washington, D.C.: Center for Strategic and International Studies, Georgetown University, 1981.

Davenport, T.R.H. *South Africa: A Modern History*. Johannesburg: Macmillan, 1977.

Dugard, John. *The Southwest Africa-Namibia Dispute*. Berkeley: University of California Press, 1973.

Duncan, Walter Raymond. *Soviet Policy in Third World*. New York: Pergamon Press, 1980.

DuToit, M.A. *South African Trade Unions: History, Legislation and Policy*. Johannesburg: McGraw-Hill, 1976.

Edwards, Allan D.; Jones, Dorothy G. *Community and Community Development*. The Hague: Mouton, 1976.

Edwards, John; Robbins, Peter. *Guide to Non-Ferrous Metals and Their Markets*. London: Kogen Page, 1979.

Entelis, John P. *Comparative Politics of North Africa*. Syracuse, N.Y.: Syracuse University Press, 1980.

Falkena, H.B. *The South African State and Its Entrepreneurs*. Johannesburg: Donker, Ltd., 1980.

Farer, Tom J. *War Clouds on the Horn of Africa: The Widening Storm*. 2d rev. ed. New York: Carnegie Endowment for International Peace, 1979.

First, Ruth; Steele, Jonathan; Gurney, Christabel. *The South African Connection: Western Investment in Apartheid*. London: Temple Smith, 1972.

Fredrickson, George M. *White Supremacy: A Comparative Study in American and South African History*. New York: Oxford University Press, 1981.

Gauze, Rene. *The Politics of Congo-Brazzaville*. Translated, edited, and supplemented by Virginia Thompson and Richard Adloff. Stanford, Calif.: Institution Press, Stanford University, 1974.

Gerhart, Gail M. *Black Power in South Africa: The Evolution of an Ideology*. Berkeley: University of California Press, 1978.

Goosen, J.C. *South Africa's Navy: The First Fifty Years*. Capetown: Flesch Publishers, 1973.

Green, Timothy. *The New World of Gold*. New York: Walker, 1981.

Grichar, J.S.; Levine, R.; Nahai, L. *The Nonfuel Mineral Outlook for the U.S.R.R. through 1990*. Washington, D.C.: U.S. Government Printing Office, 1981.

Hance, William A., ed. *Southern Africa and the United States*. New York: Columbia University Press, 1968.

Hope, Marjorie; Young, Jim. *South African Churches in a Revolutionary Situation*. New York: Orbis Books, 1981.

Horrell, Muriel *The Education of the Coloured Community in South Africa, 1652-1970*. Johannesburg: South African Institute of Race Relations, 1970.

Horwitz, Ralph. *The Political Economy of South Africa*. New York: Praeger, 1967.

Houghton, D. Hobart "Economic Development, 1865-1965." In *Oxford History of South Africa*. vol 2. Oxford: Clarendon Press, 1975.

————. *The South African Economy*. 4th ed. Capetown: Oxford University Press, 1976.

Human Sciences Research Council. *Population Projects for South Africa: 1970-2010*. Pretoria: Human Sciences Research Council, 1973.

Imports of Minerals from South Africa by the United States and the OECD Countries. Report for Subcommittee on African Affairs of the Committee on Foreign Relations of the United States Senate by Congressional Research Service. Washington D.C.: U.S. Government Printing Office, 1980.

Johnson, Richard William How Long Will South Africa Survive. New York: Oxford University Press, 1977.

Joshua, Winifred; Gilbert Stephen. *Arms for the Third World*. Baltimore: Johns Hopkins University Press, 1980.

Katzen, Leo. *Gold and the South African Economy: The Influence of the Goldmining Industry on Business Cycles and Economic Growth in South Africa 1886-1961*. Amsterdam: A.A. Balkema Publishers, 1964.

Leftwich, Adrian. *South Africa: Economic Growth and Political Change*. New York: St. Martin's Press, 1974.

Legum, Colin. *Southern Africa: The Secret Diplomacy of Detente—South Africa at the Crossroads*. New York: Africana Publishing, 1977.

Legum, Colin and Margaret. *The Bitter Choice: Eight South Africans Resistance to Tyranny*. Cleveland, Ohio: World Publishing, 1968.

Lejeune, Anthony. *The Case for Southwest Africa*. London: Tom Stacey Ltd., 1971.

Levgold, Robert *Soviet Policy in West Africa*. New York: Harvard University Press, 1970.

Metrowich, F.R. *Africa in the Sixties*. Pretoria: Africa Institute of South Africa, 1970.

Mineral Commodities Summaries Report. Washington, D.C.: U.S. Government Printing Office, annual.

Moodie, T. Dunbar. *The Rise of Afrikanerdom: Power, Apartheid and the Afrikaner Civil Religion*. Berkeley: University of California Press, 1975.

Mroz, John Edwin. *Beyond Security: Private Perceptions among Arabs and Israelies*. New York: Pergamon Press, 1982.

Myers, Desaix, et al. *U.S. Business in South Africa*. Bloomington: Indiana University Press, 1980.

Ottaway, David M. *Afro-Communism*. New York: Holmes and Meier, 1981.

Palmer, Robin; Parsons, Neil, eds. *Roots of Rural Poverty in Central and Southern Africa*. Berkeley: University of California Press, 1977.

Paton, Alan. *South African Tragedy: The Life and Times of Jan Hofmeyer.* New York: Scribner Co., 1965.

Rhoodie, Eschel Mostert. *The Third Africa.* New York: Twin Circle, 1968.

Rhoodie, Nic J. *South African Dialogue.* Johannesburg: McGraw-Hill, 1972.

Robbins, Peter, Lee, Douglas. *Guide to Precious Metals and Their Markets.* London: Kogan Page, 1979.

Rogers, Barbara. *White Wealth and Black Poverty.* Westport, Conn.: Greenwood Press, 1976.

Rosenthal, Eric. *Encyclopedia of Southern Africa.* New York: Warner, 1973.

Rotberg, Robert I. *Suffer the Future: Policy Choices in Southern Africa.* Cambridge: Harvard University Press, 1980.

Rotberg, Robert I., Barratt, John, eds. *Conflict and Compromise in South Africa.* Lexington, Mass.: Lexington Books, D.C. Heath and Co., 1980.

Selassie, B.H. *Conflict and Intervention in the Horn of Africa.* New York: Monthly Review Press, 1981.

Simson, Howard. *Social Origins of Afrikaner Fascism and Its Apartheid Policy.* Stockholm: Almquist and Wiksell International, 1980.

Singh, K. Rajendra. *Politics of the Indian Ocean.* New Delhi: Asian Books, 1974.

South African Institute of Race Relations. *Survey of Race Relations in South Africa.* Johannesburg, annual.

Strack, Harry R. *Sanctions: The Case of Rhodesia.* Syracuse, N.Y.: Syracuse University Press, 1978.

Study Commission on U.S. Policy toward Southern Africa. *South Africa: Time Running Out.* Berkeley: University of California Press, 1981.

Stultz, Newell M. *Transkei's Half Loaf: Race Separatism in South Africa.* New Haven, Conn.: Yale University Press, 1979.

Thompson, Leonard M. *The Unification of South Africa, 1902–1910.* Oxford: Clarendon Press, 1960.

Thompson, Leonard M; Butler, Jeffrey, eds. *Change in Contemporary South Africa.* Berkeley: University of California Press, 1975.

Toussant, Auguste. *History of the Indian Ocean,* translated by June Guich Arnaud. Chicago: University of Chicago Press, 1966.

U.S. House. Committee on Armed Services. Panel of Defense Industrial Base. *Capability of U.S. Industrial Base.* 96th Cong., 2d sess., September 17, 18, and 25, 1980; October 21, 22, and 24, 1980; November 12, 13, 14, 17, 18. 19, and 20, 1980; and December 3, 1980.

———. Committee on Banking, Finance and Urban Affairs. Subcommittee of International Trade, Investment and Monetary Policy. *Export-*

Import Bank and Trade with South Africa. 95th Cong., 2d sess., February 9, 1978.

———. Committee on Foreign Affairs. Subcommittee on Africa. *The Possibility of a Resource War in Southern Africa.* 97th Cong., 1st sess., July 8, 1981.

———. *U.S. Interest in Africa.* 96th Cong., 1st sess., October 16, 18, 19, 22, 24, 25, and 29, 1979; and November 13 and 14, 1979.

———. Committee on Interior and Insular Affairs. Subcommittee on Mines and Mining. *Sub-Sahara Africa: Its Role in Critical Mineral Needs of the Western World.* Committee Print no. 8. 96th Cong., 2d sess., July 1980.

———. Committee on International Relations. Subcommittee on Africa. *United States-South Africa Relations: Nuclear Cooperation.* 95th Cong., 1st sess., June 30, 1977; and July 12, 1977.

U.S. Senate. Committee on Armed Services. Subcommittee on Military Construction and Stockpiles. *Consideration of Stockpile Legislation.* 95th Cong., 2d sess., March 8 and 9, 1978.

———. Commerce, Science and Transportation Hearing, *Critical Minerals and Materials.* Serial no. 97-12. 97th Cong., 1st sess., 1981.

———. *General Stockpile Policy.* 95th Cong., 1st sess., September 9, 1977.

———. *Stockpile Commodity Legislation.* 96th Cong., 1st sess., July 10, 1979.

———. *Strategic and Critical Materials Stockpiling Act Revision.* 96th Cong., 1st sess., March 19, 1979.

———. Subcommittee on Preparedness. *Stockpile Legislation.* 97th Cong., 1st sess., March 19, 1979.

———. Committee on Banking, Housing and Urban Affairs. *Defense Production Act and the Domestic Production of Cobalt.* 97th Cong., 1st sess., October 26, 1981.

U.S. Senate. Committee on Foreign Relations. *U.S. Corporate Interests in Africa.* Report by Senator Dick Clark, 1978.

———. Committee on Foreign Relations. Subcommittee on African Affairs. *U.S. Policy toward Southern Africa.* 94th Cong., 1st sess., June 11, 13, and 16, 1975; and July 9, 10, 14, 23, 24, 28, and 19, 1975.

———. *South Africa.* 94th Cong., 2d sess., September 8, 9, 16, 22, 23, 29, and 30, 1976.

U.S. Department of the Treasury. *The Role of gold in the Domestic and International Monetary Systems,* vols. 1 and 2. Report to Congress of the Commission on the Role of Gold in the Domestic and International Monetary Systems, March 31, 1982.

Van der Merwe, Sandra. *The Environment of South African Business.* Capetown: Master Miller, 1978.

Van zyl Slabbert, Frederick. *South Africa's Options*. New York: Saint Martin's Press, 1979.

Whitaker, Jennifer Seymor. *Conflict in Southern Africa*. New York: Foreign Policy Association, 1978.

Wille, G.; Gibson, J.T.R. *Principles of South African Law*. 6th ed. Capetown: Juta, 1970.

Williams, Basil. *Botha, Smuts and South Africa*. New York: 1948.

Wilson, Monica; Thompson, Leonard M., eds. *Oxford History of South Africa*. vol. 1. New York: Oxford University Press, 1969.

―――. *Oxford History Of South Africa*. vol 2. New York: Oxford university Press, 1971.

Zwing, Lawrence, ed. *The Subcontinent in World Politics*. New York: Praeger, 1978.

Index

About the Author

Rev. Frank J. Parker, S.J., is a professor of international management and of African business in the M.B.A. program at Boston College. He is also an adjunct professor at Boston College Law School, where he teaches a course on international regional organizations. He has recently been active in the field of international human rights as a U.S. delegate to the UNESCO Executive Board Committee on Recommendations and Conventions in Paris. Father Parker is a graduate of Holy Cross College, Fordham Law School, and the University of Louvain. He has taught management as a Senior Fulbright Fellow in Cameroon, Chad, Togo, and the Central African Republic; he has also worked as a teacher and a consultant in Zimbabwe and South Africa. This is his fourth published book.